CECILE BEURDELEY

L'AMOUR BLEU

TRANSLATED FROM THE FRENCH BY
MICHAEL TAYLOR

Published in the United States of America in 1978 by:

RIZZOLI INTERNATIONAL PUBLICATIONS, INC.
712 Fifth Avenue/New York 10019

Copyright © 1978 by Office du Livre, Fribourg

All rights reserved.
No parts of this book may be reproduced in any manner whatsoever without permission of Rizzoli International Publications, Inc.

Library of Congress Catalog Number: 77-77509
ISBN: 0-8478-0129-2

This is a reprint edition distributed by Bookthrift, New York

Antonio de Pollaiuolo, *Naked Youth*, Musée Bonnat, Bayonne.

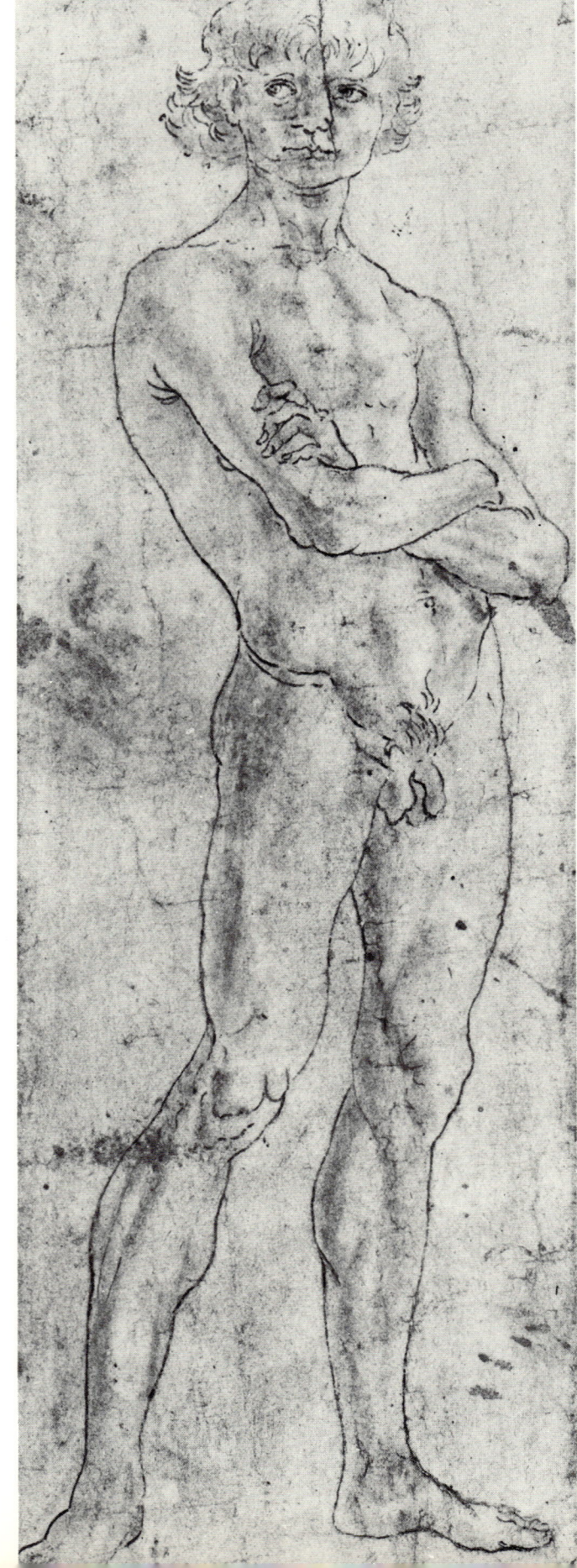

You again, front and back, Ganymede, beautiful little friend!

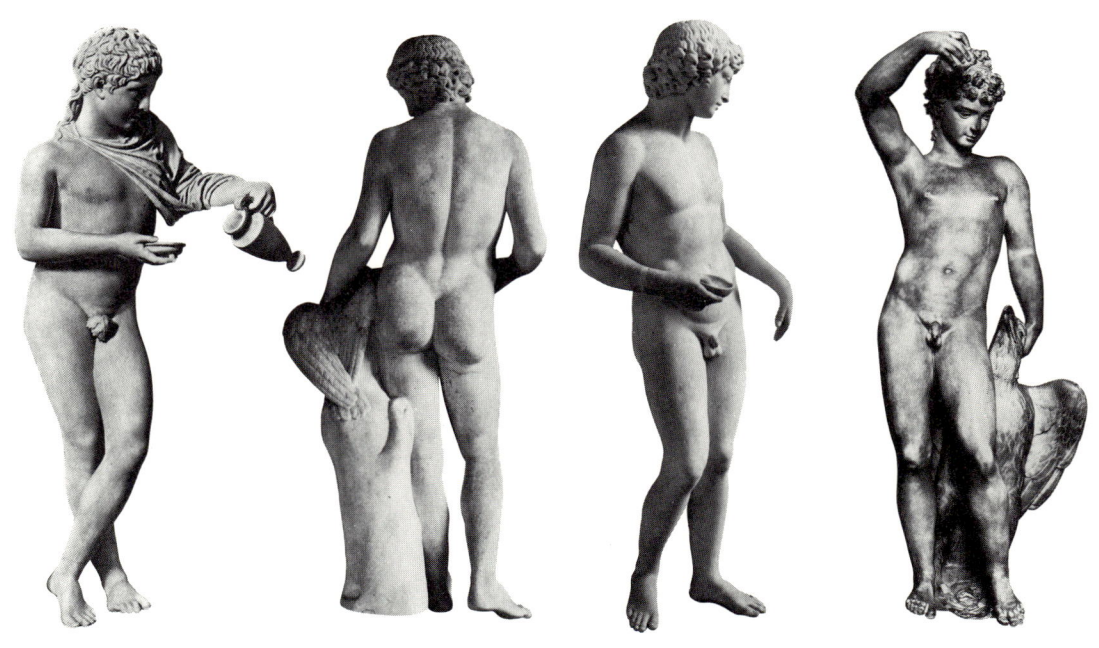

Three ancient statues representing Ganymede. The fourth is a copy from the Roman original by Benvenuto Cellini. (a) Vatican Museum, Rome. (b) and (c) Victoria and Albert Museum, London. (d) Benvenuto Cellini, *Ganymede*. Museo Nazionale del Bargello, Florence.

On a Statue of Ganymede

What! in this stodgy spa
(Respite, rest, repose and recess),
You again, front and back,
Ganymede, beautiful little friend!

Lifted by the eagle, as though
Love struck, from among the flowers.
His wing, beating strong and slow,
Churns the air, wanting you

Elsewhere than at that tyrannical
Jove, as they'd say in Revard.
His eye, taunting us, slips you
A look I wouldn't trust.

Oh, well! Stay with us, good lad.
Relieve our boredom
A little, the way you know.
Are you not our little brother?

(Verlaine, *Parallèment*)

Benvenuto Cellini, a triumphant *Ganymede*,
Museo Nazionale del Bargello, Florence.

CONTENTS

PREFACE
7

I
BUDDING YOUTHS,
OR LOVE—CHASTE AND UNCHASTE—IN ANCIENT GREECE
9

Author's comments 11—Anacreon 18—Pindar 20—Aristophanes 21—Plato 24—Xenophon 28—Aeschines 30—Artemon 31—Rhianos 32—Theocritus 32—Lucian 35—Strato of Sardis 39—Philostratus 41—Achilles Tatius 42

II
WHEN THE GODS PLAYED
43

Author's comments 45

III
LOVE, THE ROMAN WAY
53

Author's comments 55—Catullus 60—Petronius 62—Martial 64—Juvenal 67—Suetonius 69

IV
THE RETURN OF PLATO
73

Author's comments 75—Politian 88—Matteo Bandello 90—Gerolamo Morlino 92—Pietro Bassi, called Aretino 94—Michelangelo Buonarrotti 96—Richard Barnfield 99—Christopher Marlowe 103—William Shakespeare 108

V
THE PHILOSOPHERS' SIN
111

Author's comments 113—Theophile de Viau 121—Denys Sanguin de Saint-Pavin 123—Anonymous: *Alcibiades in School* 124—John Wilmot, Earl of Rochester 127—Johann Joachim Winckelmann 132—Voltaire 134—Jean-Jacques Rousseau 137—Count Giuseppe Gorani 141—Donatien Alphonse François, Marquis de Sade 144—Johann Wolfgang von Goethe 146—Author's comments: William Beckford, Collector and Writer 148—William Beckford 157

VI
AESTHETES AND POETS ACCURSED
159

Honoré de Balzac 160—Isidore Ducasse, Comte de Lautréamont 164—Author's comments: Paul Verlaine and Arthur Rimbaud 166—Rimbaud 171—Verlaine 173—Author's comments: Oscar Wilde 177—Oscar Wilde 183—Lord Alfred Douglas 187—*Teleny* 188—Aleister Crowley 192—Wald Whitman 194—Henry James 196—Paul Gauguin 198—Author's comments: Jean Lorrain 200—Jean Lorrain 202

VII
TO A HAPPIER YEAR
205

Author's comments 206—Charles-Louis Philippe 211—Paul Léautaud 214—Stefan George 216—Robert Musil 218—Frederick Rolfe [Baron Corvo] 220—Guillaume Apollinaire 223—Vsevolod V. Ivanov 225—Mikhail Kuzmin 226—Thomas Mann 230—Marcel Proust 232—Robert Desnos 237—René Crevel 238—Roger Peyrefitte 240—T.E. Lawrence 243—E.M. Forster 247—Federico Garcia Lorca 249—André Gide 251—Author's comments: Jean Cocteau and His Friends 254—Jean Cocteau 260—Maurice Sachs 264—C.P. Cavafy 268—Jean Genet 271—Marcel Jouhandeau 274—Umberto Saba 277—Kurt Malaparte 281—Charles Henri Ford and Parker Tyler 284—Julian Green 287—Gore Vidal 289—Tennessee Williams 291—Georges Eekhoud 292—William Burroughs 294—James Baldwin 297

SELECTED BIBLIOGRAPHY
299

ACKNOWLEDGMENTS
300

PHOTO CREDITS
304

PREFACE

For the Greek rhetorician and satirist Lucian, Jupiter's abduction of the young shepherd boy Ganymede was merely a delightful story. For Michelangelo it symbolized the torment of a tragic passion. Homoerotic love has been sublimated by some, while others have experienced it as a monstruous and unmentionable inclination.

This book is a survey of the different attitudes towards male homosexuality, from the authors of Antiquity, through the artists of the Renaissance, to the writers and painters of the seventeenth, eighteenth and nineteenth centuries in Europe and America. It also presents, for the first time, a number of anonymous erotic texts which have long been buried in private collections or in the rich inner recesses of the British Museum in London and the Bibliothèque Nationale in Paris. Finally, selections from contemporary authors, who can speak openly about matters their ancestors often had to veil, are given by way of contrast.

Wherever it seemed useful, we have made a point of explaining the circumstances, historical or otherwise, which lie behind a given text. Homosexuality was considered a superior form of love in ancient Greece and Rome, where it was cloaked with the prestige of art and literature. But with the spread of Judaism and Christianity all sexual activity not aimed at procreation was banned. Homosexuality came to be viewed as a vice, a perversion, an act against nature to be dealt with harshly by the laws of church and state. Nevertheless, it continued to inspire masterpieces in the plastic arts and literature. More than one artist (as can be seen from the illustrations) was stirred by the ambiguous appeal of young boys whose slender, not yet virile bodies combined the most graceful and seductive traits of both sexes. In a sense aren't painting a picture, carving a statue, composing a poem or a song to celebrate a lad's looks different ways of making love?

Claude Francin, *Ganymede*, Louvre, Paris.

I

BUDDING YOUTHS, OR LOVE–CHASTE AND UNCHASTE–IN ANCIENT GREECE

You will love boys in the sweet bloom of youth,
And long for their thighs, and long for their mouth.
(Solon)

Makron, *Ephebe and Adult*, interior of an Attic bowl. *c.* 490 B.C. Staatliche Antikensammlungen und Glyptothek, Munich.

The Argonauts (detail) from the Ficoroni cist, Praeneste. Fourth-third century B.C. Museo Nazionale di Villa Giulia, Rome.

In ancient Greece pederasty—homosexual love, as its etymology indicates (*pais* = adolescent; *erastēs* = lover)—meant exclusively love relationships with adolescent boys. Xenophon considered it an aspect of a young man's education: the lover set an example of moral rectitude and inculcated patriotism and respect for the laws in his young friend. According to Plato's pupil, Heracleides Ponticus, the inhabitants of Crete had, in some very early period, made pederasty an open social institution. It was customary for a boy's parents to ask one of their more esteemed acquaintances to seduce and carry off their son. For sixty days the youth and his adult "kidnapper" would participate in all kinds of festivities, banquets and hunting parties during which both were showered with gifts. This prolonged initiation ceremony ended with the sacrifice of a bull, after which the boy returned home having gained the right to bear the title "Illustrious" and to enjoy various privileges. Seduced for their looks, many of these lads remained faithful to their initiators—chiefly by fighting at their sides in battle. Before a fray began several of the youngest and handsomest warriors gave offerings to Eros, "the best god for exciting the ardor of war," according to the poet Phaidimos.

It was in Crete too that Zeus is said to have carried off Ganymede to make him serve as his cupbearer, so impressed was he by the young man's beauty. The Chalcideans had their own version of the story: according to them the abduction occured in Euboea—the amorous customs of the Euboeans being as notorious as those of the Cretans. For example, the city of Chalcis, the capital of Euboea, had raised a monument to Cleomachus, the warrior who had singlehandedly routed the cavalry of neighboring Eretria. There was a popular song to this hero, which Plutarch gives:

> O lad, whom fate has granted honest parents,
>   And all the gifts and talents,
> Do not turn down the warriors lusting for your youth;
> For no less than bravery doth benevolant Eros
> Flower in the cities of the Chalcideans.

These mores were by no means confined to Euboea or to Crete; they prevailed throughout Greece. In Thebes the heroism of the famous battalion of lovers who fought side by side inspired the youth of all the city—as did the story of Achilles' love for Patrocles. (Grief-stricken at the death of his young friend the Trojan hero is reported—by Lucian—to have cried out: "What could surpass the sacred intercourse with your thighs!")

There were other famous hero-lovers: Epaminondas and Cephisodoros who died in the battle of Mantineia (July 4, 362 B.C.); Aristogiton and Harmodius who stabbed Hipparchus, the brother of the tyrant Hippias, during the Panathenean festival of 514 B.C.. (Four years later Hippias was exiled. The tyrannicide couple became the heroes of democracy, and statues to them were raised in the agora).

In Plato's *Symposium,* Pausanias relates that in Elis and Boetia "... they have ... an ordinance that it is seemly to gratify lovers, and no one whether young or old will call it shameful, in order, I suppose, to save themselves the trouble of trying what speech can do to persuade the youths; for they have no ability for speaking." The Boetians, who were accused of being unmannerly and slow-witted, practiced homosexual love not only to stimulate their martial zeal, but also to polish their manners. In Megara, homophilia seems to have been a little more genteel: each Spring it was customary to honor the Athenian exile Diocles who had died while defending a young friend. A boys' kissing contest organized around his grave commemorated his many tender friendships. The bucolic poet Theocritus says that "whosoever presseth lip sweetliest upon lip, cometh away to's mother loaden with garlands." And he adds, "Happy the justicer holdeth that court of kissing! God wot he prays beamy Ganymede ... to make his lips like the touchstones which show the money-changer whether the gold be gold or dun."

Some philosophers viewed the love of boys as a superior type of love reserved for the intellectual elite. To those who argued that it was "against nature for a man to love a man" the Greek writer Lucian replied: "He-lions do not love he-lions, for they are not philosophers." He asserted, moreover, that "marriage is a boon and a blessing to men when it meets with good fortune, while the love of boys, that pays court to the hallowed dues of friendship, I consider to be the privilege only of philosophy. Therefore all men should marry, but let only the wise be permitted to love boys, for perfect virtue grows least of all among women."

Greek vase (detail). Sixth century B.C. Louvre, Paris. The palaestra, where the ancient Greeks trained for wrestling or athletics, was also a meeting place for pederasts.

Greek bowl (detail). Sixth century B.C. Louvre, Paris. Reveling sileni and satyrs in what Martial called a "chain of voluptuousness."

Clearly, as that excerpt shows, the ancient Greeks made a distinction between marriage and love. The former was simply an institution for procreating children to carry on the domestic rites. Wives lived in a separate world, had no acquaintances other than their servants and a few (female) friends, and more often than not were utterly uneducated. (Sappho was an exception, but then she was born in Lesbos.) Doubtless the Athenians would readily have concurred with Baudelaire, who wrote that "to love an intelligent woman is a faggot's pleasure."

Sexual segregation played an important role in Greek education. Parents preferred seeing their sons go to the Gymnasium and become attached to their instructors than get involved with depraved, money-loving hetaerae. "Doves with the claws of hawks," "poisoned cups of hydromel," as Diogenes called them, these professional courtesans were considered particularly dangerous. They were thought to encourage moral laxity and an immoderate love of luxury in young men. Whereas, as M.H.-E. Meier observes in his remarkable *History of Greek Love*— "by associating with the philosophers and by practicing pederasty, boys perfected their cultural education."

Socrates, Plato and Xenophon all celebrate the pure love between grown men and boys. In the *Symposium* there is a stirring speech (by Pausanias) which develops the idea that two kinds of love exist: the "Popular" and the "Heavenly". The Heavenly "partakes not of the female, but only of the male" and is "untinged with wantonness." The Popular, on the other hand, "...is the love we see in the meaner sort of men; who love women

Pan and Daphne. Museo delle terme, Rome. A marble copy of a Hellenistic group.

Lovers [Erastes and Eromenes], Greek vase (detail), fifth century B.C. Staatliche Museen Preussischer Kulturbesitz, Berlin.

as well as boys," and "where they love, they are set on the body more than the soul...." Thus, the philosophers, mentors of youth, were inspired by the heavenly Aphrodite who induces one to love friendship and noble deeds. But in fact were they not as Lucian writes, "more interested in youth and the beauty of the body than in virtue—and whatever Plato may say, it is unlikely that handsome Alcibiades after sleeping beneath the same blanket as Socrates rose intact from his embraces...." Aristophanes ridiculed these intellectuals and sophists whose favorite occupation was to go the rounds of the gymnasiums to pick up boys, and who went to their lessons accompanied by their pet little friends. At twelve a boy already appealed to them, says the great comedian; they considered him to be in the prime of life between sixteen and seventeen and already over the hill at eighteen.

At banquets a well-behaved young man would sit next to one of his relatives, to avoid having to respond to the advances of one of the guests. But according to Aristophanes such virtuousness was rare in Athens by the beginning of the fourth century B.C., and he complained that modern boys were ignorant in everything except wantonness (see p. 2). No wonder that the state of their morals left much to be desired once they grew up.

In Aristophanes' comedy *The Birds* a depraved Athenian describes his ideal of moral sophistication:

To have the father of some handsome lad
Come up and chide me with complaints like these,
Fine things I hear of you, Stilbonides,
You met my son returning from the baths,
And never kissed, or hugged, or fondled him,
You, his paternal friend! You're a nice fellow.

Some years later, towards 323 B.C., this dream almost came true, if one is to believe Addeus of Macedonia. Here is the advice he gives to a lover of ephebes (from the Greek word *efébos*, a young man between eighteen and nineteen): "When you meet a lad who catches your fancy, do not waste any time trying to disguise your intentions, but immediately grab hold of his balls with both your hands. Do not mince words, or say 'I respect you' or 'I would like to be like a brother to you'—for that sort of thing will only stand in your way."

In fact not all the "boy chasers" were that overt. Some of them preferred a more subtle approach, seeking to gain a boy's trust rather than rushing him. They would give him gifts, hang garlands on his door, sing laments in front of his home. A lover who was wise and discrete would stroke his young friend under the chin—even kisses were permitted—but "to do unto a boy that which the housewife does unto the hen when she looks to see if any eggs are on the way" was the act of one who was impure, an "old billy goat"—a raving fag, in short.

One has but to read Aristophanes, Athenaeus and the speeches of Aeschines to see that it was by no means uncommon for young, free-born citizens to earn extra change as male prostitutes. In Athens male brothels were exceedingly prosperous and had nothing to fear from outside competition. The city-state collected taxes on these houses where young slaves, usually imported from Syria or Egypt, were forced to satisfy the whims and

14

desires of their clients. (Some of the slaves were castrated, but the Greeks generally do not seem to have been as fond of eunuchs as were the Romans, the Medes and the Lydians). There was a great number of slaves: in Attica, in 309 B.C. for example, it is estimated that for a total population of half a million, there were 90,000 citizens, 45,000 foreign residents and no less than 365,000 slaves! The latter were treated rather better than their fellows in neighboring states. An Athenian who abused a slave could be fined. Rape, beatings and indecent assault were indictable offenses, but naturally the sentence was lighter when the victim was a slave.

To protect the young from "impure" homosexual solicitations, Greek lawmen apparently tried very early to control pederasty. Notwithstanding the fact that he had written obscene poems in his youth and may even have been the lover of the tyrant Peisistratus, Solon passed a law forbidding sexual relations between slaves and young citizens. Was this, as M. H.-E. Meier speculates, merely "to express his esteem for chaste homophilia"? It seems more likely that it was to protect young Athenians from disreputable acquaintanceships. Other laws forbade old men as well as slaves from entering gymnasiums and schools—for a lover over forty was considered indecent.

Were these laws respected or even enforced? Velerius Maximus relates that, at the age of eighty, Pindar fell asleep in a gymnasium, with his head resting on the knees of a boy he cherished above all others. At closing time, an attendant came to wake him up and discovered that he was dead.

Sophocles at fifty-five confessed that despite his age he often fell in love, and Euripedes at seventy-two spoke of his love for Agathon, who was forty: "A fine Autumn is a beautiful thing indeed!" Anacreon, who, it seems, "delighted in young men," confided: "I am old, there's no denying it. But so what? Among young satyrs I can still dance as well as old Silenus himself!" (See p. 19)

Sometimes homosexual love turned into criminal passion. Aeschines says that "Demosthenes, who was much inclined to lasciviousness and dressed with refined elegance, being drawn to boys as well as to women," fell violently in love with Plutarch. Fearing that the latter might be stolen from him, he tore out his eyes in a fit of rage, so that no one else would be attracted to him. Apparently this desperate ruse worked so well that Demosthenes himself was repulsed, for Athenaeus, who tells this cruel story, adds that "thereupon he took young Cnossia and installed him in his home, and made him share his own bed, whereat his wife complained bitterly." She soon took her revenge, however, by seducing the boy and becoming her husband's rival.

Philip of Macedonia was assassinated in 336 B.C. by

one of his favorites, Pausanias. The latter had been mortally angry at the king because Attalus, a relative of the Queen's, had treated him like a common prostitute and had handed him over to a gang of mule-drivers. "Incidentally" Aristotle counsels those who are in positions of power to avoid such relationships, "for in this passion," he says, "there is something which exceeds the bounds of vice."

Alexander the Great obviously ignored the wise teachings of his tutor. According to Athenaeus, he kissed the eunuch Bagoas, his favorite, on the mouth in front of his officers and had the satrap Orsines killed because the latter had mocked Bagoas by saying that "he would not talk to a man who prostituted himself like a woman." Plutarch has described the insane grief of the conqueror at the death of his beloved Hephaestion: having crucified the doctor who had not been able to save the boy, Alexander ordered his officers to cut off their hair, shave off the manes of every horse in his army and massacre every native in sight—man, woman and child—so as to celebrate with sufficient circumstance, if not pomp, the funeral of his beloved catamite.

The ancient Greeks spoke openly and uninhibitedly about matters which we call erotic. A love affair between two grown men, or between an adult and a boy, drew few comments and was even considered by many intellectuals as the noblest kind of love possible. Yet it was an insult to call someone a *pathicus* (the Roman term for the passive partner). In that patriarchal society, which has been compared to an all-men's club, and which scorned women, virility was very highly prized. Diogenes, the cynic, once said to a scented, plucked, ringleted young fop, "Aren't you ashamed that Nature had a better opinion of you than you yourself have? Nature made you a man, and you are trying to be a woman!"

Aristotle considered that the *paedico*'s (the "male" partner's) act of love with an effeminate boy was not much different from making love to a woman. On the other hand the "female" role seemed to him to be an aberration which was either congenital or which resulted from "bad habits contracted at puberty." That is why Aristotle deals harshly with adolescents who amused themselves by soliciting adults and getting themselves invited to banquets which usually degenerated into Bacchanalia. To a young exquisite who had lisped to him, "If I were as hated by my fellow citizens as you, I would hang myself," Aristotle retorted, "I would hang myself if I were as much loved by them as you."

The philosophers of Plato's and Xenophon's symposia considered the pleasurable disturbance caused by a youth's good looks not just a physical sensation, but also an intellectual delight—and even an intimation of perfection linked to religious feeling. For beauty was not a mere ornament to them; it was an expression of divinity. The winner of an event at the Olympic games, the boy crowned with roses at some festival, saw themselves as cult objects: they embodied triumphant youth, they were the springs of life and, in a way, they were the living images of divinity. The Greeks were fascinated by physical beauty. At the Olympic games they required the athletes to compete naked—much to the distress of the Romans who saw that as a proof of the moral degeneracy of the Greeks. The glorification of nudity, of course, is one of the characteristics of Greek art; and the fragility of that beauty, the ephemeral charm of youth, and love which vanishes like smoke, were the favorite themes of the poets who cherished boys. "In a single summer, the kid turns into a bearded billy goat." Strato of Sardis, the compiler of an anthology of homosexual verse, expressed the same sentiment when he lamented: "Agathon's little lizard was a rosy little finger; now it is more like an arm!" Was not homophilia in ancient Greece—as perhaps it still is—what Roger Peyrefitte has called "the dream of a love forever fled"? The lover's enjoyment of the lad he loves is so brief: no sooner has the flower of youth been plucked than already it has begun to fade.

Greek krater (See details p. 20), decorated by the painter working for the potter Kleophrades. c. 500 B.C. Museo Nazionale Tarquiniese, Tarquinia, Italy. A gymnastics instructor and an athlete holding a javelin. The accompanying inscription reads: *kalos ei* [You are beautiful, noble].

Interior of an Attic bowl representing a discobolus. Fifth century B.C. Louvre, Paris. "What I love above all else is a boy at the palaestra: his dusty body, his sturdy limbs, his soft skin." (Strato of Sardis)

ANACREON (c. 521 B.C.)

A.-E. Girodet de Roucy Trioson, Illustration for *The Odes of Anacreon*, Bibliothèque Nationale, Paris. "I have seen the portrait of Anacreon at Teos. He was the loftiest of the lyric poets in the old days... and was the delight of youths everywhere. Anacreon, you have sung entire Man most truly." (*The Idylls*, Theocritus.)

When someone asked Anacreon why his poems were always about children and not about gods, he replied: "That is because children are our gods."

Anacreon was born in Teos in Asian Greece, but he spent part of his life first at the court of the tyrant Polycrates in Samos, and next in Athens at the court of Hipparchus, the son of Peisistratus. He was a pleasure-loving, wine-loving, boy-loving poet. However, when he praised the beauty of young actors or musicians, like Smerdies, Megister or Bathyllus, it was not always his own feelings he was expressing, but those of his patron, Polycrates. This sinecure sometimes led to trouble. Once young Smerdies took Anacreon's love verses so seriously that he fell in love with the poet and ignored Polycrates. Furious with jealousy, the tyrant had Smerdies' hair shorn—a terrible disgrace, since a full head of long hair was a boy's finest asset. Anacreon pretended to believe that Smerdies had cut off his hair himself and reproached him for it. The poet was also the friend of wealthy Critias and of Xanthippos, the father of Pericles. Entertained everywhere, invited to feasts by the great families, Anacreon lived to a ripe old age. Very few of the songs and poems which have come down to us can be attributed to him with certainty.

TO A SILVER WINE CUP

O silver working Hephaestus, portray
Me not in the dress of a warrior, I pray.
Why combats for me? But as big as can be
A deep hollow wine cup fashion for me!

But carve on the same neither stars nor the Wain,
Nor hated Orion—for why should my brain
Grow dizzy with watching the fields of the sky—
The Pleiades or the fair Plowman on high?

But make for me vineyards of beautiful shapes
Lavishly tasselled with clusters of grapes,
And the frantic maids who are robbing the vine,
And the vat that imprisons or sets free the wine,

Together with lovely Lyaeus, so mighty—
Since he, only he, can subdue Aphrodite.

TO BATHYLLUS, THE YOUNGER

Thus for me draw thou Bathyllus,
My companion, as I teach thee.
Make indeed his lower ringlets
Shining and as dark as midnight,
But those on the summit sun-touched,
Free, with curling locks for my sake.
Fashion them with braids dishevelled,
Falling down in sweet disorder
Also let his fine and dewy
Eyebrows crown his forehead with a
Hue more glossy than the Dragon's.
Let his eye be black and dreadful,
But with gentleness be blended—
This from Ares drawn, and that from
Cytherea. While you fear the
Glance of Ares, Cytherea's
Holds you in suspense atremble
But his fair and downy cheek, make
Rosy hued just as an apple.
And his blush of bashful boyhood,
Make if thou hast power to hit it.
But his lip, no longer know I
In what way thou mayest fashion
That sweet burden of Persuasion—
Let the moulded wax reveal it
Speaking though enwrapt in silence.
Next his face let there be fashioned
Smooth, an ivory neck surpassing
Even that of fair Adonis.
But the space between his shoulders
Grace with Hermes' double pinions
And the thighs of Pollux give him
And a Dionysian person
But below his dainty thighs, his
Thighs the fire of youth possessing
Make thou smooth his secret members
For the Paphian rites propitious.

Oh, an envious craft thou wieldest
Since to show his back thou couldst not.
But this is by far the better.
To describe his feet, why need I?
Take as pay whate'er thou sayest
But the statue of Apollo
Taking down, make a Bathyllus
And if e'er thou go'st to Samos
From Bathyllus draw a Phoebus.

A.-E. Girodet de Roucy Trioson, Two illustrations for *The Odes of Anacreon*. Bibliothèque Nationale, Paris. (a) *Portrait of Bathyllus*. (b) *In Praise of Old Age*.

PINDAR (c. 518-438 B.C.)

According to Athenaeus, whose works are a source of information about all of ancient Greek literature, the famous Theban poet was by nature as randy as a goat. He loved Agathonidas, Diodoros the flute player, Boulagoras and other lads whose names have not come down to us. Perhaps the boy whose knees his head was resting on when he died was Theoxenus, to whom the fragment below is dedicated. In 476 Pindar went to Sicily where he spent two years at the court of Hiero at Syracuse, but he was never a paid sycophant, and he always managed to retain his independance: "I live as I please," he said once, "and not as it pleases others."

Showered with honors in his lifetime, Pindar had the satisfaction of seeing one of his poems, an ode composed to celebrate the victory of the athlete Diagoras of Rhodes at the wrestling event of the Seventh Olympiad (464 B.C.), carved in gold on the temple of Athena at Lindos.

ON THEOXENUS OF TENEDOS

Right it were, fond heart, to cull love's blossom in due season, in life's prime; but whosoever, when once he hath seen the rays flashing from the eyes of Theoxenus, doth not swell with desire, his black heart, with its frozen flame, hath been forged of adamant or of iron; and, unhonoured of brightly glancing Aphrodite, he either toileth over hoarded wealth, or, with a woman's courage, is borne along enslaved to a path that is utterly cold.

But I, for the sake of that Queen of love, like the wax of the holy bees that is melted beneath the heat of the sun, waste away when I look at the young limbs of blooming boys. Thus I ween that even in Tenedos Suasion and Charm dwelt in the soul of the son of Hagêsilas.

Krater (detail) shown on p. 16. Painted by the painter working for the potter Kleophrades, c. 500 B.C. Museo Nazionale Tarquiniese, Tarquinia, Italy. Two crowned athletes: one of them preparing to throw the discus, the other the javelin.

ARISTOPHANES (c. 448 - after 388 B.C.)

Aristophanes, the famous comic poet, poked fun at the intellectuals of his age—especially Socrates—in his witty, ribald plays. The ageing, pot-bellied philosopher (who was forty-six at the time) seemed to him a satyr surrounded by provocative boys, corrupting the youth of Athens not only by the bad example he was setting but above all by his teachings. In *The Clouds* (423 B.C.) Aristophanes satirizes the sophistic system of education that was fashionable then and looks back nostalgically to the severe discipline of the old-fashioned aristocratic method of schooling. The play tells the story of a father whose son impoverishes the family with his debts. Hoping to win the trial that his son's creditors have instituted against him, the man goes to see Socrates for lessons in disputation. Naturally Socrates prefers the son to the father. He calls in personifications of the two types of Discourse—the Just and the Unjust—and has them debate in front of the young man. The lad is of course captivated by the theories and promises of easy living which the Unjust Discourse proffers—and so he decides to follow the teachings of Socrates.

Greek amphora (detail). c. 550 B.C. Cabinet des Médailles, Bibliothèque Nationale, Paris. Amorous conversation between an adult and a young boy from Sparta.

From THE CLOUDS

JUST DISCOURSE. Very well, I will tell you what was the old education, when I used to teach justice with so much success and when modesty was held in veneration. Firstly, it was required of a child, that it should not utter a word. In the street, when they went to the music-school, all the youths of the same district marched lightly clad and ranged in good order, even when the snow was falling in great flakes. At the master's house they had to stand, their legs apart, and they were taught to sing either, "Pallas, the Terrible, who overturneth cities," or "A noise resounded from afar" in the solemn tones of the ancient harmony. If anyone indulged in buffoonery or lent his voice any of the soft inflexions, like those which to-day the disciples of Phrynis take so much pains to form, he was treated as an enemy of the Muses and belaboured with blows. In the wrestling school they would sit with outstretched legs and without display of any indecency to the curious. When they rose, they would smooth over the sand, so as to leave no trace to excite obscene thoughts. Never was a child rubbed with oil below the belt; the rest of their bodies thus retained its fresh bloom and down, like a velvety peach. They were not to be seen approaching a lover and themselves rousing his passion by soft modulation of the voice and lustful gaze. At table, they would not have dared, before those older than themselves, to have taken a radish, an aniseed or a leaf of parsley, and much less eat fish or thrushes or cross their legs.

UNJUST DISCOURSE. What antiquated rubbish! Have we got back to the days of the festivals of Zeus Polieus, to the

Aubrey Beardsley, Illustration for *Lysistrata*. Private edition for Smithers, 1896. "I will tell the Senate to choose other delegates by brandishing this rod here." (Aristophanes)

Attic bowl (detail). [Adult kissing an ephebe.] Fifth century B.C. Louvre, Paris.

Buphonia, to the time of the poet Cecydes and the golden cicadas?

JUST DISCOURSE. 'Tis nevertheless by suchlike teaching I built up the men of Marathon. But you, you teach the children of to-day to bundle themselves quickly into their clothes, and I am enraged when I see them at the Panathenaea forgetting Athené while they dance, and covering themselves with their bucklers. Hence, young man, dare to range yourself beside me, who follow justice and truth; you will then be able to shun the public place, to refrain from the baths, to blush at all that is shameful, to fire up if your virtue is mocked at, to give place to your elders, to honour your parents, in short, to avoid all that is evil. Be modesty itself, and do not run to applaud the dancing girls; if you delight in such scenes, some courtesan will cast you her apple and your reputation will be done for. Do not bandy words with your father, nor treat him as a dotard, nor reproach the old man, who has cherished you, with his age.

UNJUST DISCOURSE. If you listen to him, by Bacchus! you will be the image of the sons of Hippocrates and will be called *mother's great ninny*.

JUST DISCOURSE. No, but you will pass your days at the gymnasia, glowing with strength and health; you will not go to the public place to cackle and wrangle as is done nowadays; you will not live in fear that you may be dragged before the courts for some trifle exaggerated by quibbling. But you will go down to the Academy to run beneath the sacred olives with some virtuous friend of your own age, your head encircled with the white reed, enjoying your ease and breathing the perfume of the yew and of the fresh sprouts of the poplar, rejoicing in the return of springtide and gladly listening to the gentle rustle of the plane tree and the elm. If you devote yourself to practising my precepts, your chest will be stout, your colour glowing, your shoulders broad, your tongue short, your hips muscular, but your other parts small. But if you follow the fashions of the day, you will be pallid in hue, have narrow shoulders, a narrow chest, a long tongue, small hips and a big thing; you will know how to spin forth long-winded arguments on law. You will be persuaded also to regard as splendid everything that is shameful and as shameful everything that is honourable; in a word, you will wallow in debauchery like Antimachus....

UNJUST DISCOURSE ... young man, just consider a little what this temperance means and the delights of which it deprives you—young fellows, women, play, dainty dishes, wine, boisterous laughter. And what is life worth without these? Then, if you happen to commit one of these faults inherent in human weakness, some seduction or adultery, and you are caught in the act, you are lost, if you cannot speak. But follow my teaching and you will be able to satisfy your passions, to dance, to laugh, to blush at nothing. Are you surprised in adultery? Then up and tell the husband you are not guilty, and recall to him the example of Zeus, who allowed himself to be conquered by love and by women. Being but a mortal, can you be stronger than a god?

JUST DISCOURSE. And if your pupil gets impaled, his hairs plucked out, and he is seared with a hot ember, how are you going to prove to him that he is not a filthy debauchee?

UNJUST DISCOURSE. And wherein lies the harm of being so?

JUST DISCOURSE. Is there anything worse than to have such a character?

UNJUST DISCOURSE. Now what will you say, if I beat you even on this point?

JUST DISCOURSE. I should certainly have to be silent then.

UNJUST DISCOURSE. Well then, reply! Our advocates, what are they?

JUST DISCOURSE. Low scum.

UNJUST DISCOURSE. Nothing is more true. And our tragic poets?

JUST DISCOURSE. Low scum.

UNJUST DISCOURSE. Well said again. And our demagogues?

JUST DISCOURSE. Low scum.

UNJUST DISCOURSE. You admit that you have spoken nonsense. And the spectators, what are they for the most part? Look at them.

JUST DISCOURSE. I am looking at them.

UNJUST DISCOURSE. Well! What do you see?

JUST DISCOURSE. By the gods, they are nearly all low scum. See, this one I know to be such and that one and that other with the long hair.

UNJUST DISCOURSE. What have you to say, then?

JUST DISCOURSE. I am beaten. Debauchees! in the name of the gods, receive my cloak,* I pass over to your ranks.

*Having said this, Just Discourse threw his cloak into the amphitheatre and took a seat with the spectators.

PLATO (c. 427-347 B.C.)

Born in an aristocratic Athenian family, Plato became a student of Socrates at the age of twenty. He was not able to attend his master's last moments, being sick at the time. The death sentence pronounced against Socrates seemed so unjust to him that he voluntarily exiled himself from Athens and went to Megara. From there he journeyed to Egypt, the coast of Africa, Southern Italy and Sicily, where he stayed at the court of Dionysius the Elder. There he met the ruler's nephew, Dion, to whom he immediately felt drawn. Was this attraction purely "Platonic"? Whatever the case, Dionysius disapproved, and Plato was obliged to leave town. Unfortunately the vessel he sailed away on called in at the port of Aegina, which was at that time at war with Athens. Plato was made a prisoner and was sold as a slave. But he was recognized by a trader who bought him and set him free. Back in Athens (387 B.C.), in a gymnasium in a park named after the ancient hero Akademo, Plato organized a school of philosophy, doubtless the first in the Western world: the famous "Academy." Plato was forty at the time. In the years which followed he wrote the *Symposium*.

The selection given below is Alcibiades' account of how he tried—unsuccessfully—to seduce Socrates. Alcibiades, still a beardless youth, was notoriously handsome, ostentatious and depraved. Plato's intention here is to vindicate Socrates from the accusation of the poetaster Meletos, who had charged that the philosopher was corrupting the youth of Athens. Meletos, it seems, had been put up to it by Anytos, the leader of a powerful political party, who was in love with Alcibiades, but whom Alcibiades scorned. One night Anytos invited Alcibiades and some friends to dine; Alcibiades sent his servants over to Anytos's house and had them bring him the dinner, silver plates and all! The unfortunate host took his revenge later by using his power to destroy Socrates. Alcibiades also tells how he hoped to profit from the philosopher's wisdom—which he proposed to pay for with his own beauty. But Socrates declined, saying that it would be like trading "bronze for gold."

Frieze (detail) from the Parthenon representing Poseidon and Apollo awaiting the arrival of a procession of Panathenaea contestants. Fifth century B.C. Acropolis Museum, Acropolis, Athens.

Attic bowl, reverse side. Fifth century B.C. Louvre, Paris. The bowl shows a banquet with youths crowned with flowers. The inscription *Lysis* is probably the name of one of the banqueters.

Two selections from the SYMPOSIUM

ALCIBIADES: Observe how Socrates is amourously inclined to handsome persons; with these he is always busy and enraptured. Again, he is utterly stupid and ignorant, as he affects. Is not this like a Silenus? Exactly. It is an outward casing he wears, similarly to the sculptured Silenus. But if you opened his inside, you cannot imagine how full he is, good cup-companions, of sobriety. I tell you, all the beauty a man may have is nothing to him; he despises it more than any of you can believe; nor does wealth attract him, nor any sort of honour that is the envied prize of the crowd. All these possessions he counts as nothing worth, and all of us as nothing. I assure you; he spends his whole life in chaffing and making game of his fellow-men. Whether anyone else has caught him in a serious moment and opened him, and seen the images inside, I know not; but I saw them one day, and thought them so divine and golden, so perfectly fair and wondrous, that I simply had to do as Socrates bade me. And believing he had a serious affection for my youthful bloom, I supposed I had here a godsend and a rare stroke of luck, thinking myself free at any time by gratifying his desires to hear all that our Socrates knew; for I was enormously proud of my youthful charms. So with this design I dismissed the attendant whom till then I invariably brought to my meetings with Socrates, and I would go and meet him alone: I am to tell you the whole truth; you must all mark my words, and, Socrates, you shall refute me if I lie. Yes, gentlemen, I went and met him, and the two of us would be alone; and I thought he would seize the chance of talking to me as a lover does to

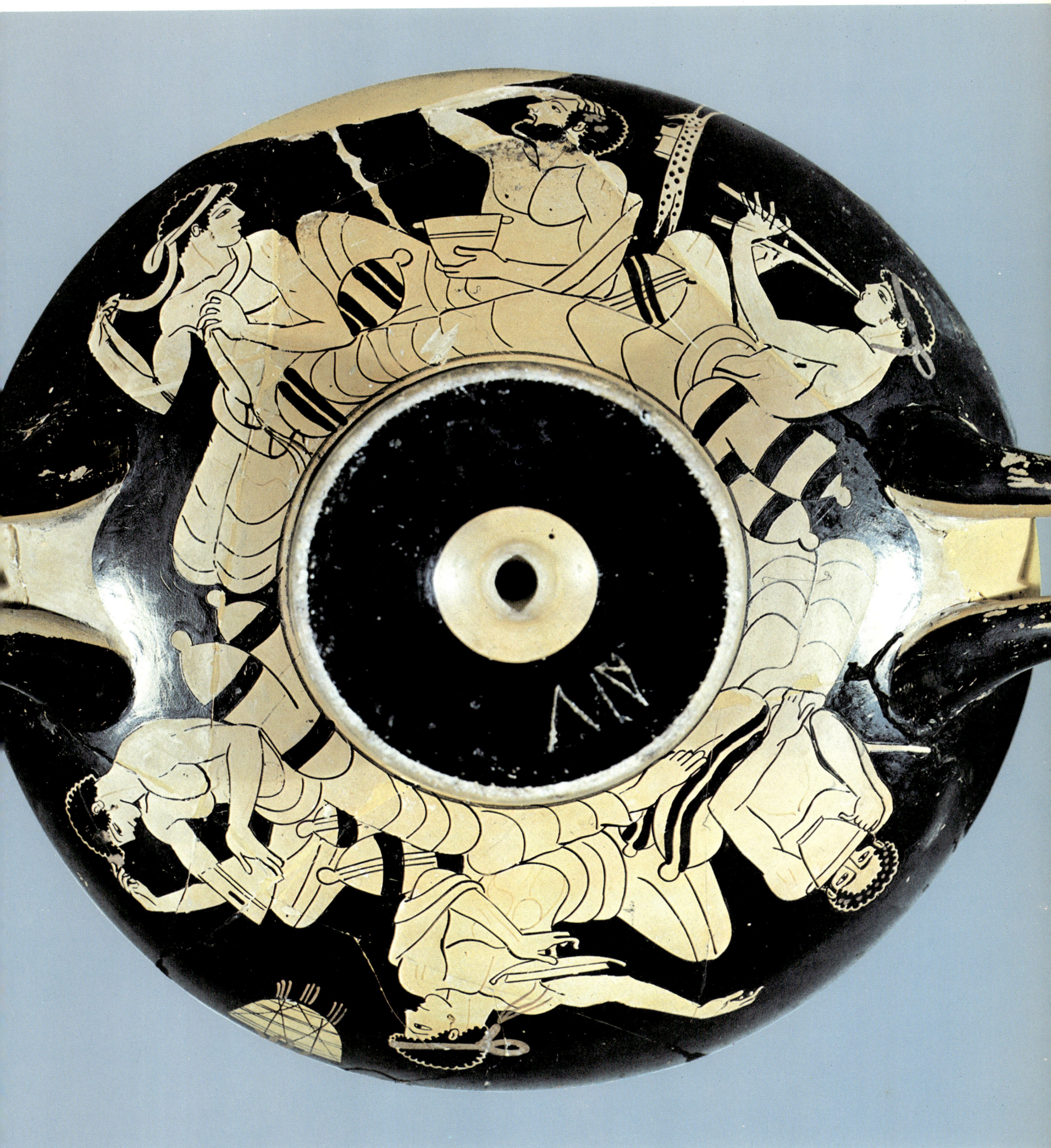

Bowl (detail) attributed to the painter working for the potter Chairias. Attic style, sixth century B.C. Louvre, Paris.

his dear one in private, and I was glad. But nothing of the sort occurred at all: he would merely converse with me in his usual manner, and when he had spent the day with me he would leave me and go his way. After that I proposed he should go with me to the trainer's, and I trained with him, expecting to gain my point there. So he trained and wrestled with me many a time when no one was there. The same story! I got no further with the affair. Then, as I made no progress that way, I resolved to charge full tilt at the man, and not to throw up the contest once I had entered upon it: I felt I must clear up the situation. Accordingly I invited him to dine with me, for all the world like a lover scheming to ensnare his favourite. Even this he was backward to accept; however, he was eventually persuaded. The first time he came, he wanted to leave as soon as he had dined. On that occasion I was ashamed and let him go. The second time I devised a scheme: when we had dined I went on talking with him far into the night, and when he wanted to go I made a pretext of the lateness of the hour and constrained him to stay. So he sought repose on the couch next to me, on which he had been sitting at dinner, and no one was sleeping in the room but ourselves....

Well, gentlemen, when the lamp had been put out and the servants had withdrawn, I determined not to mince matters with him, but to speak out freely what I intended. So I shook him and said, "Socrates, are you asleep?"

"Why, no," he replied.

"Let me tell you what I have decided."

"What is the matter?" he asked.

"I consider," I replied, "that you are the only worthy lover I have had, and it looks to me as if you were shy of mentioning it to me. My position is this: I count it sheer folly not to gratify you in this as in any other need you may have of either my property or that of my friends. To me nothing is more important than the attainment of the highest possible excellence, and in this aim I believe I can find no abler ally than you. So I should feel a far worse shame before sensible people for not gratifying such a friend than I should before the senseless multitude for gratifying him."

When he heard this, he put on that innocent air which habit has made so characteristic of him, and remarked: "My dear Alcibiades, I dare say you are not really a dolt, if what you say of me is the actual truth, and there is a certain power in me that could help you to be better; for then what a stupendous beauty you must see in me, vastly superior to your comeliness! And if on espying this you are trying for a mutual exchange of beauty for beauty, it is no slight advantage you are counting on—you are trying to get genuine in return for reputed beauties, and in fact are designing to fetch off the old bargain of *gold for bronze*. But be more wary, my gifted friend: you may be deceived and I may be worthless. Remember, the intellectual sight

Interior of a bowl: young man drawing wine. Fifth century B.C. Louvre, Paris.

Krater (detail) decorated by the painter Euphronios. *c.* 510 B.C. Staatliche Museen Preussischer Kulturbesitz, Berlin. The painter depicts ephebes famous for their athletic looks and the nobility of their minds (*kaloi*). Shown is an athlete tying his foreskin with a band, assisted by a slave boy; a second athlete is getting ready to hurl the discus.

begins to be keen when the visual is entering on its wane; but you are a long way yet from that time."

To this I answered: "You have heard what I had to say; not a word differed from the feeling in my mind: it is for you now to consider what you judge to be best for you and me."

"Ah, there you speak to some purpose," he said: "for in the days that are to come we shall consider and do what appears to be best for the two of us...."

Well, after I had exchanged these words with him and, as it were, let fly my shafts, I fancied he felt the wound: so up I got, and without suffering the man to say a word more I wrapped my own coat about him—it was wintertime; drew myself under his cloak, so; wound my arms about this truly spiritual and miraculous creature; and lay thus all the night long. Here too, Socrates, you are unable to give me the lie. When I had done all this, he showed such superiority and contempt, laughing my youthful charms to scorn, and flouting the very thing on which I prided myself, gentlemen of the jury—for you are here to try Socrates for his lofty disdain: you may be sure, by gods—and goddesses—that when I arose I had in no more particular sense slept a night with Socrates than if it had been with my father or my elder brother.

XENOPHON (*c.* 430-355 B.C.)

Another detail of the krater on p. 27. *c.* 510 B.C. Staatliche Museen Preussischer Kulturbesitz, Berlin. Two famous ephebes: Hegesias pouring unguent on to his hand, and Leagros folding his clothes.

Palaestra scenes. First half of the fifth century B.C. Louvre, Paris.

Xenophon came from a wealthy Athenian family. He too was a student of Socrates, and in a work entitled *The Symposium* (like Plato's) he recorded his conversations with the great philosopher.

He was a citizen of Athens and a member of the class of knights. He was not only an intellectual but a man of action, and took part in the punitive expedition of Cyrus the Younger against his brother Artaxerxes. Promoted to general he served under the king of Thrace and later under the king of Sparta in the war against Athens—which resulted in his being banished from his native city.

In 365 B.C. the edict of banishment was lifted. From then on Xenophon devoted himself to the Athenian cause. His work on *Hiero,* in which he condemns tyranny, dates from this period.

Despite the fact that he extolled the virtues of asceticism and contempt for pleasure, Xenophon was often troubled by the perfect physiques of young athletes.

From HIERO

31. Such was the opinion that Hiero expressed. But Simonides, with a smile, replied, "What say you, Hiero? Do you intimate that no desire for male objects of affection arises in a king? How is it, then, that you have such love for Dailochus, who is called the most beautiful of youths?"

32. "It is not assuredly, my dear Simonides," replied Hiero, "because I am so eager to obtain from him that which appears to be always ready for me, but because I long to effect that which is least of all in the power of a king. 33. For I indeed desire to have from Dailochus what human nature perhaps compels every one to desire from beautiful objects; but what I desire to have I wish to obtain with mutual affection and willingness, and to extort from him by force I feel less inclination than I should feel to do an injury to my own person. 34. To take from enemies against their will, I consider to be one of the highest gratifications; but favours from objects of affection give us most pleasure when they bestow them voluntarily. 35. From one who returns our affection, glances of the eye, for instance, are pleasing, questions are pleasing, answers are pleasing, and little contentions and resentments are the most pleasing and fascinating of all. 36. But to enjoy objects of our affection by force appears to be more like the act of a robber than that of a lover. To a robber, indeed, the prospect of gain, or the annoyance of an enemy, affords some gratification; but to snatch pleasure from an object of our desire, while that object is suffering pain, to incur hatred by the advances of love, and to lay hands on one that resents the familiarity, can such conduct be regarded as otherwise than odious and contemptible? 37. To a private individual, if the object of his affection offers him a favour, it is at once a proof that that object bestows the favour through love, since he knows that the favour is conferred without any impulse from necessity. 38. But as to a king, it is hardly ever possible for him to believe that he is loved; for we know that those who submit to our pleasure through fear, assimilate their manner, as much as they can, to that of those who comply with our wishes from love; and indeed there are none from whom conspiracies against kings proceed more frequently than from those who have affected to love them with the greatest sincerity."

AESCHINES (c. 390-314 B.C.)

Aeschines, another Athenian, the son of a schoolmaster father and a mother who served as a priestess in one of the secret religious cults, tried his hand at various trades before becoming a statesman and a well-known orator. Early in his career he denounced Philip of Macedonia; later, though, he changed his mind and became an ardent advocate of peace at any price. He was asked to negociate a settlement with the Macedonians in 346 B.C.. Upon hearing that Demosthenes and Timarchus were charging him with having sold out to Philip, Aeschines counterattacked by instigating a trial against Timarchus. He accused him not of being gay (who wasn't in Athens?) but of having prostituted and debauched himself. Timarchus was condemned on a charge of immorality and was forbidden to speak in public. Aeschines speech is especially interesting because of what it tells us about homosexual legislation in fourth-century Athens.

From AGAINST TIMARCHUS

And just here I understand he is going to carry the war into my territory, and ask me if I am not ashamed on my own part, after having made a nuisance of myself in the gymnasia and having been many times a lover, now to be bringing the practice into reproach and danger. And finally—so I am told—in an attempt to raise a laugh and start silly talk among you, he says he is going to exhibit all the erotic poems I have ever addressed to one person or another, and he promises to call witnesses to certain quarrels and pommellings in which I have been involved in consequence of this habit.

Now as for me, I neither find fault with love that is honourable, nor do I say that those who surpass in beauty are prostitutes. I do not deny that I myself have been a lover and am a lover to this day, nor do I deny that the jealousies and quarrels that commonly arise from the practice have happened in my case. As to the poems which they say I have composed, some I acknowledge, but as to others I deny that they are of the character that these people will impute to them, for they will tamper with them.

The distinction which I draw is this: to be in love with those who are beautiful and chaste is the experience of a kind-hearted and generous soul; but to hire for money and to indulge in licentiousness is the act of a man who is wanton and illbred. And whereas it is an honour to be the object of a pure love, I declare that he who has played the prostitute by inducement of wages is disgraced. How wide indeed is the distinction between these two acts and how great the difference, I will try to show you in what I shall next say. Our fathers, when they were laying down laws to regulate the habits of men and those acts that inevitably flow from human nature, forbade slaves to do those things which they thought ought to be done by free men. "A slave," says the law, "shall not take exercise or anoint himself in the wrestling-schools." It did not go on to add, "But the free man shall anoint himself and take exercise;" for when, seeing the good that comes from gymnastics, the lawgivers forbade slaves to take part, they thought that in prohibiting them they were by the same words inviting the free. Again, the same lawgiver said, "A slave shall not be the lover of a free boy nor follow after him, or else he shall receive fifty blows of the public lash." But the free man was not forbidden to love a boy, and associate with him, and follow after him, nor did the lawgiver think that harm came to the boy thereby, but rather that such a thing was a testimony to his chastity. But, I think, so long as the boy is not his own master and is as yet unable to discern who is a genuine friend, and who is not, the law teaches the lover self-control, and makes him defer the words of friendship till the other is older and has reached years of discretion; but to follow after the boy and to watch over him the lawgiver regarded as the best possible safeguard and protection for chastity.

ARTEMON
(fourth century B.C.)

Artemon wrote epigrams. A few verses extolling the beauty of an Athenian lad called Echedemus, in the series of epigrams written by Meleager of Gadara in 100 B.C., are ascribed to him.

HOT COALS

Echedemus, that graceful boy,
was peeking through
the doorway. I got him
by surprise, and kissed his lips.

But I'm still aflutter.
For I saw him in a dream
point his little bow at me,
all smiles and frowns,

then leave, leaving me
a gift or another. I'm afraid
I've put my hand into nettles,
into a wasp's nest, into hot coals.

Anonymous, *The Apollo of Piombino* [bronze statue of an ephebe]. Second quarter of the fifth century B.C. Louvre, Paris. "Oh, virginal-eyed lad, I follow your steps and you do not even know that you govern my soul." (Anacreon)

Anonymous, *Mercury* (detail). Fourth century B.C. Etruscan Museum, Vatican, Rome.

31

RHIANOS (third century B.C.)

Rhianos was a Greek poet and philologist born on Crete. He lived most of his life in Alexandria, where he published an edition of the *Iliad* and the *Odyssey*. Rhianos wrote epigrams, an epic and mythical poems in which he collected and versified heroic legends, for instance about the Third Messianian War (464-459 B.C.). Only fragments of these poems are extant today.

From MUSA PUERILIS

Boys are a labyrinth from which there is no way out; for wherever thou castest thine eye it is fast entangled as if by bird-lime. Here Theodorus attracts thee to the plump ripeness of his flesh and the unadulterate bloom of his limbs, and there it is the golden face of Philocles, who is not great in stature, but heavenly grace environs him. But if thou turnest to look on Leptines thou shalt no more move thy limbs, but shalt remain, thy steps glued as if by indissoluble adamant; such a flame hath the boy in his eyes to set thee afire from thy head to thy toe and finger tips. All hail, beautiful boys! May ye come to the prime of youth and live till grey hair clothe your heads.

(no. 93)

THEOCRITUS (310 - c. 250 B.C.)

Born in Syracuse, this Greek poet lived at the court of the Egyptian ruler Ptolemy II Philadelphus between 275 and 270 B.C.. Then he settled in Cos, the island his family had come from, and there he composed "bucolic idylls" in the manner of the lyrics sung by Sicilian herdsmen at rural poetry contests. Theocritus frequently drew his inspiration from popular legends.

XXIX THE FIRST LOVE-POEM

In sack, out sooth goes the saying, lad, and now that you and I are a-drinking we must fain be men of truth. I for one will tell what doth lie in my mind's hold, and it is that you will not that I should love you with my whole heart. I know it; for such is the power of your beauty that there's but half a living left me to love you withal, seeing my day is spent like as a God's or in very darkness according as you do choose. What righteousness is here, to deliver one that loves you over unto woe? Trust me, if you 'ld only hearken to your elder 'twould be profit unto you and thanks unto me. Listen then: one tree should hold one nest, and that where no noisome beast may come at it; but you, you do possess one bough to-day and another tomorrow, seeking ever from this unto that; and if one but see and praise your fair face, straightway are you more than a three years' friend to him, and as for him that first loved you, in three days, lad, you reckon him of those men whose very manhood you seem to disdain. Choose rather to be friends with the same body so long as you shall live; for if so you do, you will have both honour of the world and kindness of that Love who doth so easily vanquish the mind of man and hath melted in me a heart of very iron.

O by those soft lips I beseech you remember that you were younger a year agone, and as we men wax old and wrinkled sooner than one may spit, so there's no re-taking of Youth once she be fled, seeing she hath wings to her shoulders, and for us 'tis ill catching winged beasts. Come then, think on these things and be the kinder for 't, and give love for love where true loving is; and so when Time shall bring thee a beard we'll be Achilles and his friend. But if so be you cast me these words to the winds, and say, and say in your heart, "Peace, man; begone," then, for all I would go now for your sake and get the Golden Apples or fetch you the Watch-dog o' the Dead, I would not come forth, no, not if you should stand at my very door and call me, for the pain of my woodness would be overpast.

Bronze statue (detail) in the manner of Praxiteles. Fourth century B.C. National Archaeological Museum, Athens. This ephebe is wearing the ornament of the palaestrae in his hair—a curved metal claw—the attribute of the god Hermes.

From XXX THE SECOND LOVE-POEM

Aye me, the pain and the grief of it! I have been sick of Love's quartan now a month and more. He's not so fair, I own, but all the ground his pretty foot covers is grace, and the smile of his face is very sweetness. 'Tis true the ague takes me now but day on day off, but soon there'll be no respite, no not for a wink of sleep. When we met yesterday he gave me a sidelong glance, afeared to look me in the face, and blushed crimson; at that, Love gripped my reins still the more, till I gat me wounded and heartsore home, there to arraign my soul at bar and hold with myself this parlance: "What wast after, doing so? whither away this fond folly? know'st thou not there's three gray hairs on thy brow? Be wise in time, or one that is no youth in's looks shall play new-taster o' the years. Other toys thou forgettest; 'twere better, sure, at thy time o' life to know no more such loves as this. For whom Life carries swift and easy as hoof doth hind, and might endure to cross and cross the sea every day's morrow that is, can he and the flower o' sweet Youth abide ever of one date? How much less he that hath yearnful remembrance gnawing at his heart's core, and dreams often o' nights and taketh whole years to cure his lovesickness!..."

XXIII THE LOVER

There was once a heart-sick swain had a cruel fere, the face of the fere goodly but his ways not like to it; for he hated him that loved him, and had for him never a whit of kindness, and as for Love, what manner of God he might be or what manner of bow and arrows carry, or how keen and bitter were the shafts he shot for his delectation, these things wist he not at all, but both in his talk and conversation knew no yielding. And he gave no comfort against those burning fires, not a twist of his lip, not a flash of his eye, not the gift of a hip from the hedgerow, not a word, not a kiss, to lighten the load of desire. But he eyed every man even as a beast of the field that suspects the hunter, and his lips were hard and cruel and his eyes looked the dread look of fate. Indeed his angry humour made change of his face, and the colour of his cheeks fled away because he was a prey to wrathful imaginings. But even so he was fair to view; his wrath served only to prick his lover the more.

At last the poor man would bear no more so fierce a flame of the Cytherean, but went and wept before that sullen house, and kissed the doorpost of it, and lifted up his voice saying "O cruel, O sullen child, that wast nursed of an evil she-lion; O boy of stone which art all unworthy to be loved; lo! here am I come with the last of my gifts, even this my halter. No longer will I vex you with the sight of me; but here go I whither you have condemned me, where they say the path lies all lovers must travel, where is the sweet physic of oblivion. Yet if so be I take and drink that physic up, every drop, yet shall I not quench the fever of my desire.

And lo! now I bid this thy door farewell or ever I go. I know what is to be. The rose is fair and Time withers it, the violet is fair in the year's spring and it quickly groweth old; the lily is white,—it fades when its flowering's done; and white the snow,—it melts all away when the wind blows warm: and even so, the beauty of a child is beautiful indeed, but it liveth not for long. The day will come when you shall love like me, when your heart shall burn like mine, and your eyes weep brinish tears. So I pray you, child, do me this one last courtesy: when you shall come and find a poor man hanging at your door, pass him not by; but stay you first and weep awhile for a libation upon him, and then loosing him from the rope, put about him some covering from your own shoulders; and give him one last kiss, for your lips will be welcome even to the dead. And never fear me; I cannot do thee any mischief; thou shalt kiss and there an end. Then pray thee make a hole in some earthy bank for to hide all my love of thee; and ere thou turn thee to go thy ways, cry over me three times 'Rest, my friend,' and if it seem thee good cry also 'My fair companion's dead.' And for epitaph write the words I here inscribe upon thy wall:

Here's one that died of love; good wayfarer,
Stay thee and say: his was a cruel fere."

This said, he took a stone and set it up, that dreadful stone, against the wall in the midst of the doorway; then tied that slender string unto the porch above, put the noose about his neck, rolled that footing from beneath his feet, and lo! he hung a corpse.

Soon that other, he opened the door and espied the dead hanging to his own doorway; and his stubborn heart was not bended. The new-done murder moved him not unto tears, nor would he be defiling all his young lad's garments with a dead corpse; but went his ways to the wrestling-bouts and betook himself light of heart to his beloved bath. And so came he unto the God he had slighted. For there stood an image of him upon the margin looking towards the water. And lo! even the graven image leapt down upon him and slew that wicked lad; and the water went all red, and on the water floated the voice of a child saying "Rejoice ye that love, for he that did hate is slain; and love ye that hate, for the God knoweth how to judge."

LUCIAN (A.D. c. 125-192)

Born in Samosata in Syria, Lucian came from a family of modest means. He lived in Athens and wrote satiric works, before finally settling in Egypt where he became a high official. He died very old, of gout according to some authors, of a rabid dog's bite according to the Christian historians who never forgave him for attacking Christianity in his writings.

In the *Amores* Lucian tells how, during a voyage to Cnidus, he met two philosophers, Charicles and Callicratidas. The first loved women; the second preferred boys. The three travellers went to the temple of Venus, which housed a statue of the goddess by Praxiteles. Callicratidas, the gay philosopher, praised this work with such enthusiasm that he astonished his companions.

Apollo with a Lyre (detail). Middle of the fifth century B.C. Museo Archeologico Nazionale, Naples. Roman copy of a Greek statue.

Callipygian Venus, Museo Archeologico Nazionale, Naples. Roman copy of a Hellenistic original. This Venus was venerated by homosexuals and heterosexuals alike.

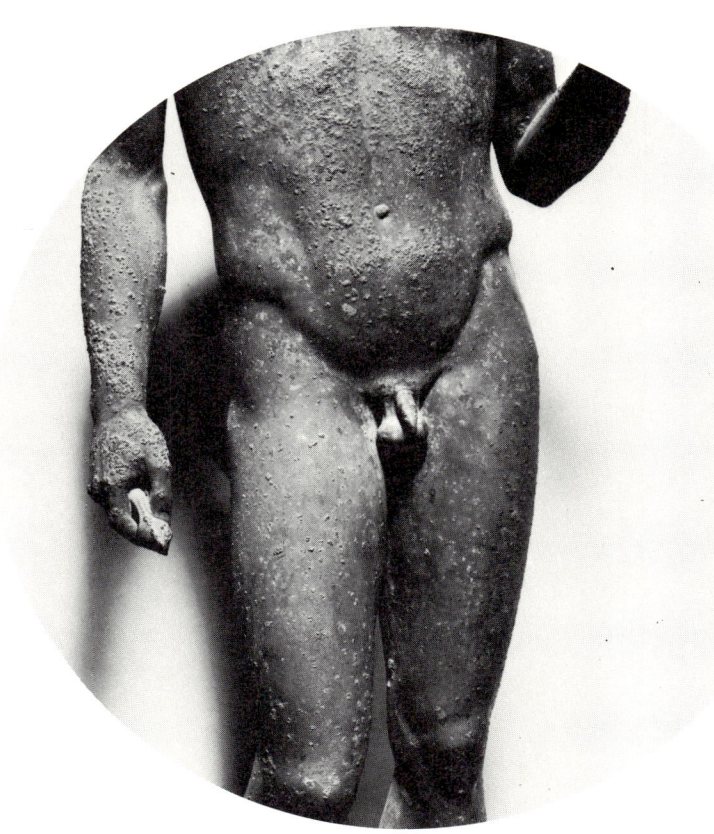

From TWO KINDS OF LOVE

"Charicles a young man from Corinth who is not only handsome but shows some evidence of skilful use of cosmetics, because... he wishes to attract the women, and... Callicratidas, the Athenian...a devotee of physical training...because of his love for boys" arrive together in Cnidus.

13. When the plants had given us pleasure enough, we entered the temple. In the midst thereof sits the goddess—she's a most beautiful statue of Parian marble—arrogantly smiling a little as a grin parts her lips. Draped by no garment, all her beauty is uncovered and revealed, except in so far as she unobtrusively uses one hand to hide her private parts. So great was the power of the craftsman's art that the hard unyielding marble did justice to every limb. Charicles at any rate raised a mad distracted cry and exclaimed, "Happiest indeed of the gods was Ares who suffered chains because of her!" And, as he spoke, he ran up and, stretching out his neck as far as he could, started to kiss the goddess with importunate lips. Callicratidas stood by in silence with amazement in his heart.

The temple had a door on both sides for the benefit of those also who wish to have a good view of the goddess from behind, so that no part of her be left unadmired. It's easy therefore for people to enter by the other door and survey the beauty of her back. 14. And so we decided to see all of the goddess and went round to the back of the precinct. Then, when the door had been opened by the

woman responsible for keeping the keys, we were filled with an immediate wonder for the beauty we beheld. The Athenian who had been so impassive an observer a minute before, upon inspecting those parts of the goddess which recommend a boy, suddenly raised a shout far more frenzied than that of Charicles. "Heracles!" he exclaimed, "what a well-proportioned back! What generous flanks she has! How satisfying an armful to embrace! How delicately moulded the flesh on the buttocks, neither too thin and close to the bone, nor yet revealing too great an expanse of fat! And as for those precious parts sealed in on either side by the hips, how inexpressibly sweetly they smile! How perfect the proportions of the thighs and the shins as they stretch down in a straight line to the feet! So that's what Ganymede looks like as he pours out the nectar in heaven for Zeus and makes it taste sweeter. For I'd never have taken the cup from Hebe if she served me." While Callicratidas was shouting this under the spell of the goddess, Charicles in the excess of his admiration stood almost petrified, though his emotions showed in the melting tears trickling from his eyes.

15. When we could admire no more, we noticed a mark on one thigh like a stain on a dress; the unsightliness of this was shown up by the brightness of the marble everywhere else. I therefore, hazarding a plausible guess about the truth of the matter, supposed that what we saw was a natural defect in the marble. For even such things as these are subject to accident and many potential masterpieces of beauty are thwarted by bad luck. And so, thinking the black mark to be a natural blemish, I found in this too cause to admire Praxiteles for having hidden what was unsightly in the marble in the parts less able to be examined closely. But the attendant woman who was standing near us told us a strange, incredible story. For she said that a young man of a not undistinguished family—though his deed has caused him to be left nameless—who often visited the precinct, was so ill-starred as to fall in love with the goddess. He would spend all day in the temple.... In the end the violent tension of his desires turned to desperation and he found in audacity a procurer for his lusts. For, when the sun was now sinking to its setting, quietly and unnoticed by those present, he slipped in behind the door and, standing invisible in the inmost part of the chamber, he kept still, hardly even breathing. When the attendants closed the door from the outside in the normal way, this new Anchises was locked in. But why do I chatter on and tell you in every detail the reckless deed of that unmentionable night? These marks of his amorous embraces were seen after day came and the goddess had that blemish to prove what she'd suffered. The youth concerned is said, according to the popular story told, to have hurled himself over a cliff or down into the waves of the sea and to have vanished utterly.

17. While the temple-woman was recounting this, Charicles interrupted her account with a shout and said, "Women therefore inspire love even when made of stone. But what would have happened if we had seen such beauty alive and breathing? Would not that single night have been valued as highly as the sceptre of Zeus?"

But Callicratidas smiled and said, "We don't know as yet, Charicles, whether we won't hear many stories of this sort when we come to Thespiae. Even now in this we have a clear proof of the truth about the Aphrodite whom you hold in such esteem."

When Charicles asked how this was, I thought Callicratidas made a very convincing reply. For he said that, although the love-struck youth had seized the chance to enjoy a whole uninterrupted night and had complete liberty to glut his passion, he nevertheless made love to the marble as though to a boy, because, I'm sure, he didn't want to be confronted by the female parts....

Charicles spoke up, saying "I will prove to you that having one's pleasure with a woman is superior to having it with a boy."

...each man thinks pleasant what he enjoys along with another, and in sharing our pleasures we find greater enjoyment. Now men's intercourse with women involves

Vase (details). Second century B.C. Vatican Museum, Rome. "Since I set eyes on Diophantos, who among all the lads of his age is like a new flower, I have neither the strength to flee nor to stay." (Meleager)

giving like enjoyment in return. For the two sexes part with pleasure only if they have had an equal effect on each other—unless we ought rather to heed the verdict of Tiresias that the woman's enjoyment is twice as great as the man's. And I think it honourable for men not to wish for a selfish pleasure or to seek to gain some private benefit by receiving from anyone the sum total of enjoyment, but to share what they obtain and to requite like with like. But no one could be so mad as to say this in the case of boys. No, the active lover, according to his view of the matter, departs after having obtained an exquisite pleasure, but the one outraged suffers pain and tears at first, though the pain relents somewhat with time and you will, men say, cause him no further discomfort, but of pleasure he has none at all. And, if I may make a rather far-fetched point, but one I should make as we are in the precinct of Aphrodite, a woman, Callicratidas, may be used like a boy, so that one can have enjoyment by opening up two paths to pleasure, but a male has no way of bestowing the pleasure a woman gives.

28. Therefore, if even men like you, Callicratidas, can find satisfaction in women, let us males fence ourselves off from each other; but, if males find intercourse with males acceptable, henceforth let women too love each other. Come now, epoch of the future, legislator of

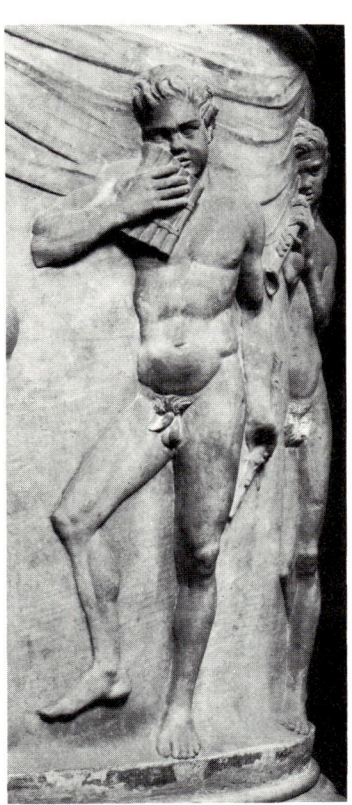

strange pleasures, devise fresh paths for male lusts, but bestow the same privilege upon women, and let them have intercourse with each other just as men do. Let them strap to themselves cunningly contrived instruments of lechery, those mysterious monstrosities devoid of seed, and let woman lie with woman as does a man. Let wanton Lesbianism—that word seldom heard, which I feel ashamed even to utter—freely parade itself, and let our women's chambers emulate Philaenis, disgracing themselves with Sapphic amours. And how much better that a woman should invade the provinces of male wantonness than that the nobility of the male sex should become effeminate and play the part of a woman!

29. In the midst of this intense and impassioned speech Charicles stopped with a wild fierce glint in his eyes. It seemed to me that he was also regarding his speech as a ceremony of purification against love of boys.

Callicratidas, after a moment's silence during which one could observe the extreme agitation of his mind mirrored in his face, then replied:

Indeed, as the wise Euripides says, it would be greatly to be desired if we had no intercourse with women but, in order to provide ourselves with heirs, we went to shrines and temples and bought children for gold and silver. For we are constrained by necessity that puts a heavy yoke on our shoulders and bids us obey her. Though therefore we should by use of reason choose what is beautiful, let our need yield to necessity. Let women be ciphers and be retained merely for child-bearing; but in all else away with them, and may I be rid of them. For what man of sense could endure from dawn onwards women who beautify themselves with artificial devices, women whose true form is unshapely, but who have extraneous adornments to beguile the unsightliness of nature?

Bowl (detail) painted by Douris. *c.* 480 B.C. Cabinet des Médailles, Bibliothèque Nationale, Paris. The scenes of revelry shown are to celebrate the return of Dionysius to Olympus.

THEOMNESTUS:

By heaven, do you think I'm a Melitides or Coroebus to cast a vote in opposition to your just verdict? For through my intense enjoyment of your narrative I thought I was in Cnidus, almost imagining this small

chamber to be that temple. But nevertheless, seeing that nothing said on a festive day is unseemly, and any jesting, even if carried to excess, is thought in keeping with the holiday spirit, I must say I admired the solemnity of the very highbrow speeches evoked by love of boys, except that I didn't think it very agreeable to spend all day with a youth suffering the punishment of Tantalus, and, though the waters of beauty are, as it were, almost lapping against my eyes, to endure thirst when one can help oneself to water. For it's not enough to look at the loved one or to listen to his voice as he sits facing you, but love has, as it were, made itself a ladder of pleasure, and has for its first step that of sight, so that it may see the beloved, and, once it beholds, it wishes to approach and to touch. If it only touches with but the fingertips, the waves of enjoyment run into the whole body. Once easily achieving this, love attempts the third stage and tries a kiss, not making it a violent one at first, but lightly bringing lips close to lips so that they part before completing full contact, without leaving the slightest cause for suspicion. Thus it adjusts itself to the success gained and melts into ever more importunate embraces, sometimes gently opening the mouth and leaving neither hand idle. For open embraces of the beloved when clothed give mutual pleasure; or else the furtive hand wantonly glides down into the bosom and squeezes for a moment the breasts swollen past their normal size and makes a smooth sweep to grasp with the fingers the belly throbbing full spate with passion, and thereafter the early down of adolescence, and—

"But why recount the thing one should not tell?"

Once love has gained so much liberty it begins warmer work. Then it makes a start with the thighs and, to quote the comic poet, "strikes the target."

54. May I for my part find it my lot to love boys in this way. But may the airy talkers and those who raise their philosophic brows temple-high and even higher, beguile the ignorant with the speciousness of their solemn phrases. For Socrates was as devoted to love as anyone and Alcibiades, once he had lain down beneath the same mantle with him, did not rise unassailed. Don't be surprised at that. For not even the affection of Achilles for Patroclus was limited to having him seated opposite

"Waiting until Aeacides should cease his song."

No, pleasure was the mediator even of *their* friendship. At any rate, when Achilles was lamenting the death of Patroclus, his unrestrained feelings made him burst out with the truth and say,

"The converse of our thighs my tears do mourn
With duteous piety."

Those whom the Greeks call "revellers" I think to be nothing but ostentatious lovers. Perhaps someone will assert this is a shameful thing to say, but, by Aphrodite of Cnidus, it's the truth.

STRATO OF SARDIS
(b. beginning of third century A.D.)

This Greek poet compiled an anthology of homosexual verse (found in *The Greek Anthology* under the Latin title, *Musa Puerilis*, [*The Puerile Muse*]) in which he included many of his own compositions.

Terracotta (detail). End of the fifth or beginning of the fourth century B.C. Louvre, Paris. Youths dancing during grape harvest.

From MUSA PUERILIS

I delight in the prime of a boy of twelve, but one of thirteen is much more desirable. He who is fourteen is a still sweeter flower of the Loves, and one who is just beginning his fifteenth year is yet more delightful. The sixteenth year is that of the gods, and as for the seventeenth it is not for me, but for Zeus, to seek it. But if one has a desire for those still older, he no longer plays, but now seeks "And answering him back."

(no. 4)

I like them pale, and I also love those with a skin the colour of honey, and the fair too; and on the other hand I am taken by the black-haired. Nor do I dismiss brown eyes; but above all I love sparkling black eyes.
(no. 5)

I hate resistance to my embrace when I kiss, and pugnacious cries, and violent opposition with the hands, but at the same time I have no great desire for him who, when he is in my arms, is at once ready and abandons himself effusively. I wish for one half-way between the two, such as is he who knows both how to give himself and how not to give himself.
(no. 200)

Lie not by me with so sour a face and so dejected, Diphilus, and be not a boy of the common herd. Put a little wantonness into your kisses and the preliminaries, toying, touching, scratching, your look and your words.
(no. 209)

Animals, being mindless, only couple with females, whereas men, having the advantage of intelligence do it differently. Therefore any man who goes out of his mind for a girl is an animal.
(no. 245)

PHILOSTRATUS (A.D. 175-249)

Born on Lemnos, Philostratus first taught rhetoric in Athens, and then moved to Rome towards the end of the reign of Septimius-Severus. An exceedingly eclectic author, he wrote a *Life of Apollonius of Tyana*, a *Lives of the Sophists*, a treatise on gymnastics and a series of fictitious love letters to a seventeen year old boy in the precious literary style affected by certain of his contemporaries.

TO A BOY

The roses, borne on their leaves as on wings, have made haste to come to you. Receive them kindly, either as mementos of Adonis or as tinct of Aphroditê or as eyes of the earth. Yes, a wreath of wild olive becomes an athlete, a tiara worn upright the Great King, and a helmet crest a soldier; but roses become a beautiful boy, both because of affinity of fragrance and because of their distinctive hue. You will not wear the roses: they will wear you.

TO A BOY

I commend you for cheating time and shaving your cheeks. That smooth skin which left you by nature's law is now restored by art; and recovery of what is lost is most agreeable. So, if you take my advice, you will let your hair grow long on your head and will take care of your locks in such a way that some come down over your cheeks a little (and anyone can readily remove this hair from your cheeks at will) and some rest on your shoulders, even as Homer says that the Euboeans wear their hair long behind—for a good head of hair is far lovelier than the tree of Athena, since in fact this acropolis also must not be seen bare or unadorned—but let your cheeks be bare and let nothing bedim their brightness, neither cloud nor mist. As eyes that are shut are not a pleasant sight, so is it with a handsome fellow's cheeks if they are hairy. So then, with drugs or with keen razors or with finger tips or with detergents and herbs or by any other means whatsoever, make your beauty longer-lasting. If you do this, you will be imitating the always youthful gods.

TO A BOY

You have done well to use the roses for a bed also; for pleasure in gifts received is a clear indication of regard for the sender. So through their agency I also touched you, for roses are amorous and artful and know how to make use of beauty. But I fear that they may actually have been restless and oppressed you in your sleep, even as the gold oppressed Danaë. If you wish to do a favour for a lover, send back what is left of them, since they now breathe a fragrance, not of roses only, but also of you.

Jacopo del Zucchi, *Psyche and Cupid* (detail). Galleria Borghese, Rome.

ACHILLES TATIUS
(fourth century A.D.)

This Greek writer converted to Christianity and became the bishop of Alexandria. The following excerpt is taken from *The Adventures of Leucippe and Cleitophon*, an erotic romance written in his youth.

From THE ADVENTURES OF LEUCIPPE AND CLEITOPHON

False are the ways of woman, words and deeds alike; and although she may seem fair to behold, it is all the result of the laborious use of pigments, and her beauty is all of perfumes, or the dye of her hair, or even of her artificial kisses; and if she be stripped of all these many devices, she is like to the jackdaw that was plucked of its feathers in the fable.

But the beauty of a boy is not fostered by the odour of perfumes, nor yet by cunning and foreign unguents. And the fresh natural odour of a boy has a sweeter smell than all the anointings and perfumery of a woman. And you can, before the consummation of your love, wrestle in close embrace with him and openly enfold him in your arms. And his embraces have no shame. There is no soft tenderness of flesh in the close pressure of love, but your bodies press hard together and wrestle in very bliss. His kisses have not the cunning artifices which a woman's kisses have; nor do they trick you with an idle deceit, but he loves as he knows best, and there is no art; his kisses are the kisses of nature. And this is the likeness of a boy's kisses—even as nectar set firm upon your lips, such is it. And in kisses you can never have satiety, but, the deeper draughts you drink, the more you thirst for love, and you would not draw away your mouth from his, till from very delight you flee from his kisses.

(from Book II, §§ 37-38)

Attic bowl: representing the embrace of Eros. Fifth century B.C. Staatliche Museen Preussischer Kulturbesitz, Berlin.

II

WHEN THE GODS PLAYED

And now I'll strum a lyre that's gay
And sing of boys with whom the gods did play....
(Ovid, *Metamorphoses*, Bk. X)

◁◁ A.-E. Girodet de Roucy Trioson, *Mercury*. Cabinet des Estampes, Bibliothèque Nationale, Paris.

Claude Marie Dubufe, *Apollo and Cyparissus*. Musée Calvet, Avignon (on extended loan from the Louvre, Paris). Apollo is holding his beloved Cyparissus, who having accidentally killed his favorite stag is pining away with grief. After his death, the youth was changed into a cypress, the tree which symbolizes sadness.

Annibale Carracci, *The Flute Lesson*. The National Gallery, London.

In Antiquity the gods battled, feasted and made love not only with goddesses but also with mortals. Pindar asserts that "gods and men spring from the same fount; a single mother brought forth both races." Small wonder, then, that they were stirred by the same passions. The ancient writers cast their dreams and desires into stories and poems which celebrate the loves of heroes and gods; the extraordinary thing is that the myths which they created retain their freshness and their power of suggestion even today.

Ganymede
The theme of Ganymede's abduction by Zeus changed into an eagle—the naked body of the young shepherd (who was said to be the most beautiful of mortals) clutched in the talons of the great bird—has inspired not only the Greeks and the Romans, but also the painters and the writers of the Western World since Antiquity. Some saw it as a pretty picture only, others as the apotheosis of youth, and still others as the tragic emblem of a devouring passion. The king of the gods had many other lovers, though none as significant as Ganymede: there was young Euphorion, for example, the son of Helen and Achilles, who tried to escape from Zeus's advances by flying away (he was born with wings); mad with rage and disappointment, Zeus struck him down with a thunderbolt, and when some nymphs had the audacity to bury the unfortunate lad, he turned them all into frogs.

Orpheus
Ovid says Orpheus was "the first among the peoples of Thrace to teach the art of loving youths and of plucking from the down of their cheeks the matchless bloom of their springtime." After losing Eurydice he gave up women and consoled himself with boys. Not only did he invent the gay pleasures with his beloved friend Calais, but he also organized the Orphic mysteries, from which

Marble replica: Greek bronze representing Hercules. Fourth century B.C. Baths of Caracalla. Farnese Collection, Museo Archeologico Nazionale, Naples. Hercules was the most virile and the most homosexual of the deified heroes.

Jean Broc, *The Death of Hyacinth.* Musée des Beaux-Arts, Poitiers.

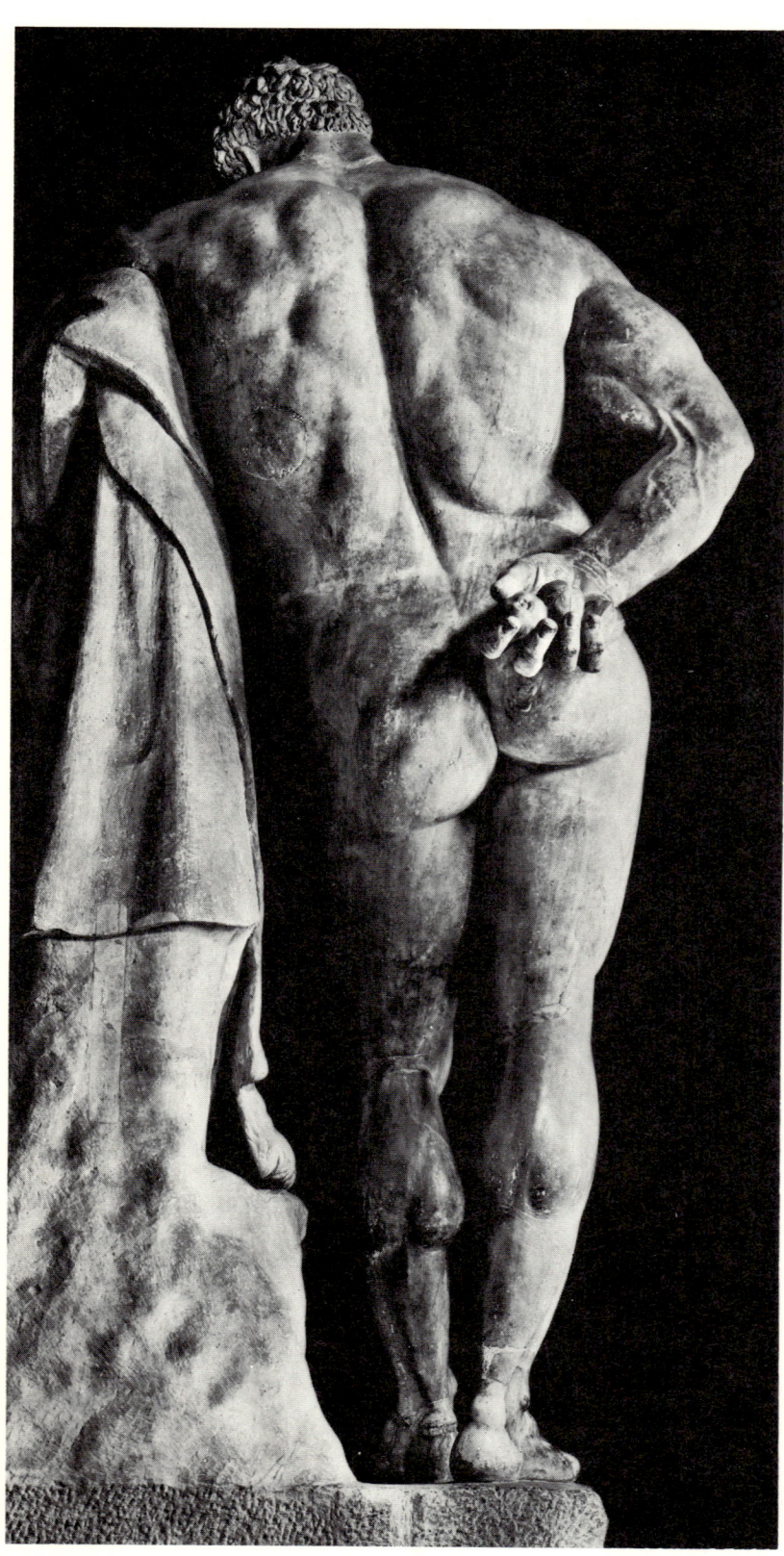

women were barred. The Thracian women (Maenads, according to Ovid) tore his body into pieces which they then threw into a river. Orpheus's lyre, and his bloody head still singing, floated over the sea to the island of Lesbos.

In another version, the poet's lyre rose up to the heavens and became a constellation. Clad in a white tunic, Orpheus's soul wandered to the Elysian Fields where it charmed the elect with its unearthly melodies. As for the Furies who killed Orpheus, Ovid asserts that they were turned into trees. But Phanocles (a Greek poet of the fourth century) maintains that they were tatooed by their husbands in revenge for Orpheus's death. Each year in Lesbos married men used to prick their wives with needles to commemorate this punishment and the awful deed which deserved it.

Thamyris

According to other legends, it was not Orpheus but Thamyris who first taught the love of boys to men. The poet Thamyris was Homer's teacher, and he is said to have been descended from Endymion, whom the goddess of the moon loved. While still in the prime of youth, Endymion had asked Zeus to put him to sleep for eternity, so that his beauty might never fade.

Thamyris had an affair with Hymenaeus, who had an incomparable voice and the frail sweetness and gracefulness of a young girl. Apollo himself fell in love with him. One day, while he was singing at the wedding of Althea and Dionysus, Hymenaeus lost his voice and died. Another legend has it that the lad died at his own wedding. In his memory the hymenaeus or hymeneal was chanted during nuptials.

But the loveliest legend of all is the one about Hesperus, who was changed into a star. Hesperus was in love with Hymenaeus. That is why the evening star— Hesperus—rises when the hymeneal is sung.

Hercules

Hercules was the most popular, the most virile, but also the gayest of the divinized heroes. He had countless affairs with men. According to the Alexandrian poet Diotimos, Hercules undertook his twelve labors out of love for Eurysthenes, a timorous, unlikeable fellow whom

Pierre Brebiette, Drawing. Cabinet des Dessins, Louvre, Paris. The metamorphosis of Cycnus, grief-stricken at the death of his beloved Phaeton, into a swan.

Gustave Moreau, *Narcissus*. Private collection. "... and already the lusty foliage, the twining flower, the avid vegetation was wrapping itself around his beloved body; while he, oblivious, was lost in the ideal contemplation of his own being." (Gustave Moreau)

Zeus protected. During the expedition of the Argonauts, Hercules was accompanied by his faithful charioteer, Iolas and by the graceful Hylas, who had been raised and "formed to his heart's desire." Naturally Hercules fell desperately in love with the curly-haired, girl-faced young boy. One day the *Argos* anchored off the shores of Myasia, and Hylas wandered off to fetch some water. Suddenly, he found himself surrounded by a band of nymphs, who liked him so much that they decided to carry him off and make him immortal. That is how Hercules lost his beloved forever.

The Metamorphoses of Budding Youths

Except for Ganymede who became a cupbearer and lived with Zeus on Mt. Olympus, most of the love affairs between gods and men ended tragically for the mortals. Filled with regret, the gods would then change their lover's corpse into a flower—a hyacinth, a narcissus, an anemone, a violet, etc.—in order to perpetuate the memory of their love every year when spring came around.

Thus, according to tradition, Thamyris is supposed to have invented pederasty out of love for Hyacinth. Hyacinth was so beautiful that even Apollo could not resist him. One day, as they were throwing the discus together; Hyacinth, with the impetuousness of youth, ran to pick up the god's discus—which rebounded, striking him in the face. Another story says that Zephyr, who was also madly in love with Hyacinth, deflected the discus in flight out of jealousy. Despite Apollo's attempts to revive him, the boy died. Filled with despair, the god lamented: "What is my crime? Is it a crime to play? Is it a crime to love...?" All he could do was to turn the youth's blood into a flower: the hyacinth whose petals are marked with his cry—the letters AI—or with his initial, Y.

Flowers crop up in a number of legends about Adonis, too. Adonis was the son of Myrrha. Myrrha was in love with her own father and managed to sleep with him twelve nights running by tricking him with the help of her nurse. On discovering the ruse, her father wanted to kill her, but she escaped—only to be turned into a tree. Ten months later, the bark of the tree cracked open and Adonis was born. He was then carried off by some nymphs. Persephone and Aphrodite fell in love with

him. But one day the goddess Artemis had Adonis charged by a wild boar, and the youth was mortally wounded. Aphrodite ran to his assistance, but tore her foot on a thorn: her blood tinted the pale flowers of the thornbush and turned them into beautiful red roses. The poet Bion says that from each one of Aphrodite's tears a rose sprang forth, and from each drop of Adonis's blood there blossomed an anemone. After Adonis died, the father of one of his companions-at-play grew despondant and hung himself from a tree, which was thereafter called *melos* (appletree, in Greek).

Narcissus was not a pederast, but he avoided women. He wanted to save his seed for his own reflection—a kind of homophilia. At his birth, the seer Tiresias had said "Narcissus will live to be old, provided that he never sets

eyes on himself." Unfortunately one day it came to pass that Narcissus, hot from being chased by the nymph Echo, suddenly grew very thirsty. Leaning over a spring to drink, he glimpsed his own reflection. So fascinated was he by it that he could not lift his eyes again, and there he remained, wrapped in self-contemplation, until he died. The flower that bears his name is supposed to have sprung up where his body lay.

Another legend says that, weary of the attentions of a young man called Ameinas, Narcissus sent him a sword as a gift. Ameinas took the hint and killed himself with the weapon. But, before dying, he called down the curses of the gods on Narcissus. Not long after that, Narcissus saw his own face reflected in a pool, fell insanely in love with himself and committed suicide. The myth of Narcissus is still relevant: even today it symbolizes the rejection of shared sexuality and procreation.

Finally there is the strange tale, associated with the appearance of the almond tree and of violets, of Agdistis and Attis. The source is Pausanias: Zeus had a "nocturnal emission," and seeded the earth in his sleep. A divine being, having both male and female organs, was born from this unconscious union. This creature was called Agdistis. Horrified at this monster, the gods cut off his private parts and threw them on the ground. Instantly, an almond tree sprang up. It so happened that a nymph was passing by, and she stopped to pick the nuts—that is to say, the fruit of the tree—which she then clasped to her breast; the next thing she knew she was pregnant. The child she gave birth to—Attis—was miraculously beautiful. A he-goat was given the task of educating him. Now Agdistis, the unfortunate eunuch, loved the lad and was terribly jealous because Attis was to marry the daughter of a king. On the day of the wedding ceremony, at the very moment that the hymeneal was being sung, Agdistis

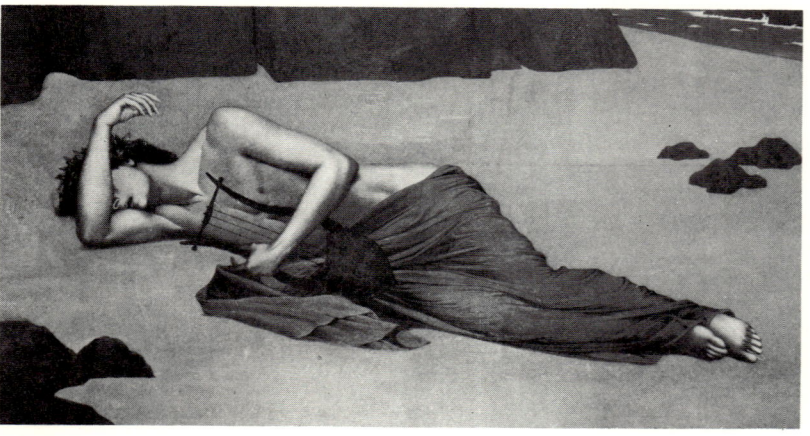

C. Famin, *The Surprise* (1832). Engraving illustrating a book by Famin in the restricted collection of the Museo Archeologico Nazionale, Naples. Private collection.

Alexandre Seon, *Orpheus Lamenting*. Louvre, Paris.

Annibale Carracci, *Study for a Bacchus*. Victoria and Albert Museum, London.

showed up, and Attis lost his mind. In a fit of madness the young bridegroom emasculated himself and died. His blood turned into a bunch of purple violets. Remorse-stricken, Agdistis asked Zeus to preserve Attis's corpse for all eternity. According to another story his hair kept on growing and, stranger still, his little finger continued wiggling. Mysteries were celebrated in honor of Attis, during which certain devotees would mutilate themselves in their sacred frenzy.

Androgynes and Ritual Transvestites

The bisexuality of the gods only enhanced their status. A bearded Venus was worshiped in Cyprus; and in Labranda in South Western Anatolia, Zeus was represented with six breasts arranged in a triangle on his chest. Some divinities, like Hera the mother of Hephaistos, could conceive independently.

The most notorious androgyne was Hermaphrodite, the son of Aphrodite and Hermes. A child of unearthly beauty, he grew up among nymphs. One day as he was walking beside a lake, the nymph Salmacis tried to seduce him, but he brushed her off. Vexed, she hid behind a tree. Thinking himself alone, Hermaphrodite disrobed and jumped into the water to bathe. Salmacis then rushed down and wrapped her arms around him, refusing to let go until the gods had fused their two bodies together. "He entered the water as a male," writes Ovid, "he came out both male and female; like unto his father in one respect, like unto his mother in certain other ways."

Although the ancient Greeks accepted the androgyne as a figure of ritual significance—since he embodied the magical power of the two sexes joined in one being—children born with marks of physical androgyny were considered monstrous and were immediately put to death. With time the symbol of the hermaphrodite lost its cultic significance and became a mere figure of multiplied erotic potentiality.

Dionysus, the god of mystic frenzies, was usually represented with effeminate features. Upon seeing Dionysus appear on stage, a character in one of Aeschylus's plays asks him: "Whence do you come, O Man-Woman? What regions do you hail from? What are those clothes you are wearing"? Seneca gave the god a woman's face, and, in the *Metamorphoses,* Ovid speaks of the two-fold nature of Dionysus. He adds that "the god does not lack virility, rather he is too frail to exhibit it." Dionysus was the offspring of Zeus and the goddess Semele. Zeus had entrusted the boy to Hermes and to the king of Orochmene, instructing them to dress him like a little girl in order to protect him from the jealous rage of Zeus's wife, Hera. Later, Dionysus was changed into a young goat, and he lived among the nymphs of the forest. As the god of wine, he originated the Bacchanalia, notorious for their orgiastic character (in 186 B.C. the senate of Rome outlawed them, deeming them too licentious).

Transvestism was often an integral part of the sacred initiation rites in the different sects. Plutarch reports various practices which seem strange indeed to our eyes. In Argos a bride wore a beard on her wedding night. In Cos a husband dressed in women's clothes. In Sparta a bride-to-be was put in the care of a woman called a *nympheutria,* who shaved off her hair, dressed her in men's robes and shoes, and made her lie down alone on a straw mat in a dark room. Then her betrothed "who was neither enfeebled with wine nor made sluggish with the pleasures of the table—for with his usual sobriety he had dined at the *phidities*—entered the room and, unclasping her girdle, took her in his arms and laid her down on the bed." Having done his duty he went off—as usual—to sleep with his young friends. This bizarre ceremony went on for months and even years, so that the husband often fathered several children before ever seeing his wife in full light.

Plutarch approves of this custom wholeheartedly, for he believed that too much familiarity between husband and wife diminished their mutual love and esteem. But wasn't the real purpose in disguising the bride as a boy to give courage to the young husband who was more accustomed to making love with men than with women?

Louise Janin, *The Rape of Ganymede* (1937).

III

LOVE, THE ROMAN WAY

Rome, which delighted in making love from behind,
Spelled AMOR—love—by inverting its own name.
(Latin distich)

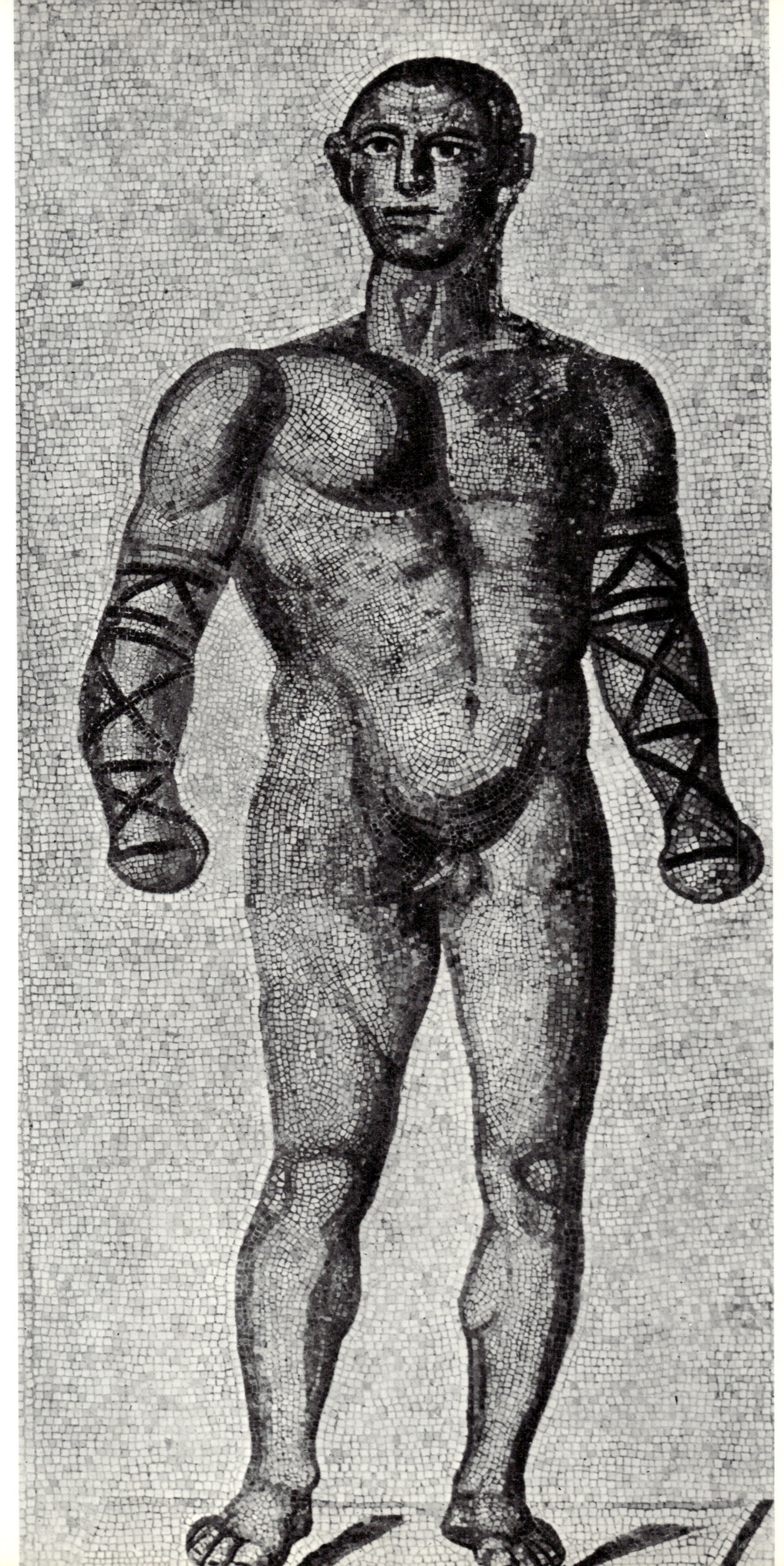

◁ C. Famin, *Naked Priapus Dancing* (1832). Engraving illustrating a book by Famin in the restricted collection of the Museo Archeologico Nazionale, Naples. Private collection.

Mosaic (details) from the Baths of Caracalla. Vatican Museum, Rome. Roman athletes and wrestlers. As Martial writes, these supermales had a double function, serving "both women and men."

The Etruscans, who settled in the region later known as Etruria sometime in the eighth century B.C., retained their matriarchal traditions for many centuries. Their women possessed a considerable degree of freedom, and participated in banquets and other festive occasions with the men. To the Greeks, who believed firmly in sexual segregation, these mores seemed scandalous. The Greek historian Theopompos of Chios is full of contempt for the Etruscans, and, without ever questioning its veracity, he reports all sorts of slanderous hearsay about them: he writes that the Etruscan wives stripped naked at banquets while their husbands buggered each other in public.

The only Etruscan texts that have come down to us (treatises on divination written in Latin) give scanty information about the customs and morals of that society. It is only by looking at the frescoes and the painted earthenware found in their tombs that we can arrive at some idea of the role of Etruscan women. In the necropolis of Tarquinia, for instance, one painting shows a man and a woman making love in front of a bull who is watching them with apparent approval; a little further on, however, the same bull is furiously charging two copulating men. What does this mean? Is it, as some archeologists believe, a condemnation of homosexuality? In any case it seems that there were fewer homosexuals among the Etruscans than among the Greeks, and the same is true of Rome during the first four hundred years of its history.

It was by way of Sicily, Southern Italy and above all the city of Tarentum (Taranto, annexed in 272 B.C.) that Rome absorbed the Hellenic influence. Homosexual mores, which seemed prestigious because they were celebrated in Greek art and literature, soon spread throughout the peninsula. One mustn't forget that Greek was the language *par excellence* of diplomacy, and that the patrician families of Rome had nurses, slaves and tutors who were Greek, and that consequently they were bilingual. Finally, for a long time Greek was the language of literature; the first works written in Latin appeared only after the capture of Tarentum. During the second Punic War (218-201 B.C.) Rome grew more isolationist, and it became fashionable to blame Hellenism for the vices and debauchery of the Romans; but with victory Rome lost its inferiority complex, and Greece became increasingly a Roman province. As a result the Hellenic influence was more marked than ever in the arts, in literature and in morals. Everyone wanted to live in the Greek style; and "Greek" sculptures, paintings and objects cluttered the wealthy patrician homes.

Cato complains that a handsome young slave fetched as high a price as a farm and that caviar from the Black Sea cost as much as a team of oxen. He cautions his sons about the Greeks, "a perverse race incapable of improving itself," and he adds: "the day that this low breed will give us its literature everything will be corrupted." However, Cato's fulminations did not stop the upper classes in Rome from reading Plato, Xenophon, Theocritus and Pindar—or from sending their sons to Athens for their education. Under the Republic, homosexuality was widespread despite the Scantine (or Scatine) Laws, proclaimed around 226 B.C., which punished homosexual acts with death. (This law seems to have been rarely—and then only arbitrarily—enforced).

Under the Empire the example came from the top, as can be readily seen from the passages taken from Suetonius's *Lives of the Caesars*, reporting the proclivities of Caesar, Tiberius and Nero for young boys. Nor must one forget Caligula's passion for the pantomime Mnester; Otho, known as Otho the Pathic, who liked to put

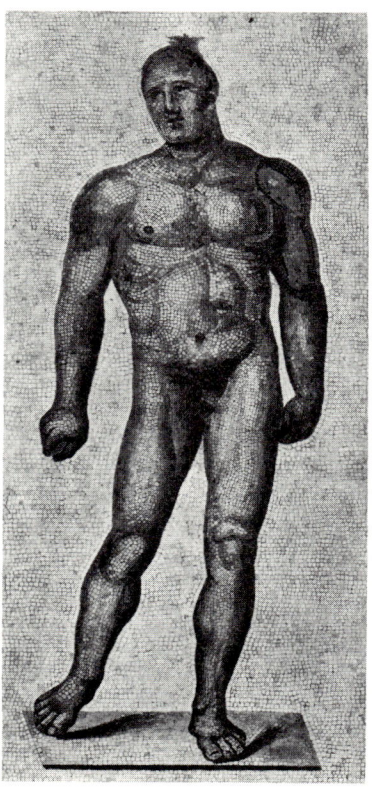

Mosaic. Timgad, Algeria. One of the young *officiosi* who offered their services in the Roman baths.

Fresco: Tomb of the Bulls. Sixth century B.C. Museo Nazionale Tarquiniese, Tarquinia, Italy. On the left a bull looks on indifferently while two men copulate with a woman (not pictured); on the right another bull is charging two men engaged in sodomy.

himself up for sale like a slave; Hadrian and his favorite, Antinoüs; Commodus and his exceptionally well-endowed cup-bearer, whom he would call "my donkey"; Heliogabalus who officially married Hieracles, a slave, and who used to kiss his "wife's" tool in public, explaining that he was merely celebrating the mysteries of Flora!

At banquets *cinaedi* [male dancers] struck lascivious poses, while *spatalocinaedi* went from couch to couch offering their services to each guest. (The *spatalocinaedi* were young men who had been carefully castrated: "when their organs were just beginning to be shadowed with hair and were therefore ripe, the testicles weighing as much as two pounds...." Juvenal, *Satire VI*). There were several kinds of enunch: the *castrati,* who were entirely amputated, the *thlibae,* whose testes had been stunted by wringing or by squeezing, and the *spadonae*, who were regularly equipped but were impotent. Slaves of this last type were highly prized by the Romans—to such a degree, in fact, that matrons had their favorite eunuchs wear black leather chastity belts.

Actors frequently underwent "infibulation," an operation which consisted in putting a ring through the prepuce in order to prevent copulation. Certain athletes and singers were infibulated to keep them from succumbing to carnal temptation and depleting their physical strength. Breaking the ring of someone who had been infibulated was a thrill sought after by both men and women, because the infibulated were supposed to be tireless lovers.

Nor were prescriptions lacking for stiffening drooping spirits. There were aphrodisiacs prepared by the witches of Thessaly and brews of medicinal herbs mixed with pepper, nettle seeds and yellow pyrethrum flowers steeped in old wine. Branched, testicle-shaped satyrium roots were reputed to be particularly stimulating, whereas the root of the water lily, recommended for the voice, was supposed to weaken sexual appetite—and excessive use could even cause impotence. Some remedies, said to be very effective, pertained to magic rather than to medicine: dried, powdered horses' testes, or a donkey's right testicle and a vulture's right lung tied together with strips of stork meat.

Some of the wealthier Romans had their private harems (called *paedagogia*) of beautiful boys dressed in filmy garments attached with silver buckles. During chariot outings these lads would wear beauty masks of soaked breadcrumb to protect their delicate complexion from the wind and sun. Usually imported from Africa, Syria or Egypt they were then sold in Rome by "child dealers" who—says Martial—" could manipulate their organs very skilfully in such a way as to attract buyers with their splendid proportions." In the male brothels, which were advertised by large phalluses, young boys (*pueri*) acted as women. *Exoleti* (from *exolescere*, being fully grown), also called *drauci*—or *agentes in paedicatione*—were bearded, hairy, well-muscled adults who usually assumed the male role, although they would also play passive if a client so desired.

The main gathering places for homosexuals in Rome were the street of the Tuscans, the barber shops and the

56

public baths where youths called *officiosi* offered themselves to the bathers. No sooner does Petronius's catamite show up in one of these establishments than he is greeted with enthusiastic applause, "for he had a tool of superb dimensions. What an active champion he was! Seeing him run around naked, a Roman knight gave him his cloak and took him home, doubtless to enjoy his good fortune all alone." To this depraved creature, Juvenal contrasts his virtuous young servant, whose demeanor "was worthy of a free-born man," and who does not go to the baths "to show off testicles big as fists, or seek to draw attention with a deep-throated voice, or pluck his arm pits, or coyly hide an outsized organ behind a jar of oil." (*Satire XII*) It must be said that Juvenal was a refined esthete about such matters: "the rarer the pleasure," he writes, "the greater its worth."

Many young men sold themselves (they were often penniless boys from the provinces, or impoverished intellectuals looking for a patron); they would lavish care on their long hair, pluck their body smooth, rub their skin with scented oils, paint their eyebrows with lamp black, dress in green gowns and walk with a provocative sway. Professionals would advertise themselves by scratching their head with their middle finger. That is why for centuries it was considered "the finger of infamy," and no one wore a ring on it.

There seemed nothing unnatural about a slave having "a meaty, fat-tipped needle stuck up his arse" (as the

Bronze figure: Young black slave carrying a load. Middle of the second century B.C. Cabinet des Médailles, Bibliothèque Nationale, Paris.

58

satirist Gaius Lucilius puts it), but it was considered a terrible insult to accuse a free-born citizen of being passive. Martial relates that a certain Amillus used to grope at boys in public view so that no one would suspect him of being a *pathicus*.

On the other hand bisexuality raised no moral problems whatsoever. Horace himself confided that he was ambidextrous—in other words, that he liked boys as well as girls—although in fact his preference seems to have gone to women. Martial declares that "males are meant for two things: women on the one hand, men on the other." Ovid states that he was not much interested in boys, for "I dislike embraces where neither surrenders to the other."

Patrician sons shared their bed with young slaves in order to satisfy the first stirrings of their manhood when they reached puberty. When he got married, a young man would give orders to have his slave's hair cut, indicating that he intended to remain faithful to his bride.

Roman marriages were not based on love; they were considered necessary for perpetuating society and family, nothing more. The Roman matron expected respect from her husband; she took part in social life, and sometimes even in politics; but, as Hadrian's son remarked to his wife who had complained of being neglected, "*wife* is a title of dignity, it is not a title to pleasure." Petronius, nicknamed the "Arbiter of Elegance," quips: "One must love one's spouse as a legitimate asset—but who wants to be condemned to loving one's asset only."

As described by Petronius, Juvenal and Martial (see selections), the homosexuality of the ancient Romans seems brutal and vulgar. When Virgil, Horace or Tibullus sang the praises of their beloved, they were usually referring to young professionals—and there was nothing Platonic about their feelings. It often happened that the boy loved was a slave—and sometimes the master really was in love, educating and eventually even setting the lad free. A special ceremony took place on such occasions: the slave wore a Phrygian cap, which symbolized his free status, and took his master's name (retaining his slave's name as his surname). Some of these freed slaves occupied important positions at court; others, like Livius Andronicus, Terence and Phaedrus became well-known authors.

As early as the first centuries after Christ, the Jews, the Christians and even some Romans who were nostalgic for the traditions of austerity and severity under the early Republic, began denouncing the turpitude of pagan Rome, the moral turmoil, the feverish gropings of the young for any form or fashion—so long as it was new—of spiritual experience. Saint Paul observed that "men have given up their natural intercourse with women and are consumed with desire for each other, and among themselves they commit acts of shame." He adds: "What these people do in hiding is shameful even to tell."

A little later Justin accused the ruling princes of granting debauchery *de facto* recognition by taxing the male brothels. Like Alexandria, Carthage and Antioch, Rome had the dubious privilege of being known as a capital of vice. What is more, Rome remained the holy city of paganism until the beginning of the fifth century, despite the presence of the Pope, who was becoming an increasingly important figure. To some minds, the fall of Rome in 410 came as a fitting retribution for its sins. The Christians had paid for their mistakes, as had the pagans, and they considered themselves lucky not to be massacred by the barbarians and not to have their city razed. Now sodomy became the abominable sin which no one dared even name. The Emperor Justinian declared: "Such a crime is the cause of famines, earthquakes and plagues. Because of it, cities have been destroyed by the fire of Heaven.... Therefore those who commit it must be punished by death; otherwise the whole Empire may fall into ruination because of them."

Bronze phallus. Jean Larcade Collection, Paris. Roman. Such objects were considered protection against the evil eye.

CATULLUS (84-54 B.C.)

One of the great Latin poets, Catullus came from Verona and belonged to a family of knights. He squandered his inheritance in the company of ne'er-do-wells and dissolute revellers. His stormy love-affair with the wife of a proconsul, whom he immortalized under the name Lesbia, lasted four years. Next he fell in love with Juventius, "the flower of indolent and lascivious youth," who came from one of the leading families of Rome. Catullus died "of exhaustion" (it is said) at the age of thirty-four.

Marble statue (detail). Second century A.D. Villa Albani, Rome. Emperor Hadrian's favorite, who drowned in the Nile and was deified.

Anonymous, *Virgilian Shepherds*. c. 1820 European neoclassical school. Private collection.

TO JUVENTIUS

I stole a kiss from you, honey-sweet Juventius, while you were playing, a kiss sweeter than sweet ambrosia. But not unpunished; for I remember how for more than an hour I hung impaled on the top of the gallows tree, while I was excusing myself to you, yet could not with all my tears take away ever so little from your anger; for no sooner was it done, than you washed your lips clean with plenty of water, and wiped them with all your fingers, that no contagion from my mouth might remain....

(XCIX)

TO AURELIUS

I will show you my manhood,
Aurelius the Pathic, and you, Faggot Furius,
who call me a profligate
on account of my little verses being rather
voluptuous. Granted, a reverent poet should
himself be chaste, but for his verses
that's another matter; they've no salt
or grace unless they're unchaste
and can set a man itching—a man, mark you,
who is hairy and cannot quiver
his backside like a boy....
And you, because you've read a thousand kisses
in my books you say I'm not a real male?
Wait, I'll show you my manhood.

(XVI [a fragment])

PETRONIUS (d. A.D. 66)

The Satyricon is a novel which describes the mores of Roman society in the reign of Nero. Encolpius, "the gay, unprincipled profligate, but never altogether worthless, narrator of the story" (as Oscar Wilde calls him) is travelling with his two companions, Ascyltos ("his comrade and rival, as immoral and good for nothing as the other, but without his redeeming touch of gentlemanliness") and Giton ("the minion, changeable and capricious, with his pretty face and wheedling ways"). They encounter Eumolpas, an old libidinous poet, who regales them with his amorous adventures, given here in the lively translation attributed to Oscar Wilde.

From THE SATYRICON

"When I went to Asia," he began, "as a paid officer in the Quaestor's suite, I lodged with a family at Pergamus. I found my quarters very pleasant, first on account of the convenience and elegance of the apartments, and still more so because of the beauty of my host's son. I devised the following method to prevent the master of the house entertaining any suspicions of me as a seducer. Whenever the conversation at table turned on the abuse of handsome boys, I showed such extreme indignation and protested with such an air of austerity and offended dignity against the violence done to my ears by filthy talk of the sort, that I came to be regarded, especially by the mother, as one of the greatest of moralists and philosophers. Before long I was allowed to take the lad to the gymnasium; it was I that directed his studies, I that guided his conduct, and guarded against any possible debaucher of his person being admitted to the house.

"It happened on one occasion that we were sleeping in the dining-hall,—the school having closed early as it was a holiday, and our amusements having rendered us too lazy to retire to our sleeping-chambers. Somewhere about midnight I noticed that the lad was awake; so whispering soft and low, I murmured a timid prayer in these words, 'Lady Venus, if I may kiss this boy, so that he know it not, to-morrow I will present him with a pair of doves.' Hearing the price offered for the gratification, the boy set up a snore. So approaching him, where he lay still making pretence to be asleep, I stole two or three flying kisses. Satisfied with this beginning, I rose betimes next morning, and discharged my vow by bringing the eager lad a choice pair of doves.

"The following night, the same opportunity occurring, I changed my petition, 'If I may pass a naughty hand over this boy, and he not feel it, I will present him for his complaisance with a brace of the best fighting cocks ever seen.' At this promise the child came nestling up to me of his own accord, and was actually afraid, I think, lest I might drop asleep again. I soon quieted his uneasiness on this point, and amply satisfied my longings, short of the supreme bliss, on every part of his beautiful body. Then when daylight came, I made him happy with the gift I had promised him.

"As soon as the third night left me free to try again, I rose as before, and creeping up to the rascal, who was lying awake expecting me, whispered at his ear, 'If only, ye Immortal Gods, I may win of this sleeping darling full and happy satisfaction of my love, for such bliss I will to-morrow present the lad with an Asturian of the Macedonian strain, the best to be had for money, but always on the condition he shall not feel my violence.' Never did the stripling sleep more sound. So first I handled his plump and snowy bosoms, then kissed him on the mouth, and finally concentrated all my ardours in one supreme delight. Next morning he sat still in his

Marble statue (detail). Third century B.C. Archeological Museum, Istanbul. A boy from Tralles in Asia Minor. Jean Cocteau's design for the jacket of *Les Enfants Terribles* was inspired by this sculpture.

Bronze statue. Discovered at Agde, France, in 1964. Louvre, Paris. Roman done in the Hellenistic manner. Pliny says that several statues of this type were "abused" by overfervent admirers.

room, expecting my present as usual. Well! you know as well as I do, it is a much easier matter to buy doves and fighting cocks than an Asturian; besides which, I was afraid so valuable a present might rouse suspicion as to the real motives of my liberality. After walking about for an hour or so, I returned to the house, and gave the boy a kiss—and nothing else. He looked about inquiringly, then threw his arms round my neck, and 'Please, sir!' he said, 'where is my Asturian?'

Although by this breach of faith I had closed against myself the door of access so carefully contrived, I returned once more to the attack. For, after allowing a few days to elapse, one night when similar circumstances had created just such another opportunity for us as before, I began, the moment I heard the father snoring, to beg and pray the boy to be friends with me again,—that is to let me give him pleasure for pleasure, adding all the arguments my burning concupiscence could suggest. But he was positively angry and refused to say one word beyond, 'Go to sleep, or I will tell my father.' But there is never an obstacle so difficult audacity will not vanquish it. He was still repeating, 'I will wake my father,' when I slipped into his bed and took my pleasure of him in spite of his half-hearted resistance. However he found a certain pleasure in my naughty ways, for after a string of complaints about my having cheated and cajoled him and made him the laughing-stock of his school-fellows, to whom he had boasted of his rich friend, he whispered, 'Still I won't be so unkind as you; if you like, do it again.' So forgetting all our differences, I was reconciled to the dear lad once more, and after utilizing his kind permission, I slipped off to sleep in his arms. But the stripling was not satisfied with only one repetition, all ripe for love as he was and just at the time of life for passive enjoyment. So he woke me up from my slumbers, and, 'Anything you'ld like, eh?' said he. Nor was I, so far, indisposed to accept his offer. So working him the best ever I could, to the accompaniment of much panting and perspiration, I gave him what he wanted, and then dropped asleep again, worn out with pleasure. Less than an hour had passed before he started pinching me and asking, 'Eh! why are we not at work?' Hereupon, sick to death of being so often disturbed, I flew into a regular rage, and retorted his own words upon him; 'Go to sleep,' I cried, 'or I'll tell your father!'

MARTIAL (A.D. c. 40-104)

Martial was born in the small town of Bilbilis in Spain (in the region of Tarragona). His family was well off and sent him to Rome to finish his studies. He had no trade or profession, and preferred to live in the shadow of more important people. He was the friend of Quintilien, the famous orator and teacher of the future emperor Hadrian, of Pliny the Younger, another brilliant orator, and of Juvenal. (See p. 67) The Emperor Domitian, who enjoyed his poems, knighted him. Under Trajan's reign, he fell out of favor and retired to Bilbilis. A rich widow lent him an estate where he ended his days in comfort, but missing Rome and his friends.

Bust of Antinoüs (detail). Second century A.D. Farnese Collection. Museo Archeologico Nazionale, Naples.

Leonard Sarluis, Painting. Felix Marcilhac Collection. Sarluis was a friend of Oscar Wilde, Jean Lorrain and Sar Peladan. The equivocal grace of the adolescents Sarluis paints here could illustrate certain antique epigrams.

EPIGRAMS

If any could by chance guarantee me the boon at my asking, hear, Flaccus, what kind of boy I would wish to ask for. First of all, let this boy be born on the shores of the Nile; no country knows better how to beget roguish ways. Let him be fairer than snow; for in swarthy Mareotis that hue is more beautiful by its rarity. Let his eyes vie with stars, and his soft locks tumble over his neck; I like not, Flaccus, braided locks. Let his brow be low and his nose slightly aquiline, let his lips rival the red of Paestan roses. And let him oft compel endearments when I am loth, and refuse them when I am fain; may he oft be more free than his lord! And let him shrink from boys, oft exclude girls; man to all else, to me alone let him be a boy. "Now I know him, you do not deceive me; 'tis in my judgment true. Such was," you will say, "my Amazonicus."

(Book IV, XLII)

There's no finer love than the love of women
For those who're so inclined. For the others,
Whose passion is all masculine,
I know a cure for what ails their heart:
All they need do is ask Menophilas
To turn around and show her ass.
    (Epigram no. 116 by Marcus Argentarius attributed to Martial)

Your door's wide open, Amillus, when you bugger your friends
(They're not so young anymore), hoping to be caught in the act;
Fearing the servants and household slaves your father gave you
Might spread unsavory rumors with all their chatter....
But he who shows off what he does *not* do before witnesses
Often does it, doesn't he, when he's behind closed doors.
(Book VII, LXII)

Aubry Lecomte, *The Sleeping Shepherd*. Lithograph. Cabinet des Estampes, Bibliothèque Nationale, Paris.

Why, Hyllus boy, have you denied to-day what yesterday you gave, hard so suddenly who erewhile were gentle? But now you plead your beard, and your years, and hair: O night, how long thou art, one night that makest an old man! Why do you laugh at me? Hyllus, who yesterday were boy, tell me how you are man to-day?

(Book IV, VII)

So shadowy is the down on thy cheeks, so soft that a breath, or the sun, or a soft breeze, rubs it away. With such a fleecy film are veiled ripening quinces, that gleam brightly when plucked by maiden fingers. Whenever I have too strongly impressed upon thy cheek five kisses, I become, Dindymus, bearded from thy lips.

(Book X, XLII)

Artemidorus possesses a young slave, but has sold his land; the land Calliodorus possesses in exchange for the slave. Say, which of those two made the better bargain, Auctus? Artemidorus has his pleasure, Calliodorus his plough.

(Book IX, XXI)

When you pluck the hairs from your chest, and legs, and arms,
And when after you have shaved, your prick's surrounded
With but a few short curls, we all know it's for your girl, Labienus;
But who's it for, tell me, when you pluck out the hairs from your arse?

(Book II, LXII)

Oh, to have a young slave whose skin is soft,
Not with pumice but with sweet youth
—To tempt me away from any female!

(Book XIV, CCV)

Aubrey Beardsley, *Bathyllus's Swan Dance*. Illustration for Juvenal's *Satire VI*. Published in 1906 by Lawrence and Bullen.

JUVENAL (c. 55-140)

The adoptive son of a rich freed slave, the satiric poet Juvenal directed his shafts against the vices of the Romans. He speaks from experience when he describes the difficulty of finding a patron. In the ninth satire, Nevolus, a parasite who is obliged to submit to the whims of his benefactors, explains why he is no longer the gay party-goer he used to be.

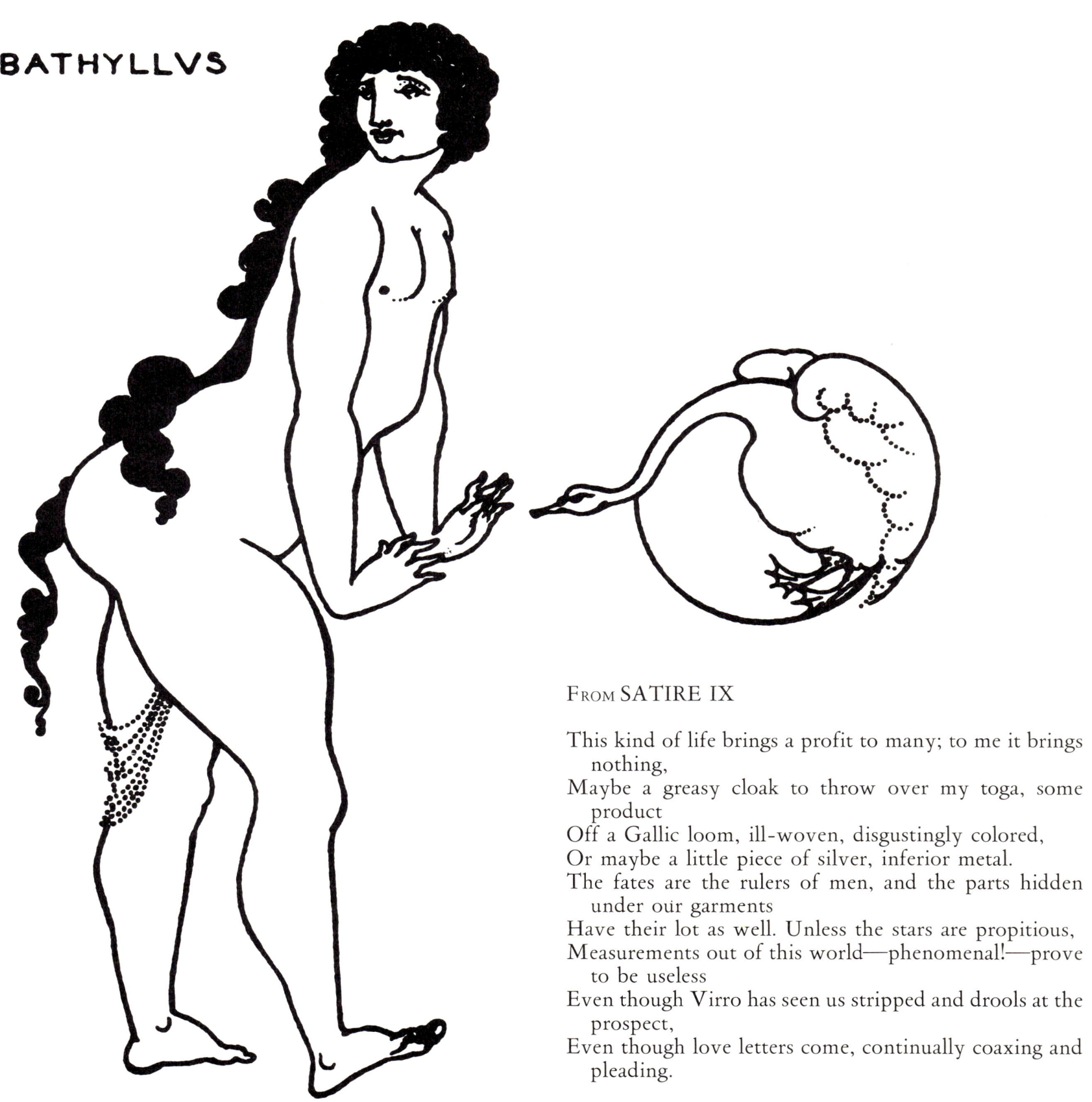

From SATIRE IX

This kind of life brings a profit to many; to me it brings nothing,
Maybe a greasy cloak to throw over my toga, some product
Off a Gallic loom, ill-woven, disgustingly colored,
Or maybe a little piece of silver, inferior metal.
The fates are the rulers of men, and the parts hidden under our garments
Have their lot as well. Unless the stars are propitious,
Measurements out of this world—phenomenal!—prove to be useless
Even though Virro has seen us stripped and drools at the prospect,
Even though love letters come, continually coaxing and pleading.

What's that phrase from the Greek—A *man is drawn to a fairy?*
What in the world can be worse than the fairy who's stingy about it?
"Oh, but I paid you once, and I paid you twice, and I paid you
Ever so many times." He's figured it out, or he hopes so,
Using every device.... Does he think this job is so easy,
Shoving it in to the point where it meets with yesterday's dinner?
Ploughing the master's field pays more than ploughing his person.
Ah, but he used to think himself such a delicate fellow,
Such a pretty boy, a Ganymede, worthy of Heaven,
Won't he ever be nice to his lowly pleasurers? Won't he
Ever be prepared to pay for his gratification?
("A Parasite")

FROM SATIRE VI

There are some women who find unmanly eunuchs delightful,
Love the soft kisses of those who are hopeless of growing a beard—
No need here for precautions. But oh, the height of their pleasure
Comes when they happen on one who was fully mature when they took him
Off for the doctors to work on, and his quill was darkened already,
So what the surgeon removes hurts no one's game but the barber's
Once the members have grown, filled out, begun to weigh something,
But if you get young boys, they really are wretchedly weakened,
Ashamed of their empty bag and the chick-peas that once were contained there.
This one, though, deprived, by his lady's will, of his manhood,
After his teens, is a noteworthy sight, outstanding Priapus
On his way to the baths. So, let him sleep with his lady,
But never let yourself think that he's impotent under the covers.
("Eunuchs")

Aubrey Beardsley, *Bathyllus*. Illustration for Juvenal's *Satire VI*. Published in 1906 by Lawrence and Bullen.

SUETONIUS (c. 69-140)

A writer of great erudition, Suetonius was the Emperor Hadrian's secretary. He was dismissed in 122 for reasons we do not know. He wrote a number of biographical and historical works including *The Lives of the Caesars*. In this long narrative he did not just report the significant events in the lives of the emperors; he also described their personality and their private behavior. He did not hesitate to travel when it was necessary to obtain information, and he used official documents, pamphlets and even graffiti as his sources.

From THE TWELVE CAESARS

49. The only specific charge of unnatural practices ever brought against him was that he had been King Nicomedes's catamite—always a dark stain on his reputation and frequently quoted by his enemies. Licinius Calvus published the notorious verses:

> The riches of Bithynia's King
> Who Caesar on his couch abused.

Dolabella called him "the Queen's rival and inner partner of the royal bed", and Curio the Elder: "Nicomedes's Bithynian brothel".

Bibulus, Caesar's colleague in the consulship, described him in an edict as "the Queen of Bithynia... who once wanted to sleep with a monarch, but now wants to be one". And Marcus Brutus recorded that, about the same time, one Octavius, a scatterbrained creature who would say the first thing that came into his head, walked into a packed assembly where he saluted Pompey as "King" and Caesar as "Queen". These can be discounted as mere insults, but Gaius Memmius directly charges Caesar with having joined a group of Nicomedes's debauched young friends at a banquet, where he acted as the royal cup-

(a) Pierre François Huges, chevalier de Hancarville, Engravings for *Monuments de la vie privée des douze Césars*, 1785. Private collection. The engravings depict scenes wholly imagined by Hancarville. (b) Nero publicly weds young Sporus. (c) Nero and Diophorus. (d) Caligula with two youths (his friends are dining in the company of respectable Roman matrons). (e) Diophorus and Nero in girl's dress. (f) Tiberius attending a sacrifice: His fancy is caught by two youths. (g) Tiberius and children.

bearer; and adds that certain Roman merchants, whose names he supplies, were present as guests. Cicero, too, not only wrote in several letters: "Caesar was led by Nicomedes's attendants to the royal bedchamber, where he lay on a golden couch, dressed in a purple shift... So this descendant of Venus lost his virginity in Bithynia," but also once interrupted Caesar while he was addressing the House in defence of Nicomedes's daughter Nysa and listing his obligations to Nicomedes himself. "Enough of that," Cicero shouted, "if you please! We all know what he gave you, and what you gave him in return." Lastly, when Caesar's own soldiers followed his decorated chariot in the Gallic triumph, chanting ribald songs, as they were privileged to do, this was one of them:

> Gaul was brought to shame by Caesar;
>   By King Nicomedes, he.
> Here comes Caesar, wreathed in triumph
>   For his Gallic victory!
> Nicomedes wears no laurels,
>   Though the greatest of the three.

("Julius Caesar")

28. Not satisfied with seducing free-born boys and married women, Nero raped the Vestal Virgin Rubria. He nearly contrived to marry the freedwoman Acte, by persuading some friends of consular rank to swear falsely that she came of royal stock. Having tried to turn the boy Sporus into a girl by castration, he went through a wedding ceremony with him—dowry, bridal veil and all—which the whole Court attended; then brought him home, and treated him as a wife. He dressed Sporus in the fine clothes normally worn by an Empress and took him in his own litter not only to every Greek assize and fair, but actually through the Street of Images at Rome, kissing him amorously now and then. A rather amusing joke is still going the rounds; the world would have been a happier place had Nero's father Domitius married that sort of wife.

The passion he felt for his mother, Agrippina, was notorious; but her enemies would not let him consummate it, fearing that, if he did, she would become even more powerful and ruthless than hitherto. So he found a new mistress who was said to be her spit and image; some say that he did, in fact, commit incest with Agrippina every time they rode in the same litter—the state of his clothes when he emerged proved it.

29. Nero practised every kind of obscenity, and at last invented a novel game: he was released from a den dressed in the skins of wild animals, and attacked the private parts of men and women who stood bound to stakes. After working up sufficient excitement by this means, he was dispatched—shall we say?—by his freedman Doryphorus. Doryphorus now married him— just as he himself had married Sporus—and on the wedding night he imitated the screams and moans of a girl being deflowered. According to my informants he was convinced that nobody could remain sexually chaste, but that most people concealed their secret vices; hence, if anyone confessed to obscene practices, Nero forgave him all his other crimes.

("Nero")

43. On retiring to Capri he made himself a private sporting-house, where sexual extravagances were practised for his secret pleasure. Bevies of girls and young men, whom he had collected from all over the Empire as adepts in unnatural practices, and known as *spintriae,* would perform before him in groups of three, to excite his waning passions. A number of small rooms were furnished with the most indecent pictures and statuary obtainable, also certain erotic manuals from Elephantis in

Egypt; the inmates of the establishment would know from these exactly what was expected of them. He furthermore devised little nooks of lechery in the woods and glades of the island, and had boys and girls dressed up as Pans and nymphs posted in front of caverns or grottoes; so that the island was now openly and generally called "Caprineum", because of his goatish antics.

44. Some aspects of his criminal obscenity are almost too vile to discuss, much less believe. Imagine training little boys, whom he called his "minnows", to chase him while he went swimming and get between his legs to lick and nibble him. Or letting babies not yet weaned from their mother's breast suck at him—such a filthy old man he had become! Then there was a painting by Parrhasius, which had been bequeathed him on condition that, if he did not like the subject, he could have 10,000 gold pieces instead. Tiberius not only preferred to keep the picture but hung it in his bedroom. It showed Atalanta committing a grossly intimate act with Meleager.

The story goes that once, while sacrificing, he took an erotic fancy to the acolyte who carried the incense casket, and could hardly wait for the ceremony to end before hurrying him and his brother, the sacred trumpeter, out of the temple and indecently assaulting them both. When they protested at this dastardly crime he had their legs broken.

("Tiberius")

Low relief, used as a sign for a brothel. Pompeii. Some of these signs bore the inscription *Hic habitat felicitas* [Here dwells felicity].

IV

THE RETURN OF PLATO

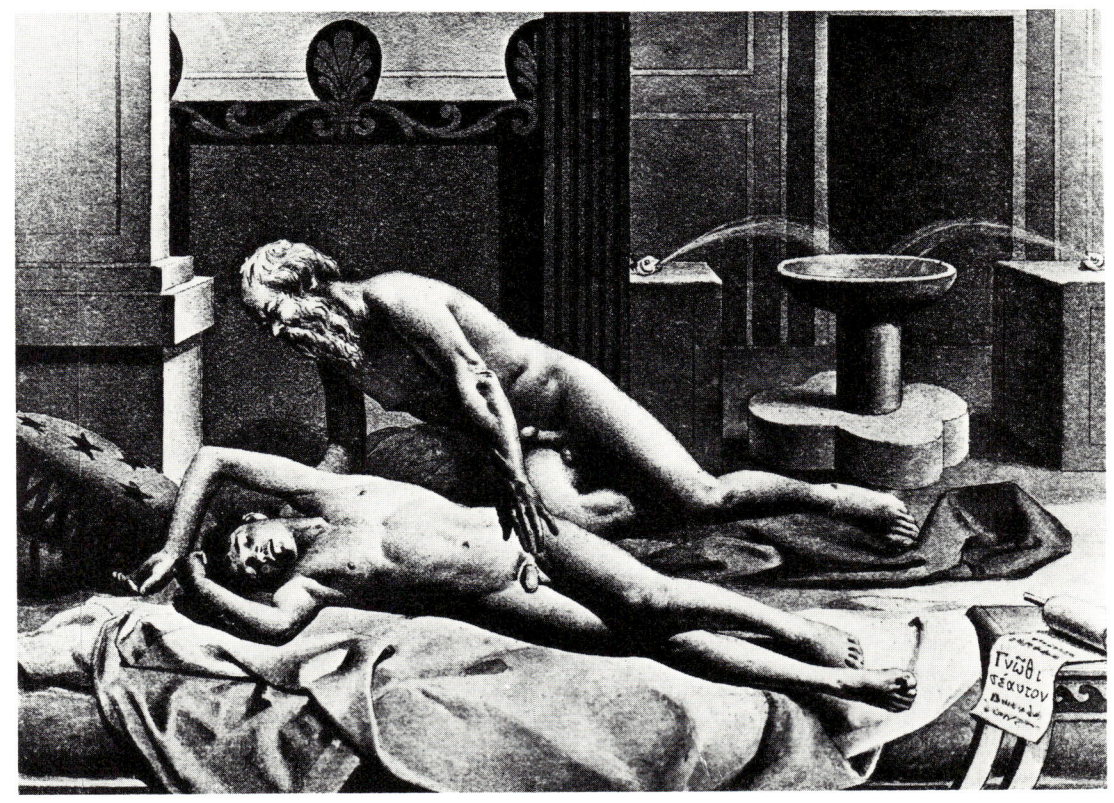

"We who are beautiful in the souls of our lovers...."
(Homer)

◁◁ *Socratic Love*, according to *De Figuris veneris*, a treatise on classical sexology by Frederich Karl Forberg, who was a philologist, a humanist and the court librarian at Coburg. Roger Peyrefitte Collection.

Luca Signorelli, *Studies of Male Nudes*. Cabinet des Dessins, Louvre, Paris.

Study for Bacchus, Italian. End of the sixteenth century. Victoria and Albert Museum, London.

In 1177 the Abbot of Clairvaux sent a warning to Pope Alexander III: "Ancient Sodom is rising from its ashes." Actually, homosexuality had not died out since the days of the Romans, despite the anathema of the Church. Ausonius says that it was widespread among the Gauls and the other "barbarians." Hoping to stamp out "that infamous vice," Charlemagne decreed death for sodomy—but to no great effect. Some 200 years later, at the Council of Rheims in 1049, the Deacon Peter, speaking in the name of Pope Leo IX, castigated the abominable practices of the laity and the priesthhood. William of Nangis wrote that in 1092 a bishop of Orleans named John had himself called "Flora" by his *concubii*; in the evenings youths who sold themselves to men would walk through the streets of the town singing ditties in his honor.

Some chroniclers, like Odoric Vital, maintained that it was the Norman invaders who infected the French lords with the "vice against nature." He wrote: "Effeminate fops prevailed throughout the land and employed themselves without restraint at their foul debauchery; catamites, deserving to be burned at the stake, indulged repeatedly in the horrible inventions of Sodom." According to this author, a hermit had predicted the accession of Robert II Curthose, the Duke of Normandy— nicknamed Shortbritches— "a prince like unto a lascivious cow, who giveth himself over to luxury and sloth, and who would lay hand upon the riches which rightfully belonged to the Church and divide them among his ruffians and infamous flatterers." In fact, the Normans had proved to be as eager for women as for men during their conquest. After laying waste the country and massacring the old, they shared boys and girls whom they "used for their pleasure" under the gazes of their forever-pregnant and indifferent wives. It should be noted, however, that in a poem about the siege of Paris, Saint-Abbon (the Abbot of Fleury, now the town of Saint-Benoît-sur-Loire, and Councillor to Hughes Capet in 988) accuses the lords of France, and not the Normans, of the "abominable vice".

In the twelfth century, male friendship was idealized and held sacred—as it often is in warrior societies. Women were considered dangerous—for they sapped the valiance of the fighters—and unworthy of spiritual

75

intimacy with men. In the epic poems of the Middle Ages the men are generally devoted body and soul to their companions-at-arms. Thus in the *Song of Aspremont* (late twelfth century), the wife of the Sarazin king Agolant questions the Duke of Naimes: "Frenchman, tell me the truth: Have ye women in your land? And are the Christians all as handsome as you?" "Lady," replies the Duke, "of that I know naught, but many a finer man there is than myself. You ask, am I married? No, lady, and I would never consider such a thing, for my heart belongs entirely to my lord."

Walter Pater has looked for examples of Platonic love in medieval chivalrous romances. He singles out the Romance of Amis and Amiles, two knights whose manly devotion to each other turns into outright passion. Amis kills his children to cure Amiles of leprosy by washing him "in the blood of innocence." Indeed, the initiation rites of the knights' fraternities, the war-like education of boys gathered together in armed bands under the leadership of young princes in gorgeous clothes, the jousts organized with the formal precision of dances and the segregation of the sexes could only encourage homosexuality—which flourished among the Crusaders and in the courts of France, England, Italy and Spain.

William of Nangis reports that in 1120, when the ship they were sailing on ran aground and left them stranded, the knights in the following of the son of Henry I all practiced homosexuality. The female poet Marie de France, who lived at the court of Henry II in England, makes Guenevere mock the young knight Lanval, who had had the temerity to resist her overtures:

I have heard it whispered many times
That to women you are not inclined;
But with low valets and that sort
You prefer to make your sport.

The medieval chroniclers speak indignantly about the depraved habits of the great lords. Froissart says of the count of Foix, Gaston Phoebus, that "he is the only one I know of who hath not lain with one of his minions.... They all do; the Duke of Berry hath his pet Take Thibaut: a varlet and a mender of dikes whom the Duke had taken into his affection no one knows why, for this varlet was a dim wit and a fool who possessed nothing and cared for nothing save what profited him; and this Duke made him rich with presents of silver and gold worth two hundred thousand francs, which the poor subjects of Auvergne and Languedoc had paid for, being taxed three or four times a year to afford the Duke his

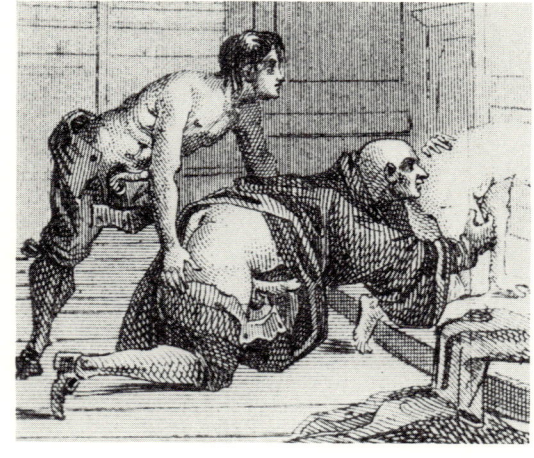

Sandro Botticelli, *The Inferno*. Illustrations for Dante's *Divine Comedy*. Bibliothèque Nationale, Paris. Eighty-five drawings from this series belonged to William Beckford (See p. 148).

Nineteenth-century English engraving. Private collection.

Miniature from the *Très riches heures du duc de Berry*. Musée de Condé, Chantilly, France. According to Jean Froissard, the Duke of Berry spent fabulous sums of money buying gifts for his *marmouset*, Take Thibaut.

Anonymous, *Portrait of Pico della Mirandola*. Galleria degli Uffizi, Florence.

Perugino, *Apollo and Marsyas*. Louvre, Paris.

unreasonable pleasures." The notoriety of Take Thibaut was such that, in his great poem *Le Testament*, Francois Villon gives his name to the Bishop of Orleans, Thibaut d'Auxigny, whom he accuses of sodomite practices. (Note that in the Middle Ages it was common practice to accuse one's enemies of "sodomy"—the usual term for homosexuality. The Knights Templar, the Albigensians, the Waldenses were all denounced as being devotees of the "abominable vice" *contra naturam*.)

Whereas the chroniclers frequently mentioned instances of homosexuality at the court of kings like John the Good, who wiled away blissful hours with his lover Lacerda during his imprisonment in England, or told with thrills of horror how Edward II was impaled (see p. 103); the great poets of the age, Dante and Petrarch and the troubadours of Provence, passionately celebrated the love of high-born ladies. As Petrarch has written, "The fountainhead of love is Beauty, and none other, and Beauty is that which striketh the eye with brightness." In the writings of these poets, Beauty is embodied in woman. But in their daily lives they also knew passions of a different sort. Dante places two poets who were the forerunners of the new lyric style—the *dolce stil nuovo*—among the sodomites in Purgatory: the troubadour Arnaut Daniel and Guido Guinizelli. The author of the *Divine Comedy* was being relatively lenient, since he did not put them in Hell with his master, Brunetto Latino, who was there, not for homosexuality as was long believed, but for "sinning against the Holy Spirit,"—considered a kind of spiritual sodomy. Brunetto Latino's mates in the *Inferno* are the "violent sodomites" like Giacomo de Rusticci, a wealthy knight whose extramarital affairs made him disgusted with women; among them too are the "many brilliant minds who have excelled in Letters and in the [Church] Doctrine, but whose lives and renown have been smirched with the same vice."

As the French scholar René Nelli writes in his study of erotic themes in the poetry of the troubadours *(L'Erotique des Troubadours)*, the ideal of courtly love held by the lyric poets from the twelfth century on "transferred the values of homosexuality, of idealized friendship in Antiquity—the values, if you like, of male Platonism—to heterosexual love." By celebrating the femininity of the young ladies of the castle, the troubadours helped to dispel the misogyny of the lords and barons of the Middle Ages. Thanks to them, women began to be considered worthy of being loved, not merely possessed. Indeed, one now had to earn the esteem of the woman one loved by performing feats of valor and demonstrating how chivalrous one was. The lover was devoted to his lady in the same way that the vassal was devoted to his lord; he had to be ready to die in her service. This upgrading of the status of women in the twelfth century was peculiar to Southern Europe. Some historians attribute it to the tempering influence of Christianity which "purified" morals; others trace it back to the poetic traditions of the Arabs who had settled in Andalusia. Now, among the Arabs, as had been the case among the Greeks, love was often pederastic: witness Ibn Dā'ūd's *Book of the Flower,* which was dedicated to a young man; whereas French courtly love, the *Fin'Amor* of the troubadours, was essentially heterosexual. And in fact, though it was frequently practiced, homosexuality is seldom mentioned in the literary works—the epics, the courtly romances and the lyrics—of the four centuries which we call the Middle Ages. With the rise of humanism in the fifteenth

century things changed. The writers, poets, painters and sculptors of the Renaissance acclaimed the Platonic—or rather the Neoplatonic—ideal of love between men.

As Walter Pater has written, the Neoplatonic school of the Renaissance sought "to make Homer and Plato utter words which Moses would have approved." For the Italian philosopher Marsilio Ficino and his followers "love is the urge to savor beauty...." and in their eyes more often than not beauty took the shape of a boy, whom one might love "in God and in Plato." Ficino was smitten with love—a very pure and chaste love—for the handsome Giovanni Cavalcanti. He wanted priests who were celebrating mass to add a passage from Plato to the traditional liturgy. Short and ugly, Ficino nevertheless was loved by the "Prince of scholars," Pico della Mirandola, who is said to have known Hebrew, Latin, Greek, Arabic and Aramaic thoroughly by the age of twenty. Pico was so stunningly handsome that the first time Marsilio set eyes on him he mistook him for an angel. Thomas More too seems to have been stirred by Pico's looks, for he describes him in more-than-flattering terms:

> of feature and shape seemly and beauteous, of stature goodly and high, of flesh tender and soft, his visage lovely and fair, his color white, intermingled with comely reds, his eyes gray, and quick of look, his teeth white and even, his hair yellow and abundant....

Another of Pico's admirers, Girolamo Benivieni, would send him very loving sonnets. The two friends—Pico and Marsilio—claimed that they shared the same soul, and each would sign his letters with both their names. They were buried in the same grave. The spiritual love these two esthetes cultivated radiates from their correspondance. In one letter Pico writes: "I hunger and thirst for Marsilio, for the joyfulness that fills his life, for the pleasure that inhabits his mind." Marsilio confides to his friend Bembo: "Bernardo, my dear, I thought that I loved myself so much that I could not possibly love myself more; but happily I was mistaken in this opinion, for, learning that you ardently love me, I have begun to love myself even more ardently" *(Epistle VIII)*.

As for the poet Politian, he claims that whenever he glimpses a certain Buonisegni, "my heart pounds like the bridegroom's when he climbs on to the promised virgin's couch." Such passionate epistles were often followed by refined gifts. Cavalcanti sent a brace of turtle-doves to Marsilio as if the latter were a young girl; Politian presented Lorenzo de' Medici with baskets of lilies and roses.

Marsilio Ficino, Pico della Mirandola and Politian met frequently, for each owned a house near Fiesole. They were invited together to extravagant festivities given by rich patrons and admirers. Each year on the November 7, Francesco Bandini held a banquet to commemorate Plato's death. Beautiful Cavalcanti would attract all the looks—he who was the "Prince of the Feast"—as he did at Lorenzo de' Medici's gatherings (where, on one occasion, he delivered a brilliant commentary on the speeches of Phaedrus). The Neoplatonic scholars had their own heroes: such as Donato Accajuolo, who was still a virgin at thirty-two, or Michael Verino "who died at the age of nineteen for having wanted to remain chaste." "Oh Paul," wrote the latter to one of his friends, "do you know that the doctors have prescribed intercourse for my health? If that is the price, I would rather not hang on to life."

Politian, who astonished his friends with his enormous range of erudition and with his multiple talents, believed that the only sin against nature was virginity. His active sex life seems to have raised eyebrows in his day, but that did not prevent him from being employed as the tutor of Lorenzo de' Medici's children. In his *Florentine Anecdotes*, Varillas reports that Politian died while playing the lute for a boy whom he loved to distraction (see p. 88).

It was no easy thing for a man in a prominent position or for a Church dignitary to remain an angel. Male prostitution flourished in Rome as well as in Florence, and well-born youths attired themselves in gorgeous finery, perfuming themselves and even sometimes curling their hair like women. There are very few writers and intellectuals of the two centuries of the Renaissance who cannot be suspected of homosexuality. Paulus Jovius was called "the Hermaphrodite" because, according to his contemporaries, he was "both man and wife." Francesco Berni, the author of Petrarchan parodies and satiric poems which originated the *bernesco* style; the physician and mathematician Gerolamo Cardano; Antonio Beccadelli, called *la Panoramita,* who dedicated his book, *The Hermaphrodite,* to Cosimo de' Medici; Aretino; Tasso; Machiavelli and countless others all tried their hands at loving—not only the opposite sex. Professor Pomponius Laetus, who liked to walk down from the Esquiline with a lantern in his hand while lecturing youths "in the manner of Socrates," was at a loss to know which way to turn.... There were so many possibilities! As one of Aretino's characters observes, if the fires of Heaven were to punish all those who indulged in the vice against nature, not a single lord or scholar would remain in all of Italy. Why, the Papacy itself.... Rumor had it that Paul II used to paint his face, and it was said that on being elected he had been disappointed at not being allowed to take the name "Formosus I" [the Well-shaped]. It was even whispered that he had died of a heart-attack in the act of sodomy. His successor Pius II nicknamed him "Maria Pientissima," but in his own youth in Siena, when he had written under the pen name Aeneas Silvius, he himself had been friends with people like Beccadelli, the author of *The Hermaphrodite*. And it was alleged that this same Aeneas Silvius—who had been crowned the Prince of Poets by the Emperor Frederick III—had contributed certain passages to that book, which was reputed to be filled with "obscenities". But like the blue-stocking literary ladies in Molière's *Précieuses Ridicules,* these

Giovanni Antonio Bazzi, known as Sodoma, *Self-Portrait* (detail). Monteoliveto, Siena.

Michelangelo Merisi da Caravaggio, *Bacchus*. Galleria degli Uffizi, Florence.

Renaissance intellectuals found the word—obscenity—the "most delightful in all creation." Finally, one might mention a certain opuscule entitled *De laudibus Sodomiae seu Pederastiae* [*In Praise of Sodomy or Pederasty*, 1548], said to be the work of the legate of Venice, Giovanni Casa, who, had it not been for his immoderate love for boys, would certainly have worn the cardinal's hat.

In the workshops of the painters and sculptors, "immoral acts," especially homosexual ones, were almost the rule. The striplings who shared the living quarters of their masters as apprentices or as servants were often shameless urchins. If they had a pretty face, or a well-proportioned body, they would sit as models. Nor was their master's attitude towards them always strictly professional. Witness Verrochio and Lorenzo di Credi whom the former appointed executor of his estate. As for Leonardo da Vinci, it was at the time that he was working in Verrochio's workshop that he was accused of committing illicit acts with a certain Jacopo Saltarelli, aged seventeen. The anonymous charge had been dropped into a *tamburo*, the special mailbox for denouncing your fellow citizens to the authorities. On April 9, 1476, Leonardo went on trial, and on June 7, the same year he was formally acquitted. In his *Notebooks*, Leonardo refers to another trouble-causing entanglement with one of his students whom he nicknamed Salai [little devil]. Vasari says that Salai was a pretty lad, "graceful and with a fine head of long, wavy hair." Leonardo, himself of "such physical beauty as transcends all praise," used to choose his students—at least that is what evil-tongues whispered—for their looks rather than for their artistic gifts. Salai, Leonardo complains in his notes, was a liar, a thief and a little glutton; but nevertheless the great painter spoiled him, showering him with beautiful clothes and gifts. On his death, Leonardo left a sizeable estate to Salai, although his principal inheritor turned out to be another one of his students, Francesco Melzi.

Homosexuality was rampant during the Renaissance, and denunciations were frequent. Thus in 1502 Botticelli—it seems that the master of madonnas was somewhat of a misogynist—was accused of having "unnatural relations" with one of his assistants. To his patron Tommaso Soderini, who had advised him one day to get married (in order to put a stop to rumors?), Botticelli replied, horrified: "Sire, I will tell you what happened to me one night. I dreamed that I had taken a wife, and this caused me such anguish that I awoke, and so afraid was I of falling back into that dream that I spent the remainder of the night wandering like a madman through Florence." Then there was Giovanni Antonio Bazzi, otherwise known as Sodoma, an eccentric painter who lived with a bizarre menagerie of animals—badgers, squirrels, monkeys and exotic birds—and who made no bones about advertising his sexual proclivities. On one occasion he won a horse-race, and the urchins who had joined in the

victory parade having asked him what name they should shout out, Bazzi replied, "Sodoma!" So loud were the cheers that the whole town was alerted; and the painter, galloping away on his Barbary horse with his little monkey hanging on for dear life behind, narrowly escaped being stoned. But the name stuck.

At the age of fourteen Domenico Ghirlandaio's student Michelangelo was granted the great honor of being admitted to the "Garden of the Medici," a school of sculpture established in the Medici gardens under the supervision of Bertoldo (a former student of Donatello's). Michelangelo was given a room in the palace, and he took his meals with the Medici—thus making acquaintance with the future Pope Julius II. Among the Tuscan humanists and artists who gathered around the Medici, the young man encountered many famous and respected figures who gaily indulged in what Savonarola called the abominable vice. But at the time that Savonarola was organizing his "bonfire of vanities"—burning paintings, licentious books, adornments, wigs and other "futilities," while little children in white dresses wearing crowns of olive leaves intoned the hymn specially composed for the occasion by Pico della Mirandola's dear friend Girolamo Benivieni—Michelangelo was in Rome sculpting a "Cupid" and a perverse, lascivious and drunken "Bacchus". "It is impossible to be more sinful with a chisel," marvelled the connoisseurs. Contrary to habit Michelangelo is said to have made this statue from a live model, whose name has not come down to us (see p. 83). The great sculptor and painter was certainly not short on models. In a letter written in 1515 to Nicolo Quaratei, he recounts that a man came to him one day asking him to accept his son as an apprentice. Michelangelo refused, whereupon the man tried to prevail on him by saying that if he took the boy he could keep him "not only in his house but also in his bed." Michelangelo replied gently that "regretfully he would forgo that consolation, not wanting to deprive the old man of it."

The love affairs which Michelangelo alludes to in his sonnets were generally unhappy ones. In 1522 the artist fell in love with Gherardo Perini, who is perhaps the vigorous youth in "Victory" trampling the old man, who resembles Michelangelo himself. (See p. 83). Two years later they broke up, and Michelangelo lamented in one of his unfinished poems:

From this very stone did I see him take wing,
He who had torn me from myself and now lets me drop.

The sculptor's other great passion was a certain Febbo di Poggio, a capricious young man who was forever asking for money. Then there are the sonnets on the death of Cecchino dei Brazzi, the son of an exiled Florentine, who died at the age of fifteen and was the idol of the aptly named banker-poet Luigi del Riccio. These poems are thought to have been inspired by Luigi's grief. Michelangelo also nourished a Platonic and very courtly passion for Vittoria Colonna, a great but rather ugly lady seventeen years his junior who died in 1547. But, as Vasari observes, "more than anyone he loved Master Tommaso Cavalieri, a gentleman from Rome who was inclined to the arts at a very tender age." This was a chaste love according to most of Michelangelo's contemporaries (except for the poet Aretino who drops poisonous hints about this friendship in his acrimonious exchange with the sculptor). Anyway, Michelangelo died holding Tommaso's hand in 1564.

It would take up too much space if we were to list all the artists of the Renaissance who are thought to have had homosexual involvements. However, we mustn't leave out Benvenuto Cellini who, though he carefully avoids referring to these incidents in his *Autobiography,* went on trial no less than three times for the crime of sodomy.

Like Caravaggio he had a fatal weakness for ne'er-do-wells encountered in taverns or on the street. To one lord who complained of Cellini's dissolute ways and marvelled at the Pope's forbearance, Paul III replied: "You must realize that men who are past-masters in the arts like Benvenuto are not subject to ordinary laws...." Admittedly, Paul III had reasons for being soft on sodomites: his bastard son Peter was rumored to have been killed for having attempted to rape a handsome bishop.

Notwithstanding the denunciations dropped into the *tamburo,* the artists of the Renaissance were able to pursue their proclivities without having to worry much about

Leonardo da Vinci, *Sketch of His Apprentice Salai (?)*. Picture Gallery, Christ Church, Oxford. According to Georgio Vasari, the lad was "graceful and had long, wavy hair."

Michelangelo, *Bacchus*. Museo Nazionale del Bargello, Florence. "It is impossible to be more sinful with a chisel," marvelled the artist's contemporaries.

Michelangelo, *Victory*. Palazzo Vecchio, Florence. The face of the old man being trampled by the victorious youth may be a self-portrait of the great artist.

legal reprisals (such as being burned at the stake). As they grew old, the painters and the sculptors solicited gratifications from their young students which they considered mere peccadilloes, "little sins which a drop of holy water washes away." So notorious were the morals of the artists that in one of his *Satires* Ariosto mentions a facetious saying among common people that "it is as dangerous to turn your back to a painter as it is to share his bed."

The intellectuals and the writers—particularly the devotees of Socratic love—viewed Antiquity as the lost Paradise which they wanted to restore in fifteenth- and sixteenth-century Italy. After centuries of Christian asceticism and harsh discipline, the aristocracy eagerly embraced the new spirit of paganism. Wealthy lords named their sons Achilles or Agamemnon; Filippo di San Gemignano changed his name to Callimachus; a member of the renowned Sanseverino family had himself called Julius Pomponius Laetus. On holidays satyrs, nymphs and crowned youths got up as ancient gods paraded through the towns on elaborate horse-drawn floats. Gradually Neoplatonic philosophy supplanted the Medieval systems of thought. Not only were the souls of the saints considered beautiful, but so were their bodies (for is not physical beauty the reflection of inner perfection?). Thus is seemed perfectly natural to paint them unclothed, like the adolescents of Arcadia, or the god Adonis, or the athletes of Greece and Rome. Saint John the Baptist was represented as a bold shepherd lad, David as a gladiator, Saint Sebastian as a strangely disquieting androgyne. According to some a painting of that saint by Fra Bartolomeo had to be removed from a church because it

Guido Reni, *Saint Sebastian* (detail). Pinacoteca, Musei Capitolini, Rome. There is a tradition (unsupported by history) that Saint Sebastian had been the Emperor Heliogabalus's favorite before his conversion.

Leonardo da Vinci, *Bacchus*. Louvre, Paris. Originally a picture of Saint John the Baptist, this painting (which did not particularly inspire religious feeling, it was said) was converted into a landscape with Bacchus by changing the cross into a Bacchic staff.

was giving the monks ideas. Before becoming a martyr Saint Sebastian may have been a Roman soldier and perhaps even a friend of Heliogabalus's (but that has never been proved). At any rate his martyrdom has inspired painters from the Renaissance up to our own time—and more often than not it is impossible to tell from their works which is greater: his sexual ambiguity or his ecstatic masochism. In Sodoma's version he appears as an updated hermaphrodite with ringleted hair and sweetly langorous limbs. The fleshier Saint Sebastians make one think of sensual pleasures, of delicious pain, rather than of the rigors of torture. As for the arrow which pierces his side, the symbolism is obvious enough. More than one mind has been haunted through the ages by sado-masochistic fantasies inspired by the saint's legend. In *Confessions of a Mask* the Japanese novelist Yukio Mishima describes his trances of vicarious feeling on seeing Guido Reni's Saint Sebastian, and he confides that in order to identify more closely with the saint he had a picture of himself taken in the same pose. Which shows how the old myths persist in our technological age even to conquering new media.

Invented by the Greeks to justify the love between men and boys, the myth of Ganymede was reinterpreted in the Renaissance to symbolize the ascent of the soul, or the "divine fury" which took hold of a saint—or even divine charity (with Christ as the eagle and the saint as the shepherd boy). For Dante Ganymede was the *mens humana*, the Intellect transported by the Supreme Being to the heights of Contemplation. The adaptation of ancient themes to sacred Christian art allowed the Renaissance artists to express their sensual delight. Sebastiano Veneziano del Piombo, who enjoyed joking, wrote to Michelangelo about the ceiling of the Sistine chapel: "It seems to me that Ganymede would look good in that place—why you could give him a halo and he would be taken for Saint John of the Apocalypse being carried up to Heaven."

Savonarola, and later the Council of Trent (1545), violently condemned this Neoplatonic culture with its saints transvestised as ancient gods and its morals reminiscent of Athens in its heyday. Aretino, whose *Licentious Sonnets* and *Ragionamenti* did not prevent him from aspiring to the cardinalate, hypocritically proclaimed his indignation at the naked bodies in Michelangelo's "Last Judgement" and, one month before the opening of the Council of 1495, he wrote an open letter to the artist declaring: "As a baptized Christian I am ashamed at the licentiousness which you display in your illustration of such a lofty theme... you show angels and saints unrobed, utterly depriving the latter of earthly modesty and the former of heavenly splendor...." Aretino complains that Michelangelo had not followed his advice, and he scolds him for not sending a preliminary sketch of the "Last Judgement." He adds with perfidiousness, "you give your word only to the Gherardoes [Gherardo Perini] and the Tommais [Tommaso Cavalieri] of this world." His parting shot is: "Your kind of painting

belongs in a tavern or some obscene bathing establishment, not in the greatest chapel of all Christianity."

The religious fervor aroused by the Reformation and the Council of Trent poisoned the lives of the artists who had enjoyed the period of freedom and artistic renewal during the late 1400s and the early 1500s. As early as 1550 one of Michelangelo's disciples, Daniel Volterra, was commissioned to cover up the naked bodies in the "Last Judgement"—a job which earned him the nickname *braghettone* [cod-piece]. After Michelangelo died, El Greco even suggested white-washing the chapel and "redecorating it with something more suitable...."

The invasions of Charles VIII and Louis XII brought back ancient art works and Italian paintings to France. Thanks to the discovery of printing the humanists were able to spread the wisdom of the ancients throughout Europe. In Germany, England and France, where it was already flourishing, homosexuality grew more refined under the influence of Neoplatonism. But after the Council of Trent, intellectuals who did not submit to the laws and doctrines of the Church were suspected of heresy. It became common practice to accuse free-thinkers, Protestants and atheists of sodomy—it was the best way of getting rid of them. All the more so as it was easy to support the allegation with proof, or a semblance of proof. Thus Montaigne's former tutor Muretus (Marc Antoine Muret), a mediocre poet and the author of numerous translations and commentaries of Catullus, Tibullus, Terence, etc., was accused in 1552 of having "anti-physical," that is to say unnatural, inclinations. He was locked up in the prison of the Châtelet in Paris, then released thanks to the intervention of friends. In Toulouse, where he then went to teach law at the university, he was re-arrested and charged with committing sodomy with one of his students, a certain Luc Menge Fremiot, some of whose poems he had published. This time he was sentenced to being burned alive, but he managed to escape and he fled to Italy where, despite his homosexual reputation, he was welcomed by Ippolito d'Este and Pope Pius V. Eventually Muretus changed his ways and entered the Church—it was said that he used to have tears in his eyes when he celebrated Mass. About the same time Richard Renvoisy, the cannon of the King's Chapel at Dijon, who had set Anacreon's odes to music, was less fortunate: he was burned at the stake in 1586 for having made the other kind of music with his little singers.

In his own writings Montaigne poked fun at the affected—and affecting—Platonism of Ficino and Pico de la Mirandola. His friendship for Etienne de la Boetie, a magistrate, poet and humanist four years younger than himself (Montaigne was twenty-six), was nevertheless "Neoplatonic" in the amorous if not the erotic sense. True, Montaigne writes that love in the "Greek style" is abhorrent—but on the other hand, the great humanist was obviously not entirely satisfied with women, for "they have neither sufficient strength of character nor intellectual capacity." He thought that marriage is simply a deal contracted "for other purposes than love." La Boetie died at twenty-nine and, grief-stricken, Montaigne gave vent to the depth of his sorrow in the words of the Latin poets:

> Since he could no longer share my days
> I resolved to give up pleasure and its ways.
>
> (Terence)
>
> O Brother who art sweeter than life,
> Will I see you no more, whom I love for all time?
>
> (Catullus)
>
> Ah, Fate has stolen half my soul away!
> What am I doing here, I who am the other twain?

The muse who whispered into the ears of the French poets of the sixteenth century was rather ribald. The frolics of the young monks and courtiers delighted writers like Rabelais and poets like Ronsard. But others—like

Domenico Cresti, known as il Passignano, Painting. Private collection. Public baths were favorite meeting places for lovers in the sixteenth century: they were among the very few places were "Socratic" yearnings could be satisfied in relative safety.

Albrecht Dürer, *Men's Bath* (detail). Bibliothèque Nationale, Paris. Note the erotic allusions—the shape of the faucet for example.

Anonymous, *Three Page Boys* (detail). Engraving, nineteenth century (?). Private collection.

most famous crowned homosexuals in history. These "little falcons," as they were called, pushed their impudence so far as to poke fun at the king's Scottish accent, and finally in 1608 their fraternity was dissolved. Nevertheless the Socratic cult of masculine beauty never lacked adepts in England. Its most illustrious celebrants were Marlowe and William Shakespeare.

Agrippa d'Aubigné—reacted to them with furious indignation. The latter's long poem *Les Tragiques* and his "Island of the Hermaphrodites" are a far cry from the serene self-examinations of Montaigne. "The way to a king's heart is through a rascal's arse," sputtered Agrippa.

"Unconformity" was just as much of a nobleman's vice at the court of England as it was in France. Here for example are a few sentences from one of the numerous anonymous pamphlets of the Elizabethan period. The author complains that the children of Saint Paul of the Chapel Royal "deck themselves out in satin and silk, and parade about in these clothes. They would do as well to wear them when they celebrate their papist mummeries. Even in the Queen's chapel these depraved boys profane the Lord's service with lascivious contortions of their effeminate limbs, and with the dazzling richness of their dress, as they mime the obscene fables invented by idolatrous and heathen poets." In the playhouses of London the female parts were acted by graceful striplings, who were in great demand among the young lords of the court—foremost among whom was James I, one of the

POLITIAN (1454-1494)

Angelo Poliziano, called Politian, the greatest poet of his age, was a friend of Lorenzo de' Medici's and the tutor of his children. Owing to his penchant for boys, his reputation was about as battered as a reputation can get. His great nose made him ugly; he was malicious by nature, and nothing vexed him more than to hear someone else praised. His contemporaries considered him a genius unlike any since Ovid. Regularly each morning more than 500 youths from all over Europe would accompany him to the hall where he taught, and after his lecture they would take him back to his rooms. In his *Florentine Anecdotes* (1685-1687), Varillas tells the story of how Politian died at the age of forty-two: "The criminal passion which raged in him for one of his high-born pupils caused him—for it could never be satisfied—to break out into a high fever. Utterly distracted, he composed a song for the youth, got out of bed and, upon fetching his lute, began singing such a piteous and tender lament that on reaching the end of the first couplet he expired; which happened on the very same day that Charles VIII crossed the Alps on his way to conquer Naples." What Varillas does not say is that Politian was buried in the church of San Marco dressed, according to his instructions, in a Dominican monk's habit. *The Fable of Orpheus* (1480), from which the following lines are taken, was written to be staged. Monteverdi's *Orfeo* (1607) was inspired by it.

From THE FABLE OF ORPHEUS
(Orpheus, lamenting his fate:)

And since my fate hath been so cruel never more shall I wish for woman's love. Henceforth I shall gather flowers, maidens in their spring when all are fair and lithe. This is a love more gentle and more sweet.

Let the love of woman bind me no longer. Let there be no longer any to prate to me of women. For dead is she who held my heart. Who would converse with me let him not talk to me of woman's love.

How wretched the man who changes his purpose for a woman, or ever for her is happy or sad! Or who barters for her his liberty, or who puts faith in her pretences or her words. She is ever lighter than a leaf before the wind. A thousand times a day she will and will not. She follows him who flees. From him who wishes her she hides, and like the wave upon the shore she comes and goes. Of this is Jove assured who scorns the sweet amorous tie that binds him and in heaven enjoys his beautiful Ganymede; and on earth Phoebus enjoyed Hyacinth. To this holy love Hercules surrenders, he who won the world and was won by fair Hylas. The married man I urge to seek divorce, and all to flee the company of women.

(Indignant at this speech, the Bacchantes attack Orpheus and tear him limb from limb.)

Agnolo Bronzino, *Portrait of the Grand Duke Cosimo I de' Medici as Orpheus*. Philadelphia Museum of Art, Philadelphia.

MATTEO BANDELLO
(1485-1561)

Bandello was born in Lombardy. His uncle, who was the general of the Dominican order, had him ordained at a very early age. Bandello pursued his studies brilliantly at Genoa, Milan and the University of Pavia. A great humanist, he was respected by the most illustrious men of his age. He frequented the courts of Galeazzo Maria Sforza, whose reputation for buggery was well established, and of the Gonzagas in Mantua (where he was entrusted with the education of Lucrezia Gonzaga). Later he was engaged as a secretary by Cesare Fregoso, who belonged to a powerful Genovese family and was a friend of the king of France, François I. In 1540 Cesare was assassinated in Venice on orders from the Holy Roman Emperor, Charles V; Bandello accompanied Fregoso's widow to the castle of Bassens near Agen in southwestern France. Henri II made Bandello bishop of Agen, on condition that half of the revenues of the diocese be handed over to young Ettore Fregoso. Bandello devoted little attention to his office, preferring literature instead. He wrote speeches in Latin, made translations, composed poems, etc., but he was above all a storyteller. Each one of his tales, which can be compared to Boccaccio's, is dedicated to a leading person of the day and were written before he was named bishop. Bandello's fame was great in England and in Spain as well as in France: Shakespeare borrowed the story of *Romeo and Juliet* from him.

From THE TALE OF PORCELLIO

(Porcellio is a poet, whose young wife suspects him of secretly committing the sin against nature.)

Presently, Porcellio fell most grievously sick, so that the physicians had scant hope of the poor old man's life, he having lost sleep and appetite, more by token that he was nearer seventy than threescore and was grown very feeble. His wife, seeing this, strove with a thousand excellent arguments to bring him to confess, and he hearkened to her, but after said that he would not do it; wherefore, seeing she wearied herself in vain, she sent to Duke Francesco, humbly beseeching him for the love of God to send some person of authority, who should persuade Porcellio, grievously sick as he was, to have some care of his soul, so he might not die like a dog, without the sacraments of the Church. The duke, hearing the pious petition of this good woman and affectionate wife, sent to the Convent delle Grazie of the Friars of St. Dominick, which was then newly built, and letting call Fra Giacomo da Sesti, an old man of very holy life, informed him of that which he would have him do. The holy man, hearing the duke's will, betook himself straightway to Porcellio's house, where telling the lady how he came by the prince's commandment to visit and confess her husband, he was received by her with the utmost reverence. Then, after she had caused him sit, she proceeded fully to acquaint him with the depravity of her husband's life, beseeching him with tears in her eyes to do his utmost endeavour to bring him to amendment. The friar shrugged his shoulders and had little mind to the task, but replied that, not to fail of his duty, he would do everything that was possible to him.

Accordingly, anxious to save a soul, which, according to his wife, was in the hands of the devil, he entered Porcellio's chamber and said, "The peace of God be upon this house and upon all those who dwell therein!" So saying, he went up to the bed and softly saluted the sick man, who feigned himself well-pleased to see him. Then, entering into various converse with him, he gave him to understand how the duke's most excellent lordship had sent him and wherefore and bespoke him with many good words, discreetly exhorting him to confess, for that he was ready to hear him at whatsoever time might be convenient to him. Porcellio, after he had thanked the duke of his courtesy and the friar for his pains, replied that he would confess then and there; whereupon, all having departed the chamber, the holy friar began with the utmost diligence to do his office and coming to the sins of the flesh, asked him shamefastly if he had ever sinned against nature. At this question, Porcellio, collecting himself, considered the friar with amazement; then, as he were scandalized, "Sir," said he, "this is a strange question to ask me. Of what speak you? Never in my life have I sinned against nature."

The priest, ashamed to have put such a question to him, passed to other things, using every pains in his power so the sick man should confess himself thoroughly; then, seeing that Porcellio had no otherwhat to say, he assigned him such penance as he thought fit and gave him absolution, concluding that the goodwife must be grossly mistaken. When he had shriven him and bestowed on him a pious exhortation, he said to him, being about to take his leave, "Messer Porcellio, I will come to-morrow to visit you and if you remember otherwhat, I will hear you; and after order shall be taken that your parish-priest shall come and give you the holy sacrament of the Eucharist, to the end that, having taken the salutary viaticum, you may abide in readiness to do whatsoever shall please our Redeemer, the Lord Jesus Christ, in whose hand abideth our life and our death," "I prithee do it," replied Porcellio, "for I will do whatsoever you shall command me;" whereupon the good father blessed him with the sign of the holy cross and departed the chamber.

The wife came to meet him and asked him if her husband was resolved to sin no more against nature; to which the holy friar courteously replied, "Madam, you may conceive that, when we hear the confession of any one, whosoever he may be and whether he be whole or sick, we do our whole duty, and it pertaineth not unto any to seek to know that which the penitent saith, nor doth it beseem us, who are of our superiors deputed to hear confessions, anywise to discover aught which may

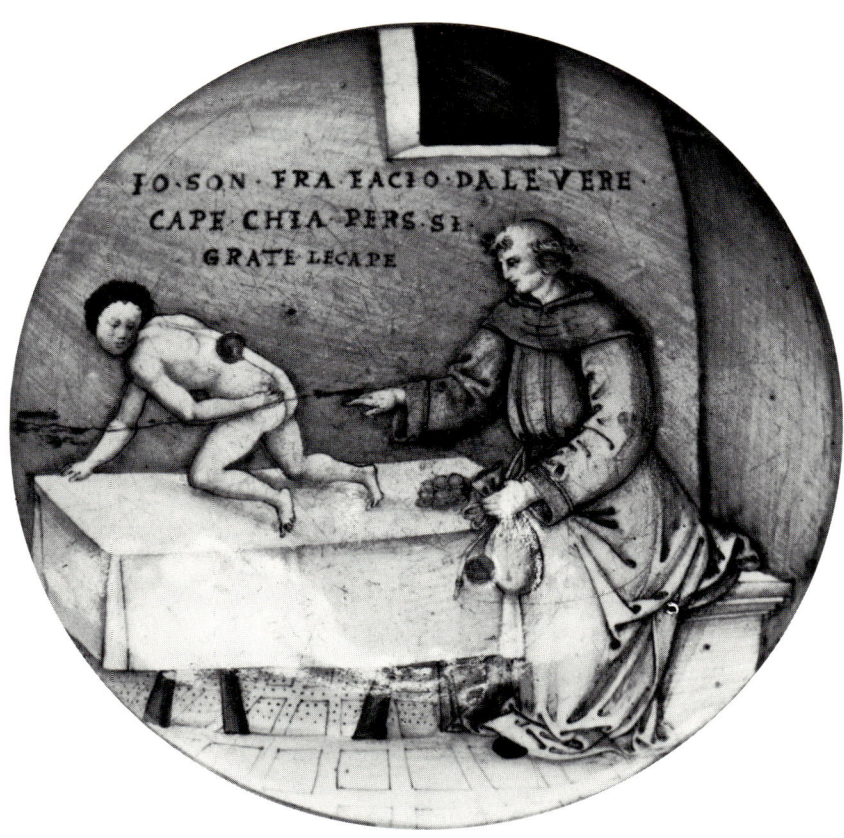

Earthenware dish. Italian, sixteenth century.
Musée de Cluny, Paris.

be told us; nay, an we should reveal a confession, we should deserve to be put to death. But so much I will and may presently say to you, that you are grossly mistaken in the strange opinion you have of your husband. He (praised be God) hath nowise that filthy vice whereof you bespoke me, nay, he is very far therefrom." Whereupon the good woman, who well knew how the case stood, said, weeping piteously, "Dear my father, I am nowise mistaken nor do I deceive myself; nay, my wretched husband it is who deceiveth himself and is ashamed to tell this frightful sin. Believe me, who know it, he is more wrapped up therein than is a chick in tow. For mercy's sake, father, come speak with him again and have no heed to that which he saith, for I assure you he hath told you a lie." "It is well, madam," answered the good friar; "I shall return hither to-morrow to cause him take the sacrament and if it be as you say, I will do that which behoveth unto me." So saying, he took leave of the lady and returned to his convent.

(The friar returned several times, but Porcellio still refused to confess.)

The good father, seeing him near unto death, could not imagine that he said otherwhat than the truth, and the priest being come, poor Porcellio received the holy sacrament and to all appearance, showed great contrition; whereat his wife was exceeding rejoiced, thinking to have saved her husband's soul. Accordingly, the friar presently taking leave, the lady accompanied him to the door, thanking him heartily for the pious office he had done her husband and beseeching him to pray God that Porcellio might abide in that his mind and return no more to his vomit. The friar mildly rebuked her, saying, "Madam, you are over-obstinate and sin in deeming ill of your husband touching that whereof he is not guilty and in impeaching him, as you do, of so shameful a vice. This is not well, nor should one do thus." The lady, hearing this, stayed the friar, who would fain have departed the house, and bespoke him thus, saying, "Father, I would not have you depart displeased with me, who have done nought to merit your displeasure, and still less would I have my husband die like a brute-beast; nay, if he have, as he hath until this present, lived worse than animals without reason, I would e'en, an it be possible, have him die as all good Christians should. That which I told you of him you must not think, indeed, that I said for jealousy or of some slight suspicion that betided me of him, for I were loath to commit myself so lightly; but I have seen all with these two eyes; nor (woe is me!) am I alone in this; nay, all in the house will render you witness thereof. As if I had not an hundred times made a great outcry thereanent! And I assure you he would not have ventured to deny it in my presence. Wherefore, father mine, take no heed to any denial he may make thereof, but, for God's sake, return to his chamber and endeavour to pluck him out of the Devil's clutches."

The holy man abode aghast at this and returning to Porcellio, said to him, "Alack, son, I know not what to think of thee; thou deniest to me to have committed the sin against nature, wherewith thou art more burthened than as thou haddest Milan Cathedral on thy shoulders, and yet I am assured that thou art a thousand times fainer unto boys than are goats to salt." Whereupon Porcellio shook his head and said as loudliest he might, "Ho, ho, reverend father, you knew not how to question me. To divert myself with boys is more natural to me than eating and drinking to man, and you asked me if I sinned against nature! Go to, sir, you know not what a tidbit is." The holy friar, stricken all aghast with this diabolical speech, shrugged his shoulders and looking upon Porcellio awhile with horror and amazement, as he were some frightful monster, said, sighing, "Woe's me, Lord God, I have let cast Christ into a fiery furnace." Therewith he departed and meeting the lady, as he went, said to her, "Madam, I have done what I might."

Meanwhile Porcellio called lustily for his wife, who ran hastily to her husband's chamber; whereupon quoth that ribald and wicked man to her, "Wife, let fetch me a bucket of water and tarry not." She asked what he would with it and he, "I would fain quench the fire about Christ, for yonder jackass of a friar telleth me I have cast him into a furnace," and told her all that passed; whereat she was grieved well nigh unto death. Porcellio presently began to amend and recovered of his sickness; whereupon, the thing being bruited abroad at court and about Milan, he was pointed at of all with the finger of scorn and was constrained to keep his house, and we may suppose that, like as he had lived as a beast, even so he died the death of a brute....

GEROLAMO MORLINO
(or MORLINI)
(first half of the sixteenth century)

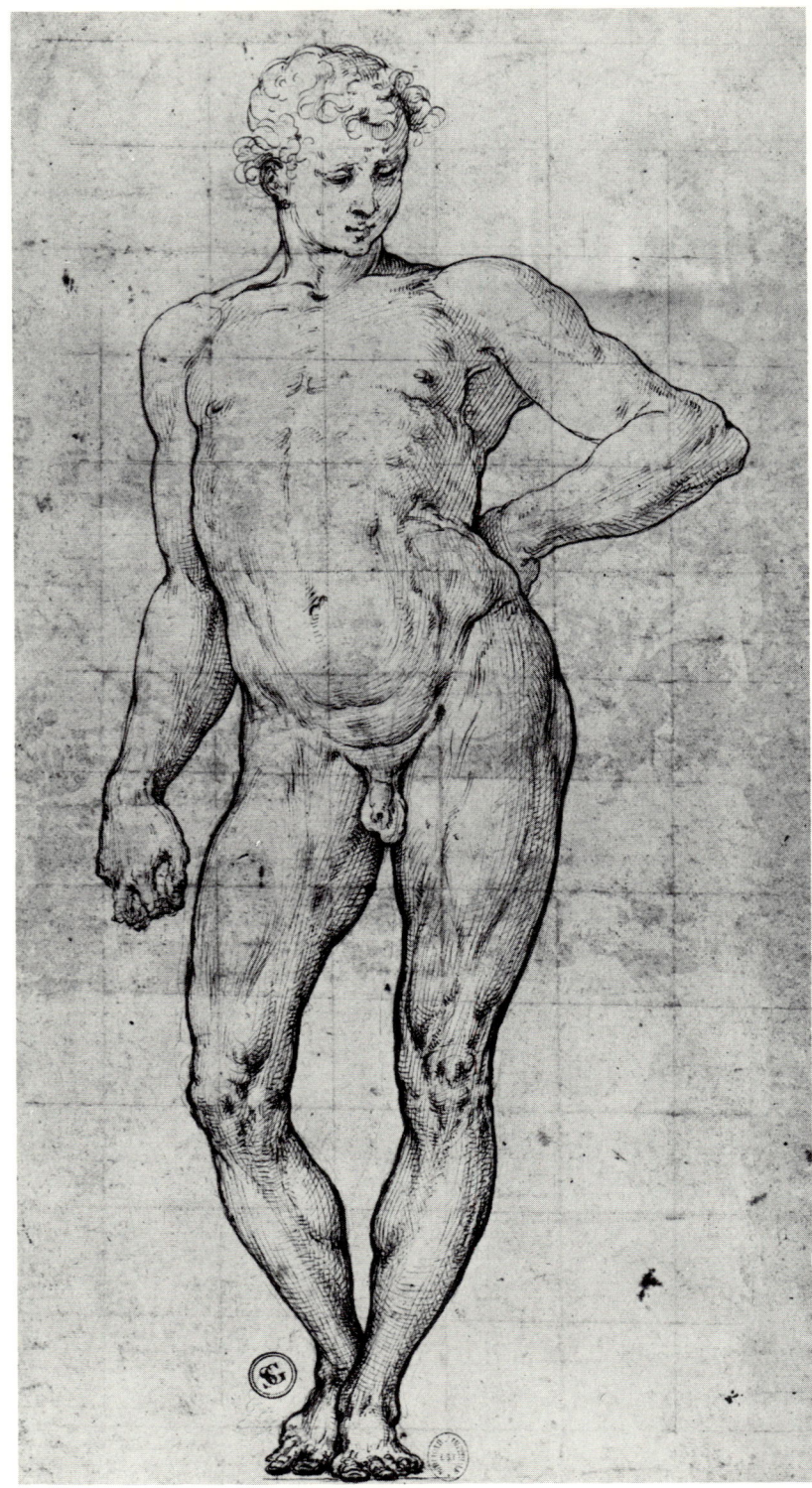

Morlino was a Neapolitan jurist. He is the author of tales, fables and ribald comedies which were burned for obscenity. The first volume of his tales was printed in 1520—and soon copies were very hard to obtain. La Fontaine borrowed from Morlino, notably in his "Tale of the Washtub."

From THE TALE OF THE YOUTH WHO WAS CAUGHT IN THE ACT OF ADULTERY AND WAS SODOMIZED AND FLOGGED BY THE HUSBAND

Now it happened that towards the eleventh hour of the night the husband returned from his business much sooner than expected. He knocked on the door of his house, shouted and even whistled loudly to announce his arrival. But no one answered. Fearing that some terrible calamity had befallen his family, he rushed at the door and burst it from its hinges with such force that neither Forculus, nor Limentius nor the goddess Cardina herself could have stopped him from crossing the threshold. He hastened to the bedroom, and there he saw his wife lying in tight embrace with a young man. This affront to his conjugal couch seems to have left him almost indifferent at first, whereas the two culprits woke up with a start and were overcome with shame and amazement. Taking in the youth's beauty and his acute dismay, the husband then began speaking. "Fear not, fair lad," he said. "Far be it from me to be so cruel as to be your executioner, and still less to deliver so pretty a boy over to the rigor of the

Pietro Bonaccorsi, known as Pierino del Vaga, *Study of a Nude*. Bibliothèque Nationale, Paris.

Albrecht Dürer, *Self-Portrait*. Cabinet des Estampes, Bibliothèque Nationale, Paris.

law. Only—so that what you have done unto my wife may in turn be done unto you—I propose to use your charms for the pleasures of my bed. You will be my catamite, and you will have to submit to all my desires. I will share you with my wife, as all of our possessions are shared between us, and in this way I will settle our difference. Verily, one and the same bed will serve for all three of us, for it seems to me that I have always lived in such perfect harmony with my wife that what pleased the one invariably had the same effect on the other."

Having made this little speech, he took off his clothes and slipped into bed. He grasped the youth in his arms, and, pressing a vigorous attack that revealed rather the will to punish than the desire to get pleasure, he subjected him to an operation very like the one the bold lad had so generously performed on the lady of the house, but using a different avenue. The boy desperately struggled to avoid the rough embrace of he whom he had thought to beguile, but in vain: he was obliged to suffer its humiliating supremacy to the very end. Meanwhile the husband found cruel delight in this pleasure which the inhabitants of Sodom had once honored, and which, in this case, was doubled by the satisfaction of revenge.

The night was spent in couplings of this kind. At the first glimmer of dawn, the husband called out to two husky servants. Ordering them to hold the young man down, he flogged his charming buttocks with a birch-rod until the boy could stand it no longer. "This is to punish you," the husband then said, "you who have hardly left childhood and have the brashness to compete with profligates who glorify in committing the crime of adultery."

At this the presumptuous young Romeo was allowed to go. Though mortified by his experience, he nevertheless felt fortunate to have had to pay with his body instead of with his head, and, as the reader may well imagine, he never spoke a word about his adventure. As for the guilty wife, the husband simply put a lock where she had been too generous.

"Now I know that I will be the only one to enter here," he exclaimed.

This tale confirms the old adage that He who lives by the sword dies by the sword. Moreover, it shows that you mustn't trust ladies with hospitable laps.

PIETRO BASSI, called ARETINO
(1492-1556)

Pietro Bassi was born in the town of Arezzo in Tuscany (whence the name Aretino). He settled successively in Perugia, in Siena and in Rome; but he was obliged to leave the Holy City for having written indecent sonnets on a set of obscene drawings by Giulio Romano. He was violently attacked on this score by Giberti, the leader of the pro-French party. To make matters worse Aretino spoke out in defense of the authors of the *pasquinate,* satiric poems which were posted beneath the mutilated statue of the Pasquino near the Piazza Navona. After narrowly escaping being killed by assassins probably hired by Giberti, Aretino moved to Venice.

He considered himself a moralist, and in his writings he delighted in laying bare the more shameful imperfections of society. Nicknamed the Divine Aretino by his admirers—intellectuals, artists and rulers who were tickled by his verses—he was called the "scourge of princes" by his detractors, because of his evil tongue and his unscrupulous cynicism. Some even went as far as to accuse him of being a vile blackmailer.

In Venice he lived with his sisters—ladies who led a rather dissolute life. It is said that he was taken by such a hysterical fit of giggling at an off-color story he was told one day that he fell over backwards and died on the spot. The short story from which this excerpt is taken is attributed to Aretino.

From THE WANDERING WHORE
(A Dialogue between Madeleine and Julia)

MADELEINE: (telling the story of her adventures with a young man from Genoa) ... One day I asked him who his familiars were, and whether they had not noticed his frequent visits to me. He replied that he had no acquaintances, other than a canon from St. Peter's to whom his parents had recommended him. He added that this cleric was a witty, handsome and pleasant-mannered youth who was greatly attached to him. Whereupon I told him, "If it will give pleasure to your friend, you may bring him to my house. I will receive him, because I love you, but you must be discrete." At this he threw his arms around me, full of gratitude, and assured me that he wished it with all his heart, for he lived on such close terms with the canon that neither withheld anything from the other. So it happened that one evening they arrived together. I liked the cleric's looks—there was a fresh and youthful air about him—though he could not compare to my young Genovese. The three of us settled down to a delightful conversation. After a while the two men ordered dinner, and after the meal we continued talking. Gradually the canon began warming up to me. Sitting on either side of me, he and the Genovese gave me a thousand caresses, which enchanted me. It was getting late, and now, having thoroughly fondled me, they carried me over to my bed and undressed me. At the whiteness of my skin, the firmness of my body and nipples, they exclaimed in admiration. Feverishly they took off their clothes, and soon I was lying between their two naked bodies, holding a swelling cock in each hand. They were both in high spirits, and I wondered who would take the first turn with me. It was my little Genovese: he climbed up on me and thrust in as he knew so well how to do. But no sooner was he in me than the cleric clambered up on top of him and entered him from behind. Now both were lying on me, pumping with a single motion, but I hardly felt the extra weight—indeed it seemed that my pleasure was doubled. They both spent in the same moment, whereupon I burst out laughing at the sport we had just had, and especially at the canon who, I saw, was ready to renew his attack. This time I was sure that he was going to mount me, but his friend seized the opportunity instead and thrust in once more. Hugging us both tightly, the canon turned us on our sides and, kindly sparing me his weight, he once again reamed my young lover. This happened a third time, with the difference that the canon turned us around so that I was in the middle. Then, spreading my buttocks, he plugged me to the hilt. Imagine, what could I do? I have never received such a shaking in all my life, rammed as I was in two places at once. After this, the canon buggered me again, while his friend turned around and buggered him. In the morning, after we had gotten up, and as I was sitting in my chair, the young man presented me with his cock, putting it in my hand so that I would guide it into my cunt. He was entering me when the canon came up behind him, bared his ass, and entered him. And now, my dear, you have my story. I do not know if yours contains such pleasant adventures; but I beg you in any case not to hold anything back from me.

Engraving after one of the erotic drawings of Giulio Romano. Bibliothèque Nationale, Paris.

Pisanello, *Madonna and Saint George* (detail). The National Gallery, London. Saint George is dressed in the extravagant fashion of the Quattrocento.

MICHELANGELO BUONARROTTI (1475-1564)

We learn from Michelangelo's correspondance with Tommaso de' Cavalieri that the artist presented this young man, whom he loved and admired, with a number of drawings, including a Ganymede and a Tityus. Ganymede being carried off by the eagle may symbolize the ecstasy of Platonic love; Tityus, whose liver is being devoured by a vulture, may represent the throes of physical passion. Passages from Michelangelo's letters accompanying these drawings are given here, as are two sonnets (translated by John Aldington Symonds) the sculptor dedicated to his friend. These poems were published in 1632 by Michelangelo's great-great-nephew who tried to make the readers believe that they had been addressed to a woman and not to Tommaso.

Michelangelo, *Adam* (detail). Sistine Chapel, Vatican, Rome.

Michelangelo, *The Rape of Ganymede*. Drawing given by the artist to Tommaso de' Cavalieri in 1532. Windsor Castle, Windsor, England. Here the rape symbolizes the action of Platonic love, which frees the souls from its physical bonds and conducts it towards felicity.

TO MESSER TOMMASO DE' CAVALIERI IN ROME

Most inadvisedly I was prompted to write to your lordship, and had the presumption to be the first to move, as though I had a debt to pay in replying to a letter of yours. Afterwards I recognized my error the more, so much did I enjoy reading your reply, for which I thank you.

Far from being a mere babe, as you say of yourself in your letter, you seem to me to have lived on earth a thousand times before. But I should deem myself unborn, or rather stillborn, and should confess myself disgraced before heaven and earth, if from your letter I had not seen and believed that your lordship would willingly accept some of my drawings. This has caused me much surprise and pleasure no less. And if you really esteem my works in your heart as you profess to do in your letter, I shall count that work much more fortunate than excellent, should I happen, as I desire, to execute one that might please you.

I'll say no more. Many things that might be said in reply remain unwritten, lest you be wearied and because I know that Pierantonio, the bearer of this, can and will supply what I lack. On the, for me, happy first day of January.

(Unsigned, from Rome, January 1st, 1533)

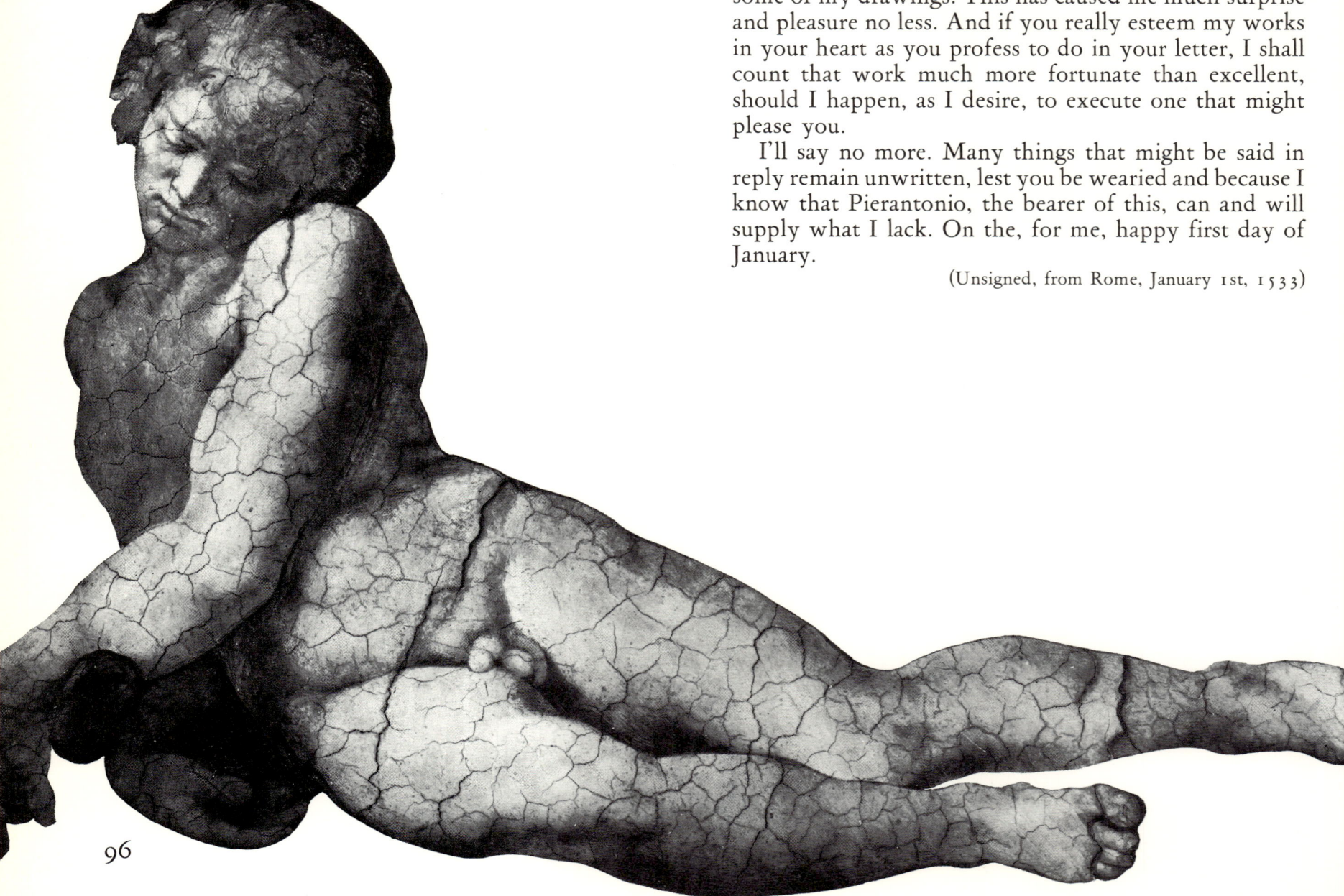

My dear lord—Had I not believed that I had convinced you of the immense, nay, boundless love I bear you, the grave apprehension shown by your letter that I might have forgotten you, as I haven't written to you would seem to me neither strange nor surprising. But there is nothing unusual in this, nor in being alarmed, when so many other things go wrong, lest this too should come to grief; since what your lordship says to me, I would have said to you. But perhaps you did this in order to try me, or in order to kindle anew a greater flame, if a greater were possible. But be that as it may, I realize now that I could [as soon] forget your name as forget the food on which I live—nay, I could sooner forget the food on which I live, which unhappily nourishes only the body, than your name, which nourishes body and soul, filling both with such delight that I am insensible to sorrow or fear of death, while my memory of you endures. Imagine, if the eye were also playing its part, the state in which I should find myself....

(Unsigned, from Florence, July 28th, 1533)

[But Michelangelo had second thoughts about this letter and did not send it. Instead he wrote:]

Though I have not yet replied to your letter, my dear lord, I do not believe that you might even contemplate accusing me of having forgotten, or having been able to forget, the food on which I live, which is none other than your name. That is why, although it is very presumptuous of me to say it, since I am vastly inferior to you, I am convinced that nothing can destroy our friendship.

(From Florence, July 28th, 1533)

SONNETS ADDRESSED TO CAVALIERI

I cannot by the utmost flight of thought
    Conceive another form of air or clay,
    Wherewith against thy beauty to array
    My wounded heart in armour fancy-wrought:
For, lacking thee, so low my state is brought,
    That love hath stolen all my strength away;
    Whence, when I fain would halve my griefs, they weigh
    With double sorrow, and I sink to nought.
Thus all in vain my soul to scape thee flies,
    For even faster flies her beauteous foe:
    From the swift-footed feebly run the slow!
Yet with his hands Love wipes my weeping eyes,
    Saying, this toil will end in happy cheer;
    What costs the heart so much, must needs be dear!
        (XXVII. "No Escape from Love," *Non posso altra figura*)

From thy fair face I learn, O my loved lord,
    That which no mortal tongue can rightly say;
    The soul imprisoned in her house of clay,
    Holpen by thee, to God hath often soared.
And though the vulgar, vain, malignant horde
    Attribute what their grosser wills obey,
    Yet shall this fervent homage that I pay,
    This love, this faith, pure joys for us afford.
Lo, all the lovely things we find on earth,
    Resemble the soul that rightly sees
    That source of bliss divine which gave us birth:
Nor have we first-fruits or remembrances
    Of heaven elsewhere. Thus, loving loyally,
    I rise to God, and make death sweet by thee.
        (LIV. "Love Lifts to God," *Veggio nel tuo bel viso*)

Companion piece to the *Ganymede* (detail) on the preceding page. Windsor Castle, Windsor, England. It too was presented to Tommaso de' Cavalieri by Michelangelo. It symbolizes the sufferings of those who abandon themselves to physical love.

RICHARD BARNFIELD
(1574–1627)

In 1574, when Barnfield was twenty, and had just graduated from Oxford, he published *The Affectionate Shepherd (or The Complaint of Daphnis for the Love of Ganymede)*. A year later he brought out *Cynthia, with Certain Sonnets* (*Cynthia* is a panegyric on Queen Elizabeth I, in the manner of Spenser's *Faerie Queen*). Ten years younger than Shakespeare, and obviously influenced by him, Barnfield mixed in the literary circles of Elizabethan London and acquired no small reputation as a poet during his lifetime. But because of his overtly homosexual themes, Barnfield has been scandalously neglected since the sixteenth century. Only two comprehensive collections of his verse have appeared since he died: the 1876 *Complete Poems*, published by the Roxburghe Club and limited to forty copies and a scholarly facsimile edition of the first printings of his major works which appeared in London in 1936.

In 1606 Barnfield retired to live the life of a country gentleman on his estate in Staffordshire. He died at the age of fifty-two on March 1, 1627.

Anonymous, *Portrait of Henri III's Minion, Saint-Mégrin*. Miniature, sixteenth century. Louvre, Paris. It was said that when he died, Saint-Mégrin gave "his soul to God, his body to the ground and his arse to the Devil."

Luca Signorelli, *The Last Judgement* (detail). The Cathedral, Orvieto, Italy. Signorelli, an ardent partisan of the Medici, enjoyed depicting muscular male figures draped in clinging clothes, which emphasize their lascivious, provocative or aggressive postures.

From THE AFFECTIONATE SHEPHERD

Scarce had the morning star hid from the light,
Heaven's crimson canopy with stars bespangled,
But I began to rue th'unhappy sight
Of that fair Boy that had my heart entangled;
    Cursing the time, the place, the sense, the sin;
    I came, I saw, I viewed, I slipped in.

If it be sin to love a sweet-faced boy,
(Whose amber locks trussed up in golden trammels
Dangle adown his lovely cheeks with joy,
When pearl and flowers his fair hair enamels)
    If it be sin to love a lovely lad;
    Oh then sin I, for whom my soul is sad....

Oh, would to God he would but pity me,
That love him more than any mortal wight;
Then he and I with love would soon agree,
That now cannot abide his suitor's sight.
    O would to God (so I might have my fee)
    My lips were honey, and thy mouth a bee.

Then should'st thou suck my sweet and my fair flower
That now is ripe, and full of honey-berries:
Then would I lead thee to my pleasant bower
Filled full of grapes, of mulberries, and cherries;
    Then should'st thou be my wasp, or else my bee,
    I would be thy hive, and thou my honey bee.

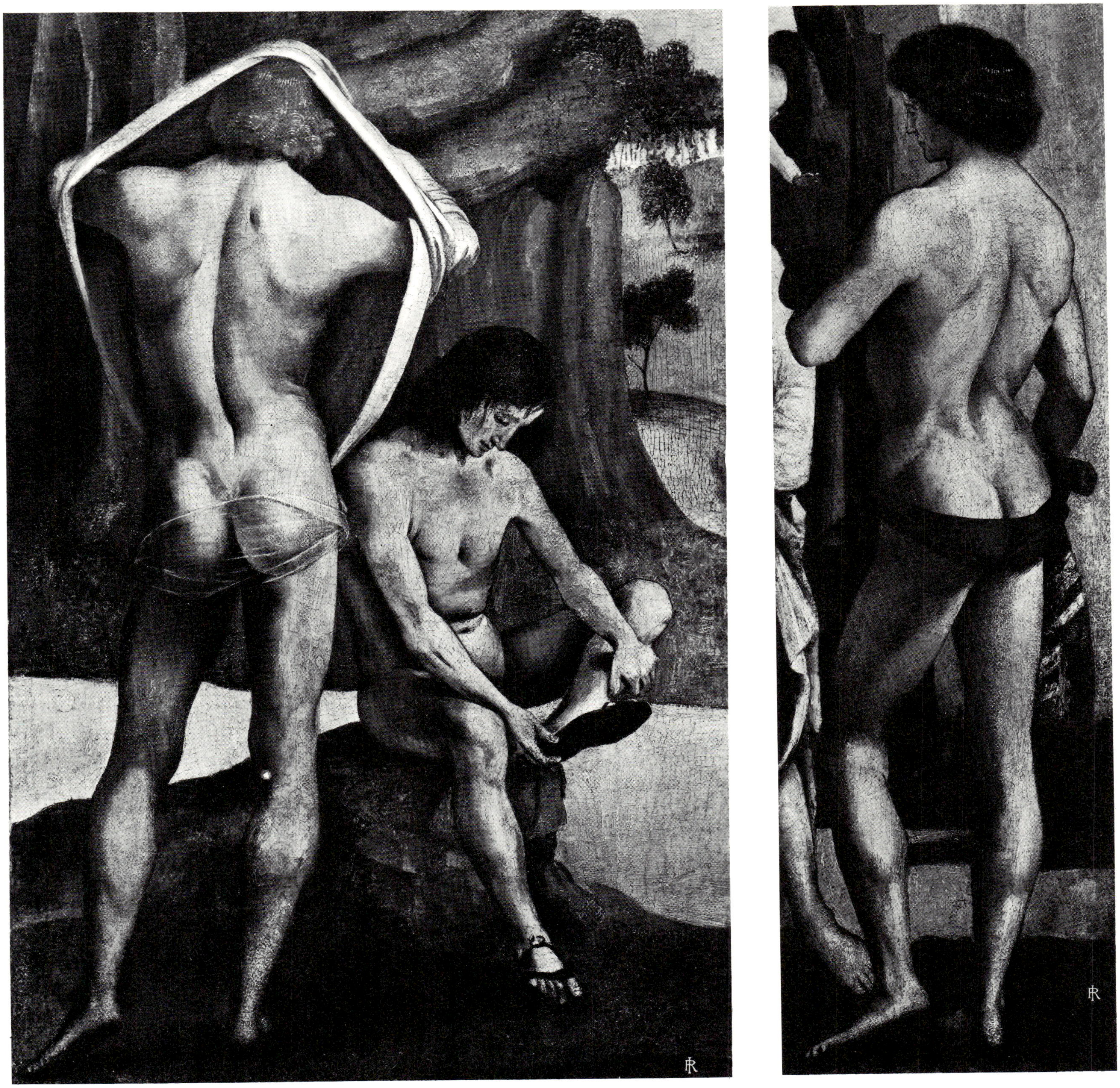

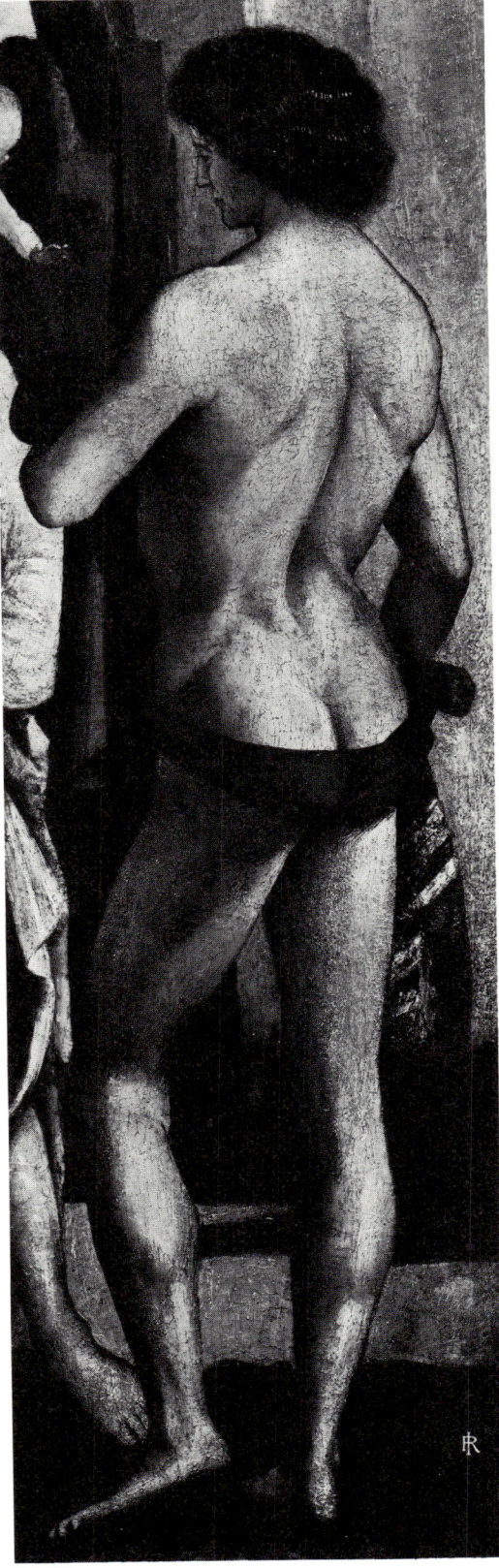

Luca Signorelli, Panels from the *Bichi Altarpiece* (details). Toledo Museum of Art, Toledo, Ohio.

I would put amber bracelets on thy wrists,
Crownets of pearl about thy naked arms:
And when thou sit'st at swilling Bacchus' feasts
My lips with charms should save thee from all harms:
    And when in sleep thou took'st thy chiefest pleasure,
    Mine eyes should gaze upon thine eye-lids' treasure.

And every morn, by dawning of the day,
When Phoebus riseth with a blushing face,
Silvanus' chapel-clerks shall chant a lay,
And play thee hunts-up in thy resting place:
    My cot thy chamber, my bosom thy bed,
    Shall be appointed for thy sleepy head.

Sixteenth-century French courtier dressed as an inhabitant of the Island of Hermaphrodites, ruled by King Woman and Queen Man. Cabinet des Estampes, Bibliothèque Nationale, Paris.

And when it pleaseth thee to walk abroad,
(Abroad into the fields to take fresh air),
The meads with Flora's treasure should be strowd,
(The mantled meadows, and the fields so fair);
    And by a silver well (with golden sands)
    I'll sit me down, and wash thine ivory hands.

And in the sweltering heat of summer time,
I would make cabinets for thee, my love;
Sweet-smelling arbors made of eglantine
Should be thy shrine, and I would be thy dove.
    Cool cabinets of fresh green laurel boughs
    Should shadow us, ore-set with thick-set yews.

Or if thou list to bathe thy naked limbs
Within the crystal of a pearl-bright brook
Paved with dainty pebbles to the brims;
Or clear, wherein thyself thy self may'st look;
    We'll go to Ladon, whose still trickling noise
    Will lull thee fast asleep amid thy joys....

But if thou wilt not pity my complaint,
My tears, nor vows, nor oaths, made to thy beauty:
What shall I do? But languish, die, or faint,
Since thou dost scorn my tears, and my soul's duty:
    And tears condemned, vows and oaths must fail,
    For where tears cannot, nothing can prevail....

CHRISTOPHER MARLOWE
(1564-1593)

"From Heaven he got his mind, from Hell his vice"—such is the reputation of Christopher Marlowe whom Swinburne considered the most audacious and inspired of the English poets. Very little is known about his life, except that he matriculated at Cambridge, and that he got his degrees there. There are some grounds for thinking that, despite his youth, he may have served as an informer in the Queen's secret police. He left Cambridge and turned his back on an ecclesiastical career to become an actor and playwright. His brilliant, adventure-filled life was cut short in a tavern brawl. After his death, his fellow lodger, Thomas Kyd, was arrested and charged with being an atheist. To clear himself, Kyd declared that all the compromising papers which had been found in his rooms had belonged to Marlowe, and that the latter had proclaimed things like "Whoso liketh not tobacco and boys is a fool," and "Saint John the Baptist was Christ's bedfellow, and used to rest his head on Christ's breast, and Christ used him as the sinners of Sodom do."

In fact, no one has ever proved that Marlowe was a homosexual, although some of his verse strongly suggests that he was at least bisexual. The tragedy *Edward the Second* centers on the overtly homosexual relationship between the king and his favorite Gaveston. In "Hero and Leander" Neptune twines voluptuously around young Leander who is swimming across the Hellespont to rejoin his beloved Hero, and in *Dido, Queen of Carthage* Jupiter fondles Ganymede who is sitting on his knees. The French author Julien Green noted in his *Journal* (1950), "Have just re-read 'Hero and Leander' with delight. The sensuality of the Elizabethans is the only one that ever seemed authentic to me. In comparison the erotic writers of today are cold and flat."

Apollo and Hyacinth, after Guilio Romano. From an illustration for *The Loves of the Gods.* Bibliothèque Nationale, Paris. Romano's work was destroyed, and the painter was obliged to leave Rome.

From THE TRAGEDY OF DIDO, QUEEN OF CARTHAGE

(HERE the curtains draw: there is discovered JUPITER dandling GANYMEDE upon his knee, and HERMES lying asleep.)

JUP. Come, gentle Ganymede, and play with me;
    I love thee well, say Juno what she will.
GAN. I am much better for your worthless love,
    That will not shield me from her shrewish blows!
    To day, whenas I fill'd into your cups,
    And held the cloth of pleasance whiles you drank,
    She reach'd me such a rap for that I spill'd,
    As made the blood run down about mine ears,

JUP What, dares she strike the darling of my thoughts?
  By Saturn's soul, and this earth-threatening hair,
  That, shaken thrice, makes nature's buildings quake,
  I vow, if she but once frown on thee more,
  To hang her, meteor like, 'twixt heaven and earth,
  And bind her, hand and foot, with golden cords,
  As once I did for harming Hercules!
GAN. Might I but see that pretty sport a-foot,
  O, how would I with Helen's brother laugh,
  And bring the gods to wonder at the game!
  Sweet Jupiter, if e'er I pleas'd thine eye,
  Or seemed fair, wall'd-in with eagle's wings,
  Grace my immortal beauty with this boon,
  And I will spend my time in thy bright arms.
JUP. What is't, sweet wag, I should deny thy youth?
  Whose face reflects such pleasure to mine eyes,
  As I, exhal'd with thy fire-darting beams,
  Have oft driven back the horses of the Night,
  Whenas they would have hal'd thee from my sight.
  Sit on my knee, and call for thy content,
  Control proud Fate, and cut the thread of Time:
  Why, are not all the gods at thy command,
  And heaven and earth the bounds of thy delight?
  Vulcan shall dance to make thee laughing sport,
  And my nine daughters sing when thou art sad;
  From Juno's bird I'll pluck her spotted pride,
  To make thee fans wherewith to cool thy face;
  And Venus' swans shall shed their silver down,
  To sweeten out the slumbers of thy bed;
  Hermes no more shall show the world his wings,
  If that thy fancy in his feathers dwell,
  But, as this one, I'll tear them all from him.
      [*Plucks a feather from Hermes' wings.*]
  Do thou but say, "their colour pleaseth me."
  Hold here, my little love; these linked gems
            [*Gives jewels.*]
  My Juno ware upon her marriage-day,
  Put thou about thy neck, my own sweet heart,
  And trick thy arms and shoulders with my theft.
GAN. I would have a jewel for mine ear,
  And a fine brooch to put in my hat,
  And then I'll hug with you an hundred times.
JUP. And shalt have, Ganymede, if thou wilt be my love.
              (act I)

Charles Paul Landon, *Daedalus and Icarus*.
Musée de Peinture, Alençon.

Aubrey Beardsley, *Man and Satyr*. Illustration
for *Le Morte d'Arthur* (1893). Published by
M. Dent, London.

Aubrey Beardsley, *The Hermaphrodite*. Illustration for *Le Morte d'Arthur* (1893).
Published by M. Dent, London.

FROM THE TROUBLESOME REIGN AND LAMENTABLE DEATH OF EDWARD THE SECOND

I must have wanton poets, pleasant wits,
Musicians that with touching of a string
May draw the pliant King which way I please.
Music and poetry is his delight.
Therefore I'll have Italian masks by night,
Sweet speeches, comedies, and pleasing shows;
And in the day when he shall walk abroad,
Like sylvan nymphs my pages shall be clad:
My men, like satyrs grazing on the lawns,
Shall with their goat feet dance an antic hay:
Sometime a lovely boy in Dian's shape,
With hair that gilds the water as it glides,
Crownets of pearl about his naked arms—
And in his sportful hands an olive-tree
To hide those parts which men delight to see—
Shall bathe him in a spring: and there hard by,
One like Actaeon peeping through the grove,
Shall by the angry goddess be transform'd:
And running in the likeness of an hart
By yelping hounds pull'd down, and seem to die.
Such things as these best please His Majesty....
(act I, scene 1)

Michelangelo Merisi da Caravaggio, *Victorious Love*. Staatliche Museen Preussischer Kulturbesitz, Berlin.

A.-E. Girodet de Roucy Trioson, Drawing. Bibliothèque Nationale, Paris.

From HERO AND LEANDER

"O Hero, Hero!" thus he cried full oft;
And then he got him to a rock aloft,
Where having spied her tower, long star'd he on't,
And pray'd the narrow toiling Hellespont
To part in twain, that he might come and go;
But still the rising billows answer'd, "No."

With that, he stripp'd him to the ivory skin,
And, crying, "Love, I come," leap'd lively in:
Whereat the sapphire-visag'd god grew proud,
And made his capering Triton sound aloud,
Imagining that Ganymede, displeas'd,
Had left the heavens; therefore on him he seiz'd.

Leander striv'd; the waves about him wound,
And pull'd him to the bottom, where the ground
Was strew'd with pearl, and in low coral groves
Sweet-singing mermaids sported with their loves
On heaps of heavy gold, and took great pleasure
To spurn in careless sort the shipwreck treasure;
For here the stately azure palace stood,
Where kingly Neptune and his train abode.
The lusty god embrac'd him, call'd him "love,"
And swore he never should return to Jove:
But when he knew it was not Ganymed,
For under water he was almost dead,
He heav'd him up, and, looking on his face,
Beat down the bold waves with his triple mace,
Which mounted up, intending to have kiss'd him,
And fell in drops like tears because they miss'd him.
Leander, being up, began to swim,
And, looking back, saw Neptune follow him:
Whereat aghast, the poor soul gan to cry,
"O, let me visit Hero ere I die!"
The god put Helle's bracelet on his arm,
And swore the sea should never do him harm.
He clapp'd his plump cheeks, with his tresses play'd,
And, smiling wantonly, his love bewray'd;
He watch'd his arms, and, as they open'd wide
At every stroke, betwixt them would he slide,
And steal a kiss, and then run out and dance,
And, as the turn'd, cast many a lustful glance,
And throw him gaudy toys to please his eye,
And dive into the water, and there pry
Upon his breast, his thighs, and every limb,
And up again, and close beside him swim,
And talk of love. Leander made reply,
"You are deceiv'd; I am no woman, I...."

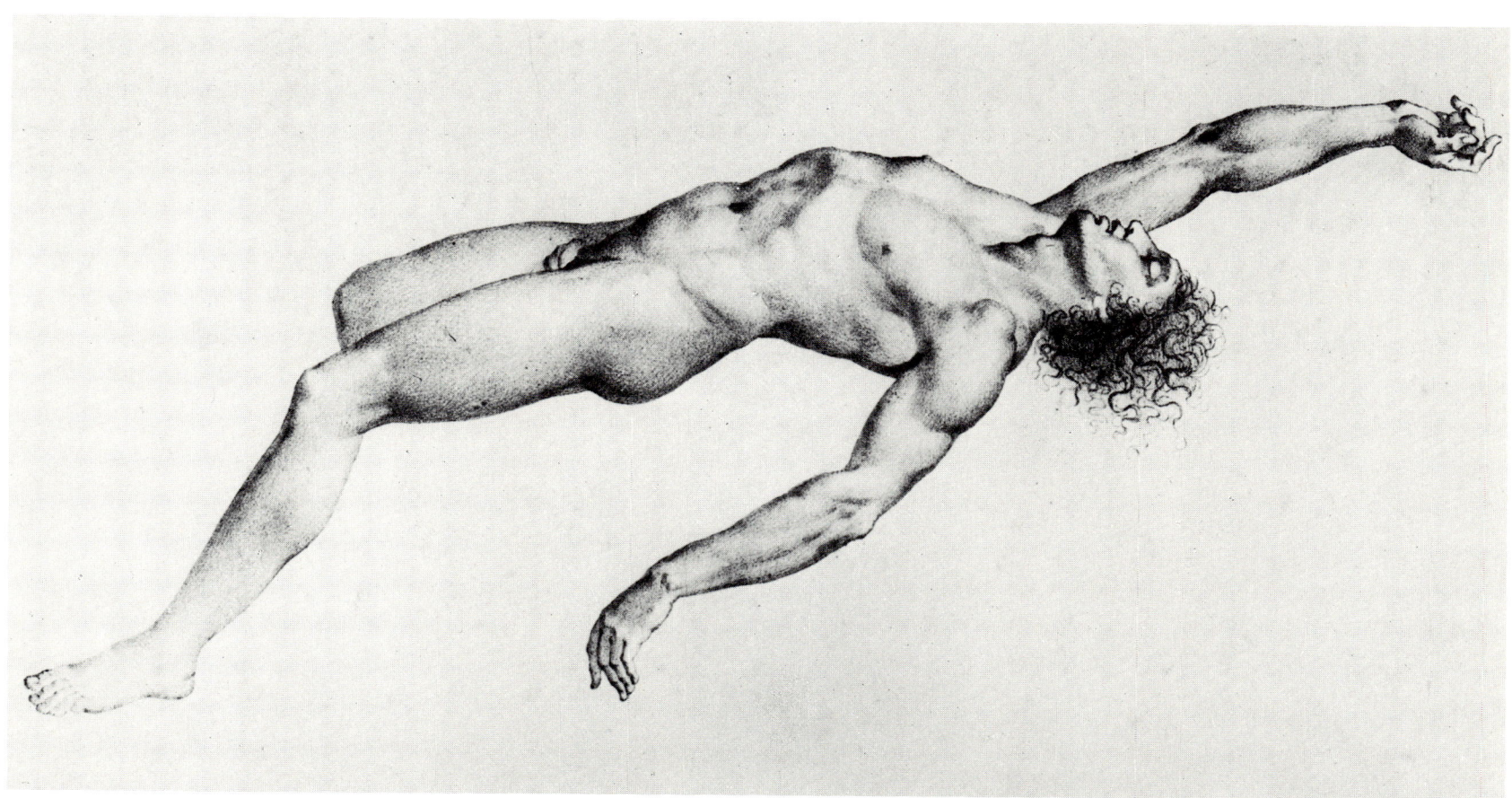

WILLIAM SHAKESPEARE (1564-1616)

No one can say for sure at what date Shakespeare composed his *Sonnets*. The first quarto edition was published in 1609 by Thomas Thorpe, then reprinted in a different order by John Benson in 1640. The first reference to these poems occurs in a work called *Palladis Tamia* (1598), by Francis Meres, who praises Shakespeare's "sugred sonnets among his private friends." Their main subject is the author's love for a handsome young man he wants to immortalize in verse. Shakespeare's mistress, the "dark ladie," cheats on him with this young, fair-haired friend. Rejection, growing old, betrayal, the complexity of the feelings of love, are the principal themes of this sequence of sonnets dedicated to the mysterious Mr. W.H. Some scholars think that W.H. was Sir William Harvey, who may have asked Shakespeare to write these poems to encourage his third wife's son, Henry Wriothesley, to marry! Others prefer William Hughes, an actor who played women's roles, or the Earl of Pembroke, William Herbert, or even a printer called William Hall. There is no end to the ingenious speculations which critics have launched on to explain those two initials. Apparently Shakespeare did not want his readers to know who Mr. W.H. was—and all one can say is that he succeeded.

20

A woman's face, with Nature's own hand painted,
Hast thou, the master-mistress of my passion;
A woman's gentle heart, but not acquainted
With shifting change, as is false women's fashion;
An eye more bright than theirs, less false in rolling,
Gilding the object whereupon it gazeth;
A man in hue all hues in his controlling,
Which steals men's eyes and women's souls amazeth.
And for a woman wert thou first created,
Till Nature as she wrought thee fell a-doting,
And by addition me of thee defeated
By adding one thing to my purpose nothing.
  But since she pricked thee out for women's pleasure,
  Mine be thy love, and thy love's use their treasure.

42

That thou hast her, it is not all my grief,
And yet it may be said I loved her dearly;
That she hath thee is of my wailing chief,
A loss in love that touches me more nearly.
Loving offenders, thus I will excuse ye:
Thou dost love her because thou know'st I love her,
And for my sake even so doth she abuse me,
Suff'ring my friend for my sake to approve her.
If I lose thee, my loss is my love's gain,
And losing her, my friend hath found that loss:
Both find each other, and I lose both twain,
And both for my sake lay on me this cross.
  But here's the joy—my friend and I are one.
  Sweet flattery! then she loves but me alone.

104

To me, fair friend, you never can be old,
For as you were when first your eye I eyed,
Such seems your beauty still. Three winters cold
Have from the forests shook three summers' pride,
Three beauteous springs to yellow autumn turned
In process of the seasons have I seen,
Three April perfumes in three hot Junes burned,
Since first I saw you fresh, which yet are green.
Ah, yet doth beauty, like a dial hand,
Steal from his figure, and no pace perceived!
So your sweet hue, which methinks still doth stand,
Hath motion, and mine eye may be deceived;
  For fear of which, hear this, thou age unbred:
  Ere you were born was beauty's summer dead.

144

Two loves I have, of comfort and despair,
Which like two spirits do suggest me still.
The better angel is a man right fair,
The worser spirit a woman colored ill.
To win me soon to hell, my female evil
Tempteth my better angel from my side,
And would corrupt my saint to be a devil,
Wooing his purity with her foul pride.
And whether that my angel be turned fiend
Suspect I may, yet not directly tell;
But being both from me, both to each friend,
I guess one angel in another's hell.
    Yet this shall I ne'er know, but live in doubt,
    Till my bad angel fire my good one out.

(a) Nicolas Hilliard, *Portrait of an Unknown Man*. Victoria and Albert Museum, London. (b) Isaac Oliver, *Portrait of Edward Herbert*. Collection of the Earl of Powis, Tate Gallery, London. The French aesthete, Robert de Montesquiou, lamented the fact that modern fashions "deprived men of their ornaments." Looking at these miniatures one can see why.

V

THE PHILOSOPHERS' SIN

Nothing less than a bonfire will stop a pen.
(Théophile Feret, *Le Verger des Muses*)

◁◁ Jean Delville, *Plato's Academy*. Jeu de Paume, Louvre, Paris.

Bartolomeo Sesi, Drawing. Galleria degli Uffizi, Florence.

Jacques Callot, *Portrait of a Nobleman*. Cabinet des Estampes, Bibliothèque Nationale, Paris.

For the righteous, evil always comes from across the borders. In the early seventeenth century in France, it was the Italians who were accused of importing the vice that "offended Nature." Was not sodomy practiced by the prelates of Rome, the noblemen of Italy and the French libertines who were votaries of the naturalist philosophy expounded by Cesare Cremonini at the University of Padua? Libertinism was more than a search for pleasure and a loosening of moral restraints; it was also a school of thought which undermined conformity and religion. Father Garasse, a French Jesuit, who was the spokesman for the upholders of morality and the Church, pointed his finger at Montaigne rather than at the Italians; he called the famous *Essays* a "cabalistic book" for free-thinkers. In any case, whether deists or materialists, the libertines and free-thinkers carefully avoided advertising opinions for which they could have been burned at the stake. Such was the fate of Geoffroy Vallée, the author of *The Scourge of Faith,* in 1574; such, too, was the fate of an Italian named Vanini, who was burned alive in Toulouse in 1619 after having had his tongue pulled out (he had dared to put in writing his doubts about the immortality of the soul).

Among the free-thinkers and libertines one found respectable men of noble birth (many of them Huguenots), learned writers, men of science, philosophers and poets; but also "dissidents" who scoffed at the established values, drifters and debauchees of all kinds. As Roger Vailland has remarked, the libertines of the early seventeenth century had discovered that "the pleasures of love have only a fortuitous link with the necessities of procreation." Some of them pushed sacrilege and audacity as far as to assert that homosexuality was natural and not "against Nature." Sodomite poets like Théophile de Viau, des Barreaux, Blot, Saint-Pavin and Charles Coypeau, known as d'Assoucy, not only represent the "reverse side of the seventeenth century," as someone has said (no pun intended); they also remind one of the vitality and the extraordinary variety of literature in that period.

Under the Ancient Régime in France the laws against sodomy were severe; only the aristocracy was relatively immune from them. The trial of Théophile de Viau aroused considerable feeling in the world of letters—just as Oscar Wilde's did three centuries later. Around 1620 the handsome, witty and vastly talented poet Théophile de Viau was considered the leading figure among the young libertines. Descended from a Protestant family which had "risen through Court appointments," he had studied at the Protestant Academy in Saumur and at the University of Leyden in the Low Lands (where he became friends with his compatriot, Guez de Balzac). After completing his studies he had entered the service of the Comte de Candale. Acclaimed as the "Prince of Poets," the "Apollo of our age," the "king of wits," he was also regarded as an extravagant libertine (he was thought to be a member of the scandalous fraternity of the "Blasphemers of the Marais du Temple"), a disciple of Vanini, an unbeliever and, what is more, a sodomite. Saint-Pavin, who was well acquainted with him, gibed:

With dexterity he composed
Lines to his Mistress's eyes
While riding upon his lover's thighs!

He was accused of corrupting youth and of having published indecent poems in an anthology called *The Satirical Cabinet* [*Le Cabinet Satirique*, 1616]. When he found out that his young queen, Anne of Austria, and her pretty friends were reading these ribald verses, King Louis XIII declared, outraged, that "such twisted beliefs and such hideous filth are unfit for a Christian."

De Viau thought it prudent to leave town. For a while he lived in London; then, in 1620, he decided that he was sufficiently protected by friends in powerful positions to risk returning to Paris. As an added precaution he announced that he wished to convert to Catholicism, "so as to be reconciled with the people of my country, and so as not to appear their enemy each time I utter some inconsequential word or commit some unimportant little act." The King's confessor declared that he himself would attend to the poet's conversion.

It was at about this period, according to the writer Tallemant des Réaux, that de Viau met Jacques Vallée des Barreaux. De Viau was to love this young man tenderly, although he denied ever having had physical relations with him. Des Barreaux, who was gifted, appealing and distinguished-looking, used to indulge in "all sorts of debauchery," to the utter despair of his pious mother, who may have feared furthermore that the same fate would befall her son as had occurred to her uncle Geoffroy Vallée in 1574. At any rate, she and her husband, a respectable councillor in Parlement, went to de Viau and begged him rather naively "to admonish their son about his obligations." The "Prince of Poets" was only too happy to oblige and hastened to initiate his young friend in all kinds of depravity, which "corrupted his mind" (says Tallemant des Réaux).

Appointed Court Councillor, a duty which he declined to perform, des Barreaux, surnamed the "Illustrious Debauchee," instead built up a reputation as a gifted poet and as a philosopher (whose mind was actually so penetrating and so keen that, according to one of his contemporaries, "when he skimmed through the great authors, even lightly, he was able to absorb their quintessence without imbuing himself in their works.") Later des Barreaux had a stormy affair with Marion Delorme; it was a heart-to-heart relationship, unlike the Marquis de Cinq-Mars's involvement with the same lady, which was an affair of vanity, or Cardinal de Richelieu's, which was merely a flirtation. Nevertheless des Barreaux acquired the reputation of being a "sodomite" and a "follower of Théophile." Epigrams like the following were whispered around town:

That nasty depravity
Which is called sodomy
Is by no means unknown
To Councillor des Barreaux.

In 1623 a new edition of the *Satirical Cabinet* was published under the slightly altered title *The Satirical Parnassus* [*Le Parnasse satirique*]; it contained a poem

Jean de Saint-Igny, *Young Nobles* (detail). Metropolitan Museum of Art, New York.

Giovanni Lanfranco, *Man with Cat.* (detail). (Reproduced by permission of Christie's, London.)

signed "Théophile" which began with the line, "Oh, Phyllis, I'm fucked! I've got the syph / Something fierce...." (See p. 122) This frank confession aroused the ire of the faction of the righteous, and especially of its commander-in-chief, Father Garasse. This fanatical Jesuit responded with a series of pamphlets attacking the libertines, those "vermin whose lips are fouled with blasphemy; whose actions are utterly infected with sodomy, and whose writings are vile displays of immodesty. They corrupt the young wherever they go; their faces are made hideous with insolence, their souls with betrayal and their bodies with the putrid sweats of the pox."

This time things had gone too far, and the attorney general, Mathieu Molé, began proceedings against the poet. De Viau managed to escape in time, but he was nevertheless condemned *in absentia* to be burned at the stake. In order to impress public opinion the sentence was actually carried out with all due ceremony in the main square of Paris (the Place de Grève) with a straw dummy. Then, on September 19, 1623, Théophile de Viau was arrested near Saint-Quentin where he had gone into hiding, and was brought back to Paris. His friends managed to stay the execution and to obtain a retrial. De Viau was locked up in the dungeon of the assassin Ravaillac in the Conciergerie, without heat or light, and with a vermin-ridden pallet to sleep on. After several months of this treatment he stopped eating. His friends again intervened with attorney general Molé, who gave orders to treat the prisoner less harshly. De Viau was allowed to read and to write, and he was even able to correspond with his supporters to prepare his defense.

Meanwhile the Jesuits were up in arms. One of them, Father Guérin, furiously assailed the poet in his sermons: "May you be cursed, Théophile.... You are a blackguard and a pig. Nay, you are worse than a pig. A pig's meat is good to boil and to bake, but yours, catif, is not good for anything except roasting to a crisp. And so it shall be. You have scoffed at holy men; soon you will see how holy men will scoff at thee!" Such homilies put the fear of god in the churchgoers—and incensed the poet's friends. Presumably with the court's tacit consent, an unfinished poem which had been found on de Viau's person at the time of his arrest was published (See p. 121). It is a moving poem—comparable to Oscar Wilde's *De Profundis*—but it was also very compromising, both for its author and for the person to whom it was adressed, a certain "Tircis." Professor Adam (in *Théophile de Viau et la Libre Pensée Française*) believes that Tircis was an attorney in Parlement; Professor Frédéric Lachèvre (in *Le Libertinage au XVIIe siècle*) suggests that he may have been des Barreaux. This last hypothesis does not seem very plausible, for des Barreaux's attitude all during the trial and after the poet was released remained that of a faithful friend. Whatever the case, Théophile defended himself vigorously and claimed that his poems had been tampered with; throughout the trial he lied boldly, denied having written everything that could possibly be denied and maintained that *The Satirical Parnassus* had been published without his consent (which was probably the truth). He went to great lengths to avoid compromising any of his friends, although it would have been easy for him to reveal the true identities of the authors of various poems which the prosecutor had unjustly attributed to him.

De Viau's luck turned when the witness Forest was called to the stand. Forest testified that he had heard the accused recite obscene couplets and brag of regularly having intercourse with boys "so as not to get the clap." At that the poet stood up and, looking his accuser straight in the eyes, he announced that Forest's real name was Sageot, and that Father Voisin had obliged this dissolute and perverse young man in ways which were suspicious, to say the least. All the more so that in 1611 in Saumur he, de Viau, had personally caught witness with his pants down—in the act of buggery, in fact—and that he had soundly thrashed him with a stick, which is why Sageot-Forest and Father Voisin vowed him such hatred. Sageot lost his head, broke down in tears and finally admitted that his testimony had been concocted by Father Voisin and Father Garasse.

Things went from bad to worse for the prosecution. Several important persons—Montmorency, Liancourt and the Duke of Buckingham (whom de Viau had met in London)—announced their support of the poet. Then des Barreaux began publishing lampoons in which he disclosed that he had been Father Voisin's "pet" pupil in the rhetoric course at La Flèche, and that the good father had made dishonest propositions to him at the very time that he had been thinking of entering the novitiate. Garasse does not seem to have been particularly impressed by these accusations. His fiery temperament, his fishmonger's disposition, had naturally inclined him to use the age-old debater's device of trying to discredit a doctrine by impeaching the individual who upholds it. But he realized that he had gone too far, and henceforth he pretended to have lost interest in the case.

Incensed by des Barreaux's disclosures, King Louis XIII wanted the sordid trial to come to a quick end. Théophile de Viau was released, but was sentenced to exile and confiscation of his property. Father Voisin was expelled from the Church. On the way to Rome where he hoped to take refuge, the priest was ambushed near the town of Dijon by de Viau's friends led by des Barreaux. The assailants kicked Voisin in the stomach with spurs, yanked his beard and then obliged him to run for more than a league to catch up with his coach and his belongings.

Despite Father Garasse's protests ("Alas, where are the burning flames of Sodom?") de Viau's banishment was not strictly enforced. Cardinal Richelieu disliked religious fanaticism and, although he was not a "bird of the same feather" (as he wrote to Baudru in 1626), he felt a certain amount of personal sympathy for the poet. De Viau was allowed to stay with the Duke of Liancourt, and later with the Comte de Bethune, the brother of the statesman Sully, at the castle of Selles in the province of Berry. Several months later he was pardoned. He returned to Paris and settled in the house of his protector the Duke of Montmorency, a "liberal who always employed men of wit and intelligence," and who lived like an Italian prince of the Renaissance. In this environment, surrounded by scholars, men of letters and artists, the poet composed verses for a woman named Caliste, who became his mistress. Caliste may actually have been a lady-in-waiting of the Queen's.

The worst ordeal for de Viau after his trial was the defection of some his friends, like Boisrobert, a notorious "bugger," who was incurably afflicted—according to Tallemant des Réaux—with cowardice. De Viau seems to have been especially pained by Guez de Balzac's scornful hostility. In their days at the University of Leyden the poet had rushed, weapons in hand, to Balzac's defense on one occasion when the latter had gotten into a scrap; thereafter the two friends had sworn eternal friendship. Filled with bitterness when Balzac turned against him, de Viau took his revenge by accusing his old friend in no uncertain terms: "If I were to waste a few drops of ink over your behaviour, I would blacken your whole life. You take the trouble to warn me of the ills which come from frequenting trollops—but if I were you I would go down on my knees and pray to God that no physician might ever discover the reason why you have avoided such ills only to fall into ones which are far worse. They say that you are a queer man—I mean the opposite of a man—and indeed it amazes me that you can be so scornful of women." And de Viau concluded, "as a matter of fact, the most shameful episode in my life was my acquaintanceship with de Balzac."

The bad treatment he had received in prison had seriously undermined the poet's health. Despite the concern of his faithful friends—de Liancourt, the Duke of Montmorency and above all des Barreaux, with whom he liked to reminisce over their "blissful days together,"—de Viau was growing weaker by the day. Just one year after being released he took to bed with a high fever and, on the September 25, 1626, he died in des Barreaux's arms after having confessed and taken communion. Perhaps de Viau believed like Oscar Wilde that "Catholicism is a religion which makes death more comfortable."

Did de Viau's trial sound a public warning, as Father Garasse wanted it to? A lot of ink was spilled over it and a lot of feeling was aroused by it, but the poet's free-thinking, loose-living friends do not seem to have been in the least discouraged by it: they kept on blaspheming and publishing obscene verses as if nothing had happened. Saint-Pavin, a crony of de Viau's and des Barreaux's (and of Madame de Sevigné's), boasted that he was the "King of Sodom." "He hath a soul even more beautiful than his wit," wrote the Marquis de Jarsay, "and never did a man of vices have so many virtues." Strangely enough, Saint-Pavin was never bothered by either the Church or the royal government. The same is true of the poet Claude de

Jacopo da Pontormo,
Drawing in red chalk.
Wicar Collection,
Musée des
Beaux-Arts, Lille.

Charles Le Brun, *Portrait of Chancellor Pierre Séguier* (detail). c. 1660. Louvre, Paris.

Eustache Le Sueur, *Ganymede Carried off by Jupiter*. Louvre, Paris.

Chauvigny, otherwise known as the Baron de Blot, who is the author of the following prayer:

All I ask of Thee, Lord,
Is to be a drinker and a fornicator,
An unbeliever and a sodomite,
And then to die
And then to die very suddenly.

The last part of this wish was apparently granted, since the poet died after a very brief illness. He had led a joyous, carefree life at the court of Gaston of Orleans, a lord who is said to have had "somewhat of a page boy's mind" and who had brazenly organized a "Congress of Rotters and Wastrels" during his wife's confinement.

During the Fronde rebellions, from 1648 to 1653, the libertines were able to engage in unbridled licentiousness, provided that they were protected by important persons like the Prince de Condé. With the return to order however, the young daredevils who went around recklessly parading their homosexual preferences provoked the ire and the irritation of King Louis XIV. In order to rid his entourage of them, the monarch established a special court known as "*la Chambre ardente*" [the Burning Chamber] for trying offenses of sodomy. No doubt the king's repugnance was sincere, but it was nevertheless prudently discrete when scandal occurred in the inner circles of the royalty. Louis XIV's own brother Philip of Orleans, for example, lived in the castle of Saint-Cloud surrounded by works of art and by effeminate courtiers such as the Chevalier de Lorraine, the Chevalier de Chatillon (one of Admiral Coligny's last descendants), the Marquis d'Effiat with his ambiguous ways, and other more extravagant figures like Maurel de Volonne who (writes La Palatine) "sold boys like horses and would go shopping in the pit of the Opera."

On orders from Louis XIV two writers, well known in literary circles, but of undistinguished birth of course, were sentenced to be burned. One of them, Jacques Chausson, was a talented profligate who picked up a little money here and there "copying and hack writing." This shady character was a notorious sodomite, and it was said that he used to provide the nobles of the court with young boys "many of whom had been kidnapped and raped by force." A certain Toussaint le Tourneur had been sold to the Baron de Bellefort for "a watch and a gold snuff-box"; Richard de la Monnerie had been sold to the Marquis de Bellai "for the price of 50 gold louis." Chausson was also accused of having uttered blasphemies and having made ungodly pronouncements. Naturally neither the marquis nor the baron were obliged to appear in court; but the accused, despite the fact that he denied all charges, was found guilty of having committed, and of having induced others to commit, the crime of sodomy. He and his associate were sentenced "to make amends in the following manner: first to be stripped of their clothes, then to be taken in a tumbril to the Cathedral of Notre Dame, and there to be publicly exhibited in prisoner's shirts and with ropes tied around their necks... and then to be led to the Place de Grève and to be bound each to a stake and each to have his tongue severed, and finally each to be burned alive."

Wearing a powdered wig and gorgeously dressed in white silk, the executioner was waiting for the two prisoners. In the jostling crowd was a poet and fellow-debauchee of Chausson's: Claude Le Petit. Le Petit watched the horrible proceedings and later described his friend's last moments in this sonnet:

Unfortunate Chausson was burned, my friend;
That famous curly-haired rascal is dead,
And his boldness is a deathless legend,
For no man e'er met with a stranger end.

Nicholas Hogenberg, *The Punishment of Sodomites*. Bibliothèque Nationale, Paris.

Parmigianino, *Study of a Nude*. Cabinet des Estampes. Bibliothèque Nationale, Paris. This artist used models whose slender bodies had a feminine gracefulness to them.

With a gay wink he sang the dire song;
He slipped on the stiff shirt without blanching;
And from high up on his crackling pyre,
He looked down on death without a tremor.

As the flames were gathering, his confessor
Waved the cross, bade him think upon his soul
—In vain! For when the awful fire reached

His legs, he fell, and then, twisting around,
So as to die no differently than he
Had lived, he bared his arse for all to see!

Claude Le Petit was the author of several satiric and licentious works, one of which was entitled *The Brothel of the Muses, or the Nine Whorish Virgins: A Satirical Capriccio by Theophile the Younger* [*Le Bordel des Muses ou les neufs pucelles putains, caprice satirique de Théophile le Jeune*]. Le Petit had no idea when he wrote the provocatively cynical sonnet just quoted that he himself would meet with the same end a few months later. Angered by the outrageous behavior of Le Petit and his friends—Edmé Boursault (famous for his squirmishes with Boileau and Molière), de Vizé (the author of the *Mercure galant*) and the grammarian Jean Rou—the King's police had confiscated a number of Le Petit's writings. The poet was tried and sentenced to have his right hand cut off before being burned on the Place de Grève. His last wish was to be allowed to speak with Baron Schildebeck, whom he had met in Germany. The request was granted, and Le Petit was able to whisper to Schildebeck where a copy of his poems had been hidden away. Having been assured by the baron that his works would be rescued and published, the poet faced death "with the same so-called fortitude that he had erroneously admired in that other wretch whose inclinations he had shared" (observed Jean Rou). The order confirming the judge's sentence stipulated that Claude Le Petit was to be "discretely strangled before being burned... for such is the mercy of justice...."

Two centuries later, under Napoleon III, the works of Théophile de Viau and Claude Le Petit were once again subjected to legal proceedings. In 1855, a Monsieur Alleaume sued the publisher Jammet for printing de Viau's licentious poems "without transcribing the obscenities into Greek." He argued that that language would at least have veiled some of the crudities which were "too shocking." Alleaume was ordered to pay court expenses. In 1865 another publisher—who happened to be named Jean Gay—was sentenced to four months prison and 500 francs fine for having published Claude Le Petit's poems. Finally, in 1868, an edition of the *Satirical Parnassus* was confiscated and declared offensive to public and religious morality. Nevertheless the romantic and the post-romantic French poets viewed the so-called burlesque poets of the seventeenth century as their forerunners. They maintained, as did Mallarmé himself, that de Viau's poems were far superior to Malherbe's (which had always been considered models of prosodic perfection). Theophile Gautier declared that the *Satirical Parnassus* was like "one of Caravaggio's pitch black heads compared to one of Latour's rosy pastels." He concluded that "there is enough art in these poems to make one weep at the thought of them being burned." For, when all is said and done, wasn't the greatest scandal in the seventeenth century the fact that these books were burned"?

THEOPHILE DE VIAU (1590-1626)

This poem was found among Théophile de Viau's belongings when he was arrested in June 1623, and it was entered as evidence at the office of the clerk of the court. Strangely enough copies of the poem could be bought in Paris a few months later. Naturally "Tircis," to whom the compromising lines were addressed, preferred to keep his true identity a secret; however, he did compose a reply "From Tircis to Théophile in Prison." In this open letter, which Frédéric Lachèvre attributes to des Barreaux (unjustly so, in our opinion), the author scolds Théophile for writing verses instead of repenting and praying. He adds that he had long been avoiding the poet's "pernicious company" and that by no means could he be considered an accomplice "in the vile practice which Théophile lauds as brazenly and as unjustly as he accuses the great city of Rome of tolerating it." In the "Complaint" de Viau does in fact allude to the "innocent pleasures" that are "not punished in Rome." For his chief accuser, Father Garasse, this could only refer to the "vice against nature"; fortunately for de Viau the court did not agree with this interpretation, although it did charge the poet with insinuating that the Holy City permitted fornication. Skillfully used by the Jesuits, the following lines—especially the sonnet "Phyllis, I'm fucked"—almost cost de Viau his life at the stake.

THEOPHILE'S COMPLAINT
TO HIS ABSENT FRIEND, TIRCIS (1623)

My friend, you know my complaint very well:
Your sloth compounded with ingratitude.
I see you napping right against my pyre,
And I marvel the flames do not wake you.

My trial will end in dire sentence soon;
They're preparing to burn my effigy,
And the few friends I've left have tried in vain
To prevent that horror, that row, those flames....

If my ill-starred fate has run the course
Of the sacred friendship you once swore,
And that, true only to human nature,
You ignore me, seeing me fall so low,

Pulled down into this fearful precipice,
Oh, then, at least pretend a little grief,
And spare me the gleeful crowd snickering
That I misjudged you whom I loved so much....

If the least glimmer of virtue still winks
In you, remember how you strove to please;
How proud you were to be Theophile's friend,
Before this disgrace I've suffered through.

How your heart unfastens and goes from me
At the first ordeal my fate inflicts on you!
My case would not be lost, you know it well,
But for the defections, the betrayals....

If only my position could improve,
And the King grant me a regular pension,
And I find a place in the provinces,
Close by, but far enough to calm my foes,

I'd celebrate my luck with such rejoicings,
Such delight at slipping free of trouble,
You'd be ashamed that in adversity
I appealed to you so many times in vain,

Jacques Bellange, Drawing of a long-haired youth. Musée Municipal, Saint-Germain-en-Laye, France.

The Drinkers. c. 1610. Winslow Ames Collection, Saunderstown, Rhode Island. This drawing has been attributed successively to Georges Lallemand, Martin Freminet and Jacques Bellange.

And chided you for resigning a fate
You should have shared with me, for ill or good.
Look into your heart, so quickly cooled. Ask it
If you are still what you once were to me.

I would have fled across the Pyrenees
With you, I would have given years to you,
I would have set my skill to spread your name
From the western brink to the incoming waves

Of dawn. In my heart I've done nothing wrong
To give you cause to abandon me;
I swear by Heaven that I've done nothing
Save love you, o Tircis, each day a little deeper.

SONNET

Oh, Phyllis, I'm fucked! I've got the syph
Something fierce, I fear it's terminal.
My poor prick's as weak as a noodle,
My breath's got an ulcerous whiff.

Thirty days I sweated, heaving glue;
Worse torment never raged so long,
Hercules would have found it too strong,
And the worst is: there's nothing to do.

My closest friends have kept away;
With my own self I daren't even play.
All this because I made a pass

At you! Oh, how I regret it now!
Dear God, if I survive I vow
I'll never fuck anything but ass.

DENYS SANGUIN DE SAINT-PAVIN
(c. 1600–1670)

Saint-Pavin was the son of Madame des Essarts and Cardinal de Guise. In 1618, he was installed as the prior of Saint-Savin des Champs, in the diocese of Le Mans. He called himself the "king of Sodom," and wrote the following lines, having become impotent, at the age of fifty-five.

EPIGRAM

If, when your page boy brings us wine,
We cast an eye upon his shape,
You fall straight off into a rage,
And call us all a lot of swine.
We've only looked. Is it a crime
To ogle a lad from time to time?
Believe me, friend, it would be wise,
When you bring out your wines to taste,
And want no one to eye your page,
To make quite sure your guests are blind.

ANONYMOUS: ALCIBIADES IN SCHOOL

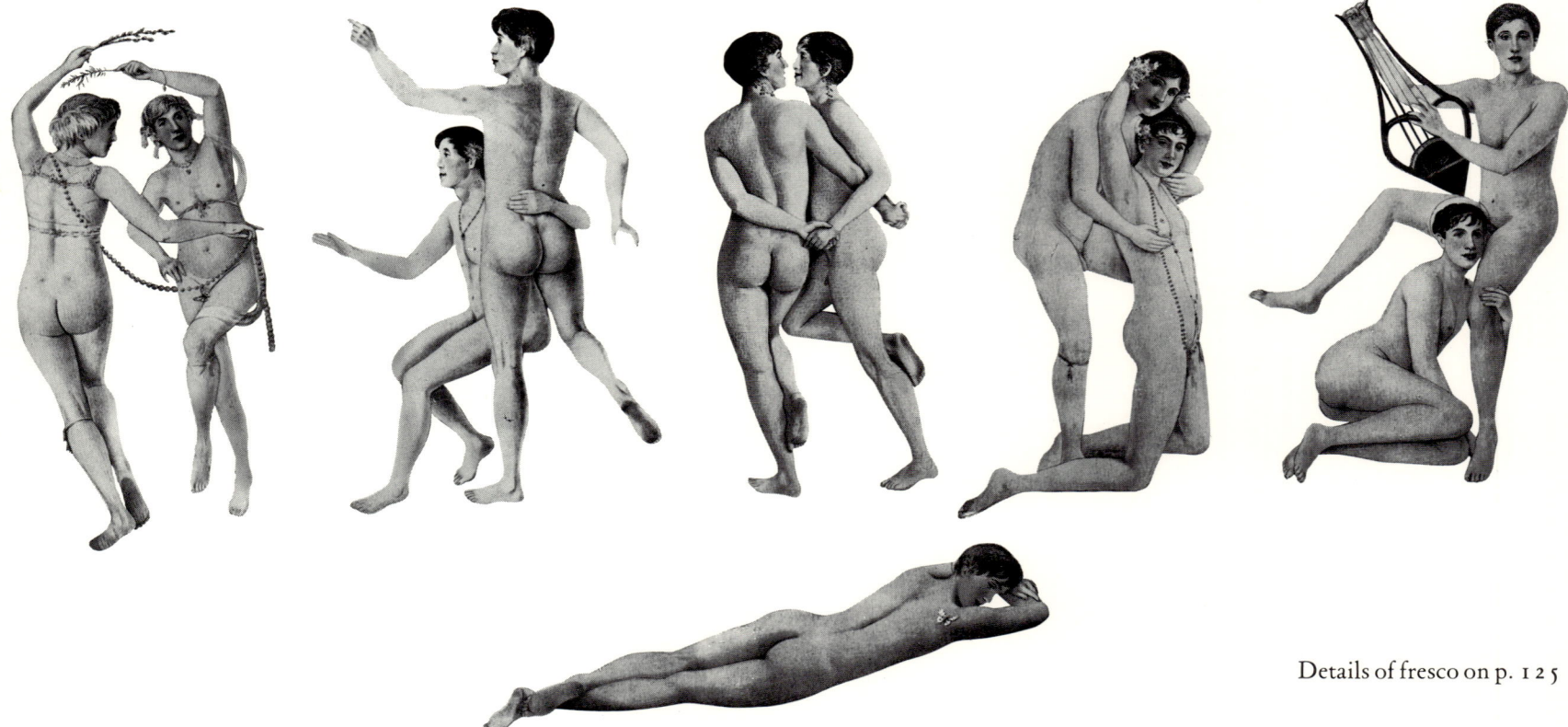

Details of fresco on p. 125

Alcibiade, fanciullo a scuola, D.P.A., Oranges was published in 1652 in the town of Oranges in southern France. Only four copies of this edition are known to be extant (one is in the British Museum, the other three in Dresden, Grenoble and Paris). In 1862 Jean Gay printed an edition in Italian, and in 1866 he published a French translation limited to 550 copies. Both editions were confiscated and destroyed, hence the rarity of copies. The initials D.P.A. (Di Pietro Aretino?) suggest that the book may have been written by the great Italian satiric poet. A study published in 1850 attributes it to another talented Italian writer, Ferrante Pallavicini, famed for his indecent literary works. Recently a letter was found in Genoa, Italy, written by the founder of the Academy "degli Incogniti," Gian Francesco Loredano, and addressed to a scholar, Father Angelico Aprosio. Loredano says that in 1630 he had had the manuscript of *Alcibiades* in his own hands, and that an edition (which has not survived) had been published in Venice in 1651. Loredano asserts that the author was Antonio Rocco, a philosophy professor in Venice. Thus the Pallavicini attribution, although it has been adopted by a number of writers including M.G. Brunt (the French translator) and Guillaume Apollinaire, may well be erroneous.

Pallavicini, who belonged to the Congregation of Canons in Rome, had written a stinging lampoon against the Barberini family, whose most illustrious member was Pope Urban VIII. The satire told the story of how God, dismayed by the various kinds of debauchery (sodomy, adultery, etc.) indulged in by his priests in the Holy City, decides to send Saint Paul to investigate matters more closely in Parma, Lucca and Rome. The Pope and the prelates take Paul for a madman possessed by the devil, and he is obliged to flee. Obviously this was pushing things too far, and the Barberinis were determined to punish the author. Pallavicini was lured into a trap by a hired thug. He was brought to Avignon, where he was tortured and chained up, his arms spread crosswise, in a dark dungeon; after a year of this treatment, he was beheaded. He was twenty-six. If Loredano really did see the manuscript of *Alcibiades* in 1630, Pallavicini could not possibly have written it: he would only have been twelve years old at the time. The attribution to Antonio Rocco seems much more plausible; after all, many of the sixteenth-century philosophers were devotees of Socratic love. The preface to *Alcibiades* states that the book was written in order to warn parents of the dangers in entrusting their sons to educators. Doubtless this is said tongue in cheek, for the book depicts the "Socratic vice" with considerable talent and in "gay, poetic accents" (as Apollinaire has said). Which is more than can be said for most of the texts published during the seventeenth and eighteenth centuries.

(Philotimus welcoming his new pupil, young Alcibiades:)
PHILOTIMUS: I shall fill the vessel of thy mind with the seed of doctrines plentiful and pleasant, such doctrines as will seem to thee supernatural. Thou shalt not encounter the stern rigor I am accustomed to use with the other children to gain their respect; nay, our first interviews will brim o'er with pleasure and sweet trust. Indeed, as a gage of my affection, and to seal the equality of our intercourse, let me bestow this, need I say honorable, kiss on thy young lips.

At this renewed attack the child, quivering and growing suddenly pale, took a hasty step backwards. "Fear not, my son," spake the master, "no man's tongue will harm thee, save when its brash impudence offends the bounds of Justice. That eloquence thou wishest to learn from me, which thy first instructors pursued so zealously, my devotion will impart to thee, but thou shalt not possess it truly until thy tongue be joined to mine. For the hand helpeth the hand, the mind assisteth the mind, the tongue aideth the tongue. Come here, come here, my ruby..." and folding him against his bosom, he punctuated each word he spake with a lingering kiss.

The child turned away a little, and looked scornful, but it was only one of those coy rebuffs which but kindle lust and add spice to wantonness. Indeed Alcibiades rebelled not and even suffered his master to fondle the shapely, small and velvet globes of his apples. Therefore the latter was feverishly visiting the lad's garden of Eden, and, in the futile transports of unsatisfied desire, nevertheless, upon touching the delicious entry with his finger, he apprehended the surpassing felicity of the blessed. This delightful play continued a short while ere Philotimus was called away upon some pressing affair; but his senses having been moved to such rapture, the merest thought of that bliss he had just quit obliged him to interrupt his business.

(Alcibiades questions his teacher: "Pray tell me whether the pleasure is keener with lads or with the wenches, and why....")
PHILOTIMUS: There is something offensive in the mingling of juices; 'tis like an untimely and unseasonable downpour which wearies and enfeebles the senses. So vast is the cunt's capacity 'tis frightening. 'Tis a labyrinth inviting one to lose oneself in its passages rather than to tarry and take one's pleasure there. Mark, on the contrary, that pretty declivity leading to the flowered garden of a boy. Doth it not enclose all the delights? Doth not the motion of those two fresh, rounded, velvety little cushions gamboling between thy thighs incline one to the pitch of wantonness? Doth it not surpass all the pleasures, both real and imagined, in a wench? Doth it not seem to thee that Nature, in giving thee these happy, happy cheeks, that plump form and that dainty softness, expressly intended to teach us her purpose, which is to fill the concavity of our body when it presseth against them? 'Tis the opposite with women. In congress the convexity of the two stomachs joining together leaveth a gap between the parts and hindereth the perfect harmony necessary to extreme bliss.

Elisar von Kupffer, *The Blessed in a World of Radiance* (details). Sanctuarium Artis Elisarion, Minusio, near Locarno. Von Kupffer, who called himself Elisarion, painted this vision of fraternal humanity on the ceiling of the Sanctuarium.

Whereas taking one's pleasure of a boy one is neither deprived of the sweetness of his kiss, nor of the delight in breathing in the perfumed breeze that escapeth between his passionate lips. Here too th' agreement is complete and the rapture entirely shared, so long as the beloved lieth in such a way that he can turn his visage and bring it close to his lover's; meanwhile, depending on the charming stripling's fancy, the spring onion is planted in his garden or quiverith in his hand....

As to know why some children discharge more frequently and plentifully than others, the reason is that, in them, the parts of their "garden" are connected to their little "finch" with subtler nerves, which improveth the circulation of the spirits; so that the wanton agitation of the "bird" accompanieth and sometimes even precedeth the transports of the "garden". Certain lads find such delight in being mounted that they become mad with desire, begging and praying and even forcing their lovers to do the thing to them. These children are keener and quicker than all others because the abundance of lascivious spirits in them maketh their motions nimble and causeth them to be hotter in action; and therefore their body constantly betrayeth the goal to which it tendeth, not to mention the wanton movements of their hips and a certain lascivious to-and-fro which is produced in them by the circulation of the spirits. There are other boys who are tranquil and modest, and have not the same immoderate urge to "chime," but notwithstanding how feebly the amorous inclination common to all creatures in them dwells, they are nevertheless as readily inclined as the others to yield to tender toyings, which they like though they'll ne'er admit to it....

ALCIBIADES: I'll submit to thy urgings. 'Tis the desire to learn above all which decideth me. Look, I am ready to satisfy thee....

Thereupon he lifted his gown and modestly took the posture the circumstances required. The master assisted him with his hand, and ere long the lad's tarse displayed ist glorious love treasures which put the sky and the stars to shame. The sun himself, vanquished by those more than celestial glories, hastened to veil his visage. What poet could e'er describe the wonders richly scattered through that epitome of the marvels of the universe. The two hemispheres, like unto two celestial spheres, with coursing blood tinted, were starred with sprightly tufts of hyacinths and privet. They quivered at the slightest touch, darkened with a thousand rubies that sparkled on a bed of milk and cinnabar. All was but delightful meadows, flowered gardens, many-hued rainbows, white beams of light and twinkling stars. Their constant, slow and amorous motions would have roused a statue of marble or bronze; ah, the majestic and beauteous spectacle of that little bud, whose folds were tight and dainty like a rose before it blossoms, a lovely floweret tinted with a thousand mottled tones among which the purest snow disputed with gorgeous purple....

How they continued their pleasant frolics, their amorous toyings, shall be related in the second part, which will be more wanton still. [This second part, entitled *The Triumph of Alcibiades,* in which the youth changes roles and becomes the active partner, never appeared.]

Details of fresco on p. 125.

JOHN WILMOT, THE EARL OF ROCHESTER (1647-1680)

John Wilmot, the second Earl of Rochester, a famous lyric poet and satirist, led a high-spirited, scandalous life at the court of Charles II. Rochester was not only a man ever on the prowl for pleasure, as Saint-Evremond put it, he was also an enormously gifted writer. Voltaire admired the "impetuous licentiousness" of this free-thinking, or rather deistic, poet who once quipped that "in a land of atheists love would make one turn to God." The manuscript of the play called *Sodom or the Quintessence of Debauchery* is now in the British Museum. The author's name is replaced by the initials "E of R", followed by a few words which indicate that this farce was acted before the royal court.

Very few English erotic writings prior to the eighteenth century—including only about twenty of Rochester's bawdy poems—have come down to us. In 1844 two French translations of *Sodom* were listed in the catalogue of the sale of Mr. Soleinne's library. One of them is entitled *Sodom* and may have been translated as early as 1682; the other is called *Le Roi de Sodome* [*The King of Sodom*] and is dated 1744. Unfortunately both handwritten texts were classified in the catalogue as "Corrupting or Unchaste" books and were subsequently destroyed by Soleinne's inheritors. Two other manuscripts in English, belonging to the private collection of the famed librarian Zachary Conrad von Uffenbach were acquired by Professor Wolff, the curator of the City Library of Hamburg, Germany, where they are still to be found. The extracts given here are taken from a limited edition of the play printed in 1904 from one of the Hamburg manuscripts.

Sodom is a bawdy comical fantasy. In act I, King Bolloxinion decides to make buggery not only legal but mandatory throughout his kingdom. His army gleefully welcomes this new measure, but the Queen and the young princesses are naturally distressed. By the end of Act V the Queen is dead, the Crown Prince has been seduced by his sister, and various other catastrophes have befallen the kingdom.

Dominique-Vivant Baron Denon, Engraving. Bibliothèque Nationale, Paris. The artist was the Director General of the Museums of France under Napoleon I and had a "secret cabinet" in his home, where he allegedly kept a collection of "treasures of the mirthful satyr."

SODOM

Dramatis Personnae

BOLLOXINION, King of Sodom
CUNTIGRATIA, Queen
PRICKET, Prince
SWIVIA, Princess
BUGGERANTHOS, General of the Army
POCKENELLO, Prince, Colonel & Favorite of the King
BORASTUS, Buggermaster-general
PINE & TWELY, Two pimps of Honour
FUCKADILLA, OFFICINA, CUNTICULA & CLYTORIS, maids of Honor
FLUX, Physician to the King
VERTUOSO, Merkin & Dildoe-maker to the Royal Family
With Boys, Rogues, Pimps & other Attendants

From ACT I
(Representing an Antichamber hung round with Aretino's Postures.
Enter Bolloxinion, Borastus, Pockanello, Pine and Twely.)

BOLLOXINION
Thus in the Zenith of my Lust I reign:
I eat to swive, and swive to eat again;
Let other Monarchs, who their scepters bear
To keep their subjects less in love than fear,
Be slaves to crowns, my Nation shall be free—
My Pintle only shall my scepter be;
My laws shall act more pleasure than command
And with my Prick, I'll govern all the Land....

POCKANELLO
Let merkin, Sir, be banisht from the court.

PINE
Just like a sapless hedge, where the land is poor.

TWELY
It is not fit, that Cunt should wear a Tower.

BOLLOXINION
As for the Queen, her Cunt no more invites
Clad with the filth of all her nasty whites.
Come, we miss-spend our time, we know not how
The choice of Buggery is wanting now.....

From collection of engravings on p. 127.

Aubrey Beardsley, Illustration for Aristophanes' *Lysistrata*. Private edition for Smithers, 1896.

BOLLOXINION
Can your perfections dare to claim a right?
Those, whom my pleasures serve, I will requite,
Henceforth Borastus, set the Nation free,
Let conscience have its force of Liberty.
I do proclaim, that Buggery may be used
Through all the land, so Cunt be not abused
That, the proviso, this shall be your Trust.
                                                    (to Borastus)
All things shall be your order to adjust.
To Buggeranthos let this charge be given
And let him bugger all things under heaven.

BORASTUS
Straight these indulgences shall be issued forth
From East to West, and from South to North.

BOLLOXINION
Let Pine assist you in this grand affair
Then to our Royal Citadel repair....

From ACT IV
(Enter Bolloxinion, Borastus, Pockanello and Buggeranthos)

BOLLOXINION
Since I have buggered human arse I find
Pintle to Cunt is not so much inclined.
What though the letchery be dry, 'tis smart;
A Turkish arse I love with all my heart.
The lust which in these animals I see
Does far exceed all human letchery.
Their cunts, by use improve their influence
Whilst ours grow void of pleasure, bound or sense.
By oft fomenting, Cunt so big doth swell
That Prick works there like Clapper in a bell.
All vacuum, no grasping flesh does hide
Or hug the brawny muscles of its side
Tickling the nerves, their rowling Eyes do glance
And all Mankind with vast delight entrance.

BORASTUS
Nature to them but one poor rule does give
But man delights in various ways to swive.

POCKANELLO
How simple was the letchery of old!
How full of shame, how feeble and how cold!
Confin'd to a formality of Law
When Women ne'er their husbands' pintles saw
But when their lust or duty did them draw
Then fuckt with an indifferent delight
As if Prick stood against their willing spright.
First rubb'd, then groan'd, then spent, and bid good night.
Now we the dictates of our sense pursue;
We study pleasures still and find out new.

BORASTUS
May as the Gods his name Immortal be
That first receiv'd the gift of buggery!

BOLLOXINION
Faces may change, but Cunt is but Cunt still
And he that fucks is slave to woman's will.
'Tis true, Borastus, should we daily bring
One dish to feast the palate of a King,
And strive with various sauces to invite
The grandeur of his critic appetite;
Yet still the meat's the same, the change does lie
All in sauces' great variety.
So 't is with Cunt's repeated dull delights
Sometimes you've flowers for sauce, and sometimes white
Or crablice which like buttr'd shrimps appear
And may be served for garnish all the year.
                                                    (enter Buggeranthos)

BORASTUS
My liege, the general—

BOLLOXINION
—brave man o' war!

BUGGERANTHOS
Great Sir, your soldiers
In double duty to your favour bound,
They own it all, and swear and tear the ground;
Protest they'll die in drinking of your Health
And creep into the other world by stealth

Intending there amongst the gods to vie
Their Sodom king with Immortality.

BOLLOXINION
How are they pleased with what I did proclaim?

BUGGERANTHOS
They practice it in honor of your name;
If lust present they want no woman's aid,
Each buggers with content his own comrade.

BOLLOXINION
They know't chargeable with Cunts to play.

BUGGERANTHOS
It saves them, Sir, at least a fortnight's pay.

BOLLOXINION
Then arse they fuck and bugger one another.

BUGGERANTHOS
And live like Man and wife, sister and brother....

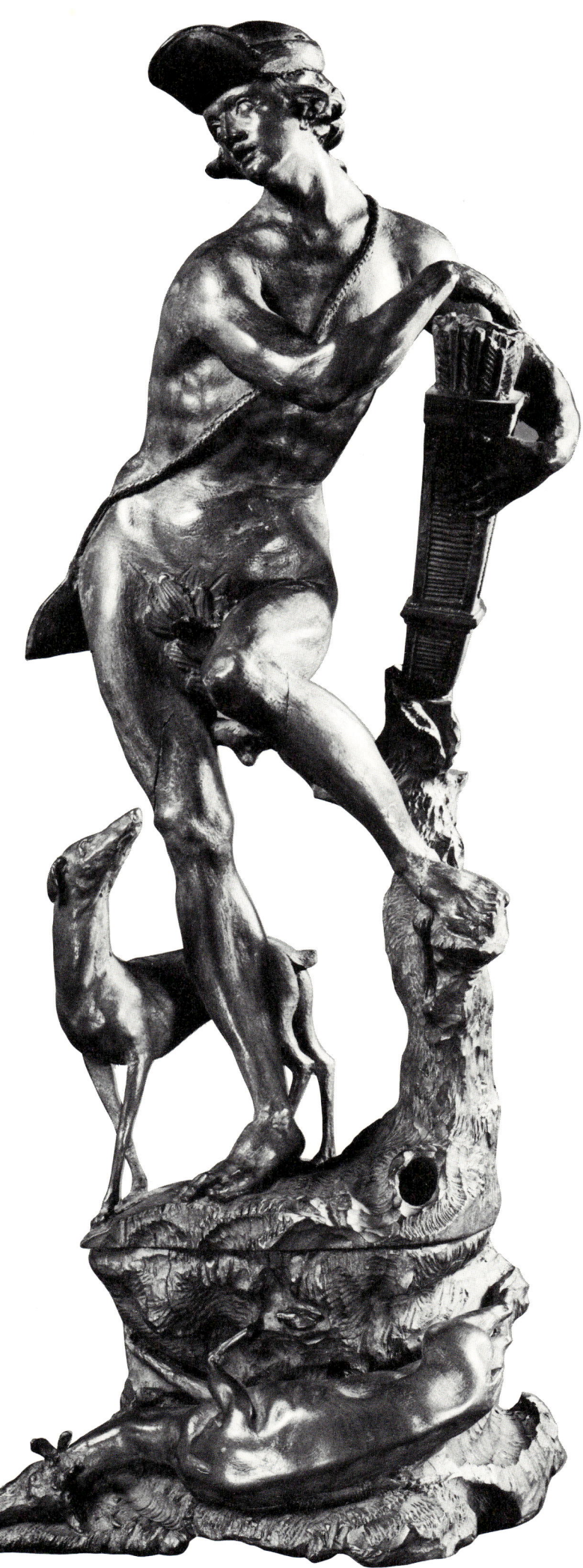

Frederich Karl Forberg, Engraving from *De Figuris veneris*. Roger Peyrefitte Collection.

François Rolland Elluin, Illustration for a work entitled *Le pot pourri de Loth* (1781). Private collection.

Anonymous, *The Hunter*. Austrian woodcut of the middle of the eighteenth century. Victoria and Albert Museum, London.

FROM ACT V, SCENE 2

(A grove of cypress trees, and others, cut in the shape of pricks,...)

(enter Flux, "man of Philosophy".)
(Bolloxinion asks him why he has been away from court so long. Flux answers that he has been "this ten days" endeavouring to cure "The tortured pains your nation does endure." A strange disease has broken out: "Men's pricks are eaten off, the secret parts/Of women withered..../The children harbor mournful discontents,/Complaining sorely of their fundaments." Furthermore, "The Queen is dead, and Pricket has a clap...." Bolloxinion asks: "Can no redress nor remedy be sought?")

FLUX
To Love and nature all their rights restore—
Fuck women and let buggery be no more.
(But Bolloxinion rejects this advice and declares: "...I'll reign and bugger still." The clouds break forth, then firey demons rise and sing).

DEMONS
Kiss, Rise up and Dally
Prig, Swive and rally;
Curse, Blaspheme and swear
Those that will witness bear.
For the Bollox singes
Sodom off the hinges,
Bugger, bugger, bugger
All in hugger-mugger,
Fire doth descend:
'Tis too late to amend.

(They vanish in smoke.
The Ghost of Cuntigratia rises.)

JOHANN JOACHIM WINCKELMANN (1717-1768)

"A lowly childhood, insufficient instruction in youth, broken, distracted studies in early manhood...." such, according to Goethe, were the beginnings of the great German scholar, archeologist and writer. In 1748 this self-taught genius became the librarian of Count Heinrich von Bünau in Nöthenitz, near Dresden. From then on, he devoted himself to studies of ancient art and culture, advocating a return to classicism. In 1754, he converted to Catholicism so as to be able to pursue his research in Rome. He lived near the painter Raphael Mengs, becoming his friend; then, he was appointed librarian to Cardinal Albani, a great connoisseur of antiquities. Next, he visited the ruins of Pompeii, and traveled to Greece where he contemplated organizing archeological excavations at Olympia. In 1764 he published his *History of Ancient Art,* which brought him world-wide renown.

Goethe, Schiller and many artists who embraced the ideals of neoclassicism were ardent admirers of Winckelmann. Walter Pater, the intellectual master of Oscar Wilde and George Moore, has observed that Winckelmann's attraction to Hellenism was not merely intellectual, which "is proved by his romantic, fervent friendships with young men. He has known... many young men more beautiful than Guido's archangel. These friendships, bringing him in contact with the pride of human form and staining his thoughts with its bloom, perfected his reconciliation with the spirit of Greek sculpture." But Winckelmann was drawn to ephebes, not to angels. While returning to Germany he became involved with a young convicted swindler ironically enough named Archangeli. He was unwise enough to show his collection of coins to this crook, whereupon Archangeli tried to strangle and rob him.

Winckelmann resisted vigorously and was stabbed five times. The fracas alerted the inn-keeper's son who came running: he found Winckelmann lying on the floor, dying. His assailant escaped, leaving the coins behind. Several months later he was arrested and executed.

The text is from a letter quoted by Walter Pater in his essay on Winckelmann in *The Renaissance.* The German scholar is writing to his beloved friend, Friederich von Berg, to whom he had dedicated his study *On the Capacity to Experience the Beautiful in Works of Art* (Dresden, 1763). Winckelmann believed that only those who are moved by the beauty of men can truly appreciate the art of Antiquity.

Guercino, *Et in Arcadia Ego* (detail). Galleria Nazionale d'Arte antica, Rome.

Saacha Alexander Schneider, *Roman Youth*. M. Manoukian Collection, Paris. This Russian painter taught at the School of Fine-Arts in Weimar. He belonged to the group of neoclassical artists who looked on Winckelmann as their master and precursor.

From A LETTER TO FRIEDERICH VON BERG

It is from you yourself that the subject is taken. Our intercourse has been short, too short both for you and me; but the first time I saw you, the affinity of our spirits was revealed to me. Your culture proved that my hope was not groundless; and I found in a beautiful body a soul created for nobleness, gifted with the sense of beauty. My parting from you was, therefore, one of the most painful in my life; and that this feeling continues our common friend is witness, for your separation from me leaves me no hope of seeing you again. Let this essay be a memorial of our friendship, which, on my side, is free from every selfish motive, and ever remains subject and dedicate to yourself alone....

As it is confessedly the beauty of man which is to be conceived under one general idea, so I have noticed that those who are observant of beauty only in women, and are moved little or not at all by the beauty of men, seldom have an impartial, vital, inborn instinct for beauty in art. To such persons the beauty of Greek art will ever seem wanting, because its supreme beauty is rather male than female. But the beauty of art demands a higher sensibility than the beauty of nature, because the beauty of art, like tears shed at a play, gives no pain, is without life, and must be awakened and repaired by culture. Now, as the spirit of culture is much more ardent in youth than in manhood, the instinct of which I am speaking must be exercised and directed to what is beautiful, before that age is reached, at which one would be afraid to confess that one had no taste for it.

VOLTAIRE (1694-1778)

In the *Philosophical Dictionary*, published in 1764 in Geneva, there is an article by Voltaire on "Socratic Love." The idea of compiling an encyclopedic dictionary had come to him during a dinner party in Potsdam. He wanted the work to be "portable,"—what we call a pocket book today. When it was published, the *Dictionary* caused such a flap that Voltaire hastily declared that he was not its author. Nevertheless in a letter to president Henault he admitted that he had in fact written half a dozen articles for it, including the one on Socratic love.

It has been said that, well before the rise of modern journalism, Voltaire was a reporter of genius: he had a flair for topicality, a passion for digging out and revealing the hidden details behind events. But, like many journalists past and present, he came to hasty conclusions at times; he had his prejudices and a strong penchant for controversy and sensationalism. Thus, in a note to the article on Socratic love he attacks a critic for "daring to quote from some musty old book in which Socrates is called *sanctus paederastus*, in other words Saint Bugger." Obviously Voltaire had passed judgement on the book without bothering to read further than its title, *Socrates sanctus paederasta* which, incidentally, he mistranslated. Gesner, the author of this work, a respectable professor from Gottingen, had actually tried to show that Socrates was the victim of slander since no great philosopher could possibly stoop to "infamous" practices.

In another note appended to the 1770 edition of the *Dictionary*, Voltaire referred to the burning of Deschauffours in 1726 for the crime of sodomy. The latter, a gentleman from Lorraine, had abducted boys and had sold them to the Marquis of Bellan and to the Baron of Belleflore, among others. At the request of the Prince of Torelly, who had a passion for castrated singers, Deschauffours had had a youth named Bizetti castrated; but the prince was disappointed in his expectations for, despite his mutilation, poor Bizetti had no gift for singing prettily. Naturally neither the marquis, the baron nor the prince were called before court. On the other hand, Jean-Baptiste Nattier, a member of the French Academy, a painter of historical scenes and the brother of the famous artist Jean-Marc Nattier, was implicated in the affair and was thrown into prison. He cut his throat in his cell after having noted in a copy of Montaigne's *Essays:* "Of the two evils, it is better to choose the lesser." Deschauffours was sentenced to be burned on the Place de Grève, "with the difference that he was strangled first," as Barbier noted in his *Journal* in April 1746.

Voltaire frequently attacked the judiciary for intolerance. In "The Price of Justice and Humanity" he wrote: "When not accompanied by violence, sodomy should not fall under the sway of criminal law, for it does not violate the right of any man." In 1810 the Napoleonic Code confirmed this opinion. (It is true that Cambacérès, who was one of the framers of the Code, was reputed to be a homosexual.)

Nothing definite is known about Voltaire's sexual behavior. To his mind physical love was one of the "trifles of life" and, at the age of twenty-five, he declared: "It seems that I am not made for passion." Be that as it may, his attitude towards homosexuality is perfectly clear: "It is a low and disgusting vice, the true punishment for which should be scorn." This did not prevent Voltaire, like a number of contemporary writers, from indulging in gay witticisms: thus, in 1732, he scribbled at the bottom of a letter to François de Moncrif, the secretary of the Comte of Clermont and the author of a ballet called *The Empire of Love:* "E vi baccio il catzo" [and I kiss your rod].

The texts we have selected include a letter from Voltaire to François de Moncrif (1733), several waggish lines of verse addressed to Frederick II, whose tendencies were no secret to Voltaire, and the article on Socratic love from the *Philosophical Dictionary*, with the note added in 1770.

Simeon Solomon, *Socrates and Agathodeamos*. Victoria and Albert Museum, London.

Caricature of the French jurist, Cambacérès—one of the authors of the Napoleonic Code. Private collection. One day Cambacérès said to Napoleon, "Excuse me, Sir, [for being late,] I was with a lady." The Emperor replied: "Next time, tell her, 'take your hat and your cane and leave me.'"

PHILOSOPHICAL DICTIONARY, "SOCRATIC LOVE"

How could it be that a vice, which if general, would extinguish the human species, an infamous crime against nature, should become so natural? It appears to be the last degree of reflective corruption, and yet it is usually found in those who have not had time to be corrupted. It makes its way into novice hearts, who are strangers to ambition, fraud and a thirst after wealth; it is blind youth, which at the end of childhood, by an unaccountable instinct, plunges itself into this enormity.

The inclination of the two sexes for each other declares itself very early; but after all that has been said of the African women, and those of the southern part of Asia, this propensity is much stronger in man than in woman. Agreeably to the universal law of nature in all creatures, it is ever the male who makes the first advances.

The young males of our species brought up together, coming to feel that play which nature begins to unfold to them, in the want of the natural object of their instinct, betake themselves to a resemblance of such objects. It is nothing uncommon for a boy by the beauty of his complexion and the mild sparkle of his eyes, for two or three years, to have the look of a pretty girl: now the love of such a boy arises from a mistake in nature; the female sex is honoured in our fondness for what partakes of her beauties, and when such resemblance is withered by age, the mistake is at an end.

> Citraque juventum
> Aetatis breve ver et primos carpere flores.
> [Ovid]

This mistake in nature is known to be much more common in mild climates than amidst the northern frosts, the blood being there more fervid and the occasion more frequent; accordingly, what seems only a weakness in young Alcibiades, is in a Dutch sailor or a Russian sutler, a loathsome abomination.

I cannot bear that the Greeks should be charged with having authorized this licentiousness. The legislator Solon is brought in because he has said,

> Thou shalt caress a beauteous boy,
> Whilst no beard his smooth chin deforms.

But who will say that Solon was a legislator at the time of his making those two ridiculous lines? He was then young, and when the rake was grown virtuous, it cannot be thought that he inserted such an infamy among the laws of his republic: it is like accusing Theodore de Beza of having preached pederasty in his church, because, in his youth, he had made verses on young Candidus, and says:

> Amplector hunc et illam.

Plutarch likewise is misunderstood, who, among his rants in the *Dialogue on Love,* makes one of the speakers say, that women are not worthy of a genuine love; but another speaker keenly takes the women's part.

It is as certain, as the knowledge of antiquity can be, that Socratic love was not an infamous passion. It is the word *love* has occasioned the mistake. The *lovers of a youth* were exactly what among us are the minions of our princes, or, formerly the pages of honour; young gentlemen who had partaken of the education of a child of rank, and accompanied him in his studies or in the field: this was a martial and holy institution, but it was soon abused, as were the nocturnal feasts and orgies.

The troops of lovers instituted by Laîus, was an invincible corps of young warriors engaged by oath, mutually to lay down their lives for one another; and perhaps, never had ancient discipline anything more grand and useful.

Sextus Empiricus and others may talk as long as they please of pederasty being recommended by the laws of Persia. Let them quote the text of the law, and even show the Persian code, yet will I not believe it; I will say it is not true, by reason of its being impossible. I do aver that it is not in human nature to make a law contradictory and injurious to nature; a law which, if literally kept to, would put an end to the human species. The thing is, scandalous customs being connived at, are often mistaken for the laws of a country. Sextus Empiricus, doubting of everything, might as well doubt of this jurisprudence. If living in our days he had seen two or three young Jesuits

La petite loge ou l'archifou.

fondling some scholars, could he from thence say that this sport was permitted them by the constitutions of Ignatius of Loyola?

The love of boys was so common at Rome, that no punishment was thought of for a foolery into which everybody ran headlong. Octavius Augustus, that sensualist, that cowardly murderer, dared to banish Ovid, at the same time that he was very well pleased with Virgil's singing the beauty and flights of Alexis, and Horace's making little odes for Ligurinus. Still the old Scantinian law against pederasty was in force: the Emperor Philip revived it and caused the boys who followed that trade to be driven out of Rome. In a word, I cannot think that ever there was a policed nation, where the laws were contrary to morality.*

(Footnote added in 1769)

*One should oblige ... to present themselves to the police once a year with a child of their own making. Because he had taken liberties with some boys from Savoy who were sweeping his chimney, Father Desfontaines was almost roasted on the Place de Grève; he was saved by protectors. A victim was required, however: Deschauffours was roasted instead. That is going too far; *est modus in rebus:* the sentence must be proportional to the offense; what would Caesar, Alcibiades, Nicomedes the King of Bythnia, Henry III of France, and so many other monarchs have said?

Deschauffours was burned at the stake on the authority of the Establishments of Saint Louis, written down in fifteenth-century French. "If anyone be suspected of ... he must be brought before the bishop; and if it be proven, he must be burned, and his chattel turned over to the baron, etc." But Saint Louis does not say what must be done to the baron if the baron be suspected of ... and *if it be proven.* It should be noted that by the word ... Saint Louis meant heretics, who were called by no other name in those times. Thus, an ambiguity caused Deschauffours, a gentleman from Lorraine, to be burned. Despréaux was indeed right to compose a satire against this ambiguity; it has resulted in more ill than can be imagined.

LETTER TO MONSIEUR FRANÇOIS DE MONCRIF

Will the author of *The Empire of Love* come to dine tomorrow, about two o'clock, in the empire of the hypochondriacs, at his sick friend's, opposite Saint-Gervais, in the rue du Long-Pont? Has he been so good as to mention the matter to his hefty gal of a wife, the Chevalier de Brassac? And if he can find that waster, La Clède, would he please bring him along too; or write if there is no hope, and the invalid is to dine without their company?

Has he had the kindness to sound out His Most Serene Highness about *Adelaïde*? I want to make a chesty effort for your prince. Adieu; I love you with all my heart, and quite effortlessly.

Hermaphrodite, Drawn after Nature by the Most Illustrious Artists and Meticulously Engraved for the Instruction of Students, attributed to Jean Michel Moreau, the Younger. c. 1772. Roger Peyrefitte Collection.

Nicolas Poussin, *The Triumph of Pan* (detail). Louvre, Paris.

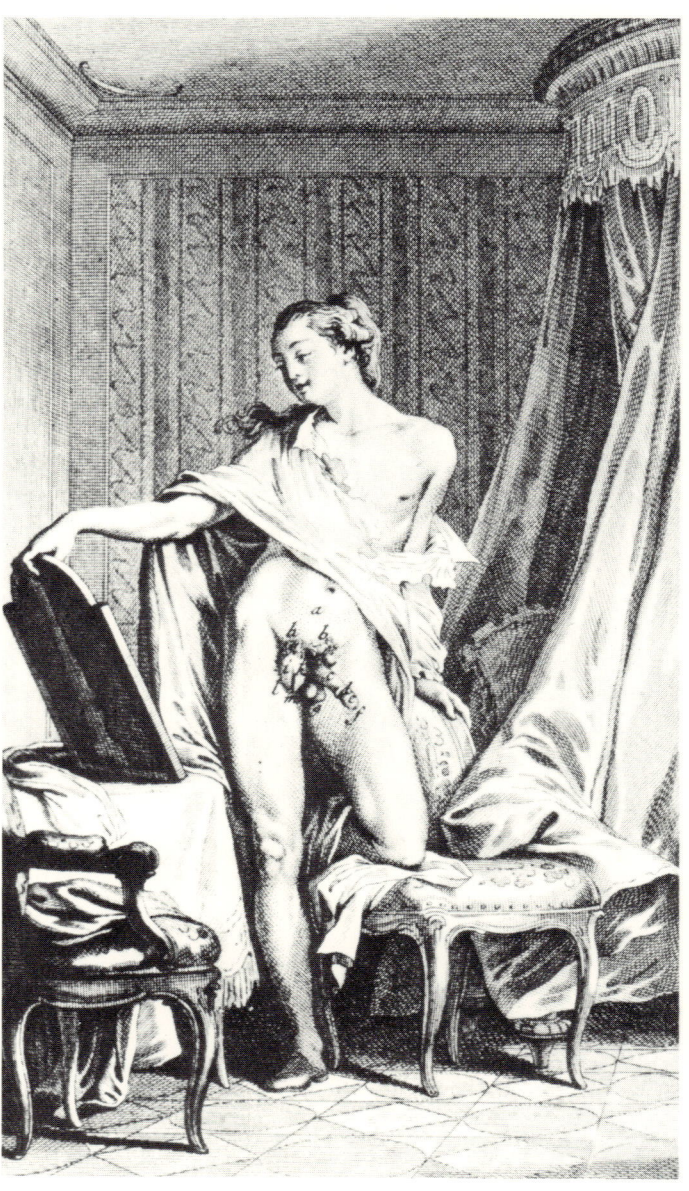

VOLTAIRE TO THE KING OF PRUSSIA,

It pleaseth me to think on Caesar
Lodg'd between his lady's arms, or knees.
The delight's as keen, you'll agree, Sir,
To recall him, young and sleeker,
Beneath or on top of Nicomedes....

(June 15, 1743)

JEAN-JACQUES ROUSSEAU
(1712-1778)

In writing his *Confessions* (between 1765 and 1770) Rousseau wanted to unearth the "secret concatenations of affection" in his youth. He stipulated that his book was not to be published until after his death; during his lifetime, however, he read passages from it to close friends. Embarrassed by the painful sincerity and the indelicacy of the narrative, the latter kept a stony silence. Embittered, Rousseau later wrote in his *Rêveries d'un promeneur solitaire:* "I am alone on the earth. The most sociable and loving of human beings has been proscribed by common consent."

In the excerpts from the *Confessions* given here, Rousseau tells how, on two occasions in his youth he rejected homosexual advances. The first time, he was in a catechumenical school preparing to receive Catholic baptism. His classmates were "horrible ruffians who seemed more like troopers of the devil than aspiring children of God." These scoundrels, who passed themselves off as Jews or Moors, would spend their lives wandering through Spain, Italy and France stopping off to have themselves baptized in homes for catechumens in order to pocket the small sum of money which the friars gave them before sending them out into the world.

The second time, Rousseau was propositioned by a priest.

From THE CONFESSIONS

During the course of these petty controversies, and whilst day after day was being wasted in arguments and idling and muttering of prayers, I had a very unpleasant little experience, which very nearly had unfortunate results for me.

There is no soul so vile, no heart so barbarous as to be insusceptible to some sort of affection, and one of the two cut-throats who called themselves Moors took a fancy to me. He was fond of coming up to me and gossiping with me in his queer jargon. He did me little services, sometimes giving me some of his food at table, and he frequently kissed me with an ardour which I found most displeasing. But, frightened though I naturally was by his dusky face, which was beautified by a long scar, and by his passionate glances, which seemed to me more savage than affectionate, I put up with his kisses, saying to myself, "The poor man has conceived a warm friendship for me; it would be wrong to repulse him." But he passed by degrees to more unseemly conduct, and sometimes made me such strange suggestions that I thought he was wrong in the head. One night he wanted to share my bed, but I objected on the plea that it was too narrow. He then

137

pressed me to come into his. I still refused, however, for the poor devil was so dirty and smelt so strongly of the tobacco he chewed that he made me feel ill.

Next day, very early in the morning, we were alone together in the assembly-hall. He resumed his caresses, but with such violence that I was frightened. Finally he tried to work up to the most revolting liberties and, by guiding my hand, to make me take the same liberties with him. I broke wildly away with a cry and leaped backwards, but without displaying indignation or anger, for I had not the slightest idea what it was all about. But I showed my surprise and disgust to such effect that he then left me alone. But as he gave up the struggle I saw something whitish and sticky shoot towards the fireplace and fall on the ground. My stomach turned over, and I rushed on to the balcony, more upset, more troubled and more frightened as well, than ever I had been in my life. I was almost sick.

I could not undestand what was the matter with the poor man. I thought he was having a fit of epilepsy or some other seizure even more terrible. And really I know of no more hideous sight for a man in cold blood than such foul and obscene behaviour, nothing more revolting than a terrifying face on fire with the most brutal lust. I have never seen another man in that state; but if we appear like that to women, they must indeed be fascinated not to find us repulsive.

I could think of nothing better than to go and inform everybody of what had just happened. Our old woman attendant told me to hold my tongue. But I saw that my story had much upset her, for I heard her mutter under her breath: *Can maledet! brutta bestia!** As I could see no reason for holding my tongue, I took no notice of her but went on talking. I talked so much in fact that next day one of the principals came very early and read me a sharp lecture, accusing me of impugning the honour of a sacred establishment and making a lot of fuss about nothing.

In addition to this rebuke he explained to me a number of things I did not know, but which he did not suspect he was telling me for the first time. For he believed that I had known what the man wanted when I defended myself, but had merely been unwilling. He told me gravely that it was a forbidden and immoral act like fornication, but that the desire for it was not an affront to the person who was its object. There was nothing to get so annoyed about in having been found attractive. He told me quite openly that in his youth he had been similarly honoured and, having been surprised in a situation where he could put up no resistance, he had found nothing so brutal about it all. He carried his effrontery so far as to employ frank terminology and, imagining that the reason for my refusal had been fear of pain, assured me that my apprehensions were groundless. There was no reason to be alarmed about nothing.

I listened to the wretch with redoubled astonishment, since he was not speaking for himself but apparently to instruct me for my own good. The whole matter seemed so simple to him that he had not even sought privacy for our conversation. There was an ecclesiastic listening all the while who found the matter no more alarming than he. This natural behaviour so impressed me that I finally believed such things were no doubt general practice in the world, though I had so far not had occasion to learn of them. So I listened without anger though not without disgust. The memory of my experience, and especially of what I had seen, remained so firmly imprinted on my mind that my stomach still rose when I thought of it. Unconsciously my dislike for the business extended to the apologist, and I could not sufficiently control myself for him not to see the ill effect of his lesson. He shot me a far from affectionate glance, and from that time on spared no pains to make my stay at the hospice unpleasant. So well did he succeed that, seeing only one way of escape, I made the same impassioned efforts to take it as hitherto I had taken to avoid it.

This adventure put me on my guard for the future against the attentions of pederasts.

(Book Two, 1728-1731)

*Cursed dog! foul beast!

Engraving from an anonymous French eighteenth-century work entitled *La Masturbomanie* (c. 1829) published by "*Branlefort, chez Poignet, rue du Bac.*" [Jerkin, at Wrist's, Bac Street]. Roger Peyrefitte Collection. The author places himself under the aegis of Socrates, Diogenes, Mirabeau, Parny and Jean-Jacques Rousseau.

Le Masturbomane.

Jean Restout, the Younger, *Study of Two Men* (detail). Nationalmuseum, Stockholm.

From THE CONFESSIONS

I think I have a fairly clear view of the sequence of events which I have described in this book. Yet I seem to recollect another Lyons journey, during this same period, which I cannot place, and during which I found myself in dire straits. One little anecdote, rather difficult to relate, will prevent my ever forgetting it. I was sitting one evening in Bellecour after a very poor supper, wondering how to get out of my trouble when a man in a cap came and sat down beside me. He had the appearance of one of those silk weavers who are called taffeta men in Lyons. He spoke to me, and I replied. We had talked a bare quarter of an hour when, with the same coolness and no change in his tone, he suggested that we should have some fun together. I waited for him to explain what this fun was to be, but without another word he made ready to give me a practical illustration. We were almost touching, and the night was not so dark as to prevent my seeing what practice he was preparing for. He had no designs on my person; at least nothing suggested that intention, and the situation would have been against it. All that he wanted, as he had said, was to have his fun and for me to have mine, each on his own account; and this seemed to him so natural that it had not even occurred to him that it might not seem the same to me. I was so alarmed at his beastliness that I did not reply, but got up precipitately and ran off as fast as I could go, imagining that the wretch was at my heels. So concerned was I that instead of making for my lodgings down the Rue Saint-Dominique, I ran in the direction of the river-bank, and did not stop till I was over the wooden bridge, trembling as if I had just committed a crime. I was addicted to the vice myself, but the memory of this incident cured me of it for some time.

On that very journey I had an adventure of almost the same kind, but one which exposed me to greater danger. Conscious that my funds were nearly exhausted, I husbanded the miserable sum that still remained. I took meals less often at my inn, and soon I took none there at all, being able to satisfy myself as well for five or six *sous* at a tavern as I did there for my twenty-five. As I no longer dined in the place, I did not feel justified in sleeping there, not that I owed very much to my landlady, but I was ashamed to occupy a room and allow her to make no profit. The weather was fine, and one evening when it was very hot I decided to sleep out in the public square. I had already settled down on a bench when a priest, who was passing and saw me lying there, came over and asked me if I had nowhere to stay. I confessed my plight, and he

139

seemed touched by it. He sat down beside me, and we talked. His conversation was pleasant, and from what he said I conceived the highest possible opinion of him. When he saw that he had put me at my ease he remarked that he had no vast lodging, in fact only a single room, but that he certainly would not leave me to sleep there in the public square. It was too late now, he said, for me to find a bed, but he offered me, for that night, the half of his. I accepted his proposal, for I had already hopes that I had made a friend who might be useful to me. We set off. He struck a light. His room seemed to me clean, though very small, and he did me the honours most courteously. He took some cherries steeped in brandy out of a glass jar, and we ate two each before going to bed.

This man had the same vice as my Jew at the hospice, but he did not display it so brutally. It may have been because he knew that I should be heard and was therefore afraid to force me to defend myself; it may have been that he was really less determined in his designs; but whatever the reason, he did not venture to propose what he wanted openly but tried to excite me without alarming me. Less ignorant than on the previous occasion, I quickly realized his purpose, and shuddered. Not knowing in what sort of house or in whose hands I was, I was afraid that if I made a noise I might pay for it with my life. I pretended not to know what he wanted, but by showing that I much disliked his attentions and was determined to put up with no more of them, I succeeded in compelling him to control himself. Then I spoke to him as mildly and firmly as I was able; and without showing him that I suspected anything, excused my display of alarm by recounting my former adventure in language that deliberately betrayed my disgust and horror, so much so that I think he felt nauseated himself. He certainly abandoned his filthy designs entirely, and we spent the rest of the night in peace. He even gave me some good and sensible advice, for he certainly was not a man without intelligence, though he was a wicked one.

In the morning, not wishing to appear put out, the priest spoke of breakfast, and asked one of his landlady's daughters, who was a pretty girl, to send some to him. She answered that she had no time. Then he turned to her sister, who did not vouchsafe him a reply. We continued to wait; no breakfast came. Finally we went into the young ladies' room. They received him with very little cordiality, and I had even less reason to congratulate myself on my reception. The elder, turning round, stepped on my toe with her pointed heel, on a spot where a painful corn had compelled me to cut a hole in my shoe; and her sister quickly pulled a chair from under me just as I was about to take a seat; while their mother splashed my face as she threw some water out of the window. Wherever I sat down they made me move so that they could look for something; never in my life had I been entertained like that. In their insulting and mocking looks, I could see a smothered fury, but I was so stupid as not in the least to understand the reason. Astounded, stupefied, and ready to believe that they were all possessed, I was beginning to get thoroughly frightened when the priest, who pretended neither to see nor hear anything, realized that there was no prospect of breakfast, and decided to leave the house. I hastened to follow him, very glad to escape from those three furies. On our walk he proposed that we should go and breakfast at a café. Although I was extremely hungry I did not accept his offer, nor did he press me very hard to do so, and we parted company at the third or fourth turning. I was delighted to see the last of everything connected with that accursed house, and he was just as glad, I believe, to have brought me so far from it that it would not be easy for me to find it again.

(Book Four, 1732)

Engraving from *La Masturbomanie* (See caption p. 138). Roger Peyrefitte Collection.

COUNT GIUSEPPE GORANI (1740-1819)

Count Gorani was born in Milan in 1744 and died in Geneva in 1819. As a writer on public affairs he was affiliated with the *Societé du Café* [the "Coffee Society"], which sponsored philosophical and political studies. This organization was supported by the French encyclopedists. Gorani was first noticed for his *Treatise on Despotism,* anonymously published in 1770. In 1792 he fraternized with the revolutionaries, and as a consequence his property was confiscated. After the fall of Robespierre, he moved to Geneva. His *Secret and Critical Memoirs of the Courts, Governments and Customs of the Principal Italian States* was printed in Paris in 1793. In this opus Gorani tells of his amazement at seeing a stunning castrato receive gifts and tributes from male admirers, including noblemen and aging prelates. The castrati, who were as much appreciated by women as they were by men, were operated before puberty in order to preserve their effeminate looks, their smooth skin and above all their high-pitched voice. They generally came from poor families; some of them made brilliant careers, like Gaetano Majorano, otherwise called Cafarelli, the son of an indigent peasant, who met triumphant success whenever he performed in Rome, and even in Paris and in London, and who became so wealthy towards the end of his life that he bought the duchy of San Donato. There was also his contemporary, Farinelli, the favorite of the king of Spain for a quarter of a century. King Philip V, who was stricken with a nervous illness, could not spend a day without hearing him sing.

In the eighteenth century, in the state of the Vatican alone, around 2000 children were castrated each year; but by the beginning of the next century, the Italians began to feel ashamed of this practice, and it declined. Nevertheless there were still some famous castrati like Cressentini who made Napoleon weep when he sang the part of Juliet, or Pacchierotti with whom Beckford fell desperately in love (see p. 150). In 1809, in the journal of his voyages in Italy, Burney claimed that there were no fewer than sixteen castrated pupils at the Naples conservatory. He mentions among others a lad called Grassetto who had submitted to mutilation of his own accord and against the advice of his friends so as not to lose his voice, which was particularly beautiful. "He is a charming singer in other respects too," adds Burney somewhat ambiguously. The last of the great castrati was Velluti who died in 1861.

Corrado Giaquinto, *Portrait of* [the Famous Castrato] *Farinelli* (detail), Museo Civico Bibliografico Musicale, Bologna.

Aubrey Beardsley, *The Priest*. Illustration for his unfinished novel, *Under the Hill* (1896), in *Savoy*, vol. 1, London.

From THE SECRET MEMOIRS
I. "THE SURPRISE"

It is common knowledge that in Rome, the cradle of the Christian religion, the theatres are packed with clerics of every order. Nor is it any secret that even the most elevated spectacles are mixed with wanton dances, and that it is the most suggestive gestures which receive the most acclaim. Wanting to distinguish itself from the secular states by an outward show of modesty, the theocratic government has retained the practice, rightly discarded by the courts of Europe, of having boys play the female parts. It has even become law, and this law is all the more respected since the Romans prefer striplings to even the most consummate actresses skilled in the art of evoking passions. I have witnessed the delirious raptures, as these lads appeared on stage, of cardinals and solemn prelates whose stern countenances had struck me but a few moments earlier. I have heard, as I had heard in Paris, but related even more shamelessly than in that capital, anecdotes and scandalous stories about the darlings of the stage, only here they were boys; in a few hours, I had learned the names of their favorite lovers, of those who aspired to their favors, and finally of those who bought them, to satisfy their vanity and their inclination. This penchant, openly recognized and acknowledged, is almost universal here. It is called the *noble sin,* the nice sin; and those who deny committing it, do so with such lack of conviction, that it appears they would be most annoyed indeed if one were to believe their protestations. These modern Antinoüses, like our backstage heroines, cause the ruin of many, for one may easily conceive that they are not overscrupulous when their own interest is concerned. The frequent and by no means hidden scandals in Rome might well refute Lucian's argument that the Greeks preferred this kind of love since boys are as yet too innocent to despoil their lovers, as do women, whose influence is the more dangerous.

Once a foreigner has acquired the trust of the Romans, they no longer restrain themselves in his presence and speak of this sort of intrigue with as much ardor, as much interest and as little reserve as the French have for their actresses. One may even visit the dressing rooms of these amphibious creatures, and it is there that one may observe how far the general corruption reaches.

I have been among the small number of the initiate; the dressing secrets of these idols have been revealed to me, but what caused me a surprise near to astonishment was to see a lady busying herself with great earnestness at dressing a young castrato she idolized. This lad was the second singer of the theatre of la Volle. Though she cherished him in the Italian manner (need I say more?), she did nothing to prevent him from receiving the tributes of a throng of worshipers who surrounded him. The singer was to play the part of a woman, and indeed it seemed that nature, in shaping him, had destined him for that very occupation. His beauty, his charms, the quality of his voice, all contributed to his glamour. Seated before a magnificent dressing table, he simpered, smiled and, now and again, would let fall a few graceful sounds which were instantly gathered up by his lovers. All those who were present, and among whom I saw the most respected prelates, whose excellent reputations were in utter contradiction with their present occupation, were striving, through a thousand attentions, to attract one of his glances. One offered him a flower, another a diamond, still others handed him different articles of the costume of the sex he was going to portray. Among these worshipers were two men of forty years, and their offerings were by no means the smallest; for you must know that the dazzling accoutrements cost not a penny to the mistress of the house or to her young Antinoüs.

I attended, I watched, I listened, I heard, and still I thought I was immersed in one of those hallucinations produced by a disordered imagination. The attentions which those mitred idiots sought to render unto that young Ganymede were accompanied by such a show of respect as you see in church valets when they are dressing a prelate. Each attempted to outshine his rivals, to deserve, or to steal, a look, and those who succeeded could hardly contain their pride. As for the young man, the most artful coquette would not have borne herself more cunningly.

At last, I left and confided my amazement to two friends who had long been living in Rome. They laughed, and assured me that such practices were common, and that the castrati vied for the adoration of the connoisseurs with other youths whose looks and talents had got them a place in the theatre, though they had not undergone the Conservatory's operation.

DONATIEN ALPHONSE FRANÇOIS, MARQUIS DE SADE (1740-1814)

Thirty years in prison for "flagrant debauchery", "cruelty" and "sodomy" gave the Marquis de Sade time to write a staggering number of works, most of which have unfortunately been destroyed. "Men were created by Nature to amuse themselves with everything on earth," the marquis would say, adding, "too bad for the victims, they are necessary." In the circumstances the victim was perhaps Sade himself. He was thrown in jail the first time for having caned a beggar woman to whom he had offered the fabulous sum of 24,000 francs for lending herself to this pleasure. The second time, he was sentenced for having organized a debauchery during which he had fed prostitutes pills of Spanish fly (an aphrodisiac said to have been invented by the Duke of Richelieu) and had then buggered them. It seems that Sade was not a homosexual so much as a fanatical sodomite. "What I would like in my bedroom," he liked to say, "is a beautiful creature in the position of the Farnese Venus." This dream was never fulfilled, and the marquis ended his days in Charenton gaol.

A number of twentieth-century authors—Apollinaire, Breton, Bataille, Vailland, Klossovski—have been fascinated by Sade. To Jean Paulhan, the marquis's works suggested "hair-raising primitive rites" and were like "the sacred books of the great religions." Michel Foucault, on the contrary, has protested against the Sade cult: "Sade bores us," he declared in a recent interview, "he is a disciplinarian, a drill sergeant of sex, a bookkeeper of arses and their equivalents."

The 120 Days of Sodom was completed on October 22, 1785. Sade had carefully written it out on a slender roll of paper made by gluing separate pages end to end. The hero, Duclos, has acquired a robust wench of twenty-five, named Justine; but his guest on the day the following excerpt is taken from prefers to be whipped by a male servant.

"As far as words are concerned, as far as girls are concerned, as far as things are concerned, Sade's universe is a universe whose skirts have been lifted up," comments Alain Robbe-Grillet.

From THE 120 DAYS OF SODOM

This extraordinary man would have nothing of the feminine but womanish dress: the wearer of the costume had to be a man; in other words, the roué wanted to be spanked by a man got up as a girl. And what was the instrument she had to use on him! don't think for a moment he was content with a birch ferule or even a cat, no, he demanded a bundle of osier switches wherewith very barbarously one had to tear his buttocks. Actually, this particular affair seeming to have somewhat the flavor of sodomy, I felt I ought not become too deeply involved in it; but as he was one of Fournier's former and most reliable clients, a man who had been truly attached to our house in fair weather and in foul, and who, furthermore, might, thanks to his position, be able to render us some service, I raised no objections and having prettily disguised a young lad of eighteen who sometimes availed us of his services and who had a very attractive face, I presented him, armed with a handful of switches, to his opponent. And a very entertaining contest it was—you may well imagine how eager I was to observe it. He began with a careful study of his pretended maiden, and having found him, evidently, much to his liking, he opened with five or six kisses on the youth's mouth: those kisses would have looked peculiar from three miles away; next, he exhibited his cheeks, and in all his behaviour and words seeming to take the young man for a girl, he told him to fondle his buttocks and knead them just a little vigorously; the lad, whom I had told exactly what to expect, did everything asked of him.

"Well, let's be off," said the bawd, "ply those switches, spare not to strike hard." The youth catches up the bundle of switches and therewith, swinging right

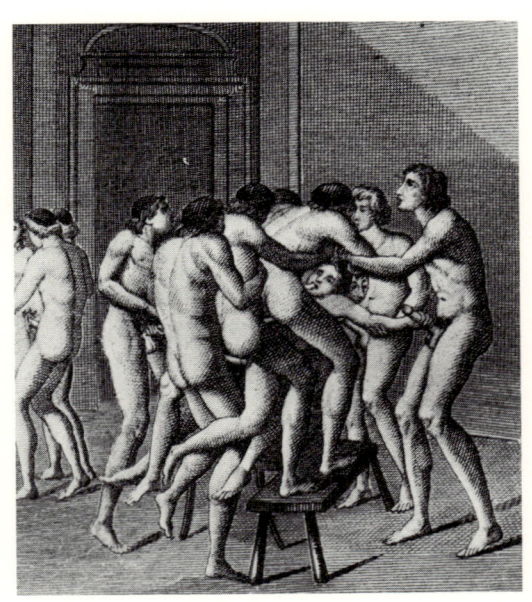

Illustrations from the first edition of the Marquis de Sade's *La nouvelle Justine ou les infortunes de la vertu, suivie de l'histoire de Juliette sa sœur* (1797). Private collection. These illustrations were made according to the author's instructions.

merrily, lays fifty slashing blows upon a pair of buttocks which seem only to thirst for more; already definitely marked by those two score and ten stripes, the libertine hurls himself upon his masculine flagellatrice, draws up her petticoats, one hand verifies her sex, the other fervently clutches her buttocks. He knows not which altar to bow down before first, the ass finally captures his primary attentions, he glues his mouth to its hole, much ardor in his expression. Ah, what a difference between the worship Nature is said to prescribe and that other which is said to outrage her! O God of certain justice, were this truly an outrage, would the homage be paid with such great emotion? Never was woman's ass kissed as was that lad's; three or four times over his lover's tongue entirely disappeared into the anus; returning to his former position at last, "O dear child," cried he, "resume your operation." Further flagellation ensued, but as it was livelier, the patient met this new assault with far more courage and intrepidity. Blood makes its appearance, another stroke brings his prick bounding up, and he engages the young object of his transports to fist it without an instant's delay. While the latter manipulates him, he wishes to render the youth the same service, lifts up the boy's skirts again, but it's a prick he's now gone in quest of; he touches it, grasps, shakes, pulls it and soon introduces it into his mouth. After these initial caresses, he calls for a third round of blows and receives a storm of them. This latest experience puts him in a perfect tumult; he flings his Adonis upon the bed, lies down upon him, simultaneously toys with his own prick and his companion's, then presses one upon the other, glues his lips to the boy's mouth and having succeeded in warming him by means of these caresses, he procures him the divine pleasure at the same moment he is overwhelmed himself: and now both discharge in harmony. Enchanted by the scene, our libertine sought to placate my risen indignation and at last coaxed a promise from me to arrange for further delights of the same kind, both with that young fellow and with any others I could find for him. I attempted to work at his conversion, I assured him I had charming girls about who would be happy to flog him and who could do so quite as well; no, said he, he would not so much as look at what I had to offer him.

"Oh, I can readily believe it," said the Bishop. "When one has a pronounced and decided taste for men, there's no changing; the difference between boy and girl is so extreme that one's not apt to be tempted to try what is patently inferior."

"Monsignor," said the Président, "you have broached a thesis which merits a two-hour dissertation."

"And which will always conclude by giving further support to my assertion," said the Bishop, "because the fact that a boy is superior to a girl is beyond doubt or contention."

(from the 18th Day)

JOHANN WOLFGANG VON GOETHE (1749-1832)

In his youthful *Letters from Switzerland*, Goethe gives a beautiful description of the sexual indeterminacy (from which adult homosexuality often springs) of pubescent boys. He tells how he was stirred by the sight of his friend Ferdinand's naked body. In *Faust: Part Two,* as the angels come to bear away the immortal part of Faust in a shower of rose petals, Mephistopheles is overcome with lust for those pretty, boyish creatures. It has been said that there was as much of Mephistopheles in Goethe as there was of Faust.

From LETTERS FROM SWITZERLAND (1775)

I sought occasion and got Ferdinand to take a swim in the lake. What a glorious shape has my friend; how duly proportioned are all his limbs: what fulness of form; what splendour of youth! What a gain to have enriched my imagination with this perfect model of manhood! Now I can people the woods, the meadow, and the hills, with similar fine forms! I can see him as Adonis chasing the boar, or as Narcissus contemplating himself in the mirror of the spring.

But alas! my imagination cannot furnish, as yet, a Venus, who holds him from the chace, a Venus who bewails his death, or a beautiful Echo casting one sad look more on the cold corpse of the youth before she vanishes for ever! I have therefore resolved, cost what it will, to see a female form in the state that I have seen my friend.

From FAUST: PART TWO

MEPHISTOPHELES: (...) Comes something strange to pierce me, and engender
This joy in looking on their youthful splendour?
What weighs upon me, that I cannot curse?...

ANGELS. We come, and yet you shrink as we advance?
Lo, we approach, and, if you can, then stay.

(The Angels hovering assemble, until the whole space is filled with their company.)
MEPHISTOPHELES (who is crowded into the proscenium).
Us spirits you call damned, and look askance.
Witch-masters, you, par excellence;
For man and maid you lead astray.—
What an adventure curst and dire!

Louis Boulogne, the Younger, *Studies of Angels* (details). Cabinet des Dessins, Louvre, Paris.

Pierre Puvis de Chavannes, *The Little Fisherman*. Roy Miles Collection, London.

Is this love's elemental game?
All of my body is on fire,
My neck can hardly feel a spurt of flame.—
You hover to and fro; but, pray you, settle:
A shade more earthly tame your limbs' high mettle;
Indeed it suits you well, this serious style,
But just for once I'd like to see you smile,
Something my hope of lasting joy to raise,
I mean the sort that lives in lovers' gaze:
A dimpling of the mouth and it is done.
With you, tall youth, I'd choose in love to fall,
This parson-visage suits you not at all,
Then give a wanton loving look, just one.
You could with decency appear more nude,
The surplice vaunts too much the acolyte—
And now they turn, and from behind are viewed—
Ah, how the rascals stir the appetite!....
        (pulling himself together)
How is't with me?—Like Job, the man seen whole,
With boil on boil, and sick of his own soul,
His triumph, clear view of himself to win,
When trusting in himself and in his kin;
Saved are the devil's limbs by his control,
The love-spell cannot pierce beneath his skin;
The cursed flames already are burnt out,
And I, as is your due, curse you and all your rout.

CHORUS OF ANGELS.
Over whom, most holy fire,
You have swayed and stood,
Henceforth will his life aspire
In bliss with the good.
Joined in maturity,
Rise and extol.
Ether wins purity,
Breathes now the soul.
    (They rise up, bearing away with them the
        immortal part of Faust.)

MEPHISTOPHELES (looking around him).
What may this be? And whither are they gone?
You innocents now fool me and outbrave,
And with your booty heavenwards are flown;
For this you picked and nibbled at the grave!
Filched from me is this lofty prize unmatched,
A soul pledged mine, by written scroll it gave,
This have they robbed from me, adroitly snatched.
  To whom then shall I carry my complaint?
Who will restore to me my well-earned right?
Fooled in old age are you, by fraud and feint,
And have deserved it: yours a wretched plight.
This thing have I most woefully mishandled,
And wrecked a deep-laid scheme in shameful sort,
Absurd amours, in gloating fancy dandled,
Have had the weathered devil for their sport.
And if to such a mad and puerile playing
The shrewd old master devil can descend,
No trifling folly this, beyond gainsaying,
That mastered him and beat him in the end.

WILLIAM BECKFORD, COLLECTOR AND WRITER (1760-1844)

Born in 1760, William Beckford, "England's wealthiest son," as Byron called him, lived on the borderline between two worlds: the free, well-educated and incredibly affluent aristocracy of the English countryside, and the rising industrial—and sternly moral—bourgeoisie of the eighteenth century. Through his mother, the daughter of George Hamilton and the granddaughter of the sixth Earl of Aberson, he was descended from the Stuarts. His father, twice lord mayor of London, belonged to a family of merchants from the colonies, who were rich—they owned huge sugar cane plantations in Jamaica—but still too close to the buccanners for respectability. He died shortly after his son's birth.

Very early, little William's remarkable intelligence impressed his household. At the age of five, he learned to play the harpsichord from eight year old Mozart (The tune of "Non più andrai" in *The Marriage of Figaro* is said to have been Beckford's inspiration). William Chambers, who introduced the Chinese style to England, tutored him in architecture. Alexander Cozens taught him painting. (This curious personage, who painted, was a stage designer and a writer, claimed to be the illegitimate son of Peter the Great and an Englishwoman.) A fanatic of necromancy, he instilled a taste for magic, the occult and the mysteries of the Orient in the boy; he even encouraged him to take up Arabic. "How could I ever have imagined someone like you, so utterly suffused by the same rays that penetrate me? It is strange, it is passing strange that so perfect an agreement can exist," gushed the young disciple to his master, whose letters he religiously stashed away in a "drawer lined with aetherial blue."

George Romney, *Portrait of William Beckford* (detail). Bearstedt Collection, Upton House, National Trust, England.

Schnorr von Carolsfeld, *The Trumpet Player*. Hamburger Kunsthalle, Hamburg.

His family tutor, the Reverand Lettice, worried about this morbid influence. He convinced William's mother to send the boy to stay with his uncle, Colonel Hamilton, who lived in Geneva (1777). But the invigorating Swiss climate does not seem to have cured the young traveler of his melancholy ruminations. Back in Fonthill, the neo-classical mansion inherited from his father, he set out with his mother to make the rounds of the great estates. After all, he had to learn how to manage his own immense properties, and it was time that he became an accomplished gentleman. In Somerset, Gloucestershire, Yorkshire, the Lake District, everywhere he was warmly welcomed. It was at the castle of Powderham, in Devonshire, that he first encountered love in the person of another William, who was eight years his junior: William Courtenay. The latter was the only male offspring of the earls of Avon, and was descended from a long line of Courtenays whose branches in England, Scotland and France went back to three Emperors of Constantinople. Young Courtenay had been raised in the midst of a flock of sisters, whose frivolous pastimes he shared. The painter Romney has depicted him as a pretty, languid-looking lad, his dreamy brow framed by ringlets, standing slender-bodied with a graceful sway to his hips. Beckford, by then a budding young man of nineteen, was drawn to this child as Narcissus was drawn to his own reflection. In one of his letters he described the feelings which Courtenay inspired in him at their very first meeting: that night he dreamed that an "angelic Spirit" brought him the lad by the hand and whispered to him:

> Rest happy ... no one shall disturb you for ages. The great power—source of all felicity—has abstracted you from both the multitude of his creatures—as examples of perpetual tenderness—and has alloted this cave—sunk deep in the center of the Earth, for your abode. Those piles of nuts are destined for your nourishment if ye freely renounce the lustre of the Sun for each other. Our transports proved how entirely we consented. The shadow vanished—all was still and silent—the form of my C(ourtney) alone was luminous—his voice—the only sound—which echoed throughout the cavern....

Deeply in love by the time he left Powderham, Beckford did not even bother hiding his feelings. He proclaimed his satisfaction "at finally loving someone other than myself." He wrote to Courtenay from Fonthill, "what a miserable thing that I cannot set eyes on you every day, nay every hour, for you are the only being to whom I can disclose the strange, mad passion that pounds in my heart... that dear shape which ever comes to haunt me at sunset. Ah, Great Power, which created us both, how rapidly our affection for each other has prospered! Surely we must have been inseparable friends in some other life, otherwise how could this sudden love for one another have come about, this love that each passing hour increases...."

Beckford's mother—the "Begum" as he called her—began to worry once again. This time she urged her son to make the "grand tour" which every young man of his age and social position was supposed to set out on. In 1780, he left England, accompanied by Lettice and the son of

Alexander Cozens, John Robert. They visited Ostende, Spa, Coblenz, Florence, Rome, Naples and Venice. In each place new discoveries and adventures awaited Beckford, but nothing could make him forget his passion. "One image alone has the power to hold me.... I beg you,

follow me to Rome without losing another hour. From Rome I go to Naples, where I will carry my heartache around for an entire month. The 15th or the 16th of December will see me back in Venice, and there my fate will be very quickly sealed."

These nostalgic outbursts did not prevent Beckford from striking up with the young castrato Pacchierotti, whom he later brought to England. He also fell in love with a young Venitian who belonged to the famous Vandramin family. This episode remains shrouded in mystery. Many years afterwards, in 1838, Beckford recalled his involvement with the youth he called "my pagan idol": "It was an entirely spiritual passion, like those friendships which we revere in ancient history and in the Scriptures. I experienced, on that occasion, that which David felt for the brother of his heart, the son of Saul...."

Venice was hardly a puritanical city; nevertheless the affair was a scandal there. Perhaps it was not as Platonic as Beckford liked to remember? At any rate the warning of his friend, Count Bartolomeo Benincasa, leaves little room for doubt: "To what end can such an irregular and deviate inclination possibly tend? Is it *fatum*? Is it a spell cast on you by some baleful genie? You talk to me about your 'beatific vision'.... 'Pon my honour, I admonish you: the more you taste of such bliss, the less such a friendship is to be countenanced. You have organs, Sir, and they are not indifferent."

"Beatific vision" was Beckford's expression for the object of his passion. In fact it designated the ideal of pleasure, the quest for which was the chief occupation of his life. By the time he was twenty, he had already forged a hermetic vocabulary that he would still be using forty years later.

The attempts to "distract the unfortunate young man from his unknown, impossible and intolerable passions," by Benincasa and above all by Lady Hamilton, the wife of Beckford's cousin, at last persuaded William to leave Italy. After a stay of several months in Paris, he arrived in London, where, naturally, he again saw his "adorable Kitty," William Courtenay.

Shortly after his return to England, on Christmas 1781, Beckford organized an astounding party at Fonthill. It was a profane, almost sacrilegious, celebration exclusively dedicated to "enjoying all that wealth and power can bring." The guests were young and high-spirited; they included Louisa Beckford, the wife of his cousin Peter (who was doubtless also William's mistress), her sister Harriet and her friend Sophia Musters. Sophia's lover, George Pitt, and the two sons of the Earl of Dunmore, Alexander and Archibald Hamilton, respectively aged fourteen and twelve, also attended. Alexander

Chevalier Sequeira, *Self-Portrait.* Collection of the Duke of Hamilton. Sent by Franchi to William Beckford in 1826 with the following note: "B. Sequeira... today brought me this little memento to send you, thereby showing that if he cannot kiss you in person at least he kisses your name—because of the great pleasure and *saudade* he experiences in recollecting Your Excellency." (*England's Wealthiest Sons* by Boyd Alexander)

Elisar von Kupffer, *Odalisque.* Sanctuarium Artis Elisarion, Minusio, near Locarno.

Elisar von Kupffer, *Klarismus* [Supreme Clarity]. Sactuarium Artis Elisarion, Minusio, near Locarno. William Beckford would doubtless have hailed the artist's vision of this place, where naked youths offer themselves to the fond looks and caresses of adults.

Cozens and another painter, Jacques de Loutherbourg (the son of the miniaturist), were put in charge of the decorations. It was a dazzling, magical affair, full of sophisticated surprises; now a concerto, now the music of an organ, now the sweet voices of concealed singers wafted over the revellers. Besides Beckford's beloved Pacchierotti, there were two Italian musicians—Rauzzini and Tenducci—who kept up a constant bewitching background of melody which drifted under the high arched ceilings, down endless hallways and staircases to the underground rooms and chambers stretched with shimmering exotic silks. For these privileged guests there were a thousand opportunities to abandon oneself to voluptuous delights. No one knew, or cared, where right shaded into wrong, where innocence turned into perversity. The delirious festivities went on for three whole days, turning Fonthill into the "Palace of the Five Senses" which Beckford describes in *Vathek*. "Langourous and tender gazes, words whispered into ears, enchanting smiles accompanying fond confidences, the sweet redolence of roses, everything prompted an extraordinary sensual delight...."

It was immediately after this party that, on returning to London, Beckford is supposed to have written *Vathek* in three days. That hardly seems possible. No matter, *Vathek* claims to be an inspired novel, rather than a deliberate literary work; Beckford considered it to be the manifestation of a "superior power" which had revealed itself to him during the unholy Christmas celebration at Fonthill. This attitude towards literary creation in a man of the eighteenth century strongly foreshadows romanticism.

In London, Beckford found regular opportunities to carry on his love affair with Courtenay, thanks to his sitting sessions for Romney, who worked on his portrait every Saturday. Cozens encouraged the relationship, as did Louisa Beckford, who was curiously made a party to her cousin-by-marriage's passion: Beckford wrote to her on one occasion, "I ... have been this night blessed with the complete enjoyment of our lovely Kitty. Doubt not her sincerity when she assures you of her affection. I am persuaded she loves you to the full extent of her...."

On turning twenty-one, Beckford inherited his father's immense estate; he was assured of 120,000 pounds yearly income. His marriage in 1783 to Lady Margaret Gordon, the daughter of the Earl of Amboyne, did not in the least hinder him from continuing his affair with Courtenay. Obviously tolerated by Lady Margaret, the relationship pursued its passionate course until, one October evening in 1784 at Powderham, it ended resoundingly.

Probably irritated by a certain reticence in his friend, Beckford left his wife's room and locked himself in with William Courtenay in the latter's bedroom. Bitter reproaches, shoutings and cajolings could be heard from behind the closed door; William's tutor was awakened, and he rushed to inform the boy's father. The latter came running, brandishing his cane. Soon the whole house was in a turmoil. Lady Margaret, who was pregnant, vainly pleaded for her husband's innocence. Beckford was accused of being a "monster" and a "corruptor"—which was merely a foretaste of the accusation that William's uncle, Chief Justice Lord Loughborough, was to level against him. Another uncle, a stern Scotsman, joined Courtenay's irate father in trying to extract a full confession from "dear little William." Outside a storm raged all night. At dawn, Beckford and his wife rushed back to Fonthill in their carriage.

The rumors of scandal spread from castle to castle and finally reached London. In November, the first stories began to appear in the press. *The Morning Herald, The Intelligencer* and *The Advertiser* reported that Loughborough had obtained a court decision of *flagrante delicto*. In the wake of this affair came a black legend about unholy goings-on at Fonthill: sacrilegious masses, witchcraft and extravagant orgies. Beckford was ostracized by the society which had adulated him in earlier days. But the "monster" stood up to all the attacks: the rejection by his class, the newspaper charges, the striking of his name from the list of Peers. He was supported by his wife, who defended him with extraordinary magnanimity. To put a stop to the rumors, Beckford's friends urged him to leave England. Six months passed before he finally agreed; in July 1785, accompanied by his wife, he sailed to the Continent to settle in Vevey, Switzerland. On May 28, 1786, Lady Margaret died of puerperal fever, leaving Beckford with two daughters. The British press pounced on this new tragedy, insinuating that Beckford's wife had

died of ill-treatment; Beckford was obliged to get a certificate of good conduct from the town of Vevey.

After the scandal and its tragic aftermath, Beckford and Courtenay never saw each other again. Beckford's passion, in fact, turned into hostility: he wrote to a friend in Lausanne that Courtenay was "a pansy if there ever was one; he dresses like a doll and paints his face like a whore." Several years later, indeed, William Courtenay became one of England's most notorious homosexuals.

Cases of homosexuality appear to have been numerous in eighteenth-century England. Shortly before the Beckford affair, Lord Tylney and Edward Onslow had both been involved in famous scandals, and public opinion had also been roused to a fine pitch of outrage by the Marquess of Townshend's flamboyant love life. To escape prosecution, these young aristocrats had been obliged to exile themselves in Italy. Less wealthy offenders could of course not afford this solution; they were often sentenced to death and executed. For example, in 1818 a certain John Attwood Eglerton was hung for having engaged in sodomy with a stable boy. It took the jury only ten minutes to reach their verdict.

Many writers, however, took a more broad-minded view—witness the following quatrain by Charles Churchill:

> Women are kept for nothing but the breed;
> For pleasure we must have a GANYMEDE,
> A fine, fresh HYLAS, a delicious boy,
> To serve our purposes of beastly joy.

Was this a purely disinterested apology for sodomy? One rather doubts it

Vagabondage in Europe

After Lady Margaret's death, Beckford thought of going to Jamaica but, discouraged by rough seas, he went no further than Portugal where he resided three times between 1787 and 1799.

In Lisbon he lived in grand style, loaded with honors and attentions of every kind. His influence at the royal court seems to have been considerable: "When I was in Portugal," Beckford later said, "I had as much influence and power as if I had been the King." How could the Queen and her retinue possibly entertain suspicions about such a devout personage who regularly attended mass, lifting his eyes up to Heaven and piously crossing his hands over his chest? None of this prevented Beckford from slipping away during the sermon to cavort with two young musicians, Polycarpo and Gregorio. "How tired I am of keeping a mask on my countenance," Beckford noted in his *Journal* on returning from mass one day. "How tight it sticks—it makes me sore." But deep down inside himself he derived a peculiar enjoyment from the unholy conjunction of devotion and sacrilege, of the "pleasures of the mass" and profane escapades, of ethereal voices and the somewhat less ethereal attractions of the choirboys. Split between the two—God and Satan—he lived his double life with extraordinary intensity and lucidity.

The Marquis of Marialva, a generous and devoted host, wished to give Beckford his daughter in marriage. Instead, the Englishman fell in love with the marquis's son Don Pedro, a graceful, excitable lad of thirteen who had been raised in the hot-house atmosphere of his own home. The couple spent exquisite moments, walking together through the groves of orange and laurel trees. "D. Pedro and I... become every day more and more attached to each other...." wrote Beckford; "we run hand in hand along the alleys, bounding like deer and leaping up to catch at the *azareiro* blossoms which dangled over our heads." To leap and gambol, to recapture the soul and the nimbleness of childhood, seems to have been an ideal which obsessed Beckford. Again and again, the words "child" and "childishness" crop up in his writings. At twenty he had written to Alexander Cozens: "How firmly am I resolved to be a Child for ever"! It seems that in his love affairs it was a vision of childhood that he was searching for; a vision that was powerfully erotic, and which forever eluded him, since it was really a memory of himself as a child. Thus his homosexuality was to a great degree narcissistic. His impossible quest isolated him from other men, cutting him off from them as effectively as did the ostracism of his countrymen.

His feelings for D. Pedro mingled friendship, tender fondness, pedagogical concern—and intense desire: "Tomorrow! Tomorrow! He loves me. I have tasted the sweetness of his lips; his dear eyes have confessed the secret of his bosom," he scribbled in a fever of anticipation on the eve of spending a day with the boy.

So as not to alarm D. Pedro's family, Beckford pretended to be interested solely in the youth's education, in the moulding of his character. In this he succeeded so well that Marialva immediately asked him to take care of a favorite nephew of his who was a pupil in a boy's school in Paris. "Rare sport, thought I," confided Beckford to his journal with rich irony. Meanwhile his passion for D. Pedro had become so strong that, fearing new complications, his friend and private physician Doctor Verdeil pressed him to leave Portugal.

Another episode in Beckford's love life in Lisbon was his relationship with Gregorio, the young musician mentioned above. Gregorio Fellipe Franchi, born in Lisbon in 1770, was the son of Loreto Franchi, a Neapolitan singer in the service of Queen Maria I of Portugal. Beckford had met the lad at the College of Music, where all the Portuguese musicians, singers and choirboys were trained, in May, 1787. Franchi became as devoted to him as a dog and was delighted to make himself useful to Beckford, who wrote: "I have need of some young sweet-breathed animal to enliven my spirits, to run in the citron thickets and bring me flowery branches, to arrange my prints, transpose my songs, and write down the musical ideas which rush into my mind in happy moments." A skillful pianist and singer, as intelligent as he was affectionate, as delightful in persona-

Francis Danby, *Apocalypse Subject*. (May have been executed for William Beckford). Professor Robert Rosenblum Collection, New York. This work was probably exhibited at the Royal Academy in 1829 with the following quotation from the Book of Revelation: "Then I saw another mighty angel coming down from heaven, wrapped in a cloud, with a rainbow over his head... and his legs were like pillars of fire...." (Rev. X: 1-2)

lity as he was in looks—which was no drawback—Franchi fitted Beckford's ideal in every respect. In 1788, the boy joined him in Madrid and promised to serve him for life. Although he married and had a daughter, he promptly left his family to follow his tyrannical friend and master to England. The voluminous correspondance which he and Beckford exchanged was always written in Italian, for discretion's sake. In his letters Beckford called himself Barzabà (doubtless from the Syrian *bar sabâ*, meaning voluptuary). "Barzabà is slobbering, Barzabà is good-natured, Barzabà is anything you wish; but in certain circumstances there is no energy that is too strenuous for him."

Franchi's devotion survived all of Beckford's fits of anger and eccentricities, whereas Don Pedro was dropped in 1787 (actually Beckford saw him twice more in Paris, in 1814 and in 1819, only to break with him for good). Unfortunately the "Portuguese orange" as Beckford's friends called Franchi never adapted to the climate of London; and he died, crippled with arthritis, in 1828. Beckford had him buried in the small cemetary of Marylebone.

Up until 1788 Beckford's tendencies were bisexual (although the word hardly conveys the diversity and the profusion of his encounters). We learn from his *Journal* that in the space of eight months he fell in love successively—or simultaneously—with no less than four boys and as many young women. In Madrid he wreaked havoc among both sexes. He fell in love with the daughter of the Duke of La Vauguyon; he fell in love with Madame de Santa-Cruz—and, at the same time, with her young husband the Prince of Listenais. He once declared that he was "resigned to meet with ... whichever would most please Providence." Such as the twelve year old brother of the ambassador of Tripolitania: "The little boy's name is Mohammed. There is a languid tenderness in his eyes, a softness in the contour of his face, and something bewitching in his smile that enchanted me."

After 1788 his homosexual inclination prevailed, apparently to the exclusion of the other side of his nature, for henceforth no woman was to enter his life.

In 1789 Beckford found himself in Paris; from the windows of his apartment on the rue de Grenelle he watched the first disturbances of the French Revolution. Was he at all concerned by them? Not a single reference to those tragic events is to be found in his *Notebooks*. On the contrary, he speaks only of the good food, the amenities of Paris and the Opera where he occupied the Prince de Condé's box. "What do I care about aristocrats and democrats; I am an autocrat"!

Fonthill

Nevertheless Beckford managed to get a safe conduct back to England from the Revolutionary authorities. He returned to the Gothic novel setting of Fonthill Abbey and immediately set to work turning it into an Oriental palace. Crates packed with treasures arrived from all over Europe; a look at the Wallace Collection gives one a rough idea of their fabulous contents.

Inevitably Beckford's Jamaican revenues were soon swallowed up; but, despite his friends' concern Beckford went on blithely spending his guineas, twice rebuilding the Abbey tower after it collapsed: It was precisely the unfinished character of Fonthill that interested him, its myriad possibilities for new inventions and new aesthetic delights. Meanwhile, his private demon, Barzabà, continued to consume him. Doubtless his devoted factotum Franchi was often hard put to satisfy his imperious requirements. Nor was he always able to lay his hands on a "beatific vision," and consequently he frequently had to fall back on his carefully picked servants, whom he nicknamed Marion, Miss Long, the Doll, Bijou, Miss Butterfly, Countess Pox and Madame Bion. The latter was in fact his valet Richardson, about whom Beckford once complained, "What most confounds and disgusts me is a certain kind of frigidity and insipidity like Mme Bion's (the devil take you, you blond beast)." These dismal involvements were probably compensated by other adventures: Beckford's numerous forays to Paris may not just have been for the purpose of buying paintings and art objects. Apart from these trips, Beckford lived in comparative solitude at Fonthill, with only a few parasites, like the dwarf Pierrot (Pierre Colas de Grailly) and the talented watercolorist Father Ange-Denis Macquin, for company. He never invited any of his illustrious contemporaries there, not even those he strongly admired—William Blake for example, whose works he collected and kept until the end of his days.

The reconstruction of Fonthill had cost Beckford 270,000 pounds, three-quarters of his fortune, and as he grew old even his pleasure in the Abbey began to wane. Eventually he sold it with no regrets, eager to start a new life. He settled in Landsdown Crescent, near Bath, in two secluded cottages which he filled with his paintings, his most precious treasures, his books, his spaniel and his dwarf. As always he surrounded himself with the finest of everything, creating a sort of refined court around him. Draped in his old "cloak of science and wit," he nevertheless moderated his ways. In his seventies, still faithful to his dreams, he tended his garden of rare exotic plants and climbed his tower each day. From the little Greek temple built on a nearby hill, he looked out over the sea, and over the downs as far as Fonthill—whose ill-starred tower had just collapsed for the third time. He had survived so many of his contemporaries, so many events; now he was approaching death, his final trial. He faced it with complete lucidity. On Sunday, April 21, 1844, he wrote to his daughter: "Liston [his doctor] congratulated himself that I had improved, but he is wrong; no sooner had he left than a horrible chill shook me from head to foot. Oh, that the interval could be cut short—cut short—the fatal interval.... I can no longer bear the waiting." As he refused to see a priest, his doctor, who was a believer, tried to convince him of the consolations

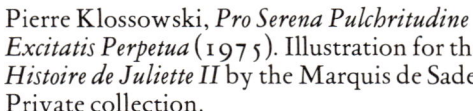

Pierre Klossowski, *Pro Serena Pulchritudine Excitatis Perpetua* (1975). Illustration for the *Histoire de Juliette II* by the Marquis de Sade. Private collection.

of religion, hoping to bring peace to his soul. The dying voluptuary seems to have listened attentively, joining his two hands in a gesture of acquiescence. On May 2, 1844, he breathed his last, passing away so gently and so quietly that his watchers did not even notice him going.

From VATHEK

...Not long afterwards a band of these unfortunate children came to the palace, decked out by their tender mothers in the way most calculated to heighten their beauty. But while the heart of everyone else went out to these lovely children Vathek was examining them with a treacherous greed, and selecting fifty of them to sacrifice to the Giaour. When he had mentally made his choice he assumed an air of benevolence and proposed that his young favourites should be given a festival in the plain, for he said that they, more than all others, should have cause to rejoice that he had been restored to health.

The Caliph's kindness won all hearts, and was soon known throughout Samarah. Litters were made ready, camels and horses were brought out, and women, children, old men, and young people took their places as they wished. The cavalcade went forward, followed by all the confectioners of the town and the suburbs. The people followed on foot in crowds, and everyone rejoiced, not one remembering what the last journey in this direction had cost several of them.

It was a beautiful evening; the air was fresh, the sky untroubled, and the flowers put forth their sweetest perfumes. Nature at rest seemed to rejoice in the rays of the setting sun, whose soft light gilded the summit of the Mountain of the Four Springs, beautified its slopes and bathed the leaping flocks in refulgence. Not a sound was to be heard save the murmuring of the fountains, the note of the reed-pipes and the voices of the shepherds calling to one another on the hill-sides.

The scene was made still more attractive by the poor children who were going all unawares to their doom. Suspecting nothing, they went forward towards the plain ful of childish pranks. Some chased butterflies, others picked flowers or gathered up shining pebbles, and a few rambled away for the greater pleasure it gave them to overtake their companions again and salute them with kisses.

Already it was possible to discern the horrible gulf at the bottom of which was the ebony portal. It cut across the plain like a black line, and was thought by Morakanabad and his colleagues to be one of those strange works which the Caliph was pleased to make. Unhappy men! Little did they know the purpose it was to serve! Vathek, not wishing that this fatal place should be too closely examined, caused a halt to be called, and had a wide circle traced out on the ground. The guard of eunuchs then set about measuring the course for the foot-races, and got ready the rings which were to serve as targets for the archers. The fifty boys hastily undressed and displayed to the admiring multitude the pleasing contours of their delicate limbs. Their eyes sparkled with joy, which was reflected in those of their relatives, who each gave encouragement to the young competitor that interested him most: the games of these sweet and innocent children took up the attention of everyone.

...then the Caliph, standing on the verge of the chasm, shouted with all his might: 'Let my fifty little favoured ones draw near, coming in the order of the success they have won in the games! To the first I will give my diamond bracelet, to the second my emerald collar, to the third my girdle of topaz, and to each of the others a part of my raiment, even to the shoes on my feet.'

At these words the applause broke out with redoubled force, and the generosity of a prince who would strip himself naked to amuse his subjects and encourage the young was lauded to the skies. Meanwhile the Caliph, disrobing garment by garment, and lifting his arm as high as possible, made each of the prizes sparkle; but while with one hand he presented the gift to the eager child, with the other he pushed the recipient into the chasm, where the Giaour, incessantly growling, repeated without intermission the word: 'More! More!'

This horrible arrangement was so quick that each child who ran forward could have no suspicion of the fate of those who had gone before; and the lookers-on were prevented from seeing anything by the darkness and the distance at which they stood. At length, Vathek, having cast the fiftieth victim to his doom, thought that the Giaour would come and take him and give him the golden key. Already he thought himself as great as Suleiman, and was fain to believe that he would have no account to render of his behaviour, when, to his great surprise, the chasm closed up and he felt the earth under his feet as firm and solid as usual. His rage and despair were indescribable. He cursed the perfidy of the Indian, called him by the most infamous names, and kicked the soil as though to make himself heard. He continued thus until, worn out, he fell to the ground like one senseless. His viziers and the great ones of his court, who were nearer to him than the others, thought at first that he was sitting down on the grass to play with the children; but, being seized with a certain anxiety, they went forward and saw the Caliph quite alone. 'What do you want?' said he, with an air of bewilderment. 'Our children! Our children!' they cried. 'You are fine fellows to want to make me responsible for the accidents of nature,' he answered; 'your children were playing near the precipice which was here, and fell in; and I should have fallen also, had I not leapt backward.'

The Master and the Pupil. Nineteenth-century English engraving. Private collection.

VI

AESTHETES AND POETS ACCURSED

The low and narrow brow, the pupils wide,
Of passive creatures perverse gods desire....
(Jean Lorrain, *Le Sang des Dieux*)

Elisar von Kupffer, Painting. Sanctuarium Artis Elisarion, Minusio, near Locarno.

Illustration for the 1867 edition of Balzac's *Lost Illusions* published by Michel Levy. "In this friendship which was already an old one, one of the two friends loved the other idolatrously: it was David, Thus Lucien ordered him about like a woman who knows that she is loved."

HONORÉ DE BALZAC
(1799-1850)

In *By Way of Sainte-Beuve,* Proust quotes Oscar Wilde's remark, "The greatest sorrow of my life? The death of Lucien de Rubempré in *Splendeurs et misères des courtisanes.*" Proust, who was himself a great admirer of Balzac, singles out the passage in *Lost Illusions* where the ex-convict Vautrin, disguised as a Spanish priest, first encounters young Lucien de Rubempré who is about to commit suicide (see selection). The poet's beauty, his elegant clothes and the bouquet of yellow flowers he is clutching remind the fake priest of another young man whom he has loved and protected, Rastignac. Proust writes, "Everything, from the manner in which Vautrin stops Lucien whom he does not know, attracted by his physical appearance alone, to his unconscious gesture of taking the youth's arm, discloses, surely, the very different and very definite purport of his theories of domination, of lifelong association, etc., which, in the eyes of Lucien and perhaps even in his own, color an unavowed thought.... But the most beautiful passage is undoubtedly the marvellous one in which the two travellers pass by the ruins of Rastignac's castle. I would call that the 'Tristesse d'Olympio' of homosexual love."

In *Splendeurs et misères des courtisanes*—in the chapter entitled "Vautrin's Last Incarnation"—Balzac describes a "queer's row" in a prison. It is a virtual foreshadowing of Jean Genet's novels. In another book, *Sarrasine,* he tells the story of a young man's unhappy passion for a castrato. Thus Balzac was interested in "those whose ways are peculiar," whom he also called the "third sex." When excerpts from *Lost Illusions* were published in *L'Estafette,* they were severely criticized. Jules Janin found the novel "repulsive." Albert Second, the *Figaro*'s critic, wrote that the book was a "disgusting diatribe." But Balzac also had admirers, including the Marquis Astolphe de Custine, the author of the famous *Travels in Russia.* "You portray hideous figures with the brush strokes and the colors of a Rembrandt... [your book] is full of ideas, and is as new as the dreadful world which you reveal," wrote Custine, who was personnally well acquainted with that "dreadful world." On November 6, 1824, he had been found, naked and badly beaten, in a field near St. Denis. Custine imprudently went to the police and lodged a complaint. The investigation revealed that he had been ambushed by some soldiers with whom he had made an assignation. The soldiers denied the charge of sodomy, but admitted that they had wanted to give the poor marquis a lesson. As a result of this scandal, Custine was turned down for the peerage he had set his heart on. Louis XVIII is said to have declared mockingly, "Monsieur de Chateaubriand's candidate seems to use a hard instrument for his enemas." Chateaubriand advised Custine to challenge his libelers to a duel for honor's sake, but Custine choose to forget the incident in the arms of a young Englishman, Edouard de Sainte-Barbe, whom Stendhal once described as "truly very Petronius-like...." and with whom Custine lived peacefully.

Countess de Menou, *Portrait of Astolphe de Custine* (1846). Private collection. De Custine, author of *Travels in Russia*, once wrote to his friends, "I am afflicted with an ill I cannot confess."

From LOST ILLUSIONS

.... The stage-coach from Bordeaux to Paris was speeding along and no doubt the passengers would soon be getting down in order to walk up this long hill. Lucien did not want to be seen, so he hurried down a little sunken lane into a vineyard where he began to pick flowers. When he returned to the main road he had in his hand a big bunch of stonecrop, a yellow flower which grows on the pebbly soil in vineyards. He emerged just behind a traveller dressed entirely in black, with powdered hair, wearing shoes of Orleans calf-skin with silver buckles, his face tanned and seamed as if it had been accidentally scorched when he was a child. This traveller, in a patently clerical garb, was walking slowly and smoking a cigar. On hearing Lucien jumping on the road from the vineyard, hytranger turned round and seemed to be struck by the poet's profoundly melancholy beauty, his symbolic bouquet and his elegant clothes. He looked like a hunter coming upon a prey long and vainly tracked. In naval fashion, he waited for Lucien to reach him and slackened his pace as if he wished to survey the plain below the slope. Lucien did likewise and noticed a little barouche drawn by two horses and a postilion who was leading them.

"You have let the stage-coach pass by, Monsieur. You will lose your seat unless you care to get into my carriage to catch up with it, for the stage-coach goes quicker than the local omnibus." The traveller pronounced these words with a markedly Spanish accent and his offer was made with exquisite courtesy....

The Spanish priest seemed so genuinely affectionate that the poet did not hesitate to open his heart to him. And so, as they travelled from Angoulême to Ruffec, he

Portrait of Lucien de Rubempré, hero of Balzac's *Lost Illusions*, from the 1867 edition. (See caption p. 160) 'As with most shrewd and intelligent men, his hips were shaped like a woman's.'

Illustration for the 1867 edition of Balzac's *Lost Illusions*. (See caption p. 160) "Child," said the Spaniard, taking Lucien by the arm

A.-E. Girodet de Roucy Trioson, *Endymion Sleeping*. Louvre, Paris. In his novella, *Sarrazine*, Balzac tells the story of a castrato called "La Zambinella," and he says that his hero might have modelled for Girodet's Endymion.

recounted his whole life, leaving out none of his misdeeds and finishing up with the latest disaster for which he was responsible. At the moment when he was ending his story, the more poetically delivered because Lucien was repeating it for the third time in a fortnight, they arrived at a point on the road near Ruffec, where the Rastignac family had their domain. The first time he mentioned this name, the Spaniard gave a start....

The priest halted his barouche, wishing out of curiosity to walk along the little avenue from the main road to the manor-house. He looked at it all with more interest than Lucien would have expected from a Spanish priest.

"So you know the Rastignacs?" Lucien asked him.

"I know everyone in Paris," said the Spaniard, getting back into the carriage.

"And so, for lack of ten or twelve thousand francs, you were going to drown yourself. You're a child, you know nothing of men or things. A man's destiny is worth whatever price he puts on it, and you value your future at only twelve thousand francs. Well, I shall presently pay a higher price for you...."

"I've fished you out of the water, brought you back to life, and you belong to me as a creature belongs to its creator, the afreet to the genie, the icoglan to the sultan, the body to the soul! My strong arm will maintain you on your road to power, and yet I promise you a life of pleasure, honour and continuous festivity.... You'll never lack for money. You will shine and show off while I, bending low in the mud of the foundations, shall be propping up the brilliant edifice of your fortune. I myself love power for power's sake! I shall always be happy to see you enjoying the things which are forbidden to me. In short, I shall live in you!... And in any case, the day when this pact between a human being and a demon, a child and a diplomat, no longer suits you, you can still go and find some little pool, like the one you mentioned, to drown yourself in: you'll be slightly more or slightly less than what you are today—an unhappy or a dishonoured man...."

Although there was much that was repulsive in his physiognomy, this effect was attenuated by his manners which were at once brusque and ingratiating; and it was evident that for Lucien the priest was doing his best to be seductive, wheedling, almost feline. Lucien noted all these details with an anxious air. He felt that this instant must settle the question of life or death for him, for they had come to the second relay stage after Ruffec. The Spanish priest's latest words had set many chords in his heart vibrating; and, be it said to Lucien's shame and that of the priest who, with perspicacious eye, was studying the poet's handsome face, they were the most harshly resonant since they responded to sentiments of depravity. Lucien could see himself in Paris once more, snatching again at the reins of domination which his unskilled hands had let fall, and taking his revenge! The comparisons he

had recently been making between provincial and Parisian life—his most urgent motive for suicide—were fading from his mind. He would be back again in congenial surroundings, but this time under the aegis of as deep and wicked a schemer as Cromwell.

"I was alone before: now there will be two of us," he was thinking.

The more he had laid bare his past misdeeds, the more interest the cleric had shown. His indulgence had increased in proportion to Lucien's misfortunes, and he had shown no astonishment....

"My child," said the Spaniard, taking Lucien by the arm. "Have you pondered over Otway's *Venice Preserved*? Have you understood the deep friendship between man and man which binds Pierre to Jaffeir, makes them indifferent about women and alters all social relationships for them? ... I'm putting that question to the poet in you."

"The Canon knows something about drama too," Lucien thought to himself. "Have you read Voltaire?" he asked.

"I've done better than that," said the Canon. " I put him into practice."

"Don't you believe in God?..."

"So now I'm the atheist!" said the priest with a smile. "Let's get down to facts, my boy," he went on, putting his arm round Lucien's waist. "I'm forty-six. I'm a nobleman's natural child, and so I have no family; and yet I have a heart. But learn this, write it down in your impressionable brain: man is terrified of solitude. And of all solitudes, moral solitude is what terrifies him most...."

ISIDORE DUCASSE, COMTE DE LAUTRÉAMONT
(1846-1870)

Isidore Ducasse was born in Montevideo in 1846. He spent a cheerless childhood, oppressed by the petty bourgeois atmosphere of his home and the austere discipline of his Spanish Jesuit school and Uruguay's violent folklore. He seems to have suffered a great deal during his early education. He developed an exceptional gift for mathematics, and as a result his father sent him to Paris in 1867 to prepare for the Ecole Polytechnique. A year later Isidore decided to give up his studies, and devoted himself to writing instead; he composed the first of the songs in *The Lay of Maldoror*, which he published anonymously at his own expense. He lived alone, working and reading intensely. The critics ignored his *Lay*. Albert Lacroix, the only publisher who had dared print it, was obliged to withdraw the book from circulation because of "stylistic excesses..." which Ducasse refused to amend. The young writer adopted the pseudonym Comte de Lautréamont, which a novel by Eugène Sue had suggested to him. In 1870 he dropped out of sight, frequently changing address and hardly writing anymore. He died on the November 23, 1870, in a squalid hotel near Montmartre. No one came to his funeral. His death, which he had been awaiting, was even more lonely and enigmatic than his life had been.

From THE LAY OF MALDOROR

O incomprehensible pederasts, it is not I will hurl curses at your degradation; it is not I will cast scorn upon your infundibuliform anus. It is enough that the shameful and almost incurable diseases which beset you carry with them their unfailing punishment. Legislators of stupid institutions, inventors of narrow morality, go from me, for I am an impartial spirit. And you young boys, or rather young girls, explain to me how and why (but keep a reasonable distance, for I too am unable to resist my passions) revenge has so ripened in your hearts, as to have affixed such a crown of wounds to humanity's thigh. By your conduct you make it blush for its sons (whom myself I revere); your prostitution, offering itself to the first comer, exercises the logic of the deepest thinkers, while your exaggerated sensibility keeps the measure of even womanly stupefaction. Are you of a more or less terrestrial nature than your fellows? Have you a sixth sense which is lacking in us? Do not lie, and say what you think. It is not a question I put to you; for since I frequented the sublimity of your grandiose intelligence as an observer, I know all about it. Be blessed by my left hand, be sanctified by my right hand, angels protected by my universal love. I kiss your faces, I kiss your breasts, I kiss with my smooth lips the various parts of your harmonious and perfumed bodies. Why did you not tell me at once what you were, crystalizations of higher moral loveliness? I had myself to divine the innumerable treasures of tenderness and chastity which the throbbing of your stifled hearts concealed. O breast, garlanded with roses and wild grasses, I had first to open your legs and my mouth to hang from the insignia of your modesty. But (important consideration) do not forget each day to wash

Auguste Rodin, Frontispiece for an edition of Baudelaire's *Fleurs du Mal* (1918). Bibliothèque Nationale, Paris.

Richard Edmont Flatters, *The Fall of the Damned*. Cabinet des Estampes, Bibliothèque Nationale, Paris.

with warm water the skin of your parts, for if not, venereal chancres will infallibly sprout upon the cloven commissures of my unsatisfied lips. Oh! if instead of being a hell the universe had but been an immense celestial anus, behold the gesture I make close to my belly; yes, I would have dug my yard through its bleeding sphyncter, shattering the very walls of its pelvis with my impetuous movements. Disaster would not then have blown entire dunes of moving sand upon my blinded eyes; I would have discovered that subterranean place where sleeping truth lies, and the rivers of my viscuous semen would thus have found an ocean in which to hurl themselves. But why do I surprise myself regretting an imaginary state of things, which will never receive the seal of final accomplishment? There is no point in giving ourselves the trouble of constructing fugitive hypotheses.

Meanwhile, let him who burns with ardour to share my bed, come and find me; but I put one rigorous condition upon my hospitality; he must not be more than fifteen. If he for his part think I am not thirty, what does that matter? Age does not diminish the intensity of the feelings, far from it; and though my hair is become white as snow, it is not on account of age; on the contrary it is due to the reason you know of. For myself, I do not love women! Nor even hermaphrodites! I need beings who resemble me; upon whose brow human nobility is more deeply, more ineffaceably marked! Are you sure that those who wear long hair are of a nature similar to my own! I do not think so, and I will not give up my opinion.

(*5th canto*)

PAUL VERLAINE (1844-1896) AND ARTHUR RIMBAUD (1854-1891)

In June 1869, twenty-eight year old Verlaine met Mathilde Mauté de Fleurville, "the young girl in the pink radiance of her mysterious candor," "blossoming with innocence and straightforwardness." She might have been a heroine out of one of the Comtesse de Ségur's novels. Verlaine had already published *Les Chansons des rues et des bois*, *Les Fêtes galantes* and *Poèmes saturniens;* and he had become something of a celebrity in the literary world of Paris. But despite his successes he drank heavily. A closet queen, he fretted guiltily over his *garçonnades* [passing affairs with boys] and over his love for young Lucien Viotti, a classmate of Mathilde's half-brother, Charles de Sivry. Twice during the month of July following his first encounter with Mathilde, Verlaine got into a drunken rage and tried to kill his mother. Afraid that he was heading for catastrophe, he decided that his salvation lay in marriage. He asked Charles de Sivry to ask Mathilde to marry him. She accepted, and the wedding took place on August 11 of the following year. A month later Verlaine, who had been drafted into the 160th battalion of the National Guard, resumed his drinking and began beating his wife. Viotti, "the frail and melancholy youth," disappointed by what he considered his friend's betrayal, enlisted and soon after was killed at the battle of The Hague. In his *Memoirs of a Widower*, written twelve years later, Verlaine recalled this lover whom he had dropped in order to marry Mathilde: "... your voice comes back to me, deep and throaty, as in the past. And your whole, elegant, subtle twenty year old self, your charming head (like Marceau's, but handsomer), the exquisite proportions of your ephebe's body under your gentleman's clothes reappear behind a veil of slow tears."

Verlaine hated his father-in-law, the "stinking old dotard," the "bourgeoisissimo," as he called him; nevertheless during the Paris Commune Monsieur Mauté put the Verlaines up and gave them an allowance (he also helped Louise Michel, who had been his daughter's teacher, during her detention and her exile in New Caledonia). Fired from his job at City Hall because he had worked for the Commune's press office, Verlaine moped around, bored and despondent. He had not published a thing since his wedding. Then, one day, he received a letter, with several poems enclosed, from a youth in Charleville named Arthur Rimbaud. He had been recommended by Bretagne, a comrade in debauchery of Verlaine's, a bacchanalian poet who pretended to be interested in the cult of Heliogabalus. Verlaine was astounded by the poems of this seventeen year old and found them "frighteningly beautiful." He sent off a quick reply: "Come, dear great soul, we are expecting you, we are calling to you." He enclosed a money order—for Rimbaud had let him know that he was penniless. The boy would come and live at the Mauté's house, Verlaine decided.

On September 10, 1871, Verlaine found the boy-poet conversing with his wife in Madame Mauté's sitting room: "His head was positively a child's, plump and fresh, while his growing adolescent's body was quite bony and clumsy-looking; his voice slurred over words a little with a thick Ardennes accent, so that it almost sounded as if he were speaking in dialect, and he squeaked and growled incongruously, like any boy whose voice is changing." Rimbaud greeted the older poet with stony silence, casting surly looks at him. He was furious at seeing the author of *Fêtes galantes* in such bourgeois surroundings, and he determined to lure him away from his home and from his big-bellied wife (Mathilde was pregnant, and about to give birth), the very sight of whom made him sick. A brutal, violent youth, audacious, yet tender and affectionate when he wanted to be, Rimbaud soon became the protector of ten-year-older Verlaine and the dominant partner in the relationship. He was dirty, slovenly, deliberately crude. He delighted in shocking people; once, when, to her horror, Mathilde noticed that he had lice in his hair, Verlaine retorted that Rimbaud liked to keep them "so as to be able to throw them on priests." Verlaine's friends, Lepelletier (who detested Rimbaud), Cros and Cabaner, joked about the "little blond alleycat" the poet had brought from Charleville. In its coverage of the premiere of François Coppée's first play, one newspaper reported that Verlaine and "Mademoiselle Rimbaud" had attended. Mallarmé, who met Rimbaud at a wine shop frequented by a group of artists who called themselves the *Vilains Bonshommes* [the Nasty Fellows], left a portrait of the lad which is hardly flattering: "He was like a common wench grown indefinably haughty, or wild; a laundry girl I

Ignace Fantin-Latour, *The Table Corner* (detail). Jeu de Paume, Louvre, Paris. Rimbaud is sitting next to Verlaine. It is said that, while posing for this painting, the young poet did not open his mouth once.

might add, since his enormous hands were reddened with chilblains from passing too often and too abruptly from hot to cold." Even among the merrymaking *Vilains Bonshommes,* Rimbaud made himself obnoxious. One night he threatened to cut the photographer Carjat's throat. As a result, Verlaine stopped going to these bohemian meetings with his young friend.

Exasperated by their unruly guest, the Mautés asked Rimbaud to leave. The boy drifted between the homes of the poet Charles Cros, the composer Cabaner and a certain Forain, whom Rimbaud nicknamed *Gavroche* and *Little Brown Kitty.* In his absence, Verlaine would get drunk every evening and start beating his wife, who had just given birth to a son. One night early in 1872, he roughed up the baby and tried to strangle Mathilde. This was going too far: Monsieur Mauté moved to Périgueux with his daughter and his grandson and began separation proceedings in Mathilde's name.

Verlaine and Rimbaud moved in together and during the following month were inseparable. They spent their days in Montmartre and in the cafés of the Trudaine quarter engaged in endless conversations. Rimbaud vehemently expounded his ideas about poetry, the ideas he had outlined a year earlier in a rambling letter to his rhetoric teacher, Georges Izambard: "You move along in the right track," he had written to the pedagogue, who taught that each of us owes a debt to society. "I also follow the principle: cynically I am having myself *kept.* I dig up old imbeciles from school: I serve them with whatever I can invent that is stupid, filthy, mean in acts and words. They pay me in beer and girls. I am degrading myself as much as possible. Why? I want to be a poet and am working to make myself a *seer:* you will not understand this, and I don't know how to explain it to you. It is a question of reaching the unknown by the derangement of all the senses. The sufferings are enormous, but one has to be strong, one has to be born a poet, and I know I am a poet."

Despite his boasts it seems that Rimbaud had had few sexual experiences before coming to Paris. The first time he ran away from home, his mother had exclaimed: "I can't understand it, he is usually so quiet and well behaved!" Rimbaud's involvements with girls seem to have been infrequent and disappointing. In a letter to his

167

Paul Verlaine, *Rimbaud in 1875*. Viollet Collection, Paris.

F.-A. Cazals, *A Soirée at Paul Verlaine's in 1889*. Private collection. From left to right: H. d'Argis, Verlaine, G. Vicaire, Sophie Arlay, Rachilde, L. Tailhade, Villiers de L'Isle-Adam, F. Clerget, J. Moréas, Jules Tellier, Paterne Berrichon and Cazals himself holding à top hat in his hand.

Paul Verlaine, Drawing (detail). Viollet Collection, Paris. The poet was imagining a meeting with Delahaye in Douai or in Arras towards 1877.

friend Paul Demeny (in which he declared that a poet must be "the great invalid, the great criminal, the great outcast"), he copied a poem which was full of disgust and anger at his heterosexual experiences:

O my little lovers,
    How I hate you!
Plaster with painful blisters
    Your ugly tits!...
And yet it is for these mutton shoulders
    That I have made rhymes!
I would like to break your hips
    For having loved!

Rimbaud encountered other disappointments in Paris. His initial enthusiasm was soon worn down by the petty passions and backbitings he discovered in that city. Always timid, he felt like an outsider. He had hoped to revolutionize the literary world with Verlaine. Less than six months later, the latter was backing down and, anxious to avoid a permanent separation from his wife, he was begging Rimbaud to return to Charleville, at least for a while. Thus Mathilde would return to the conjugal domicile, and Rimbaud would stagnate in Charleville.

"Shit, shit, shit," wrote the younger poet angrily to Verlaine, who had promised to call him back to Paris as soon as his domestic problems were "settled." True to his word, Verlaine wrote to Rimbaud two months later, enclosing a money order for the return fare to Paris. "One last word, though ... try to make yourself a little more presentable than before, at least in the beginning: clothes clean, shoes polished, hair combed, no surly looks: all necessary if you're to join in tigerish plans: I will wash, brush, etc. for you (if you want)." (The style of Verlaine's letters to "Dear Rimbe" was peculiar. One of them ends in a curious mixture of French and English, "I am an *old cunt ever open* or *opened,* or whatever, I don't have my list of irregular verbs here.")

Verlaine had mentioned "tigerish plans." Indeed, the two lovers' reunion turned out to be insanely violent. Rimbaud "punished" Verlaine by slashing him with a knife; a few nights later Verlaine turned on Rimbaud, stabbing him in the thigh, which was at least a change from running after Mathilde with a knife. On July 7, 1872, Mathilde fell ill, and Verlaine went out to look for a doctor. On the way, he met Rimbaud who convinced him to leave town immediately. And so, without a word of explanation to Mathilde, the two friends set off. They caused a disturbance in the station at Arras and were put on the next train back to Paris. The next morning they again set out, this time for Charleville, where they did not stop, having meanwhile decided to push on into Belgium. Alarmed by this wild escapade, Verlaine finally wrote to his wife, "My poor Mathilde, do not be distressed, do not cry; this is only a nightmare I am having, I will come back one day...." Kind-hearted and naive, Mathilde was convinced that she would be able to induce Verlaine to return to her eventually (in spite of his love letters to Rimbaud which she had discovered after he had left). She decided to go to Brussels with her mother-in-law to urge her fugitive husband to return home. The two women finally found Verlaine in a hotel, and husband and wife spent the night together. The poet later celebrated their reunion in his poem, "Birds in the Night."

> I see you still. I pushed the door open:
> You were lying in bed, as though tired.
> But, oh, light body bouyed by love,
> You bounded to me, naked, tearful, joyous.

Mathilde proposed moving to New Caledonia, where Louise Michel had been exiled. Verlaine was frightened at the idea of such a move, but nevertheless agreed to take the train back to Paris that very day. But on reaching the French border he realized that conjugal life was already boring him, and he slipped off the train to hurry back to his "darling Rimbe." He mailed an angry and cruel note to Mathilde: "You miserable carrot-patch fairy, you mousy princess, you have done everything you could to me, you have killed my friend's heart; I am going back to Rimbaud, if he still wants me." Verlaine never saw Mathilde again.

The next months were calm. Verlaine composed the poems of *Romances sans paroles,* and Rimbaud immersed himself in the study of "magics, alchemies, mysticisms, false perfumes and naive musics." But the savage passion of their first days together had vanished, the days of:

> The happiness of bleeding in the arms of a friend,
> The need to cry a long while upon his breast,
> The need to talk to him, low and with few words,
> The dream of drifting together, endlessly together.
> *(Parallèlement)*

Soon they ran out of money. Verlaine's drunken rages, his mystical crises and jeremiads exasperated Rimbaud, who finally went back to Charleville on November 20, 1872. Unable to stand his solitude, Verlaine fell ill early in January and wrote to Mathilde, begging her to come to London. She refused, but Verlaine's mother rushed to his side, as did Rimbaud, to whom she had sent the fare for the journey across the Channel.

Verlaine soon recovered, and once again the two friends set out on their wild wanderings. They went to Ostend and to Antwerp, then back to London and their old financial worries. Verlaine finished *Romances sans paroles,* and dedicated it to Rimbaud; meanwhile Rimbaud had started working on *A Season in Hell.* On July 3, as Verlaine was returning to their room after doing some shopping, Rimbaud, seeing him with a bottle of oil and a herring in his hands, burst out laughing, and jeered, "What an idiot you look like!" Verlaine blanched angrily, turned around and without saying a word or taking the time to pack his belongings, walked out, going straight to St. Catherine's Dock, where he took the first boat to Antwerp. He sent a letter to Rimbaud, explaining, "...that violent life, and all those senseless scenes your freakish nature imposed on me.... Only, since I loved you enormously *(Honni soit qui mal y pense),* I want you to know that if in the next three days I am not back with my wife under perfect conditions I will blow my brains out." Two days later Verlaine, who had even told Madame Rimbaud of his intentions, admitted to his friend Matuszewicz, "It's too stupid to kill oneself like that."

Rimbaud, meanwhile, was in a panic. He wrote to Verlaine admitting his errors and begging his friend, "Please come back, I am crying all the time." But three days later he had got possession of himself: "This time it is you who are wrong.... Do you think that your life will be any pleasanter with others than with me? Think it over. Certainly not. If you do not want to come back or let me come to you, you will be committing a crime, and you will regret it for years and years, for you will have lost all your freedom, and you will have troubles perhaps worse than any you have yet experienced. After that, think back on what you were before you met me...." Naturally Verlaine gave in, and the bizarre couple, accompanied by Verlaine's mother, settled down together again at the Hotel de Courtrai in Brussels. But almost immediately, Rimbaud decided that his relationship with that "poor brother" had to end. He annouced that he was leaving for Paris. A violent scene ensued, with each of them swearing never to see the other again. Early next morning, Verlaine went out and bought a revolver. He returned drunk and took a shot at Rimbaud, wounding him in the hand. Several years later, he described the scene to the journalist Antoine Retté: "Rimbaud was standing next to the door, his arms crossed on his chest in defiance. Oh, the evilness, the cruelty in his fallen archangel's eyes.... I had said everything I could to make him stay with me. Without even looking my way, he answered, 'fuck off.' I was wild, and I thought to myself, there's nothing for it. I have to kill him." Rimbaud went to have his wound dressed. That evening at 7 o'clock, Verlaine and his mother accompanied him to the station. There Verlaine made another threatening gesture, and afraid, Rimbaud called to a policeman who was standing nearby. Verlaine was arrested. Rimbaud was searched, and one of Verlaine's poems was found in his pocket (see selection); together with a report from the Paris police, this told the judge all he needed to know about the relationship between the victim and the accused. Although Rimbaud later withdrew his complaint, Verlaine was nevertheless sentenced to two years in jail.

The stormy affair had lasted two years: the two poets had actually lived together for only seven months. In prison Verlaine tried to forget the "misery of loving." Encouraged by frequent visits from the chaplain, he returned to his childhood faith. Rimbaud, too, had decided to turn over a new leaf: "Ah, the boundless selfishness of adolescence, the studious optimism; and how the world seemed full of flowers that summer!" He was impatient to find "the place and the formula." In his distress, he refused the comforts of mysticism or religion, the "artificial paradises" of drugs and wine. Instead, with his usual relentless energy he set about becoming a man of action and of science. As soon as Verlaine was released from jail, he rushed to Stuttgart to see his "beautiful, radiant sin," but Rimbaud greeted him with sarcasm, nicknaming him *Loyola*. In a letter to Delahaye, Rimbaud gives an account of their meeting: "Verlaine showed up the other day with a rosary in his paws. Three hours later we had abjured his god and had made the 98 wounds of Our Lord bleed again. He stayed two and a half very reasonable days...." The two poets wrote to each other occasionally, Rimbaud, as always, pestering *Loyola* for money. Verlaine refused his requests, and on December 12 he wrote to Rimbaud for the last time, asking him to change the tone of his letters or to stop writing.

Rimbaud soon repudiated his past and bid farewell to poetry and to the passions of his youth. It was not despair which prompted him: on the contrary, he was convinced, despite his withdrawn, emotional (he blushed easily) and shy nature, that he was really an exceptional person and that a great destiny awaited him. In this frame of mind, he set out for Africa and adventure, sure that he was going to make a fortune. He deemed himself a "materialist." The reality turned out to be far from glorious: a determined but unlucky trader and gun runner, Rimbaud was gradually worn out by hard work, the harsh climate and illness; and he died miserably of a cancer in a hospital in Marseilles in 1891.

Rimbaud has been severely judged by the critic Etiemble, who has compared him to "those who, tormented by puberty, skilled in transferring their carnal difficulties into a revolutionary apocalypse, become reconciled in their mid-twenties with the most dubious aspects of the society which as adolescents they had rightly rejected." Can one really say that Rimbaud became reconciled with the established values of society? Rather was not this poet of genius a fierce individualist? A misfit, a homosexual, an anarchist and at the end an adventurer?

After spending two quiet years in London, Verlaine was once again possessed by the "frenzy of love." This time the object of his passion was a snub-nosed schoolboy he had failed in English (for Verlaine had meanwhile become a teacher). The poet writes of the lad's graceful way of walking down stairs, of his skill at skating, "like some tall young girl," of his "little martial air" when he rode on horseback, of his "voice in the Bois de Boulogne." One dreadful evening the boy confessed to him that he had slept with a woman, and as he was describing the event, he seemed to Verlaine "like a lily swept by passion; after the storm had passed, he stood straighter and appeared more virile." Verlaine bought his young lover a farm and even considered adopting him, but in 1888, the youth died of typhoid.

> Six years it lasted, then the angel flew away.
> Since then I have wandered alone, wild, as though drunk!

Henceforth Verlaine spent most of his time cruising in bars and cafés with his friend "Bibi la purée" (see p. 172). When his mother died, he wrote miserably, "now the only mother I have is the welfare office." He drifted from hospital to hospital, had an affair with a prostitute and then other affairs with fading Parisian beauties like Eugénie Krantz and Philomène Boudin (whom he even thought of marrying).

While Rimbaud was dying in Marseilles, Verlaine was beginning to acquire belated literary renown. He was invited to lecture in the French provinces, in London, at Oxford, in Manchester and in Amsterdam; newspapers began asking him for contributions. Things were going so well that in 1894 he announced his candidacy to the prestigious Académie française. He was not elected, but was named "Prince of Poets." At the urging of Maurice Barrès and the Comte de Montesquiou, a committee was set up to administer a regular pension for Verlaine. The poet died in Eugénie Krantz's apartment whispering "François," the name of the painter Cazals, who had been his last great, though purely Platonic, love. "The reason that I have fallen so many times," Verlaine had written on the occasion of Villiers de L'Isle-Adam's death, "is that I am a fairy; that explains many things."

RIMBAUD   O SEASONS, O CASTLES

In this poem Rimbaud celebrates the joy of surrendering to the person you love. These lines, which are part of *A Season in Hell,* were probably composed in May or early June, 1872. In an earlier draft, Rimbaud had written:

> I belong to him, each time
> His cock crows....

O seasons, O castles
What soul's without stain?

O seasons, O castles,

I have studied the magic lore
Of Happiness no man eludes.

Oh, hurrah for him, each time
His Gallic cock sings.

But! I'll have no more desire,
He has taken charge of my life.

That Charm! it took body and soul,
And scattered every effort.

What can be understood from my words?
He makes them escape, fly off!

O seasons, O castles!

(And, if misfortune sweeps me along,
I am certain of his downfall.

Alas, his scorn must
Deliver me to promptest death!

—O Seasons, O Castles!)

Paul Verlaine, Drawing of Rimbaud. Viollet Collection, Musée Arthur-Rimbaud, Charleville-Mézières.

ANTIQUE

This poem was published in *Illuminations* in 1886. In his preface to his friend's book, Verlaine wrote that the prose poems in it had been written between 1873 and 1875.

Graceful son of Pan! Under your brow crowned with flowers and berries, your eyes, precious balls, move. Spotted with dark streaks, your cheeks look hollow. Your fangs glisten. Your chest is like a lyre and tinklings move up and down your white arms. Your heart beats in that abdomen where your double sex sleeps. Walk at night and move gently this thigh, then this other thigh and this left leg.

171

SONNET TO THE ASS-HOLE

These lines were found in the *Album Zutique* under the title, "Sonnet to the Ass-Hole." Scholars think that the first eight lines were written by Verlaine and the last six by Rimbaud. The *Album Zutique* was begun in 1871 by Dr. Antoine Cros, who invited poets like Verlaine, Rimbaud, Richepin, Valade, Cabaner, etc., to contribute parodies and facetious poems to it.

Dark and wrinkled like a deep pink,
It breathes, humbly nestled among the moss
Still wet with love that follows the gentle
Descent of the white buttocks to the edge of its border.

Filaments like tears of milk
Have wept under the cruel wind pushing them back
Over small clots of reddish marl,
And there lose themselves where the slope called them.

In my dream my mouth was often placed on its opening;
My soul, jealous of the physical coitus,
Made of it its fawny tear-bottle and its nest of sobs.

It is the fainting olive and the cajoling flute,
The tube from which the heavenly praline descends,
A feminine Canaan enclosed in moisture.

VAGABONDS

In 1878 Verlaine identified himself as the "poor brother" of the following poem from *Illuminations*. He wrote to Charles de Sivry, "I have reread *Illuminations* [Painted Plates], by the gentleman you know, as well as his *Season in Hell,* where I am portrayed as a satanic doctor (which is false)."

Poor brother! What terrible nights I owed him! "I had no deep feeling for the affair. I played on his weakness. Through my fault, we would return to exile and slavery." He believed I had a very queer form of bad luck and innocence, and he added upsetting reasons.
With a jeer I answered my satanic doctor and left by the window. Along the countryside, streaked with bands of rare music, I created phantoms of a future night parade.
After that vaguely hygienic distraction, I lay down on straw. And almost every night, as soon as I was asleep, my poor brother would get up, his mouth and his eyes protruding—just as he dreamed himself to be—and would drag me into the room yelling his dream of a sad fool.
In deepest sincerity, I had pledged to convert him back into his primitive state of a sun-child,—and we wandered, sustained by wine from caverns and traveler's crust, with me impatient to find the place and the formula.

Félix Regamey, *Verlaine and Rimbaud in London*. September, 1872. Viollet Collection.

Aubrey Beardsley, Frontispiece for Oscar Wilde's *Salome* (detail). John Lane, the publisher, found this drawing too indecent and refused to print it.

VERLAINE

THE GOOD DISCIPLE

The following poem, written in May 1872, was found in Rimbaud's wallet by a Brussels policeman (see p. 170).

I am elected, I am damned!
Surrounded by an unknown blast.
O terror! *Parce, Domine!*

What hard Angel pounds me thus
Between my shoulders while
I fly up to Paradise?

Fever, adorable malignancy,
Excellent delirium, blessed terror,
I am martyr and king alike,
Falcon I soar, and swan I die!

You Jealous One who called to me,
Here I am, all of me!
Crawling towards you, still unworthy
—Climb up on my loins, and trample me!

THOUSAND AND THREE

Verlaine wrote this poem in a hospital in 1891 and included it in the privately printed series of poems called *Hombres*. He intended *Hombres* to be the counterpart of another series, called *Femmes* [Women]. This translation is taken from a book entitled *Hashish and Incense*, which is a selection of poems from both series, privately printed in England in 1925 (in the original, lines 13 and 14 read: "Their vigorous cocks and joyous asses/Gladden the night, and my prick, and my behind....").

My lovers do not belong to the two rich classes:
They are the suburban and rural workmen.
Their fifteen and twenty years, unrestrained, are prodigious
With their brutal force and gross ways.

I sense them in their work clothes, overalls and shirts:
They do not smell of perfume, but blossom with health
Pure and simple; their heavy walk is nimble
For all that with youthful and grave elasticity.

Their frank and sly eyes crackle with cordial
Malice, and naïvely deceitful words
Flow—not without a gay oath to spice them—
From their mouths fresh with solid kisses;

Their vigorous ways and joyous manners
Gladden the night, and my soul, and my body
Under the lamp and at dawn, their joyous flesh,
Resuscitates my tired desire never conquered....

173

CRIMEN AMORIS

In a copy of his book *Jadis et Naguère* dedicated to Comte Kessler, Verlaine made the following annotation in the margin next to "Crimen Amoris": "Written in the prison of the Petits Carmes, Brussels, August 1873 (and not in one of the easy cells either) on a piece of wrapping paper from a cheese (from the canteen), and with a match stick dipped in the house coffee…PV." This is one of the finest poems that Rimbaud inspired; it was composed before Verlaine's crisis of repentance. The poet is haunted by the figure of Rimbaud, who appears to him as a wayward and seductive angel. This adolescent satan tries to abolish the distinction between good and evil and is destroyed for having wanted to commit this crime of love.

The following excerpt was translated for this anthology by Stewart Lindh.

To Villiers de L'Isle-Adam

The most beautiful among all the fallen angels
Wore his sixteen years like a crown of dark flowers
He stood with his arms crossed over jewels and silk,
Dreaming, his eyes filled with flames and tears.

In vain, the frenzy around him rose,
In vain, the Satans, the satyrs, the harpies
Could not uproot him from his sorrow.
His heart had broken from the orgy.

He resisted all the small rainbows of flattery,
And over a forehead outlined with gold
Sadness spread the wings of a black butterfly.
Oh, endless and terrible despair.

He spoke to those around him, "Leave me alone."
Then, having embraced each approaching form farewell,
He withdrew in one long delicate motion,
Leaving behind in their hands patches of torn silk….

What is he saying with his voice of distance and echo,
With words mixed with the crackling of fire,
And offering a message that the moon enlarges to hear:
"I am that one who will be God!…

"Enough, too much of a bickering struggle!
What must be done is to join again
The Seven Sins with the Three Holy Virtues.
Enough, too much of stale and rigid struggles!

"As for Jesus who believed himself right
In maintaining the balance in this duel,
I believe Hell, whose very den is here,
Sacrifices itself to universal Love!"

The torch fell from his opening hand,
And a comet howled across the sky,
Illuminating an enormous quarrel of golden eagles
Drowned in a black estuary of smoke and wind.

CES PASSIONS

This poem from *Parallèlement* was published in *La Cravache* in 1889 under the title "L'Abîme." It is a hymn to homosexual love, which Verlaine depicts as a rite reserved for superior men. The version given here, a brilliantly imaginative rendering, is by Stewart Lindh.

These passions that only two men name love
Are love as well, tender and wild,
With their curious differences
That lovers in daylight do not share.

Expanding deeper than ordinary feelings,
These passions array themselves in shimmering
Waves of blood and soul, joined at such a price
To themselves that lovers following the well-worn path

To pleasure are nothing but a private joke,
An erotic need, no more than a pack of pale
Proverbs, babble
Spilling from the mouths of spoiled children.

"Poor pathetic banal love, dull spirited, thick
With normality, stale breathing and dragging
About a lead appetite, without mentioning
The house of stupidity and its little blessings…."

In turn, these men, to answer their desires
Complete the supreme action, ream the dark halo of
  ecstasy:
Matching the lip, heating the mouth, filling
In the vase with flowers of fire.

These passions cast a mirrored architecture.
Their forms conceal no fainting spells or
Crying fits. No, they make courageous
Play, then aching with warm fatigue they clutch

And drop into the cool waves of sheets,
Tossing back and forth
All night in stormy dreams. So sleep,
Lovers, while around you a world

Blind to delicate sights such as yours,
Builds new noises or dulls its heart
Inside a lenghtening stupor without
Any knowledge or jealousy of you.

Waking now, fresh, laughing towards another
Adventure, these proud exiles of pleasure.
Good fortune to you, pure souls in the long
Struggle to free the body from nature's
Breathing prison.

Antoine Wiertz, *The Suicide*. Musées Royaux des Beaux-Arts de Belgique, Brussels.

Antoine Wiertz, *Satan, the Most Beautiful of All the Angels*. Musées Royaux des Beaux-Arts de Belgique, Brussels.

RENDEZ-VOUS

".... Your voice trumpets in my soul,
Your eyes are flaming in my heart.
The world calls it infamy,
But what do I care, my vanquisher!

"I have the sadness, I have the joy,
And I have the love, one more time,
The sneering tearful love,
O you, beautiful as a little wolf!

"You came to me, savage boy;
It is you—prettiness and gift of gab—
Wily of mouth and body
Who does violence to me, utterly....

"I await you like the Messiah,
Come, cast yourself into my arms;
A rare greeting, carefully prepared,
Awaits you; come, you will see!"

Phosphorus flares in his eyes,
And his lips, smiling perversely,
Are aroused on the feather
Of the pen he holds to write these lines....

(Parallèlement)

OSCAR WILDE (1854-1900)

Oscar Fingall O'Flahertie Wills Wilde was born in Dublin on October 16, 1854. He was the second child of whimsical and eccentric parents. His father, Sir William Wilde, an internationally renowned oculist, the founder of a famous hospital and an amateur archeologist, was notorious for his unbridled love life, his numerous illegitimate offspring, his propensity to drink and his uncleanliness. At thirty-six this adventurous, faunish little man of science married a young, statuesque, beautiful, though rather virile-featured poetess, Jane Francesca Elgee. "Speranza" (her pseudonym) wrote political articles and manifestoes for *The Nation,* the journal of the "Young Ireland" party; however, a political trial put an end to this work. Though physically dissimilar to the point of grotesqueness, she and her husband shared the same liberal opinions and had the same flair for eccentricity.

Presumably, Oscar's birth was a disappointment for Lady Wilde, who had wanted a daughter: she dressed him in petticoats and covered him with jewelry and perfume as if he really were a girl. She continued to do so even after her third child, a daughter named Isola, was born four years later. The bizarre Wilde family split into two clans, the one masculine, comprising Sir William and his eldest son, Willie; the other feminine, consisting of Speranza, Isola and Oscar.

Oscar attended Trinity College in Dublin where he studied the Greek classics and was awarded the Berkeley Gold Medal in 1874 for an essay on Greek poetry. The same year he won a scholarship to Magdalen College, Oxford, and there he became acquainted with the writings of Swinburne, Ruskin and Walter Pater. He soon became an ardent apostle of the "Aesthetic Movement." During holidays he visited Italy and Greece, broadening his knowledge of classical art. Even before graduating from Oxford in 1878 with a degree in art history, he began to be known as one of the leading figures of the new hedonist philosophy. He dressed in silk stockings and breeches, wore a velvet jacket and an ample cravat. In London, he walked down the streets holding a lily or a sunflower, the favorite emblems of the Pre-Raphaelite painters Dante Gabriel Rossetti, Sir John Millais and Sir Edward Burne-Jones. His various heterosexual affairs belied the rumors that were going around

Anonymous, *Oscar Wilde in 1875*. Guillot de Saix-Viollet Collection.

about his homosexual inclinations based on supposedly unmentionable affairs at Magdalen College. There are grounds for believing that he contracted syphilis from a prostitute. His teeth blackened and his hair began to discolor, presumably from doses of mercury, which was the standard nineteenth-century treatment for syphilis. Some people were repulsed by him. "The great white slug," as one of his detractors called him, had his mother's hulking build, massive hands, a ponderous jaw and a pasty complexion. Notwithstanding, Wilde was convinced he was handsome, or at least he was determined to appear handsome; he would refer to his imperial expression, caress his body and brush his hair, painstakingly arranged in the manner of Nero. Indeed, he was not an unattractive figure. He seems mainly to have appealed to actresses, such as Ellen Terry, Lilly Langtry, the Polish star Helena Modjeska and the great Sarah Bernhardt.

On May 29, 1884, Wilde married Constance Lloyd, the wealthy daughter of a Dublin barrister, whom he had met three years earlier. Constance was "as white and as

W. P. Frith, *A Private View* (1881). C.J.R. Pope Collection.

Aubrey Beardsley, *Oscar Wilde at Work*, a caricature. Guillot de Saix-Viollet Collection.

One of the young models who frequented the sanctuary built in 1927 by Elisar von Kupffer, who lived there with his friend, the philosopher Eduard von Mayer. Minusio, near Locarno.

beautiful as a lily." She adored Oscar, who seems to have been very much in love with her too. During their honeymoon in Paris he sent her extravagant bouquets each time he spent more than an hour away from her. The young couple was the darling of London society. Then came two children, both sons: Vyvyan in 1885, and Clarence in 1886. Wilde was physically repulsed by his wife's pregnancy: "In a short while, her flower's gracefulness withered. She became disfigured, deformed. She moped about the house, clumsy and unhappy, her features drawn, her complexion mottled, her body hideous, diseased by our love.... Oh, nature is despicable; it takes beauty and sullies it.... it profanes the soul's altar. How can one call that intimacy love? How can one idealize it? Love is not possible for an artist unless he is sterile." Perhaps there were other reasons for this disgust? Possibly a renewed outbreak of syphilis had strained his relationship with Constance.

At any event, after the birth of his second son in 1886, Oscar Wilde began to turn towards men. That year he met a seventeen year old student who was already an experienced homosexual, Robert Baldwin Ross. "Little Robbie," as Wilde called him, may have initiated the thirty-two year old aesthete into the ways of Socratic love. Robbie, a journalist and an art-lover, soon became an enthusiastic fellow-member of Wilde's circle, sharing his older friend's eccentric tastes. Wilde, nevertheless, carefully preserved a facade of respectability. To help pay for his extravagances, he took a job as the editor of a fashionable ladies' magazine called *Women's World*. He traveled frequently and spent much of his time in Rome and in Paris, where he was considered something of a curiosity by the French literary establishment. His Parisian counterpart, Robert de Montesquiou, the prince of the French aesthetes and a homosexual himself, referred to him unkindly as "the horrid Antinoüs." On the other hand, the young and charming writer, Pierre Louÿs, who did not by any means share Wilde's proclivities, was enthralled by the Englishman in spite of himself. André Gide, who met Wilde through Pierre Louÿs, wrote to Paul Valéry, "Oscar Wilde, the aesthete, is admirable, admirable...." Apparently, the admiration was reciprocal, for Wilde gushed back:"... you listen with your eyes ... you have the narrow lips of someone who is incapable of telling a lie...."

Virtually idolized by his disciples, Oscar Wilde no longer bothered concealing his true nature and began flaunting his scandalous behaviour. He stopped eating at home and spent less and less time there; finally, in 1893, he rented a suite at the Savoy, to which he invited young poets, many of them students, as well as less educated—and sometimes even illiterate—youths. He would offer them a meal, a few pounds or a cigarette case (sometimes engraved with the recipient's name) in return for their "services." One of his guests, nineteen year old Charles Parker, a gunner in the Royal Artillery, who had probably been supplied by one of the Savoy's staff, later at the trial, related how Wilde, after inviting him to dinner, had brought him up to his rooms. Wilde had then come to Parker's place in Chelsea a few days later. "He asked me to make believe I was a woman and he was my lover. I had to keep up this pretence. I would sit on his knees, and he toyed with me as a man does with a girl...." The two had made so much noise that they had woken up one of the lodgers in Parker's house.

One summer afternoon in 1891, a poet friend, Lionel Johnson, brought Lord Alfred Douglas to tea at Oscar Wilde's. The third son of the Marquess of Queensberry, Alfred Douglas was twenty-two years old. He was a student at Oxford. His gift for verse, his handsome looks

and his title made a considerable impression on Oscar Wilde. Douglas was no less impressed: Wilde was older and more experienced; he was rich, admired and famous. Bosie (Douglas's childhood nickname) was flattered to be seen in Wilde's company. Wilde courted him assiduously, sending him notes, letters and telegrams at the slightest pretext. "He is the only man I know," wrote Douglas, "who had the courage to put his arm around the shoulders of a former convict and to go down to Piccadilly like this...." Notwithstanding their difference in age, Bosie was too much of an individual to submit to Wilde's sadistic wit, his cruel words and his crushing hauteur. Contrary to what happened in his other relationships, Wilde assumed the role of the "victim" in his affair with Alfred Douglas. The psychological attitude was the same one Verlaine had displayed with Rimbaud; Wilde himself has described it in detail in *The Picture of Dorian Gray*. Emotionally Wilde became Douglas's puppet, even deriving a masochistic enjoyment from his dependence. André Gide has described a scene he witnessed in Algiers: in a "hissing, withering, savage voice" Douglas rapped out a few sentences, then turning on his heels, went out. Wilde turned very pale and, after a moment's silence, moaned to Gide, "He's terrible. Isn't he terrible?" "Even in those words," remarked Gide, "his admiration for Douglas and a kind of lover's infatuated pleasure in being mastered, were manifest." Wilde was later to accuse Douglas in *De Profundis* of being his evil genius and of having incited him into extravagant expenditures of money and, to the detriment of his art, of time.

Intoxicated by his successes, Wilde spent all the income he got from his writing in traveling and in debauchery. With its violent scenes and its frequent partings, his relationship with Douglas recalls Verlaine's affair with Rimbaud—with the difference that Wilde and Douglas apparently felt no sexual jealousy for each other, for neither ever felt it necessary to conceal his secondary involvements from his partner. In Worthing, where they holidayed towards the end of the summer of 1894, they cruised along the beach together, picking up young workers and newspaper vendors who were only too happy to be of service to the "Lord" and his illustrious friend. Partly as a matter of taste, partly from his eternal inclination to be provocative, Wilde loved to go slumming. In London he frequently took bizarre-looking characters out to dinner and was delighted when his guest's Cockney accent drew scandalized looks from elegant fellow diners. He frequented a tranvestite brothel run by Alfred Taylor in Pimlico. Fortunately he was not in attendance on the night when the police raided the premises. His reputation suffered though when he testified for Taylor at the latter's trial. In Algiers, Wilde and Douglas sought out their pleasures among the young Arab boys "whose bodies are dark, wild and lascivious," as André Gide, who accompanied them one night, wrote in *If It Die*....

Lord Douglas had introduced Wilde to a jobless young man named Wood. As usual, Wilde invited Wood to dinner and then took him back to his suite. In the pocket of an old jacket which Douglas had left behind, Wood found a compromising letter by Oscar Wilde, and he stole it, hoping to blackmail Wilde. Wilde eventually got the letter back. He had written: "...it is a marvel that those red rose-leaf lips of yours should have been made no less for music of song than for madness of kisses." As a precaution, Wilde had the letter translated into French by Pierre Louÿs, so that if necessary he could claim it was a prose poem.

In 1895 two of Oscar Wilde's plays, *An Ideal Husband* and *The Importance of Being Ernest,* opened at the same time. It was a year of triumph for Wilde, but it ended disastrously. Douglas's father, the irascible Marquess of Queensberry, who had quarreled with all of his children, became extremely annoyed about the rumors concerning his son and "that fellow Wilde," as he invariably referred to the writer. He wrote threatening letters to Alfred, ordering him to put an immediate stop to his "repulsive and odious intimacy" with Wilde. "What a funny little man you are," replied Lord Douglas scornfully. This only nettled Lord Queensberry further. He came to the premiere of *The Importance of Being Ernest* holding a bouquet of carrots and turnips. A few days later, happening to pass in front of Wilde's club, he handed the doorman a card on which he had written: "Oscar Wilde poses as a sodomite."

At the urging of Lord Douglas, who detested his father, Wilde decided to enter a libel action against the "scarlet marquess." It was an insane notion, since all the evidence was against Wilde. "The one disgraceful, unpardonable, and to all time contemptible action of my life was to allow myself to appeal to society for help and protection," wrote Wilde in *De Profundis*. On the opening day of the trial, Wilde arrived in court in a two-horse carriage, accompanied by the two sons of the accused. On the last day, May 25, he walked out between two policemen, having been sentenced to two years in jail. His airy manner had irked the judges. To the attorney general, who had asked him if he had kissed one of Douglas's servants, a young man named Granger, he had replied, "Oh, indeed not! he was too ugly."

The accuser had become the accused. Wilde had of course not foreseen this reversal of roles. Nevertheless counts of indictment had been piling up against him during the trial. They were all based on charges of "immoral acts" committed with young men. Taylor, who was a co-defendant, had introduced Wilde to a number of boy-prostitutes. These youths—valets, stable-boys, grooms and newspaper vendors—were called to the witness stand, and their testimony proved fatal to Wilde's case. It is amazing that Douglas was not charged too. Two of his poems were read in court, "In Praise of Shame" and "The Two Loves"; Wilde was asked to give his interpretation of the the line, "The Love that dares not speak its name."

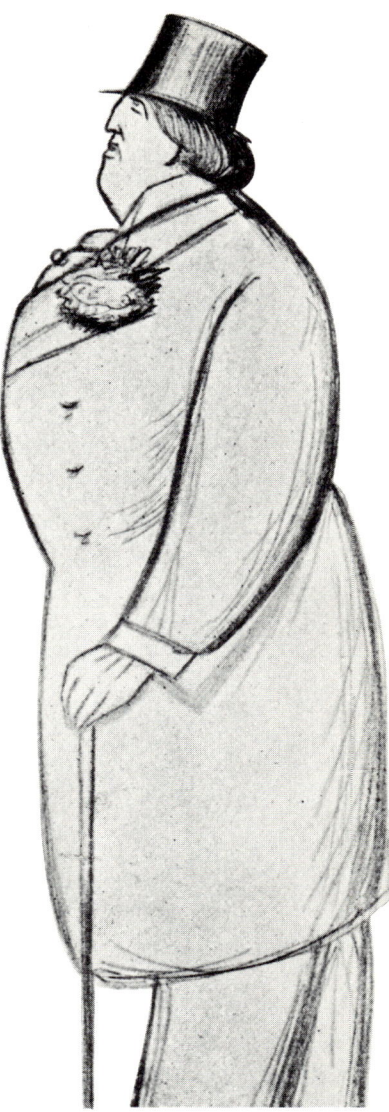

Henri de Toulouse-Lautrec, *Oscar Wilde and R. Coolens*. Musée Toulouse-Lautrec, Albi. The painter went to London especially to attend Oscar Wilde's trial.

Max Beerbohm, *Oscar Wilde*, a caricature. Guillot de Saix-Viollet Collection.

"...in this century [it] is such a great affection of an elder for a younger man as there was between David and Jonathan, such as Plato made the very basis of his philosophy, and such as you find in the sonnets of Michelangelo and Shakespeare. It is that deep, spiritual affection that is as pure as it is perfect.... on account of it I am placed where I am now.... The world mocks at it and sometimes puts one in the pillory for it." (Loud applause, mingled with some hisses.)

Despite the intervention of those friends who had stood by him during the trial, Wilde was sentenced to two years hard labor. In Reading Gaol, where he was simply prisoner C33, he sewed sacks and wore his fingers raw shredding ropes into oakum. He was eventually allowed a pen and paper, on the grounds that his behavior was so outstandingly good. As he sat writing in his cell, he had the sorrowful, hurt look of a lady who had been slighted, according to one of his warders. In the form of a letter to Lord Douglas, he began writing the scathing two-hundred page indictment later published under the title *De Profundis*.

Wilde was released on May 19, 1897, and, despite his grudges, he immediately went to see Lord Douglas. He decided to settle in France, in the village of Berneval, near Dieppe; it was there that he wrote "The Ballad of Reading Gaol" that summer. Aubrey Beardsley, who was vacationing in Dieppe with his mother and his sister, carefully avoided meeting Wilde. Wilde's only comment was, "That was cowardly of Aubrey."

Jean-François Matet, *Oscar Wilde in a Parisian Cabaret*. Georges Foussier-Viollet Collection.

John Singer Sargent, *Portrait of Graham Robertson*. Tate Gallery, London. What could be more "Dorian Gray" that this portrait?

One evening Wilde was taken by some friends to a brothel in Dieppe. It was a distasteful experience, and he vowed never to repeat it. Soon the isolation of his Normandy village began to weigh on him. Unknown to his friends, he secretly resumed his affair with Bosie. After meeting in Rouen, the two friends traveled to Naples and spent the winter there together. "I cannot live without the atmosphere of love," wrote Wilde. "(Bosie) gave me love; in my solitude and shame, after struggling for three months against the hideous world of the Philistines, I naturally turned to him." Yet Mrs. Wilde had agreed to give him a regular pension of £150 on the condition that he refrain from seeing Douglas.

The spring of 1899 found Wilde in Rome with his old friend, Robert Ross. Like many homosexuals, Wilde had always been attracted by Catholicism, and he had contemplated converting to it. Ross, who was skeptical about his friend's religious sentiments, tried to discourage Wilde from going over to the Church of Rome. Wilde later accused him of having stood at the entrance to the church brandishing a sword of fire to prevent him from entering.

Wilde made regular trips to Paris. Sometimes Bosie would be waiting for him, and the two friends would go slumming together in the city's most sordid cafés. Wilde took to drinking absinthe (like Verlaine). He knew that it was killing him. "But why should I go on living?" He stopped writing, explaining that "I used to write in the days when I did not know what life was about; now that I know I have nothing to write. Life is not meant to be written about; it is meant to be lived. I have lived."

In October, 1900, the earaches he had suffered from in prison began to return. He was unable to afford the necessary operation. Lord Douglas sent him a check, but by the time it reached him Wilde had lost the courage to go through with the operation. On November 30, he died in a little hotel in the rue des Saints-Pères, where he had registered under the name Sebastian Melmoth. Ross was with him, as was a priest, Father Cuthbert Dunne. Wilde took the sacraments, thus making the conversion he had been putting off for so long.

Ross was obliged to argue with the police to keep them from removing Wilde's body to the morgue. He arranged for the author's temporary burial in the cemetary of Bagneux on the outskirts of Paris. Lord Douglas came to the funeral and paid for the expenses.

OSCAR WILDE

The following texts were read during Wilde's trial by the public prosecutor, who wanted to show that the accused had attempted to influence youths to follow the path of vice and to "shape them according to his depraved tastes."

From THE PICTURE OF DORIAN GRAY

Suddenly I found myself face to face with the young man whose personality had so strangely stirred me. We were quite close, almost touching. Our eyes met again. It was reckless of me, but I asked Lady Brandon to introduce me to him. Perhaps it was not so reckless, after all. It was simply inevitable. We would have spoken to each other without any introduction. I am sure of that. Dorian told me so afterwards. He, too, felt that we were destined to know each other.

"Tell me more about Mr. Dorian Gray. How often do you see him?"

"Every day. I couldn't be happy if I didn't see him every day. He is absolutely necessary to me."

"How extraordinary! I thought you would never care for anything but your art."

"He is all my art to me now," said the painter, gravely. "I sometimes think, Harry, that there are only two eras of any importance in the world's history. The first is the appearance of a new medium for art, and the second is the appearance of a new personality for art also. What the invention of oil-painting was to the Venetians, the face of Antinoüs was to late Greek sculpture, and the face of Dorian Gray will some day be to me. It is not merely that I paint from him, draw from him, sketch from him. Of course I have done all that. But he is much more to me than a model or a sitter. I won't tell you that I am dissatisfied with what I have done of him, or that his beauty is such that Art cannot express it. There is nothing that Art cannot express, and I know that the work I have done, since I met Dorian Gray, is good work, is the best work of my life. But in some curious way—I wonder will you understand me?—his personality has suggested to me an entirely new manner in art, an entirely new mode of style. I see things differently, I think of them differently. I can now recreate life in a way that was hidden from me before. 'A dream of form in days of thought:'—who is it who says that? I forget; but it is what Dorian Gray has been to me. The merely visible presence of this lad—for he seems to me little more than a lad, though he is really over twenty—his merely visible presence—ah! I wonder can you realise all that that means? Unconsciously he defines for me the lines of a fresh school, a school that is to have in it all the passion of the romantic spirit, all the perfection of the spirit that is Greek. The harmony of soul and body—how much that is! We in our madness have separated the two, and have invented a realism that is vulgar, an ideality that is void. Harry! If you only knew what Dorian Gray is to me! You remember that landscape of mine, for which Agnew offered me such a huge price, but which I would not part with? It is one of the best things I have ever done. And why is it so? Because, while I was painting it, Dorian Gray sat beside me. Some subtle influence passed from him to me, and for the first time in my life I saw in the plain woodland the wonder I had always looked for, and always missed."

"Basil, this is extraordinary! I must see Dorian Gray."

PROSECUTOR: "Now I ask you, Mr. Wilde, do you consider that that description of the feeling of one man towards a youth just grown up was a proper or an improper feeling?"
WILDE: "I think it is the most perfect description of what an artist would feel on meeting a beautiful personality that was in some way necessary to his art and life...."
(The following letter was then read aloud:)

Dearest of all Boys,
    Your letter was delightful, red and yellow wine to me; but I am sad and out of sorts. Bosie, you must not make scenes with me. They kill me, they wreck the loveliness of life. I cannot see you, so Greek and gracious, distorted with passion. I cannot listen to your curved lips saying hideous things to me. I would sooner—than have you bitter, unjust, hating.... I must see you soon. You are the divine thing I want, the thing of grace and beauty; but I cont'know how to do it. Shall I come to Salisbury? My bill here is £ 49 for a week. I have also got a new sitting room.... Why are you not here, my dear, my wonderful boy? I fear I must leave—no money, no credit, and a heart of lead.
                                            Your own Oscar

PROSECUTOR: "Is that an ordinary letter?"
WILDE: "Everything I write is extraordinary. I do not pose as being ordinary, great heavens! Ask me any question you like about it."
PROSECUTOR: "Is it the kind of letter a man writes to another?"
WILDE: "It was a tender expression of my great admiration for Lord Alfred Douglas."

DE PROFUNDIS

When Wilde was released from prison in 1897 he handed over to his friend Robert Ross a twenty-page manuscript written on blue prison stationary. It was the text of a long letter addressed to Lord Douglas. Ross had it typed in two copies and claimed that he had sent one of them to Lord Douglas, who denied ever having received it however. After Wilde's death, Ross published extracts from the letter under the title *De Profundis*. He donated the entire manuscript to the British Museum, stipulating that it was not to be made available to the public before 1960. One of the typewritten copies was given to Wilde's son, Vyvyan Holland; but this version, which Mr. Holland published in 1949, was incomplete and not always in agreement with the manuscript in the British Museum, from which the following excerpts are taken. In the typewritten versions, Ross had deleted the passages in which Wilde criticized Lord Douglas most severely. In 1918 Lord Douglas entered a libel suit against Ross's friend Arthur Ransome, who had just written a biography of Wilde. Ross testified on behalf of the accused and read the expurgated passages out loud in court. That is how Lord Douglas finally became acquainted with Wilde's criticism of him. The resentment and the hatred he conceived for Ross may easily be imagined.

I will begin by telling you that I blame myself terribly. As I sit here in this dark cell in convict clothes, a disgraced and ruined man, I blame myself. In the perturbed and fitful nights of anguish, in the long monotonous days of pain, it is myself I blame. I blame myself for allowing an unintellectual friendship, a friendship whose primary aim was not the creation and contemplation of beautiful things, entirely to dominate my life....

But most of all I blame myself for the entire ethical degradation I allowed you to bring on me. The basis of character is will power, and my will power became absolutely subject to yours. It sounds a grotesque thing to say, but it is none the less true. Those incessant scenes that seemed to be almost physically necessary to you and in which your mind and body grew distorted and you became a thing as terrible to look at as to listen to: that dreadful mania you inherit from your father, the mania for writing revolting and loathsome letters: your entire lack of any control over your emotions, as displayed in your long resentful moods of sullen silence, no less than in your sudden fits of almost epileptic rage: all these things in reference to which one of my letters to you, left by you

Simeon Solomon, *Greek Acolyte*. Birmingham Museum, and Art Gallery, Birmingham. "Don't you find," said André Gide about Julian Green, "that his rosary makes a hellish noise"? What would the Nobel Prize winning French novelist have said about this painting by Oscar Wilde's friend?

lying about at the Savoy or some other hotel and so produced in Court by your father's Counsel, contained an entreaty not devoid of pathos, had you at that time been able to recognise pathos in its elements or its expression:—these, I say, were the origin and causes of my fatal yielding to you in your daily increasing demands. You wore me out. It was the triumph of the smaller over the bigger nature. It was the case of that tyranny of the weak over the strong which somewhere in one of my plays I describe as being 'the only tyranny that lasts.'

And it was inevitable. In every relation of life with others one has to find some *moyen de vivre*. In your case, one had either to give up to you or to give you up. There was no alternative. Through deep if misplaced affection for you: through great pity for your defects of temper and temperament: through my own proverbial good nature and Celtic laziness: through an artistic aversion from coarse scenes and ugly words: through that incapacity to bear resentment of any kind which at that time characterised me: through my dislike of seeing life made bitter and uncomely by what to me, with my eyes really fixed on other things, seemed to be mere trifles too petty for more than a moment's thought or interest:—through those reasons, simple as they may sound, I gave up to you always....

Of course, you had your illusions, lived in them indeed, and through the shifting mists, and coloured veils saw all things changed. You thought, I remember quite well, that your devoting yourself to me, to the entire exclusion of your family and family life, was a proof of your wonderful appreciation of me and your great affection. No doubt to you it seemed so. But recollect that

Jean-Jacques Henner, *Saint Sebastian*. Musée du Luxembourg, Paris.

Oscar Wilde with Lord Alfred Douglas in 1894 (detail). Guillot de Saix-Viollet Collection.

with me was luxury, high living, unlimited pleasure, money without stint....

I remember again, when an execution was put into my house, and my books and furniture were seized and advertised to be sold, and bankruptcy was impending, I naturally wrote to tell you about it. I did not mention that it was to pay for some gifts of mine to you that the bailiffs had entered the house where you had so often dined. I thought, rightly or wrongly, that such news might pain you a little. I merely told you the bare facts. I thought it proper that you should know them. You wrote back from Boulogne in a strain of almost lyrical exultation. You said that you knew your father was 'hard up for money' and had been obliged to raise £1,500 for the expenses of the trial and that my going bankrupt was really a 'splendid score' off him as he would not then be able to get any of his costs out of me! Do you realise now what hate blinding a person is? Do you recognise now that when I described it as an atrophy destructive of everything but itself, I was scientifically describing a real psychological fact? That all my charming things were to be sold: my Burne-Jones drawings: my Whistler drawings: my Monticelli, my Simeon Solomons: my china: my library with its collection of presentation volumes from almost every poet of my time, from Hugo to Whitman, from Swinburne to Mallarmé, from Morris to Verlaine: with its beautifully bound editions of my father's and mother's works, its wonderful array of college and school prizes: its *éditions de luxe*, and the like: was absolutely nothing to you. You said it was a great bore: that was all....

LORD ALFRED DOUGLAS
(1870-1931)

During Oscar Wilde's trial the public prosecutor quoted from two poems by Lord Douglas, "In Praise of Shame" and "Two Loves." These youthful works were later published in a bilingual (French-English) collection of Douglas's poetry printed in Paris in 1896. In the following year Douglas, who was wintering in Naples with Wilde, wrote a second work, *The City of the Soul*. It was a fertile period for both writers: Wilde was completing "The Ballad of Reading Gaol." After his release from prison, Wilde's "reunions" with Douglas never lasted very long. Wilde was secretly bitter about Douglas, and the latter looked upon his older friend with pity rather than with admiration. Two years after Wilde's death, Douglas married Olive Custance; the charming, beautiful and very wealthy daughter of a colonel, she herself wrote poems. The marriage was not a success however, despite the birth of a son. Douglas and his wife maintained separate quarters and were bound to each other only by esteem.

For years Douglas was haunted by the tragic outcome of his liaison with Wilde. He vowed to get even with Ross, who had publicly accused him of being responsible for his friend's misfortunes. He resorted to the scurrilous tactics his father had used against Wilde: he harrassed Ross, calling him a "blackguard" and (irony of ironies) a "notorious pederast." Exasperated, Ross sued him for libel. Douglas was jailed, then released and given five weeks to furnish evidence to support his allegations. This he managed to produce just eight days before court was reconvened. How did he do it? He preferred not to say, explaining that it was a "gift from Providence, into whose

hands he had placed himself, having recently converted to the Catholic faith." Several years earlier he had indeed been captivated by Pope Pius X's encyclical against modernism [*Pascendi Domini*]. After the trial, Douglas took up journalism. He edited two rather uninteresting and unsuccessful reviews, *Academy* and *Plain English*, in which he published base and violent diatribes against "Jews, Colored and the Irish." In 1923 he accused Winston Churchill of having fabricated false reports about the Battle of Jutland in order to make a killing on the Stock Exchange with the connivance of a group of Jewish financiers. He was promptly sued for libel, and this time he was sentenced to six months in prison. He died seven years later, at the age of sixty-one.

A great sportsman, though "pretty in a girlish way" (as he himself said), Lord Douglas was a hard, capricious, vindictive, insanely proud and unscrupulous man. He vented his prejudices and his racism with extraordinary agressiveness. He was, all in all, a dislikeable person; but there is no question that he was a poet of talent. He has given us, at least, a moving testimonty of "the Love that dare not speak its name."

IN PRAISE OF SHAME

Unto my bed last night, methought there came
Our lady of strange dreams, and from an urn
She poured live fire, so that mine eyes did burn
At sight of it. Anon the floating flame
Took many shapes, and one cried, "I am Shame
That walks with Love, I am most wise to turn
Cold lips and limbs to fire; therefore discern
And see my loveliness, and praise my name."

And afterward, in radiant garments dressed,
With sound of flutes and laughing of glad lips,
A pomp of all the passions passed along,
All the night through; till the white phantom ships
Of dawn sailed in. Whereat I said this song,
"Of all sweet pleasures Shame is loveliest."

From TWO LOVES

..."Sweet youth
Tell me why, sad and sighing, thou dost rove
These pleasant realms? I pray thee speak me sooth
What is thy name?" He said, "My name is Love!"
Then straight the first did turn himself to me
And cried, "He lieth, for his name is Shame,
But I am Love, and I was wont to be
Alone in this fair garden, till he came
Unasked by night; I am true Love, I fill
The Hearts of boy and girl with mutual flame."
Then sighing said the other, "Have thy will,
I am the Love that dare not speak its name."
(September, 1892)

These two poems were read during Oscar Wilde's trial.

TELENY (1893)

This novel, entitled *Teleny or the Reverse of the Medal*, was first published anonymously—and secretly—in 1893 (a second edition appeared in 1906). A version in French, limited to 300 copies, was privately printed for the "Ganymede Club" in 1934. In his preface to this edition, the British bookseller, Charles Hirsch, related how, one day around 1890, Oscar Wilde, to whom he used to sell forbidden books (like *Alcibiades in School*), gave him a sealed package containing a notebook, explaining that a friend would come by to pick it up. Indeed, not long after that a young man presented one of Oscar Wilde's cards to the bookseller and claimed the package. A few days later he brought it back, saying, "A friend will call to fetch this, on behalf of the same person." This little comedy was repeated three times. At last, the package being no longer sealed, Hirsch took out the notebook and read it, unable to resist his curiosity. He was impressed by the high literary quality of the text; it seemed to him to be the work of several hands (perhaps Oscar Wilde and his friends?). Hirsch heard nothing more about the notebook until the day when a publisher named Smithers released it secretly under the title, *Teleny, or the Reverse of the Medal: A Physiological Romance of Today*. The prologue had been deleted, and a new episode (given here in its entirety) had been added.

Des Grieux, the young protagonist of the novel has fallen in love with Teleny, a youthful musician of great promise. One evening, after a concert, Des Grieux follows Teleny who is walking along the Paris quays with a friend. Unable to bear the sight of his love walking with another person, Des Grieux tries to commit suicide by jumping into the river. But Teleny, who knew that he was being followed, rushes up in time to stop him and brings him back to his home.

Alastair, Drawing for the 1914 edition of Oscar Wilde's poem, "The Sphinx." Private collection. Gabriele d'Annunzio (according to his recent biographer, Philippe Jullian) was fascinated by this German painter who dressed like the "feathered androgynes" he drew.

Simeon Solomon, *Bacchus*. Robert Walker Collection, Paris. Solomon shared Oscar Wilde's taste for luxury, drink and boys. Swinburne, although he admired his art, found his behavior too provocative and avoided him.

From TELENY

At last they reached the Quai de ————, so busy in the daytime, so lonely at night. There they seemed to be looking for somebody, for they either turned round, scanned the persons they met, or stared at men seated on the benches that are along the quay. I continued following them.

As my thoughts were entirely absorbed, it was some time before I noticed that a man, who had sprung up from somewhere, was walking by my side. I grew nervous; for I fancied that he not only tried to keep pace with me but also to catch my attention, for he hummed and whistled snatches of songs, coughed, cleared his throat, and scraped his feet.

All these sounds fell upon my dreamy ears, but failed to arouse my attention. All my senses were fixed on the two figures in front of me. He therefore walked on, then turned round on his heels, and stared at me. My eyes saw all this without heeding him in the least.

He lingered once more, let me pass, walked on at a brisker pace, and was again beside me. Finally, I looked at him. Though it was cold, he was but slightly dressed. He wore a short, black velvet jacket and a pair of light grey, closely fitting trousers marking the shape of the thighs and buttocks like tights.

As I looked at him he stared at me again, then smiled with that vacant, vapid, idiotic, facial contraction of a *raccrocheuse*. Then, always looking at me with an inviting leer, he directed his steps towards a neighbouring *Vespasienne*.

"What is there so peculiar about me?" I mused, "that the fellow is ogling me in that way?"

Without turning round, however, or noticing him any further, I walked on, my eyes fixed on Teleny.

As I passed by another bench, some one again scraped his feet and cleared his throat, evidently bent on making me turn my head. I did so. There was nothing more remarkable about him than there is in the first man you meet. Seeing me look at him, he either unbuttoned or buttoned up his trousers.

After a while I again heard steps coming from behind; the person was close up to me. I smelt a strong scent—if the noxious odour of musk or of patchouli can be called a scent.

Alastair, Two drawings. Bibliothèque Nationale, Paris. They were published by Oscar Wilde's friend, Robert Ross, in 1914. Alastair was then twenty-four.

Donald Friend, Plate from *The Antipodeans* (1966). Eddy Batache Collection, Paris.

The person touched me slightly as he passed by. He begged my pardon; it was the man of the velvet jacket, or his Dromio. I looked at him as he again stared at me and grinned. His eyes were painted with khol, his cheeks were dabbed with rouge. He was quite beardless. For a moment, I doubted whether he was a man or a woman; but when he stopped again before the column I was fully persuaded of his sex.

Some one else came with mincing steps, and shaking his buttocks, from behind one of these *pissoirs*. He was an old, wiry, simpering man as shrivelled as a frost-bitten pippin. His cheeks were very hollow, and his projecting cheek bones very red; his face was shaven and shorn, and he wore a wig with long, fair, flaxen locks.

He walked in the posture of the Venus de Medici; that is, with one hand on his middle parts, and the other on his breast. His looks were not only very demure, but there was an almost maidenly coyness about the old man that gave him the appearance of a virgin-pimp.

He did not stare, but cast a side-long glance at me as he went by. He was met by a workman—a strong and sturdy fellow, either a butcher or a smith by trade. The old man would evidently have slunk by unperceived, but the workman stopped him. I could not hear what they said, for though they were but a few steps away, they spoke in that hushed tone peculiar to lovers; but I seemed to be the object of their talk, for the workman turned and stared at me as I passed. They parted.

The workman walked on for twenty steps, then he turned on his heel and walked back exactly on a line with me, seemingly bent on meeting me face to face.

I looked at him. He was a brawny man, with massive features; clearly, a fine specimen of a male. As he passed by me he clenched his powerful fist, doubled his muscular arm at the elbow, and then moved it vertically hither and thither for a few times, like a piston-rod in action, as it slipped in and out of the cylinder.

Some signs are so evidently clear and full of meaning that no initiation is needed to understand them. This workman's sign was one of them.

Now I knew who all these night-walkers were. Why they so persistently stared at me, and the meaning of all their little tricks to catch my attention. Was I dreaming? I looked around. The workman had stopped, and he repeated his request in a different way. He shut his left fist, then thrust the forefinger of his right hand in the hole made by the palm and fingers, and moved it in and out. He was bluntly explicit. I was not mistaken. I hastened on, musing whether the cities of the plain had been destroyed by fire and brimstone.

As I learnt later in life, every large city has its particular haunts—its square, its garden for such recreation. And the police? Well, it winks at it, until some crying offence is committed; for it is not safe to stop the mouths of craters. Brothels of men-whores not being allowed, such trysting-places must be tolerated, or the whole is a modern Sodom or Gomorrah.

"What! there are such cities now-a-days?"

Aye! for Jehowah has acquired experience with age; so He has got to understand His children a little better than He did of yore, for He has either come to a righter sense of toleration, or, like Pilate, He has washed His hands, and has quite discarded them.

At first I felt a deep sense of disgust at seeing the old catamite pass by me again, and lift, with utmost modesty, his arm from his breast, thrust his bony finger between his lips, and move it in the same fashion as the workman had done his arm, but trying to give all his movements a maidenly coyness. He was—as I learnt later—a *pompeur de dard,* or as I might call him, a "spermsucker"; this was his speciality. He did the work for the love of the thing, and an experience of many years had made him a master of his trade. He, it appears, lived in every other respect like a hermit, and only indulged himself in one thing— fine lawn handkerchiefs, either with lace or embroidery, to wipe the amateur's instrument when he had done with it.

The old man went down towards the river's edge, apparently inviting me for a midnight stroll in the mist, under the arches of the bridge, or in some out-of-the-way nook or other corner.

Another man came up from there; this one was adjusting his dress, and scratching his hind part like an ape. Notwithstanding the creepy feeling these men gave me, the scene was so entirely new that I must say it rather interested me.

ALEISTER CROWLEY
(1875-1947)

Aleister Crowley's parents were devout members of the sect of the Plymouth Brethren, which had been founded in 1830 in opposition to the Anglican Church. His father was an engineer. When he died, eleven year old Aleister declared that he had become a follower of Satan. He went to Cambridge, where he wrote and published anonymously in 1898 a book of erotic verse called *White Stains* (he never disowned this piece of juvenilia). After briefly considering a diplomatic career, he decided to devote himself to magic instead. He joined the fraternity of the Golden Dawn, and claimed to be a reincarnation of Cagliostro and of Pope Alexander VI (Borgia), which may explain his attraction to sex in all its possible shapes and forms. An enthusiastic sportsman, he joined the 1902 Chopo Ri expedition in the Himalayas. Later, he married and had a child. He published *The Book of Law* which extolls the principle, "Do what thou wilt." He proclaimed himself "He Who Is Above the Gods," and described at length in his *Confessions* how he had attained perfection. This "autotheography" was followed by poems and by studies of the unconscious. With his shaved head, his hypnotizing eyes, his magic ring, his poetry and his knowledge of esoterica, he spellbound his disciples. Even today he continues to fascinate people: he appears on the cover of one of the Beatles' albums standing between Mae West and a Hindu holy man.

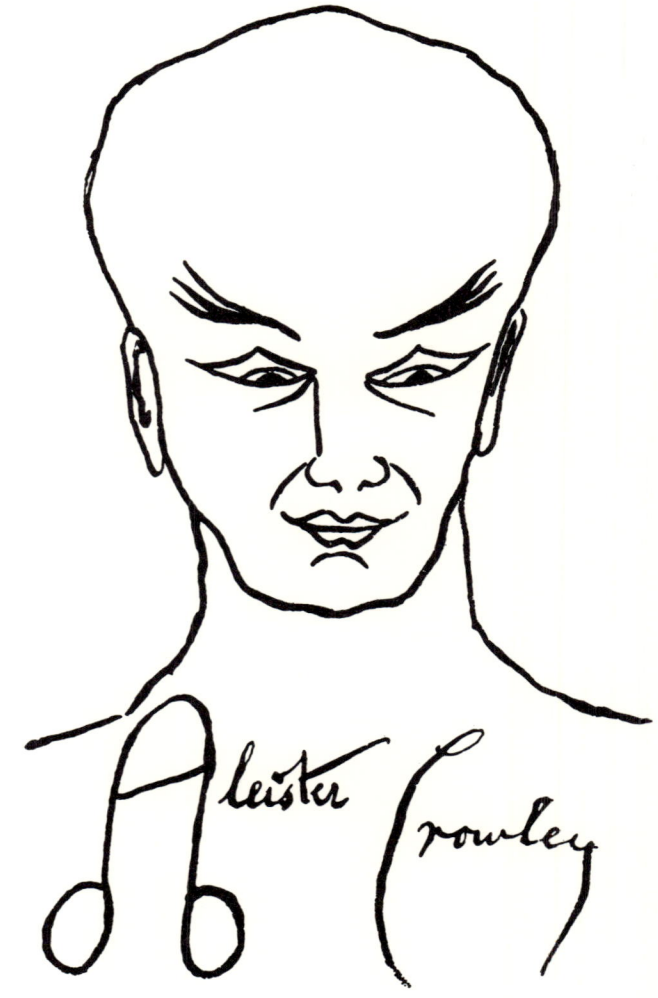

FROM WHITE STAINS

Let my fond lips but drink thy golden wine,
   My bright-eyed Arab, only let me eat
   The rich brown globes of sacramental meat
Steaming and firm, hot from their home divine,
And let me linger with thy hands in mine,
   And lick the sweat from dainty dirty feet
   Fresh with the loose aroma of the street,
And then anon I'll glue my mouth to thine.

This is the height of joy, to lie and feel
   Thy spicéd spittle trickle down my throat;
This is more pleasant than at dawn to steal
   Towards lawns and sunny brooklets, and to gloat
   Over earth's peace, and hear in ether float
Song of soft spirits into rapture peal.

("Go into the Highways and Hedges, and Compel Them to Come In")

Aleister Crowley, *Idealized Self-Portrait*. This picture was reproduced by Grant and Symonds in *The Confessions of Aleister Crowley*.

David Hockney, *Gregory Standing Nude* (1975). Galerie Claude Bernard, Paris.

Thomas Eakins, *The Swimming Hole* (1883). ▷▷ The Fort Worth Art Museum, Fort Worth, Texas. "I have known but one artist," said Walt Whitman, "and that is Thomas Eakins." The painter and the poet admired each other deeply.

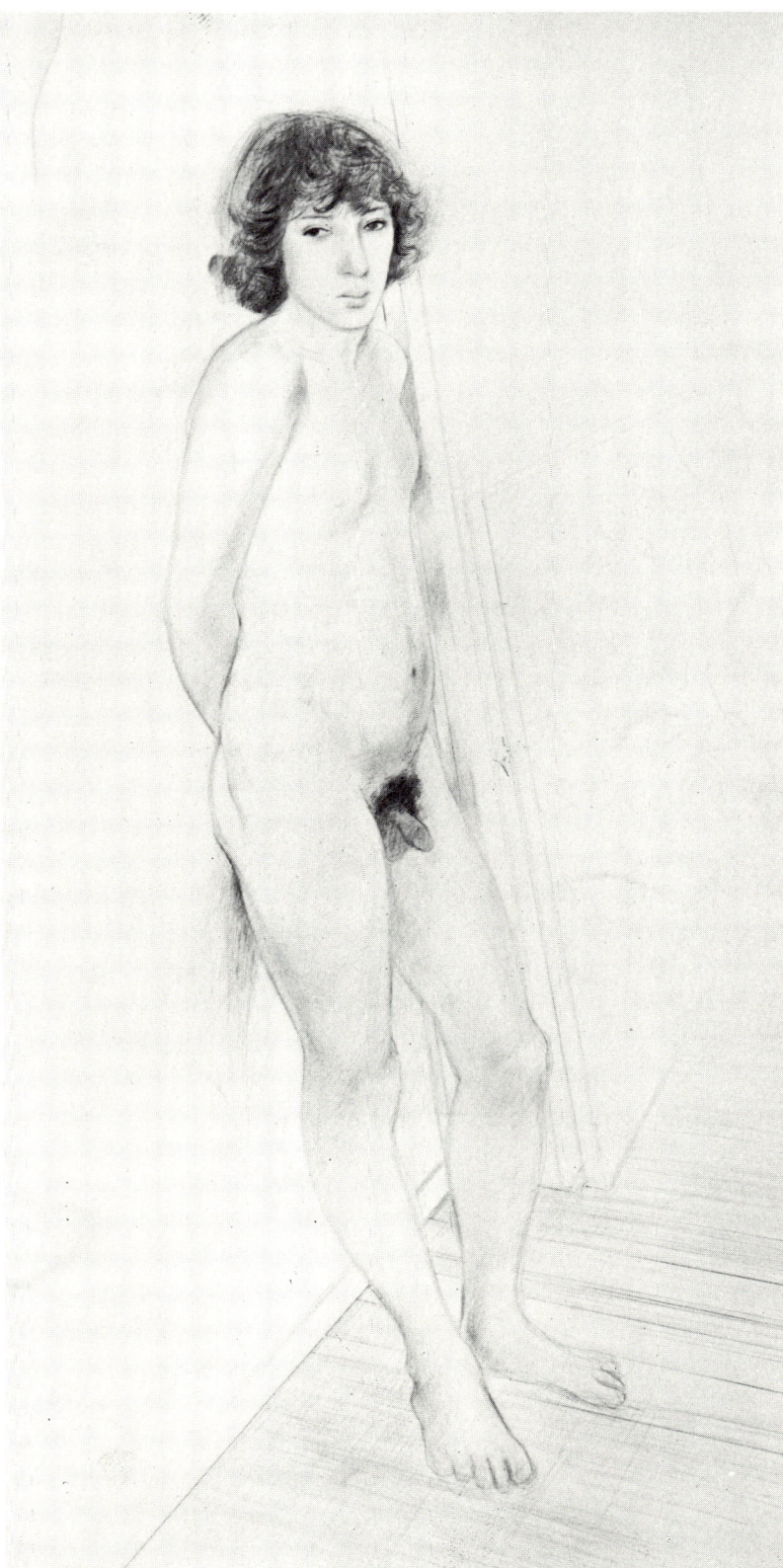

From WHITE STAINS

Of man's delight and man's desire
    In one thing is no weariness—
To feel the fury of the fire,
    And writhe within the close caress
    Of fierce embrace, and wanton kiss,
And final nuptial done aright,
    How sweet a passion, shame, is this,
A strong man's love is my delight!

Free women cast a lustful eye
    On my gigantic charms, and seek
By word and touch with me to lie,
    And vainly proffer cunt and cheek;
    Then, angry, they miscall me weak,
Till one, divining me aright,
    Points to her buttocks, whispers "Greek!"—
A strong man's love is my delight!

Boys tempt my lips to wanton use,
    And show their tongue, and smile awry,
And wonder why I should refuse
    To feel their buttocks on the sly,
    And kiss their genitals, and cry;
"Ah! Ganymede, grant me one night!"
    This is the one sweet mystery:
A strong man's love is my delight!

To feel him clamber on me, laid
    Prone on the couch of lust and shame,
To feel him force me like a maid
    And his great sword within me flame,
    His breath as hot and quick as fame;
To kiss him and to clasp him tight;
    This is my joy without a name,
A strong man's love is my delight.

To feel again his love grow grand
    Touched by the languor of my kiss;
To suck the hot blood from my gland
    Mingled with fierce spunk that doth hiss,
    And boils in sudden spurted bliss;
Ah! God! the long-drawn lusty fight!
    Grant me eternity of this!
A strong man's love is my delight!

Envoi

Husband, come early to my bed,
    And stay beyond the dawn of light
In mighty deeds of lustihead
    A strong man's love is my delight!

        ("A Ballad of Passive Pederasty")

WALT WHITMAN (1819-1892)

You cannot separate Walt Whitman's life from *Leaves of Grass*, that lusty, exuberant book of poems which he kept adding to until his death.

Whitman himself seems like the symbol of "sublimated homosexuality." His ideal of comradly love is lyrically described in a series of poems entitled "Calamus" (the calamus is a kind of marsh lily commonly found in the United States; Whitman makes it into a phallic symbol). Besides his poems, there are many testimonies to Whitman's pure, though passionate, relationships with young men of various (and sometimes very poor) backgrounds.

Whitman saw himself as the prophet of mankind, the bard of democracy, forever sympathetic to the sufferings of his "brothers." In winter he commiserated with shivering cabdrivers, sitting next to them and giving them gloves and coats. Brooklyn typographers and East River bargemen were his friends. He listened to the stories of their lives, he questioned them about their trades (he himself had been an apprentice typographer in the difficult days of his youth), he lent them books and recited Shakespearian soliloquies to them. His often proclaimed intention was to plant the seeds of comradship "as thickly as the trees growing on the banks of the rivers of America." He dreamed of founding "The City of Future Friends," where various "types of virile affection" could blossom one day.

During the Civil War he volunteered as a nurse. According to Sir John Burroughs, "he had a ruddy face, and wore clean clothes with a flower or a leafy twig pinned to his lapel. In summer, as he crossed the meadows on his way to visit the wounded at the hospital, he gathered huge bunches of dandelion flowers mixed with red and white clover, which he then scattered over the invalids' beds to remind them of the sun and the great outdoors."

Whitman always carefully concealed his true nature, so as not to shock his puritan-minded contemporaries; nevertheless it is unmistakeably revealed in the ambiguities of some of his poems.

WHEN I HEARD AT THE CLOSE OF THE DAY

When I heard at the close of the day how my name had been receiv'd with
    plaudits in the capitol, still it was not a happy night for me that follow'd,
And else when I carous'd, or when my plans were accomplish'd,
    still I was not happy,
But the day when I rose at dawn from the bed of perfect health,
    refresh'd, singing, inhaling the ripe breath of autumn,
When I saw the full moon in the west grow pale and disappear
    in the morning light,
When I wander'd alone over the beach, and undressing bathed,
    laughing with the cool waters, and saw the sun rise,
And when I thought how my dear friend my lover was on his way coming,
    O then I was happy,
O then each breath tasted sweeter, and all that day my food nourish'd me more,
    and the beautiful day pass'd well,
And the next came with equal joy, and with the next at evening came my friend,
And that night while all was still I heard the waters roll slowly
    continually up the shores,
I heard the hissing rustle of the liquid and sands as directed to me
    whispering to congratulate me,
For the one I love most lay sleeping by me under the same cover
    in the cool night,
In the stillness in the autumn moonbeams his face was inclined toward me,
And his arm lay lightly around my breast—and that night I was happy.

WE TWO BOYS TOGETHER CLINGING

We two boys together clinging,
One the other never leaving,
Up and down the roads going, North and South excursions making,
Power enjoying, elbows stretching, fingers clutching,
Arm'd and fearless, eating, drinking, sleeping, loving,
No law less than ourselves owning, sailing, soldiering, thieving, threatening,
Misers, menials, priests alarming, air breathing, water drinking,
    on the turf or the sea-beach dancing,
Cities wrenching, ease scorning, statutes mocking, feebleness chasing,
Fulfilling our foray.

                                  ("Calamus")

From SONG OF MYSELF

I mind how once we lay such a transparent summer morning,
How you settled your head athwart my hips and gently turn'd over upon me,
And parted the shirt from my bosom-bone, and plunged your tongue to my bare-stript heart,
And reach'd till you felt my beard, and reach'd till you held my feet.

Swiftly arose and spread around me the peace and knowledge
that pass all the argument of the earth,
And I know that the hand of God is the promise of my own,
And I know that the spirit of God is the brother of my own,
And that all the men ever born are also my brothers, and the women my sisters and lovers,
And that a kelson of the creation is love, ...

HENRY JAMES (1843-1916)

In several of his novels, and particularly in *The Ambassadors* and *The Europeans,* Henry James portrays refined, but weak and introverted characters whom he then confronts with handsome and carefree youths, full of *joie de vivre*. At literary evenings and social gatherings, James had often encountered and enviously observed these "glowing male tigers," these "young pagans," as he called them. As a child he himself had been considered a sissy by his mother and his brothers. At the age of seventeen he suffered an "obscure hurt" while helping to put out a fire. His biographer, Leon Edel, thinks it was a strained back, but other scholars claim that James had lost his manhood and compare him to Abelard. In his *Memoirs,* James declares that this "extraordinarily intimate" infirmity kept him from military service during the Civil War.

James apparently fell in love with several women during his life, but always from afar and Platonically. He never married and is not known to have had any affairs. Somerset Maugham, always something of a backbiter, relates that Hugh Walpole once made a pass at James, who backed away in panic, crying, "I cannot, I cannot." Bernard Shaw poked fun at the writer's affected way of greeting his friends by embracing them and kissing them on both cheeks. One wonders what Shaw would have said on reading the letters James wrote to the young American sculptor, Hendrik Andersen (see below). When James met Andersen in Rome in 1899, he was fifty-six and the sculptor was a splendid young man of twenty-eight; Andersen was not a very gifted artist, but his youthful looks appealed to the great writer enormously. James bought a small bust from Andersen and invited him to his house in Rye, Sussex. Andersen stayed only three days, but they were idyllic and unforgettable days, if one is to believe the passionate letters which James wrote to his young friend between 1899 and 1915. After this brief honeymoon, the two men seldom saw each other however. Was Henry James a homosexual "vestal virgin," or had Andersen initiated him? Had he discovered physical love too late in life? Unfortunately, these questions can never be answered. It is perhaps worth noting that, at the time of Oscar Wilde's trial, James had declined to sign a petition requesting Wilde's release.

From LETTERS TO HENDRIK ANDERSEN

I was absurdly sorry to lose you when, that afternoon of last month, we walked sadly to the innocent and kindly little station together and our common fate growled out of the harsh false note of whirling you untimely away. Since then I have *missed* you out of all proportion to the three meagre little days (for it seems strange they were only *that*) that we had together. I have never (and I've done it three or four times) passed the little corner where we came up Udimore hill (from Winchelsea,) in the eventide on our bicylces, without thinking ever so tenderly of our charming spin homeward in the twilight and feeling again the strange perversity it made of that sort of thing being so soon *over*. Never mind—we *shall* have more, lots more, of that sort of thing!...

The sense that I can't *help* you, see you, talk to you, touch you, hold you close and long, or do anything to make you rest on me, and feel my participation—this torments me, dearest boy, makes me ache for you, and for myself; makes me gnash my teeth and groan at the bitterness of things.... I wish I could go to Rome and put my hands on you (oh, how lovingly I should lay them!) but that, alas, is odiously impossible.... I am in town for a few weeks but I return to Rye April 1st, and sooner or later to *have* you there and do for you, to put my arms round you and *make* you lean on me as on a brother and a lover, and keep you on and on, slowly comforted or at least relieved of the first bitterness of pain—this I try to imagine as thinkable, attainable, not wholly out of the question. There I am, at any rate, and there is my house and my garden and my table and my studio—such as it is!—and your room, and your welcome, and your place everywhere—and I press them upon you, oh so earnestly, dearest boy, if isolation and grief and the worries you are overdone with become intolerable to you.... I will *nurse* you through your dark passage.... I embrace you with almost a passion of pity.

Charles Demuth,
In Vaudeville: Bicycle Rider.
Corcoran Gallery of Art,
Washington, D.C.

PAUL GAUGUIN (1848-1903)

Gauguin wrote *Noa Noa* in Tahiti in 1893. Rewritten and slightly altered by his friend Charles Morice, the notebook was published in 1901. The version from which the following excerpt is taken is that of the original manuscript which was published in 1954. Gauguin, who had always been drawn towards women, is suddenly overwhelmed by the beauty of his young native companion.

Paul Gaugin, *D'où venons-nous? Que sommes-nous? Où allons-nous?* [Where do we come from? What are we? Where are we going?] (detail). The Museum of Fine Arts, Boston.

From NOA NOA

It happened once that I had need of rosewood for my carving. I wanted a large strong trunk, and I consulted Totefa.

"We have to go into the mountains," he told me. "I know a certain spot where there are several beautiful trees. If you wish it I will lead you. We can then fell the tree which pleases you and together carry it here."

We set out early in the morning....

Both of us went naked, the white and blue *paréo* around the loins, hatchet in hand. Countless times we crossed the brook for the sake of a short-cut. My guide seemed to follow the trail by smell rather than by sight, for the ground was covered by a splendid confusion of plants, leaves, and flowers which wholly took possession of space.

The silence was absolute but for the plaintive wailing of the water among the rocks. It was a monotonous wail, a plaint so soft and low that it seemed an accompaniment of the silence.

And in this forest, this solitude, this silence were we two—he, a very young man, and I, almost an old man from whose soul many illusions had fallen and whose body was tired from countless efforts, upon whom lay the long and fatal heritage of the vices of a morally and physically corrupt society.

With the suppleness of an animal and the graceful litheness of an androgyne he walked a few paces in advance of me. And it seemed to me that I saw incarnated in him, palpitating and living, all the magnificent plant-life which surrounded us. From it in him, through him there became disengaged and emanated a powerful perfume of beauty.

Was it really a human being walking there ahead of me? Was it the naïve friend by whose combined simplicity and complexity I had been so attracted? Was it not rather the Forest itself, the living Forest, without sex and yet alluring?...

On Tahiti the breezes from forest and sea strengthen the lungs, they broaden the shoulders and hips. Neither men nor women are sheltered from the rays of the sun nor the pebbles of the sea-shore. Together they engage in the same tasks with the same activity or the same indolence. There is something virile in the women and something feminine in the men.

This similarity of the sexes make their relations the easier. Their continual state of nakedness has kept their minds free from the dangerous pre-occupation with the "mystery" and from the excessive stress which among civilized people is laid upon the "happy accident" and the clandestine and sadistic colors of love. It has given their manners a natural innocence, a perfect purity. Man and woman are comrades, friends rather than lovers, dwelling together almost without cease, in pain as in pleasure, and even the very idea of vice is unkown to them.

In spite of all this lessening in sexual differences, why was it that there suddenly rose in the soul of a member of an old civilization, a horrible thought? Why, in all this drunkenness of lights and perfumes with its enchantment of newness and unknown mystery?

The fever throbbed in my temples and my knees shook.

But we were at the end of the trail. In order to cross the brook my companion turned, and in this movement showed himself full-face. The androgyne had disappeared. It was an actual young man walking ahead of me. His calm eyes had the limpid clearness of waters.

Peace forthwith fell upon me again.

We made a moment's halt. I felt an infinite joy, a joy of the spirit rather than of the senses, as I plunged into the fresh water of the brook.

"*Toë, toë* (it is cold)," said Jotefa.

"Oh, no!" I replied.

This exclamation seemed to me also a fitting conclusion to the struggle which I had just fought out within myself against the corruption of an entire civilization. It was the end in the battle of a soul that had chosen between truth and untruth. It awakened loud echoes in the forest. And I said to myself that Nature had seen me struggle, had heard me, and understood me, for now she replied with her clear voice to my cry of victory that she was willing after the ordeal to receive me as one of her children.

We took up our way again. I plunged eagerly and passionately into the wilderness, as if in the hope of thus penetrating into the very heart of this Nature, powerful and maternal, there to blend with her living elements.

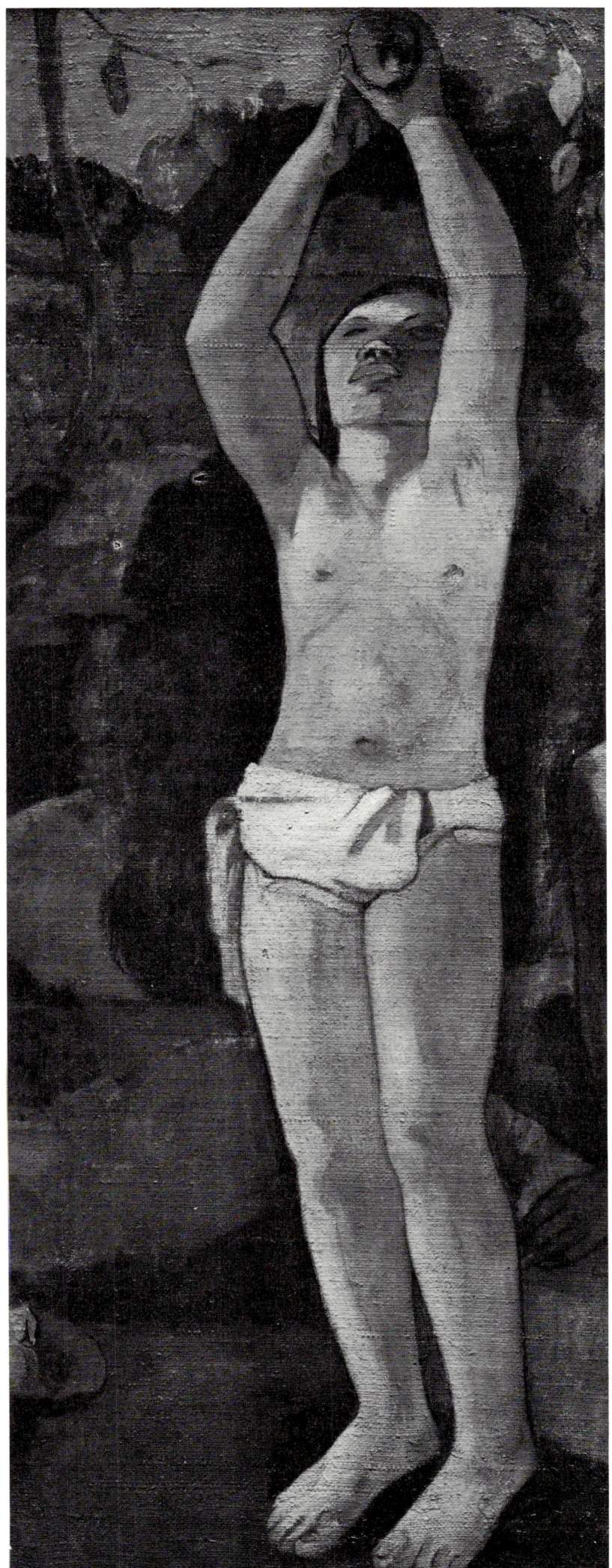

With tranquil eyes and ever uniform pace my companion went on. He was wholly without suspicion; I alone was bearing the burden of an evil conscience.

We arrived at our destination.

The steep sides of the mountain had by degrees spread out, and behind a dense curtain of trees, there extended a sort of plateau, well-concealed. Jotefa, however, knew the place, and with astonishing sureness led me thither.

A dozen rosewood trees extended their vast branches. We attacked the finest of these with the ax.

We had to sacrifice the entire tree to obtain a branch suitable for my project.

I struck out with joy. My hands became stained with blood in my wild rage, my intense joy of satiating within me, I know not what divine brutality. It was not the tree I was striking, it was not it which I sought to overcome. And yet gladly would I have heard the sound of my ax against other trunks when this one was already lying on the ground.

And here is what my ax seemed to say to me in the cadence of its sounding blows:

Strike down to the root the forest entire!
Destroy all the forest of evil,
Whose seeds were once sowed within thee
   by the breathings of death!
Destroy in thee all love of the self!
Destroy and tear out all evil, as in the autumn we
   cut with the hand the flower of the lotus.

Yes, wholly destroyed, finished, dead, is from now on the old civilization within me. I was reborn; or rather another man, purer and stronger, came to life within me.

This cruel assault was the supreme farewell to civilization, to evil. This last evidence of the depraved instincts which sleep at the bottom of all decadent souls, by very contrast exalted the healthy simplicity of the life at which I had already made a beginning into a feeling of inexpressible happiness. By the trial within my soul mastery had been won. Avidly I inhaled the splendid purity of the light. I was, indeed, a new man; from now on I was a true savage, a real Maori.

Jotefa and I returned to Mateïea, carefully and peacefully bearing our heavy load of rosewood—*noa, noa!*

The sun had not yet set when, very tired out, we arrived before my hut.

Jotefa said to me,

"*Païa?*"

"Yes!" I replied.

And from the bottom of my heart I repeated this "yes" to myself.

I have never made a single cut with the knife into this branch of rosewood, that I did not each time more powerfully breathe in the perfume of victory and rejuvenation: *noa, noa!*

JEAN LORRAIN (1855-1906)

"He was an aesthete, in both the loftiest and the broadest sense of the term."

(Octave Uzanne)

Sem, *Jean Lorrain,* a caricature. Viollet Collection.

J. Chaplin, Two drawings. 1915. (a) *The Heroes Are Decorated.* (b) *Peace Through Victory* (detail). François Duchêne Collection, Paris.

Nothing in Jean Lorrain's family background, his childhood or his early education could possibly have allowed one to predict his colorful career. Paul Duval (his real name) was born in the Normandy town of Fecamp in 1855. He came from seafaring stock on his father's side, while his mother's family had traditionally entered the legal profession. The boy was sent first to the Imperial Lycee at Vanves, next to the Dominican school at Arcueil, where he developed his gift for writing. His loneliness and his youthful aspirations found a natural outlet in poetry. The following lines, addressed to his friend Withold de K., were composed in 1872:

When you will be gone, far from these boarding school walls,
Will you think back on the poet, the dreamer,
Who loved you with a love that was true. I confess
I studied daisy petals in spring, to learn my love's fate.

Back in his small home town, he wandered for hours on end along the sea coast, frequented the bars along the port, and scandalized people with his free and easy manner. A Platonic and unrequited love for Judith Gautier, the daughter of the great poet Théophile Gautier, seems to have confirmed his "painful suspicion of woman's coldness."

He dreamt of living in Paris. At last he succeeded in persuading his father, who had taken it into his head that his son was going to become a dairy farmer, to let him go. On reaching the capital, Lorrain (as he had now decided to call himself) immediately plunged into what was then called "*la Bohème artiste,*" the bohemian world of artists and writers. He met leading literary figures like Félix Fénéon, Léon Bloy, the poet and dramatist François Coppée, the novelist Joris Karl Huysmans and the popular authors Paul and Victor Margueritte. Oscar Métenier, the son of a district police commissioner, became a close, and as it later turned out, a very useful friend.

But Lorrain's circle of Parisian acquaintances was by no means confined to the world of the arts and letters. At the same time that he was discovering his vocation as a poet (a book of his poems called *Le Sang des Dieux* was published in 1882), he was also being initiated into the low life of the city. In disguise he began frequenting disreputable dives along the banks of the Seine, and he got to know the petty thieves, the whores and pimps who congregated there. His homosexual tendencies had undoubtedly emerged into the open by this time. He confided to his friend Oscar Métenier that he was in love with a blond sailor named Ophelius, "whose thickheadedness delights me even more than his very artistic ugliness." Ophelius resembled Botticelli's allegory of *Spring,* a figure which fascinated Lorrain.

Soon the young writer had created a legend, a shimmering wall of fact and fantasy which surrounded and protected his true self. He perpetually defied and scandalized society. On one occasion he signed himself up as a dancer at the Alco on the avenue de Choisy, one of the roughest spots in Paris. "Returned to the city at last on July 15," he wrote to his friend. "Spent four wild days at the fair on the Esplanade des Invalides with all my friends the wrestlers, the burglars, the cut-throats, the clowns, the pimps, etc...." But at heart he yearned for healthier pleasures: "I would like to be a strapping fat butcher, vigorous and sound in body and soul, an incredible animal, a fornicating devil who is the steady friend of some buxom kitchen wench." In another letter he observed: "Basically, fucking is a sport for idle minds. When you work, it's goodbye ass!"

As a journalist, Lorrain wore himself out tracking down off-beat stories. One of his modern critics (Pierre

Kyria) notes: "The paradox is that Lorrain resorted to journalism in order to support himself as an aesthete, but as an aesthete he became a slave to journalism." Lorrain himself admitted, "What I want is to be able to live the life I please. Literature sustains my vices...."

Except for a few poems and his best novels, Lorrain's work was written entirely for periodicals. His stories, prose-poems and descriptions of gallery openings, exhibitions, horseraces, suburban dancing gardens, duels and opium dens gained him rapid notoriety. He became the talk of fashionable Paris; everybody knew, lionized and feared him. Gorgeously attired, laden with jewelry, exhaling a powerful odor of ether mixed with perfume, his eyes thickly outlined with black makeup, he looked like a decadent Byzantine emperor. Then suddenly he would disappear and change. Who among his elegant acquaintances would have recognized him in his worker's garb, or in his rough corduroy outfit, his cap pulled down over one eye, as he slipped away to seek his pleasures among the furtive and brawny denizens of the night?

His insolence and dissoluteness were viewed with irritation in some quarters; but, full of the fighting spirit, Lorrain continued his provocations. One day in a fashionable restaurant in the rue du Bac he declaimed the following lines at the top of his lungs:

> I spent the night between two fellows from the docks,
> Who took turns, and cured me of the hots!....

The novelist and critic Rachilde called him a "Braggart of Vice"; less elegantly, he baptized himself the "Fuckanthrope." Thoroughly cynical, he proclaimed that "all tastes are in nature, as are all distastes." And, "What is a vice? It is a taste that is not shared."

Within a span of ten years Lorrain produced the bulk of his work: *Sonyeuse*, 1891, *Buveurs d'âmes*, 1898, *Monsieur de Bougrelon: Contes pour lire à la chandelle*, *Loreley*, 1897, *La Mandragore*, 1899, *Histoires de femmes* and *Vingt masques*, 1906.

Meanwhile he traveled, discovering the south of France, Spain, North Africa, Italy. He was particularly taken by Venice. Like the globe-trotting poet Valéry Larbaud and the novelist Paul Morand, he was a born traveler.

Feeling more and more confined in Paris, Lorrain moved to Nice in 1900, attracted by the "madness of the perfumes and the other madnesses" there. "You cannot imagine the gale of love which Spring unleashes over this country," he wrote. "One is followed and accosted in the streets and on the country roads; one is solicited at every hour of the day and the night; the air is thick with the smell of roses and come.... In the evening, when you walk along the quais, sailors hail you from their dingies; you risk spending the night at the bottom of some dark hold if you accept their invitations...."

Louis Bertrand reports that Lorrain enjoyed a tremendous popularity along the waterfront during the early years of the century. "The honorable brotherhood of boatmen, not to mention the honorable corporation of coachmen, had become his devoted comrades. As soon as they saw him, they would call and shout to him...." Whereupon Lorrain would turn to his company and artlessly exclaim, "You see how everybody loves me!"

At the turn of the century Nice was the magical, and sometimes sinister, "pearl" of the Riviera, the elegant haunt of predators and princesses. It was here that Lorrain wrote his most famous books: *Monsieur Phocas, Le Vice errant, La Maison Philibert, Le Crime des Riches, Hélie, garçon d'hôtel.*

Soon his health, which had always been rather fragile, began to fail. After a brief illness, he died at the age of fifty-one of an "intestinal perforation resulting from the deterioration of his tissues due to his addiction to ether" (in the words of his physician, Doctor Pozzi).

Lorrain's novels and poems are thoroughly imbued with the often perverse spirit of the 1890s: the aesthetic spirit of J.K. Huysmans and his super-refined hero des Esseintes, the spirit of painters like Gustave Moreau, G. de Feure, Charley Toorop, and Sir Edward Burne-Jones. Vladimir Noronsoff, the hero of *Le Vice errant* (1902), organizes a banquet in honor of Adonis, during which he presents his guests with three naked men adorned with extraordinary tattooes.

Pride, sensuality and perversity are the hallmarks of Lorrain, but so are loneliness and disgust. "Did Lorrain really have the means to carry out his aesthetic vision?" Pierre Kyria wonders. "He made money by writing for papers; in a way he was a 'nouveau riche' of aestheticism: he was always reaching for, and therefore never truly possessed, luck, leisure and wealth."

From LE VICE ERRANT, "AN ASIAN COURT"

One day the prince's landau failed to come for me. I waited another day, but again it did not come. On the third day, wondering what the matter was, I went over to the villa.

Noronsoff was holding court in his fabulous bathroom. He was garbed in an incredible Turkish caftan of pink silk; pearls and turquoises were clustered on his fingers. All the elegant riffraff of Nice was there: the Russians gone to seed, the Englishmen on the run, the Italians looking for adventure. There was even a madam, who sold works of art on the ground floor of her establishment and live "conversation pieces" upstairs; and a former coachman, who had set up business as a pimp. The doors were guarded by a squad of white muzhiks, who formed a sort of living fresco against the painted frescoes on the walls.

Sprawled over the cushions of his couch, the prince was listening with relish to a German someone had brought along, a vast, chubby Bavarian whose skin bulged like a mound of lard. With short choppy gestures and with comical earnestness, this fellow was describing a police raid on a certain house of ill repute, a sanitary roundup which was the scandal of the week and which he, Herr Schappmann, had had the misfortune to be caught in. He had been arrested along with the underage residents and the patrons of the establishment, but he had had the wits to demand that the German consulate be informed and had been released on the spot. The police had detained only French citizens....

"Were there really only minors in the house? The papers had mentioned props and instruments of every description, and even a Great Dane trained to perform peculiar tricks. Rumor had it that a fat gentleman had been seen scurrying on all fours through one of the suites dressed in nothing less than a pink satin corset. Some people whispered that he was a druggist from Cannes, a family man and a churchwarden to boot; others claimed that he was a foreigner staying at the Hotel Westminster. But perhaps you were this mysterious gentleman, Monsieur Schappmann, for the man in the corset was very corpulent." The prince tormented the desperate Bavarian, unnerving him with detailed and embarrassing questions. It was great fun to watch Herr Schappmann shake with self-righteous moral indignation and shudder at each one of the prince's insinuations like an enormous oyster at a squirt of lemon juice.

The audience roared with laughter at the prince's questions. Meanwhile, with his favorite monkey huddled in his lap, Noronsoff now and then extended his arm towards a crystal bowl on a low pedestal table, from which he fished iced strawberries with a solid gold fork.

And after I had forbidden him to eat iced foods! It is true that ten minutes later, he had emptied the dish it was removed and a samovar was installed in its place, whereupon Noronsoff proceeded to gulp down cups of boiling hot tea: an internal sauna I feared would have the most calamitous effect on his worn innards.

All the while Noronsoff was toying with the hair of the eldest of Countess Schoboleski's sons, Nicholas, who was sitting on the couch next to him. The prince's hand strayed lovingly in the sixteen year old boy's curly blond fleece. The lad heard everything that was being said, and one wondered what his mother thought of this. She was there, regally seated in the first row, her youngest son standing between her knees, leaning fondly against her. Together they made a charming picture: he dressed in black velvet, she all in white.

From LE VICE ERRANT, "TRIMALCION'S FEAST"

A vast, bizarre center-piece of infinitely perplexing size and shape covered almost the entire surface of the table. It was studded with magnolia blossoms, white roses and purple carnations, beneath which one glimpsed a sort of covering sheet of golden gauze, a voluminous veil, yellow and luminous, strangely lifted and pushed out in various places; one sensed that something was alive underneath it. Whatever it was was breathing, but was obviously making an effort not to release its breath too noisily. At this mysterious living thing, more than one smile had frozen, more than one brow was knit. Feeling

Gustave Moreau, *The Suitors* (detail). Musée Gustave Moreau, Paris. Jean Lorrain particularly admired this figure's "youthful skin offered to our view in a swirl of bluish drapery."

203

indefinably threatened, everyone picked at his food, the women fearing for their modesty, the men for their dignity. They all knew that Noronsoff was capable of anything.

"Perhaps those are snakes writhing under that gauze?"

"Or bullfrogs, like the ones at the zoo."

"Perhaps a deer!"

"Yes, that's surely it, a live deer. They are going to slaughter it in front of our eyes."

"How horrid! I won't see it."

"Perhaps rats."

"What a sinister thought!"

"Oh, do be quiet!"

"No, I'd say it's a boar."

"Absolutely. A tame one."

"The idea! it makes me quite ill."

"Oh, posh! it's parrots. They are going to come out from under there suddenly and jump on our knees."

"Just my luck, I can't bear parrots."

"Let us hope, at least, that the dinner isn't poisoned."

"No?"

"I wouldn't go so far as to say arsenic, but perhaps rhubarb. He's quite capable of it, you know."

"Spanish fly, more likely."

"Oh, that's very Marquis de Sade!"

"Well, my dear, where do you think you are?"

"Heavens, baron, where have you brought me?"

Speaking in hasty monosyllables, everyone tried to make light of his anxiety. Fortunately, the atmosphere was livened by a gypsy orchestra playing czardases and Hungarian marches in the next room.

The only guest who showed any spirit was La Mariska. She had a last emerged from her black mood and, with avid lips and sparkling eyes, she leaned towards the prince and laughed with abandon as she drained glass after glass of bubbly wine. Vladimir's words seemed to excite her; she let herself succumb to them and to the delicious effect of the champagne, and soon she was as giddy and frisky as a spring filly.

The third course had just been removed by the liveried footmen who had brought in silver baskets piled high with enormous fruit on beds of crushed ice and placed them between the candelabra, when four muzhiks entered and stationed themselves at either end of the table. Prince Noronsoff stood up.

"I would have liked to offer you Countess Schoboleska and her sons. I have had to fall back on other specimens of humanity. But fear not, ladies, your modesty will be quite safe: my specimens are tattooed."

And he winked at the muzhiks, who whisked away the flowers and the golden veil on the center-piece.

The spectacle brought the guests to their feet: lying on an immense mirror, three men, entirely naked, were held down by the tightly knotted meshes of an immense net, in which their torsoes were caught like great, muscular fish. A single cry echoed through the dining hall: unkempt hair, rough and broken finger nails, foot calluses and haled hands and necks revealed plainly that the men were fishermen or dockhands. It was too much: outraged ladies left the room hurriedly asking for their coats and carriages; gentlemen, with faces taut and pale, exchanged clipped phrases: what was the proper thing to do? Slap the prince? Hand him one's card? A few women, who had been milling around, joined in shrilly: "He's mad, he's sick."

In the midst of all this confusion and uproar, the three naked men remained motionless, while the gypsies continued playing.

La Mariska had gotten up too. She had taken out her lorgnette and, leaning over the strange center piece, was studying it with the tranquil absorbtion of an interested connoisseur.

The three were sturdy fellows, Riviera darkies, whose chocolate skins were curiously tattooed. One of them lay on his stomach; he sported the famous tattoo known as the "fox hunt," which Pierre Loti described in *Mon frère Yves*: outlined in blue, dogs and horses, the pack and the riders, raced around his shoulders, his chest and his torso chasing after the fox, who had holed up in his lair. The other was on his back, hands crossed over his face. From his knees to his shoulders a vulture, its wings half-closed, had been traced. The bird's beak was in the middle of his chest, the wing tips tapered down his thighs, and the claws were fastened around an unusual perch. The third fellow, who was reclining on his side, had decorated his epidermis with architectural sketches: an arch of triumph framed his loins, one of the fountains of the Place de la Concorde plumed over his stomach. Each drawing was accompanied by a lewd comment.

The dining hall was now almost entirely empty. Everyone had left, except for a few curious females and two or three blasé men of the world. His yellow eyes lit with pleasure, the prince had surveyed the general panic and disarray with obvious enjoyement. Now, intrigued by her placidity, and perhaps a trifle anxious, he cast sidelong glances at La Mariska. She was still plunged in her examination. "These are interesting tattooes," she said at length, "but Monsieur's are much better." She waved towards the Yankee. She had replaced her lorgnette and had taken the prince's arm.

The few remaining guests followed them into the salon....

"Shall I dance for you now?" asked La Mariska.

"No, that would be cruel. Everyone has gone. Those dolts were incapable of appreciating their good fortune. And yet it was one opportunity in a thousand."

Felicien Rops, Humoristic drawing. Editions Jacques Damase, Brussels.

VII

TO A HAPPIER YEAR

"Men must begin to have esteem for themselves. Once
that is accomplished, all the rest will follow."
(Nietzsche)

Pierre Loti, Photograph Gérard Lévy Collection, Paris. Includes a dedication to his physical education teacher.

Bernard Buffet, *Transvestite* (1955). (Reproduced by permission of Maître Loudmer, Paris.)

During the years that preceded World War I, homosexuals were considered inverts, unmanly "deviants," queers, pansies or, in the words of the French writer, Charles-Louis Philippe, "five-legged sheep" (the French expression, *mouton à cinq pattes*, designates a freakish or extraordinary person). Although psychological novelists like Robert Musil, Thomas Mann and Marcel Proust depicted the "perversions" of a society they viewed as decadent, and although writers like Stefan George celebrated various kinds of Platonic affection for boys, it was really only after the war of 1914-18 that a small number of intellectuals found the courage to speak out and proclaim their homosexuality.

André Gide printed twelve copies of *Corydon*, his fervent plea for pederasty, as early as 1911; but it was only when a larger edition came out in 1924 that he dared to sign his name to it. Jean Cocteau denied being the author of *The White Paper* when it appeared in 1930, but he illustrated the 1933 edition with his own drawings (although still not openly recognizing it as his work). "I have always been drawn to the 'stronger sex' which I believe can in all justice be called the 'fair sex,'" he declared. "My misfortunes have been caused by a society which considers the rare bird a criminal and obliges us to repress our inclinations." In 1939 Marcel Jouhandeau published *On Abjection* anonymously, but nevertheless signed the complimentary press copies. All of these writers publicly identified themselves (however cautiously) with the homosexual cause because, as Cocteau declared, they could no longer accept being merely "tolerated." They refused to continue being treated as objects of contempt, and they demanded that their basic dignity as human beings be recognized. In this they largely succeeded: Gide was awarded the Nobel Prize for Literature in 1947; Cocteau was admitted to the Académie française in 1955. Back in 1891, Pierre Loti's nomination to this august honorary body had presented problems. One member had complained to his colleague Ernest Renan: "Mon cher, we cannot vote for Loti, he is a pederast."

"Oh, is that what they say?" Renan had replied.

"I assure you, there is no doubt about it."

"Well, then; we shall see what we shall see," shrugged the philosopher of positivism (and the author of *The Life of Jesus*).

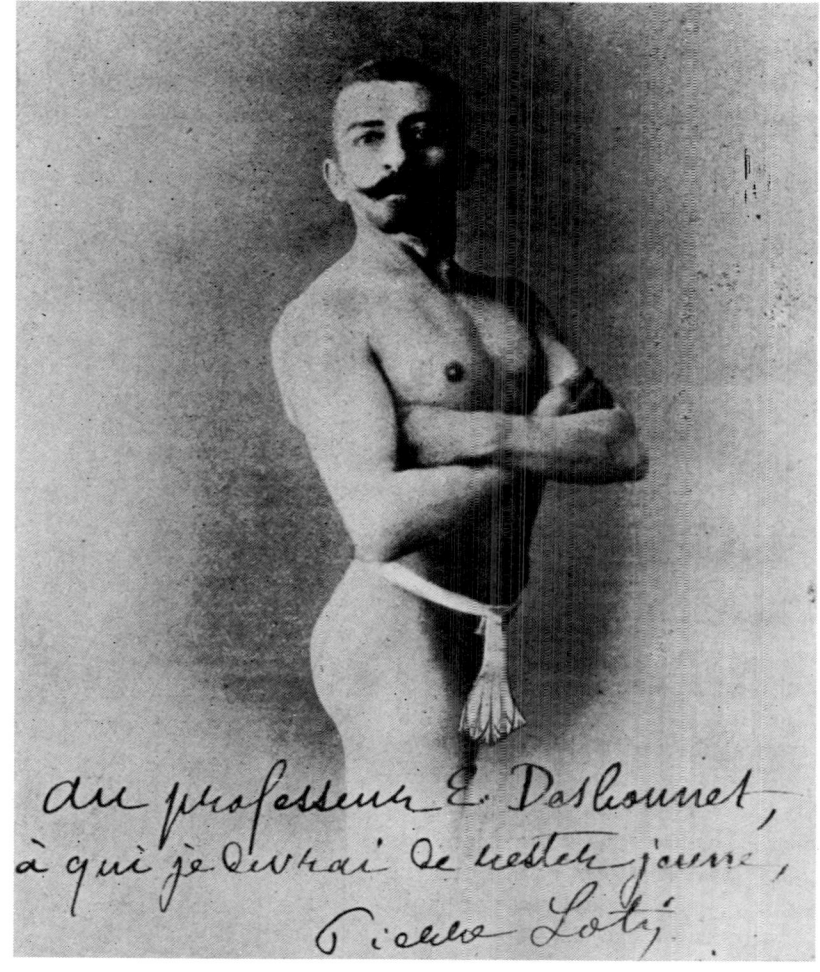

The first serious attempts to gain acceptance for homosexuality were made in the medical field. In 1886 the famous German neuropsychiatrist and professor of psychiatry at the university of Vienna, Baron von Krafft-Ebing, wrote in the preface to *Psychopathia sexualis* that homosexuals "in most cases have great spiritual and social qualities and are often exceptionally sensitive people." The pioneer sexologist even wondered whether homosexuality might not be innate. Some years later William James (the philosopher, and elder brother of Henry James) observed in *The Principles of Psychology* (1890) that most men probably contain the seeds (no pun intended) of the "unnatural vice." Although Sigmund Freud did not propose any definite solution to the question of homosexuality, he too believed that all men possess both male and female characteristics and are potentially bisexual;

nonetheless he was forced to admit that "homosexuality is a path that is forbidden by society."

Towards the beginning of the century a number of doctors and psychiatrists began to campaign for liberalized laws on homosexuality. The German doctor, Magnus Hirschfeld, launched a vigorous attack against article 175 of the German penal code, which punished any sexual act between two men with five years in prison. Later, he directed an important survey on homosexuality: 3,000 students from Berlin and 5,721 workers were interviewed. The publication of this investigation got Hirschfeld ten days in jail and a stiff fine—which did not discourage him from founding an "Institute for Sexual Research" in 1918 or from organizing the International Congress for Reform of Sexual Legislation (which met in 1929, 1930 and 1932). To the journalists who came to interview him (among them Willy, the husband of the famous French woman novelist Colette), he explained that "homosexuality is a natural phenomenon produced by an infinite number of causes independant from will." A homosexual himself, Hirschfeld considered himself "the shepherd of that strange flock." He was encouraged and supported in his lonely struggle by the British man of letters and psychologist, Havelock Ellis (who suffered from impotence and was married to a lesbian). In 1898 Ellis published the first of his *Studies in the Psychology of Sex*, the sixth volume of which took up the subject of *Sexual Inversion*. The book had been considered so scandalous that it had become the object of legal proceedings, but it had nevertheless succeeded in breaking the conspiracy of silence which had stifled discussion of sexual matters in England. In 1933 Hitler closed down Hirschfeld's Institute and ordered all of its files and papers, as well as its 20,000 volume library, burned. (In the night of June 29, 1934 Ernst Roehm, a notorious homosexual and the founder of the SA—the *Sturmabteilung*, the Nationalist Socialist brown shirt militia—was ruthlessly purged, along with his friends, followers and favorites. During the war homosexuals in Germany were interned in concentration camps and were obliged to wear a pink triangle; they were singled out for particularly sadistic treatment by the camp guards.)

It was Kinsey (whose first findings were published in 1948) who brought about a real change in the situation: he made it clear that the prevailing moral standards were unrelated to the reality of sexual behaviour. His work had a considerable impact on public opinion and especially on legislators in America and other Western countries. A biologist and a zoologist by training, Kinsey had undertaken an enormous survey of the sex life of 12,000 adult Americans from various backgrounds. The result had amazed even Kinsey himself. But that was nothing compared to the astonishment his fellow citizens experienced on learning that in America—the land of the pioneers, of record-breaking athletes and of Tarzan-type super-machos—37% of the adult male population had engaged in homosexual acts leading to orgasm; 25% had had prolonged sexual relationships with other men, and 4% had admitted to being exclusively homosexual. The Kinsey Report administered a severe blow to the image of the virile American male—all the more so that homosexuality was apparently more widespread among miners, lumbermen, cattlemen and hunters than among artists and intellectuals, the traditional "sissies" of American society.

The report was attacked with vehemence, but no one could impugn the sincerity of its author—who was a family man, a good citizen and an upstanding Christian. However, in a recent book entitled *The Modernization of Sex,* Paul Robinson suggests that Kinsey launched his

Gösta Adrian Nilsson, *Berns Salonger* (1916). Kulturhistoriska Föreningen För Södra Sverige Kulturen, Lund, Sweden. It was in this bar that the Swedish painter met his sailor friends.

Charles Demut, *Distinguished Air* (1930). Whitney Museum of American Art, New York. Gift of the Friends of the Whitney Museum of American Art, Charles Simon (and Purchase).

enormous investigation out of affection for one of his students who had died two years before he began working on the study. Whatever the case, Kinsey's findings were greeted with derisive laughter in the Latin countries. But a similar study, directed by Aldo Leoni of the Sacred Congregation of Rites in Rome, revealed that homosexuality was as widespread in the Catholic countries of Europe as it was in Protestant North America.

The relatively liberal Napoleonic Code (drawn up in 1810), which is still the basis of French law, does not specifically mention homosexuality (it only deals with the protection of minors against indecent assault)—an omission which may be explained by the fact that one of the principal framers of the Code (Cambacérès) was a homosexual. In most of the other European countries the "unnatural vice" used to be punished by death (in England this law was only rescinded in 1861, and in Scotland it was kept on the books until 1891). Thanks to

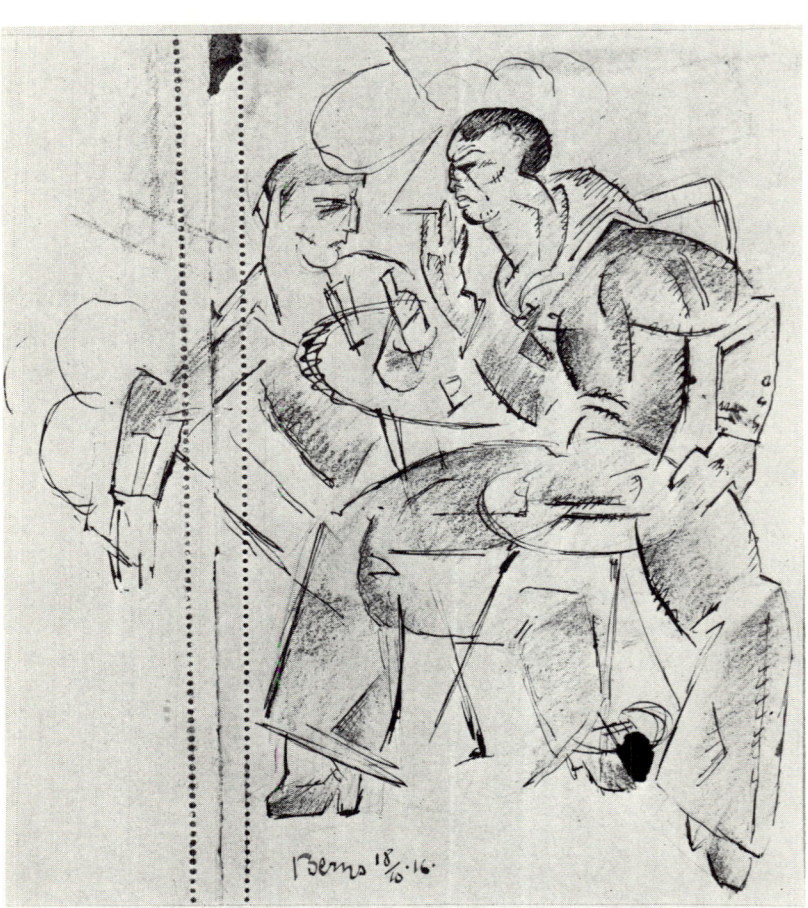

a series of reforms during the last two decades, French law now provides that any publicly offensive sex act committed with *a person of the same sex,* or any prurient or "unnatural" act committed with a *minor of the same sex,* aged between fifteen and eighteen, is punishable by a prison sentence of from six months to three years and a fine of up to $ 3,000. When the partner is not of the same sex the penalty is lighter: from three months to two years in prison and a fine of not more than $ 1,000. Since 1967 British law is substantially the same as French law on this point, except for certain cases (when more than two persons of the same sex are involved, for example) which are still very severely punished.

In Russia at the turn of the century homosexual offenders could be sent to Siberia. Nevertheless a number of writers like the poets Vsevolod Vyacheslavovich Ivanov, and Mikhail Kuzmin were well-known homosexuals (as was the statesman Georgi Vasilyevich Chicherin). After the Revolution, Soviet authorities declared that the "bourgeois vice" no longer existed in Russia. Strangely enough it soon reappeared under a new name, the "obscurantist vice." Even homosexuals who had been followers of Lenin were persecuted: Kuzmin's books were banned and the poet Kliuv died in transit between two prison camps. Under Stalin other homosexuals (like Kuzmin's lover, Yuri Yurkun) were deported or executed. In present-day USSR the "anti-social vice" is punishable by from three to eight years hard labor. Nevertheless, if the accounts of some Western tourists are to be believed, homosexuals have no trouble making contacts in the Moscow public toilets, or at the Odeon subway station.

In the United States homosexual offenses (variously designated as "sodomy," "unnatural offenses," "sexual perversion," "obscenity," etc.) fall under the provision of laws governing public morality. Even when both partners are consenting adults, they are generally charged as accomplices in crime, although some states (such as Illinois) consider that non-violent sex acts between consenting adults do not fall under the scope of criminal jurisdiction. However the civil service, the diplomatic corps and the military still discriminate against convicted homosexuals. In 1975 Sergeant Matlovich, a much-decorated Vietnam war hero, was discharged from the

209

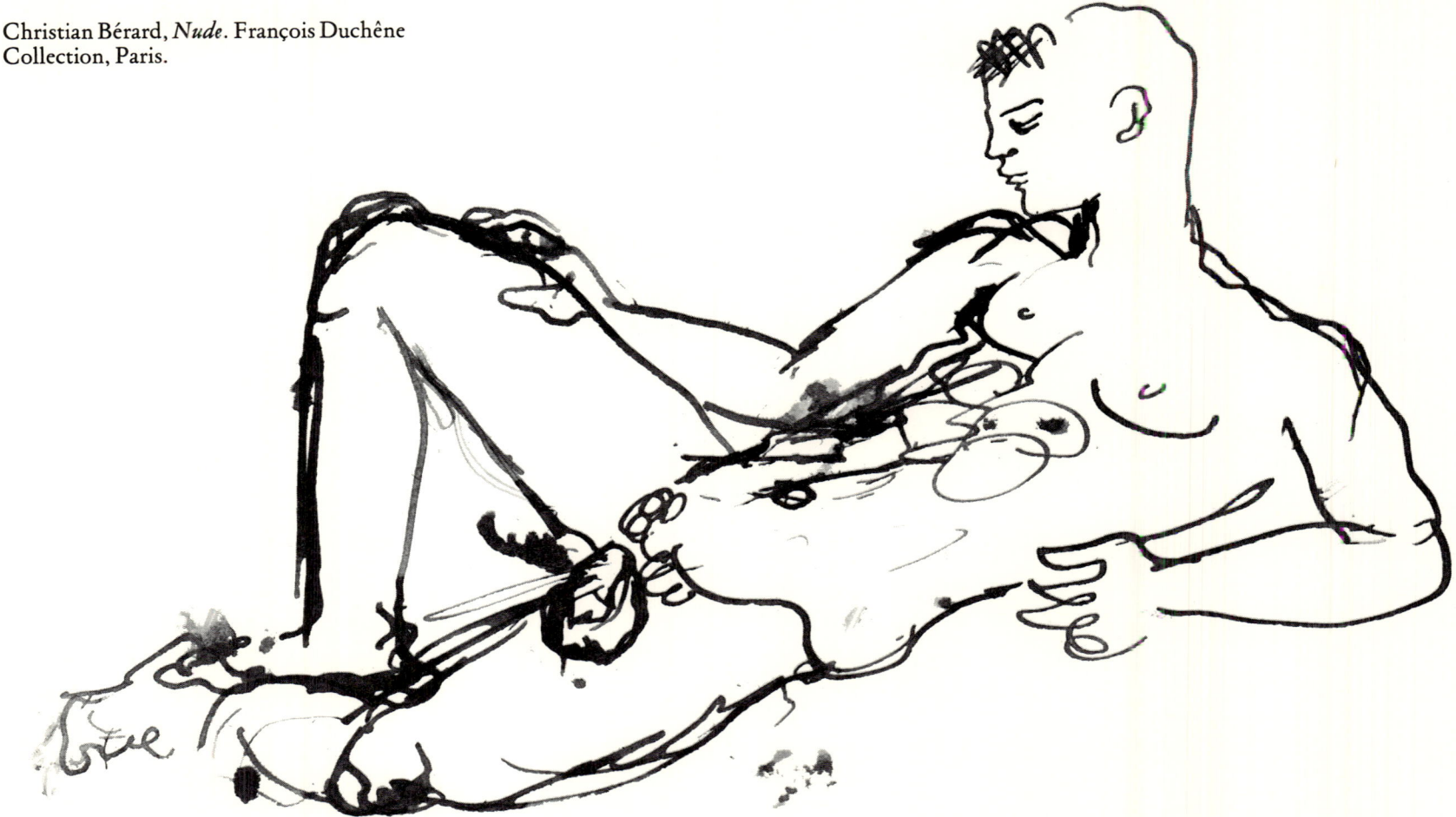

Christian Bérard, *Nude*. François Duchêne Collection, Paris.

Air Force after having publicly declared that he was a homosexual. On the other hand, a recent nationwide, front-page, news story revealed that the Secret Service officer who had protected President Ford from an assassination attempt was a militant homophile.

In *The Homosexual in America*, published in 1951, Donald Webster Cory voiced a strong protest against anti-homosexual discrimination in American society and urged gays to organize. By the late '60s gay liberation groups like the Mattachine Society (from the name of a Spanish comic figure who wears a mask and always speaks the truth) were active. In 1952 the gay magazine, *One*, began publishing out of Los Angeles; its avowed aim was to give homosexuals in America a voice. One of its first subscribers was Dr. Kinsey. Two years later the literary review, *Arcadie*, was founded in Paris (*Arcadie* now has a circulation of 10,000). Since 1960 numerous homophile magazines in America and elsewhere have published interviews, poems, short stories and writing by gay authors. The most interesting and literate of these publications are *Gay Sunshine* (San Francisco) and *Rutag Rag* (Boston).

The oldest of the homophile reviews is undoubtedly *Der Kreis* [The Circle], which began publishing in Zurich, Switzerland, in 1936. As for the term "homophile" it was first adopted by a convention in Holland to designate those who are almost exclusively attracted by members of their own sex (as distinct from *homosexual*, which now implies physical contact). In Holland, where homophiles benefit from open recognition by church and state authorities, a review named *Dialog* was launched in order to promote a wider public understanding of homosexuality and to fill in the gap between public opinion and a progressive sexual legislation. Also, the Cultur en Ontspanning Centrum [the Center for Cultural Activities and Leisure], founded in 1946, sponsors homophile gatherings in Amsterdam night clubs (though it has gone on record as disapproving homosexual weddings).

There are, therefore, grounds for hoping that—thanks to the above organizations, publications and movements—homosexuality will eventually be considered "normal," and the homosexual will no longer be derided and despised by society—while he, in turn, will no longer have to resort to provocative, scandalous (or just plain shoddy and sad) "hip," "camp," etc. self-advertisements. A critic of recent homosexual literature has voiced skepticism about the chances for homosexuals of ever finding happiness. But literature always tends to give a somber view of things, a view which, in this case, is hardly borne out by the various polls; they indicate that most men in Western societies are "fairly happy."

CHARLES-LOUIS PHILIPPE
(1874-1909)

Illustrations accompanying Charles-Louis Philippe's article on the Fersen case in *Le Canard Sauvage* (1903): (a) "My regards to Monsieur le Baron, Madame la Baronne" by Auguste Roubille. (b) "Black masses and choir boys" by Hermann-Paul. (c) "Ah, vicomte, how dare they prosecute our dear Baron...." "Marquis, this gouvernment has no respect for anything," by Félix Vallotton. (d) "Ah, the medical examination.... Doctors understand nothing about poetry." by Paul Iribe. (e) Frank Kupka, *Two Rapes*. Illustration for *Le Canard Sauvage* (1903).

In 1903 Charles-Louis Philippe, the author of populist novels like *Bubu of Montparnasse,* gave his opinion (see excerpt) of the Adelsward Fersen case for a magazine called *Le Canard Sauvage* ("The Wild Duck" or "The Unruly Rag," since the French word for duck—*canard*—is also slang for newspaper).

Adelsward Fersen was a young poet in fashion in the literary and social circles of Paris. To celebrate his engagement to a young girl he had fallen in love with, and to give a fitting end to his career as a guiding spirit of the "sodomite mecca," he threw an extravagant party for his comrades and fellow-celebrants in "pink masses and black masses" and other amusements. The affair was such a success that Fersen was arrested, charged with corrupting minors and sentenced to six months in jail. His engagement was broken off. Fersen tried to shoot himself in the head, but only managed to wound himself. After a long convalescence, he set out on a series of mad travels, "exhausting every human pleasure" in the words of the journalist and novelist Willy, who adds that Fersen became the very image of "errant vice." Fersen finally settled in Capri with a young Italian named Nino Cesarini, whom he cherished. It was in the idyllic setting of this Mediterranean island that he met Baron Krupp. (Krupp committed suicide a few years before the war to avoid facing a scandal like the one Fersen had lived through.) As for Fersen, worn out by too much opium and morphine, he died suddenly in 1909—leaving his possessions to Nino Cesarini and lamented by numerous disciples on Capri.

a

b

c

THE FIVE-LEGGED SHEEP

There are some sheep who are called five-legged sheep. These sheep are sheepier than the others, since they have an extra leg. They are exhibited at fairs, which is a bit crude. Really, a temple should be raised to them: it is the fifth leg that makes one a god. We are all familiar with them. There is the little dauber who goes to the School of Applied Arts and wears his art in his hair. He even wears velvet pants and carries a cane, which adds to his hair. Sometimes he looks at other men; he judges them according to their hair.

There is the poet. There are even portraits of the poet. I recommend the Mariani album to the reader. Monsieur Edmond Rostand has struck a fine pose in profile which shows the shape of his head, his nose, his eye and his neck to advantage. Surely, we all thought, this is the bearing of a poet. Along came Monsieur de Montesquieu, and his "simplicity." His head inclined ever so slightly, his arm resting on its elbow, one finger laid against his temple—the miracle of that index pointing to his genius—there he was, pure, noble, unemphatic, so far removed from ordinary human worries that one senses that this man was close to God.

None of them held a candle to you, Jacques d'Adelsward. No, you had corsets, the finest cravats, jewels, bracelets, silks and velvets, and blond hair more beautiful than ours. You played badminton; you served your laughter "like so many shuttlecocks." You trod on our common mud in your exquisitely-fitted pumps. We expected you to become Sully-Prudhomme and François Coppée; even that was too modest a goal for your

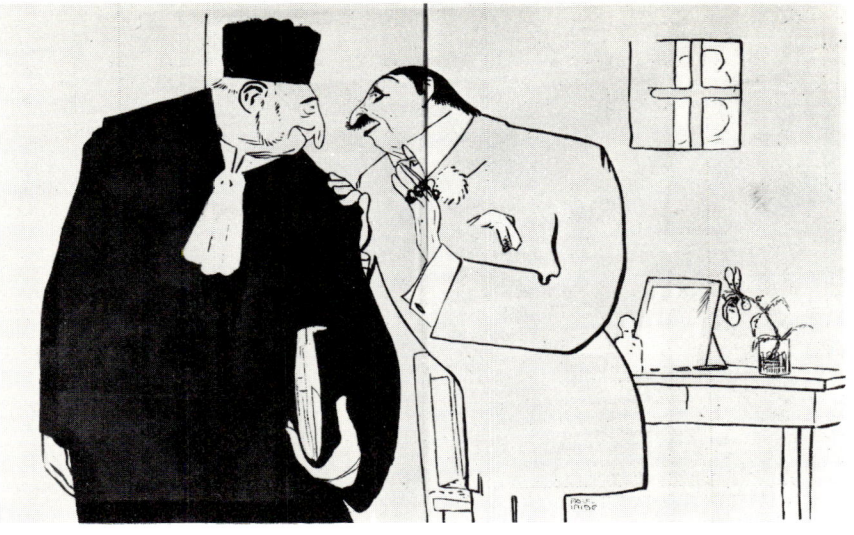

youthful brilliance. Ah, your Soarings and Orgies! You had Satan and God. You had the temple, the altar, the black masses.

But it is best not to speak of all that. I remember one autumn evening in my childhood. Two tramps were sitting on the edge of a ditch: one had his arms around the other's shoulders; they were sitting close together, holding hands and kissing. Life was as hard on them as an endless highway, but their hearts were joined. They had no wives, or mothers or brothers; so each was the other's wife, mother and brother. I was fifteen—you learn a lot of things in school at that age. So I understood. I hid behind a hedge so as not to be seen, and I saw that it is good for a man to be everything to another man.

And there are others, Jacques d'Adelsward. Bighearted men disconcerted by Nature who carry their strange passion through the world like a burden. They have need neither of Edmond Rostand's prefaces, nor of corsets, jewels and black masses. They bear themselves feverishly, but simply. Who among us would condemn them? Who would dare condemn a fellow human in his flesh and blood?

In the end you would have made us disgusted with them and with Oscar Wilde, who suffered so much. Your misfortune came at the right time. Consider yourself lucky to be brought back into the ranks of those we love. You were so sure that you were above the ordinary human condition. We will help you come back to it. Do not think that you have been dishonored. We have other passions. And any passion is great and good and normal, since it exists.

(*Le Canard Sauvage,* July 26-August 1, 1903)

PAUL LÉAUTAUD (1872-1956)

Léautaud was an assistant editor for the prestigious Paris publishing firm, Mercure de France, from 1908 to 1940. His *Literary Journal*, which spans most of his life, is remarkable for its meticulousness, its frankness and its corrosive wit. In it Léautaud confesses that he had been tempted more than once to bring boys back to his home, although he denies being "that way inclined." The following excerpt is from an entry made in the year 1904.

1904

Saturday, September 17. — Nine o'clock in the evening. At the entrance to the Etoile metro station. Two street lads. I watch them. They separate. I keep on watching. One of them, rather good features, rolls a cigarette and, as I am smoking, strolls over to ask me for a light. I ask him why his friend has left.

"He's waiting for someone."

"A man or a woman?"

"A man," he says. "English."

"What for?" I insist.

He doesn't know.

"Look," I say, "you understand what I am getting at, don't you?"

"Sure," he replies, looking at me with a quick smile.

"Well, you agree then?"

"Yes."

"Ah. But how do you go about it? Where do we go?"

Whereupon he calls his friend over. The other lad then suggests the park of the Bois de Boulogne or some hotel, God knows what sort of a place, rather far, in the rue Saussure. The three of us walk down the long avenue leading towards the Bois. Quite a conversation. One of the boys is sixteen, the other seventeen. The one I had planned to ... really has a fairly pretty face, he looks fifteen. We reach the entrance to the Bois, and I begin to have second thoughts. We sit down on a bench. Offcolor stories. I tell them the one about the boots, from the *Italian Tales*. Talk about going to my place. We start walking towards the metro. Meanwhile it occurs to me that if they know my address they might come and bother me in the future. I say something about getting a carriage... We walk back to the Place de l'Etoile. All my thinking about the risks has dampened me somewhat. Besides, it is obvious that the lads will provide only the innocent pleasures, hand or mouth. Otherwise: virgins. Telling them that I have to go to the bathroom I try to slip away. They catch up with me, and make a little scene. They are right of course: I had kept them for two hours and for nothing. Wasted their evening. Again I'm taken by the desire to use them, at least one of them, the one I like. But I start worrying again, besides it's getting late. Finally we say goodnight, almost at the spot where we had met; ...

Donald Friend, Plate from *The Antipodeans* (1966). Eddy Batach Collection, Paris.

STEFAN GEORGE (1868-1933)

Arno Breker, *Comrades* (detail). Charles Despiau once said that this sculpture was "as moving as a dying Adonis."

Pierre Yves, Trémois, *For the Apocalypse* (1961). The artist's collection.

Stefan George was born near Bingen in the Rhineland in 1868. In 1888 he went to study in Paris. There, he wrote a translation of Baudelaire's works and became associated with Mallarmé and the French Symbolists. He developed a view of poetry as Teaching and Prophecy, which is reflected in his early writings: *Algabal* (1892), *The Book of Eclogues and Eulogies* (1895), *The Year of the Soul* (1897).

Back in Germany, he founded a literary school of his own, the *George-Kreis*, a coterie of admirers who looked up to him as their guru and Master.

In 1902 George met Maximilian Kronberger (whom he was to call Maximin in his writings). This youth, who was only fourteen at the time, was a fledgling poet. What Beatrice was to Dante, Maximim became to Stefan George: the embodiment of all his yearnings for divine perfection, beauty, happiness and peace. Having accomplished his "mission" of spiritual and poetic inspiration, the lad, who was perhaps too pure and unearthly to linger in this world, died at the age of sixteen. George's later work—*The Seventh Ring* (1907), *Der Stern des Bundes* (1914) and *Das neue Reich* (1928)—is haunted by the boy's fleeting passage through the poet's life. Not wanting to mar his flawless literary image with what they considered irrelevant biographical details, George's followers kept Maximin's real identity secret.

Stefan George's nationalism, his intense concern with preserving the purity of the German language, his cult of virile beauty, his lofty isolation and his contempt for the materialism of modern society appealed to the rising National Socialist generation in Germany. Indeed the Third Reich tried to claim George as one of its great poets, but George himself was opposed to the political developments which his ideas are sometimes thought to reflect.

George died at Minusio, near Locarno, Switzerland on December 4, 1933.

216

THE LYRE PLAYER

How he advanced, with a white fillet twisted
Around his locks, a sumptuous garment weighing
His slender shoulders, how he struck his lyre,
Uncertainly at first with youthful shyness,
Astonished even the austere and the aged.
And how he kindled cheeks to yearning scarlet,
How many women flung him strings of jewels
And priceless clasps, while he, who was still new
To such ovation, bowed—will be remembered
Wherever fruit grows on the holy tree.
The girls are full of endless eager talk,
And every boy in secret anguish, worships
The hero of his sleepless, starlit hours.

(from *The Book of Eclogues and Eulogies*)

ADVENT I

To some you are a child,
To some a friend, to me
The god whom I divined
And tremblingly adore.

You came at last when sick
With waiting, weary of
My prayers, I began
To lose myself in night.

I knew you by the beam
Which flowed into my dark,
The step to which the seed
Replied with sudden bloom.

(from "Maximin," in *The Seventh Ring*)

ROBERT MUSIL (1880-1942)

In his *Journal*, written between 1937-41, the Austrian engineer, philosopher and (mainly) novelist, Robert Musil, notes that the cruelty, brutality and abasement of the Nazis are already present in seed in the microcosmic boarding-school setting of his first novel, *Young Törless* (1906). This is not an autobiographical work, according to Musil, still less is it the chronicle of a "special" friendship; rather, it is a depiction of the moral, intellectual and physical confusion experienced by a teenager. Törless, the protagonist, is a boarder in an Austrian academy. He wants to be accepted by the "tough" clique in his class, although he is filled with fear and disgust at his older classmates' bullying of a weak and cowardly lad named Basini. To his shame, Törless, who has so far known only "the secret, melancholy sexuality of adolescence," is physically drawn to Basini. "The viler and more unspeakable Basini's offers became, the more intensely they contrasted with the painfully delicate emotions which they provoked in Törless." In later years, however, Törless came to value this youthful episode. "It left something durable in me: the little dose of poison that preserves the soul from too tranquil, too self-assured a state of health, giving it instead a life which is subtler, keener and more intelligible."

From YOUNG TÖRLESS

Törless unlocked the door, and they went in. With his back to Basini, he lit the little lamp.

When he turned round, Basini was standing there naked.

Involuntarily Törless fell back a step. The sudden sight of this naked snow-white body, with the red of the walls dark as blood behind it, dazzled and bewildered him. Basini was beautifully built; his body, lacking almost any sign of male development, was of a chaste, slender willowyness, like that of a young girl. And Törless felt this nakedness lighting up in his nerves, like hot white flames. He could not shake off the spell of this beauty. He had never known before what beauty was. For what was art to him at his age, what—after all—did he know of that? Up to a certain age, if one has grown up in the open air, art is simply unintelligible, a bore!

And here now it had come to him on the paths of sexuality ... secretly, ambushing him ... There was an infatuating warm exhalation coming from the bare skin, a soft, lecherous cajolery. And yet there was something about it that was so solemn and compelling as to make one almost clasp one's hands in awe.

But after the first shock Törless was as ashamed of the one reaction as of the other. "It's a man, damn it!" The thought enraged him, and yet it seemed to him as though a girl could not be different.

In his shame he spoke hectoringly to Basini: "What on earth d'you think you're doing? Get back into your things this minute!"

Now it was Basini who seemed taken aback. Hesitantly, and without shifting his gaze from Törless, he picked up his coat from the floor.

"Sit down—there!" Törless ordered. Basini obeyed. Törless leaned against the wall, with his arms crossed behind his back.

"Why did you undress? What did you want of me?"

"Well, I thought..."

He paused hesitantly.

"What did you think?"

"The others..."

"What about the others?..."

"But it's not the beatings they give me that I'm afraid of!"

"Oh? What is it then?"

By now Törless was speaking calmly again. He was already annoyed at his crude threat. But it had escaped him involuntarily, solely because it seemed to him that Basini stood up to him more than to the others.

"Well, if you're not afraid, as you say, what's the matter with you?"

"They say if I do whatever they tell me to, after some time I shall be forgiven everything."

"By the two of them?"

"No, altogether."

"How can they promise that? *I* have to be considered too!"

"They say they'll manage that all right."

This gave Törless a shock. Beineberg's words about Reiting's dealing with him, if he got the chance, in exactly the same way as with Basini now came back to him. And if it really came to a plot against them, how was he to cope with it? He was no match for the two of them in that sort of thing. How far would they go? The same as with Basini? ... Everything in him revolted at the perfidious idea....

At last he was back in bed. He was not thinking of anything at all any more, for thinking came so hard and was so futile. What he had discovered about the secret contrivings of his friends did, it was true, go through his mind, but now as indifferently and lifelessly as an item of foreign news read in a newspaper.

There was nothing more to be hoped from Basini. Oh, there was still his problem! But that was so dubious, and he was so tired and mangled. An illusion perhaps—the whole thing.

Only the vision of Basini, of his bare, glimmering skin, left a fragrance, as of lilac, in that twilight of the sensations which comes just before sleep. Even the moral revulsion faded away. And at last Törless fell asleep.

No dream disturbed him. There was only an infinitely pleasant warmth spreading soft carpets under his body. After a while he woke out of it. And then he almost screamed. There, sitting on his bed, was Basini! And in the next instant, with crazy speed, Basini had flung off his night-clothes and slid under the blankets and was pressing his naked, trembling body against Törless.

Otto Meyer-Amden, *The Drawing Lesson* (1920). Private collection.

As soon as Törless recovered from the shock, he pushed Basini away from him.

"What do you think you're doing—?"

But Basini pleaded. "Oh, don't start being like that again! Nobody's the way you are! They don't despise me the way you do. They only pretend they do, so as to be different then afterwards. But you—you of all people! You're even younger than me, even if you are stronger. We're both younger than the others. You don't boast and bully the way they do ... You're gentle ... I love you ..."

"Here, I say! I don't know what you're talking about! I don't know what you want! Go away! Oh, go *away*!" And in anguish Törless pushed his arm against Basini's shoulder, holding him off. But the hot proximity of the soft skin, this other person's skin, haunted him, enclosing him, suffocating him. And Basini kept on whispering. "Oh yes ... oh yes ... please ... oh, I should so gladly do whatever you want!"

Törless could find nothing to say to this. While Basini went on whispering and he himself was lost in doubt and consideration, something had sunk over his senses again like a deep green sea. Only Basini's flickering words shone out in it like the glint of little silvery fishes.

He was still holding Basini off with his arms. But something made them heavy, like a moist, torpid warmth; the muscles in them were slackening ... he forgot them .... Only when another of those darting words touched him did he start awake again, all at once feeling—like something fearful and incomprehensible—that this very instant, as in a dream, his hands had drawn Basini closer.

Then he wanted to shake himself into wakefulness, wanted to shout at himself: Basini's tricking you, he's just trying to drag you down to where he is, so that you can't despise him any more! But the cry was never uttered, nor was there any sound anywhere in the whole huge building; throughout the corridors the dark tides of silence seemed to lie motionless in sleep.

He struggled to get back to himself. But those tides were like black sentinels at all the doors.

Then Törless abandoned his search for words. Lust, which had been slowly seeping into him, emanating from every single moment of desperation, had now grown to its full stature. It lay naked at his side and covered his head with its soft black cloak. And into his ear it whispered sweet words of resignation, while its warm fingers thrust all questionings and obligations aside as futile. And it whispered: In solitude you can do what you will.

Only in the moment when he was swept away he woke fleetingly, frantically clutching at the one thought: This is not myself! It's not me! ... But tomorrow it will be me again! ... Tomorrow....

219

FREDERICK ROLFE [BARON CORVO] (1860-1913)

Although raised as a Protestant, Frederick Rolfe converted to Catholicism at the age of twenty-five and hoped to become a priest. His unruly, temperamental nature worried his superiors however, and they refused to ordain him. Rolfe became a school teacher, but clung doggedly to the notion of priesthood. He felt out of place in normal society, unlike other men—as for women, they inspired feelings of repulsion in him—all of which were good reasons, he believed, for serving God (or at least the Church). But the Church saw matters differently, and Rolfe was obliged to seek other consolations: he turned to photography (inventing an underwater camera and a color film process), took up painting, wrote poetry (illustrated by himself) and published tales, much appreciated in certain circles. At the turn of the century, he wrote bizarre historical chronicles on such subjects as the lives of the Borgias. Next he became the private secretary of a former dean of Jesus College, Oxford (Dr. Hardy, the only friend with whom he did not quarrel). He went to Venice for a month's vacation, promptly fell in love with the city and decided to stay. Welcomed at first by the British residents there, who offered him hospitality, he soon made himself thoroughly unpopular, putting off even his most devoted friends. Reduced to poverty, unable to pay his hotel bill, he scribbled insulting letters to his former hosts and fell ill. He was transported to the British Hospital where he stayed several months. But he never really recovered his health and died three years later.

"The Desire and Pursuit of the Whole is called Love," says Plato. Borrowing its title from this celebrated aphorism, Rolfe wrote his best-known novel while staying at the Van Somerens' splendid rented palace in Venice. Nicholas Crabbe, the protagonist, lives on a boat and falls in love with a young girl (named Ermenegilda Falier) of rather uncertain gender. The minor characters in the book are cruel caricatures of Van Someren's friends. Rolfe made the mistake of reading several pages from the manuscript to his hostess, who was outraged and demanded that he cut some passages—or that he leave forthwith. Rolfe left, and the novel was eventually finished on his deathbed. A.J.A. Symons, who made Baron Corvo famous with a book about him, found the manuscript of *The Desire and Pursuit* in an attic in 1925. No one had dared publish it, for fear of being sued for libel.

FROM THE DESIRE AND PURSUIT OF THE WHOLE

Nicholas Crabbe had forgotten as much Greek as any man of culture need know. He had read his Plato with the rest of us, and (like the rest of us) as an intellectual gymnastic, without receiving particular influence from Plato's now-obsolete notions. He certainly had no ideas about love, as that game is practised in decent society. The human female was to him a mysterious individual very much unlike himself. At the back of his mind, even when he brought her interest (and he never never had met one who had not her fixed price), he knew that she was something rather weak, rather tender, something to which it is a duty to be kind and helpful and attentive. On the whole, then, he treated the human female (meritorious or meretricious) on those lines. When, however, she laughed and talked and acted with him as an equal, he was by no means slow to caper along with her. And his frankness and simplicity and carelessness and unsuspicious personality used to get him into the most awful trouble. That is the worst of the human female. She comes brazenly out; and jests and jousts with the male. He lets himself forget how strong he is. Suddenly, unknowingly, unintentionally, he hurts her. She runs back into her stronghold of feminality, and fills the circumambient air with howls. She is a martyr. He knows himself to be a foolish, much-wronged beast.

Such, in the main, had been Crabbe's relations with women. His natural bent was for treating them as

Hippolyte-Jean Flandrin, *Naked Youth by the Seaside* (1855). Louvre, Paris

goddesses in niches, with stately chivalry, and on his knees. He didn't in the least admire their physical beauty, as a rule. He looked upon them as he looked upon those very venerable black Madonnas who invariably work miracles. The form and ornament of them made him simply sick, "usque ad nauseam," by reason of its vapid bunchiness and vacuous inconsequent patchworkiness. You should have heard him on the pathetically anakoly- those bonnets of spinsters and fashionable horse-faced dowagers. You should have observed his furious forbearance with the scraggy ladies of rectors, or with the tailor-made females who still hoped to allure a man with their motley mangy boas and hybrid hand-bags and clinking beads and heterogeneous high heels and foolish fat stockings and hard waists (o Aphrodite Anadyomene) and tabby hats like crumpled wrecks of flea-bitten birds' nests of felt plastered with the scratchings of rag-bags and gigantic withered old cauliflowers. But sometimes he did admire a young girl, at a distance, and only for her fresh wholesome youth, her lithe strength, her dainty adroitness. And, then, an appalling prevision of what she would have to hide, of what she was likely to become, made him wipe her from the mirror of his mind. He never had wanted one of these creatures for his very own. He never had tried to conceive himself irretrievably committed to the company of any one of them. Yet he knew that he was very far from being perfect in his loneliness. He used to gaze at other men, courting, marrying, living in apparent happiness; and he would wonder whether that was the right way. Anon he would distinguish a great gulf fixed between him and other men; they were content with so little, with what came to hand, with what they could get: he was not content with anything at all, the object of his desire and pursuit being simply the Unique and the signory of it.

He had tried friendship, with adolescents, with juniors, with seniors. Youths adored him for his strength, his wit, his extraordinary expertness, and left him for their own mates. Men of his own age, being human and entirely overwhelmed with the fulness and weight of the illimitable confidence which he generously lavished upon them, invariably took the most dastardly advantage of him, robbed him, wounded him, and departed, leaving him half-dead. Old men patronized him, or inspired him with pity and terror. Friendship was a failure, as it had been given him to try. People said that he asked too much of it. Certainly he did ask a lot. He asked for loyalty—the loyalty which demands and concedes no limit of self-sacrifice for the satisfaction of one's friend. He asked for honour—the honour which can quarrel freely for the sake of avoiding stagnation and as freely make peace for the sake of pleasurable repose: but never on any account will even listen to a single syllable from outsiders in one's friend's despite. And he asked for eternal, unflinching fidelity.

You see now, perhaps, what he was after? He was after his other (not his better) half. You behold him, a passionate pilgrim desiring and pursuing the whole. Pursuing? Yes—hastening slowly. Open wide was his heart, and extended his arms and his breast bared, yearning with every fibre of body and soul, burning with eager desire to pursue, to attain, to unite with, melt, and dissolve in, the mate who should make, with him, One....

Ermenegilda Falier, however, was not an ordinary girl. She was a "sport," a freak of Nature who had made a very fine and noble sketch of a boy and failed to finish it. Her hair was cropped, always had been cropped. She was seventeen years old: but her pectoral muscles were as richly flat and vigorous as those of the Eros of Praxiteles on the newly-found "Fanciulla di Arzio" which everyone makes such a fuss about. She had no more waist than a boy who has rowed all his life standing, and stretching to thrust, in the mode Venetian, filling and clothing his reins with that ripping belt of lovely muscle which Michelangelo admired (and is said to have invented)—that girdle which no "strong man" has ever yet achieved with idiotic spring-dumb-bells or gum-elastic-exercisers. And hip, the horrible meaningless crupper, adored by kallipygs shaped like a little egg slipping off a big egg slipping off an inverted bluebell, accentuating hypertrophy caused and cultivated by straight-fronted corsets—she was close-packed, neat, rounded, and supple as the Narcissus of Pompeii. And her hard-palmed agile hands with the corn on the thumb-joint—and her long, large, sensitive, shapely springing feet. She should be a boy. She should be a servant. She should serve, serve only—oh yes, but she should surely serve. As she wished.

David Hockney, *Randy* (1974). Private collection, Paris.

GUILLAUME APOLLINAIRE
(1880-1918)

The son of a capricious Polish woman and an Italian who may have been a prelate (or more likely an officer), Wilhelm Apollinaris de Kostrowitzky, later known as Guillaume Apollinaire, always kept the circumstances of his birth a mystery (all that is known for sure is that he was born in Rome on August 20, 1880). His early years were difficult ones. Financial and emotional insecurity dogged him; perhaps as a result he immersed himself in living, writing and studying with extraordinary intensity. He began to compose poems, tales and short stories out of the lessons and images he picked up in his travels, adventures and usually unhappy love affairs. Enormously complex, he was in turns sentimental and purely physical, exuberant and moody, outrageously conceited and excruciatingly shy. In 1902, with the publication of his story, "The Heresiarch," in the important avant-garde review, *La Revue Blanche*, he became established in the literary and artistic bohemia of Paris. His friends included the poets André Salmon and Max Jacob, the irreverent fire-brand Alfred Jarry, and the painters Picasso, Picabia, Dufy, Derain and Marie Laurencin, who inspired many of his lyrics and with whom he had a stormy love affair. To earn his living he worked as a ghost writer, as a messenger at the Paris stock exchange and as a research assistant at the Bibliothèque Nationale (where he was employed to help compile a vast catalogue of "restricted" books in the library's collection of pornography. Many of the more erudite and witty comments in this work are Apollinaire's. As a result he became a connoisseur of erotica and later helped to edit a series of erotic classics for a Paris publisher. He himself wrote several masterpieces in the genre).

He volunteered for active military service during World War I, was wounded in the head in 1916 and returned to Paris and to literary life. He published a book (*Le Poète assassiné*), gave his blessing to the emerging Dadaist movement and got married. A few months later, on November 9, 1918, he died, a victim of the great Spanish influenza epidemic.

Ernst Josephson, *The Sun-God*. Private collection.

THE SOMODITE'S MINION

Louis Gian, son of a modest oil merchant in Nice, never showed the least piety; unlike the rest of his schoolfellows, who, at least at the time of their first communion, gave proofs of a touching devotion to the church.

The limping vicar of Saint-Réparate had said to him one day during catechism class, as he wiped his glasses on his dirty cassock:

"Louis! You will come to no good, because you are a hypocrite. To look at you, one would take you for an angel. But what's the truth? You're as low as a kneeling bedbug. You make fun of me. I know all about it, and you may go on doing it. But God is not mocked. You may find this out sooner than you wish."

Louis Gian listened to the vicar's admonition standing before him humbly, his eyes lowered. But the moment the priest's back was turned, the graceless boy mimicked his halting gait, and sang ironically:

"Five and three make eight. Five and three make eight."

The young man from Nice did not improve with the years. Until the age of fourteen he hardly went to school at all, but spent his time under the bridges of the Paillon and at the castle, debauching at first boys of his own age, then little girls.

At the age of fourteen, he was apprenticed to a shirtmaker, and left the old quarter of Nice, with its perfumes of fruit and spices, mingled with the rankness of raw meat, sour dough, dried codfish and latrines, for a shop in the new town. From the first days the owner and his wife, who, like all good people of Nice, did not let their apprentice go short of work, either by night or by day, kept a close eye on him.

The owner's wife had hair as red as an orange, but the owner smelled of *pissaladière*. Louis Gian was enticed away from them at carnival time by a meticulous Russian, whom he had to call General, and who in return called him Ganymede.

When he discovered that the Russian was both exacting in his requirements and miserly, Louis first robbed and then left him.

He next bestowed himself on a brutal and lasciviously greedy Turk.

The Turk, however, ruined himself at Monte Carlo, and was duly replaced by an American. Louis Gian had understood that to maintain himself fruitfully, he must devote himself, like a rounded map of the world, to all nationalities.

Yet, in his good fortune, he failed to keep that serenity which is the privilege of the virtuous. He despised his former companions, and would walk by them pretending not to see them. First, they returned insult for insult. They did not fail, when they met him, to make a certain gesture which consists of placing the left hand at the elbow of the bent right arm, and shaking the right clenched fist. Or again, as he walked by, they mouthed the obscene letter z of the silent alphabet of insult used by the people of Nice, the Monégasques and the people from La Turbie and Menton.

Finally, Louis Gian's misconduct became as abhorrent to the Heavens as to his friends. He who pisses against the wind wets his shirt; and it pleased God finally to punish the sins of the sodomite's minion in a manner fitting the offence.

Louis Gian one day insulted a former friend who had apostrophized him, telling him to mend his ways. There was a quarrel which led to blows and threats of revenge.

Four young men, who were really not much better than Louis Gian himself, lay in wait for him one night when he had gone alone to the theatre. They got drunk on Corsican wine, the reputation of which has fallen so greatly since the sixteenth century, then lay in wait for him in front of the villa where he lived with an unsavoury Austrian.

When Louis Gian arrived after midnight, they fell upon him, gagged him, and then hauled him to the town gate, where they impaled him on one of its spikes, and ran off nudging one another obscenely.

The impaled one died, voluptuously perhaps. He was as beautiful as Atys. The fireflies glowed round him....

VSEVOLOD V. IVANOV
(1866-1949)

Vsevolod Vyacheslavovich Ivanov got married very young to the sister of a boy with whom he was madly in love. He traveled to Germany and lived there. In 1893 he moved to Rome to study the classics. There he met Lydia Zinovieva Annibal. Though she was a lesbian, Lydia had gotten married too (in order to get away from her family), but she soon grew disappointed with her husband. Both mismatched, Lydia and Ivanov promptly fell in love with each other. They divorced their respective spouses and married in 1899. By then Ivanov's first poems were appearing in print and were being well received by the critics. Lydia and Ivanov returned to Russia together and settled in St. Petersburg, where their apartment became a gathering place for the city's intelligentsia. Kuzmin, who lived in the same building, became a close friend. According to Ivanov homsexual love was the only kind of love that would enable humanity to reach a higher spiritual level and cast off its savagery and brutality. While Lydia was busy writing novels whose heroines were invariably lesbians, her husband fell in love with the poet Sergei Gorodetsky and dedicated several poems to him in a book entitled *Eros*. Lydia died in 1907, a loss for which nothing could console Ivanov, who stayed on in Russia until 1924, when he married Lydia's daughter by her first marriage. From then until his death he lived in Italy, where he held professorships at several Italian universities.

INCANTATION

When Magical Midnight wafts darkness upon bright candle flames
The turnkey of the deepest depths, Magical Midnight,
Granting to parched lips the sweet intoxication of dew,
The guiding sovereign of inexorable encounters,
The undoer of the Sun's pledges, Mother Night,
The deaf-mute daugther of the blind prisoner Chaos:

Come, lie down with me to our repast of languor,
You alone, and share my fiery-black cup!
The pupils of my eyes are vacant, my dark wells are dry:
Come, my nocturnal one, and quench my torrid noon!
Come, my son, my brother! Our wife awaits us:
Night, our Magical Mother—secluded, quiet, drunken, avid....

(1906)

MIKHAIL KUZMIN
(1875-1936)

The Russian poet, Mikhail Kuzmin, came from provincial nobility; his family were Old Believers. At an early age he recognized and accepted his homosexuality. His first love was his classmate, Chicherin, who later became a great Soviet statesman. In 1906 Kuzmin published his novel *Wings*. It tells the story of how a young man from the provinces, Vanya, discovers that the man he admires to the point of love, the Hellenist Stroop, is having an affair with a sauna attendant. Horrified, Vanya flees Stroop and tries to forget him. But during a trip to Italy, where he again encounters Stroop, Vanya realizes that he has always loved him. Fully conscious of what this means, he agrees to continue his travels with the Hellenist, who becomes his mentor. *Wings* raised a storm of scandal when it appeared. G.S.Novopolin, the author of a book on pornography in Russian literature, wrote: "It is true that such practices occur in the Caucases and in certain aristocratic circles in our large cities. But no one before has dared publicize this unnatural vice." In *Literature and Revolution*, Trotsky castigates Kuzmin's writing, calling it decadent, bourgeois and unworthy of Soviet society. In 1928 Kuzmin was still able to organize a public reading of his poetry in Leningrad. Hundreds of admirers, including many homosexuals, acclaimed him, covering him with flowers. In 1929 Kuzmin, who was obliged to make translations to earn his living, published his last book of poems. He died on the eve of the Stalinist purges in 1936.

From WINGS

"We are Hellenes: the intolerant monotheism of the Hebrews is alien to us—their rejection of the visual arts, their slavish attachment to the flesh, to the getting of heirs, to seed. In the whole of the Bible there is not a single indication of a belief in bliss beyond the grave, and the only reward mentioned in the Commandments (and that, be it noted, for showing respect to those who gave us life) is 'that thy days may be long upon the land.' According to the Jews a sterile marriage is a stigma and a curse, and those bound in such a union forfeit the right to worship in the temple; yet it is a Jewish legend which tells us that childbirth and toil are a punishment for sin, not the purpose of life. And as human beings put sin behind them, so will they put behind them childbearing and toil. The Christians have some inkling of this: according to them a woman must purify herself with prayer not after marriage, but after giving birth, while a man is released from all such observances. Love needs no justification outside itself; nature too is without trace of the idea of finality. The laws of nature are of an order quite different from the laws of God, so called, and the laws of man. The law of nature does not say that a given tree must bear fruit; it says that in certain conditions the tree will bear fruit and that in other conditions it will not only fail to bear fruit, but will wither and die just as simply and naturally as it would have born fruit. That a heart will stop beating if it is pierced with a dagger—*there's no finality, no good or evil in that.* And the only man capable of breaking the law of nature is he who can kiss his own eyes without tearing them from their sockets, and see the back of his own head without a mirror. And when they say to you 'unnatural,' be content to look at the blind fool who has said such a thing and go your way, not behaving as do those sparrows which fly up at the sight of a scarecrow in a vegetable garden. People go about like the blind, like the dead, when they might create for themselves a life

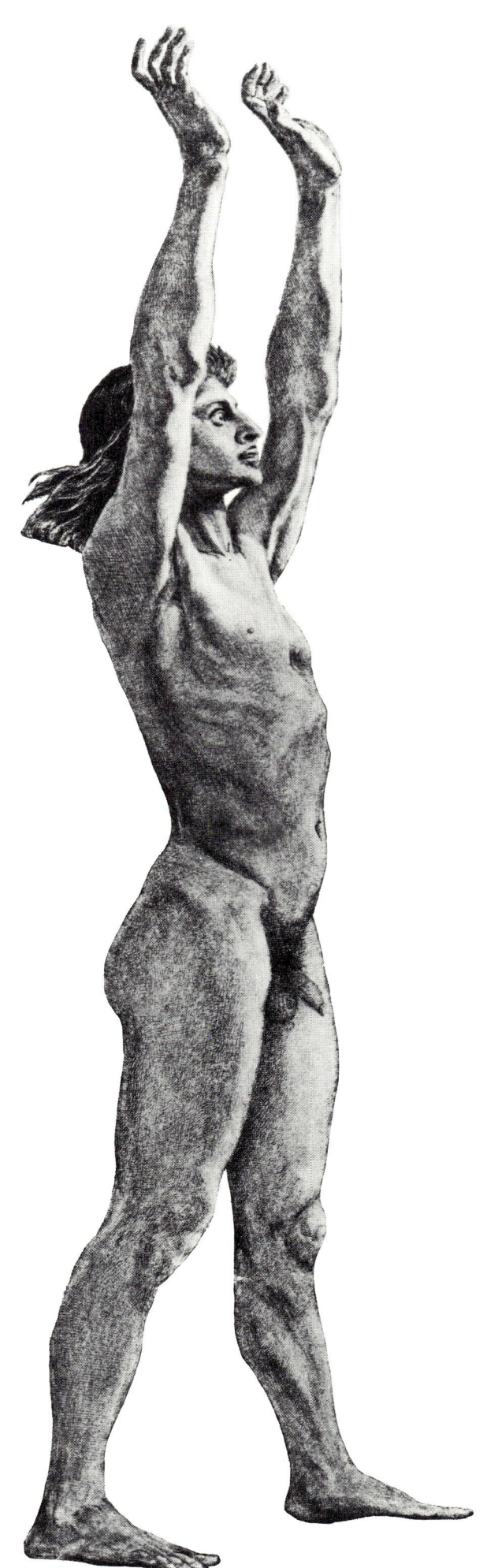

The Poles (detail). Illustration for the 1797 edition of *L'Histoire de Juliette ou les prospérités du vice* by the Marquis de Sade, published in Holland.

Max Klinger, *And Yet* (detail). Engraving from the series *On Death, Opus XIII*. Bibliothèque Nationale, Paris. "We are all lovers of the Beautiful," wrote Kuzmin referring to the works of Max Klinger.

burning with intensity in every moment, a life in which pleasure would be as poignant as if you had just come into the world and might die before the day were done. It is with such greed that we must fling ourselves upon life. Miracles crowd upon us at every step: there are muscles, sinews in the human body which one cannot look upon without a tremor! And those who would bind the idea of beauty to the beauty of a woman seen through the eyes of a man—they reveal only vulgar lust and are furthest of all from the *true idea* of beauty. We are Hellenes, lovers of the beautiful, the bacchants of the coming day. Like the visions of Tannhäuser in Venus' Grotto, like the inspired revelations of Klinger and Thoma, somewhere lies our ancient kingdom, full of sunlight and freedom, of beautiful and courageous people, and thither we sail, my argonauts, over many a sea, through mist and darkness. And in things yet unheard we shall descry ancient roots, in glittering visions yet unseen we shall know our own dear land!..."

They were walking along the road which followed the far side of the Cascine; through the trees they could see meadows dotted with farms and a range of low mountains beyond. They passed a restaurant, deserted at that time of day, and walked on through a region which grew ever more rustic. Here and there, a shiny-buttoned watchman would be sitting on a bench, and in the distance boys in cassocks frolicked under the watchful eye of a plump abbot.

"I'm so grateful that you agreed to come," said Stroop lowering himself to a bench.

"If we're going to talk, we'd better do it walking: I think better that way," observed Vanya.

"An excellent idea."

And they began to walk, now pausing, now moving forward again through the trees.

"Why did you deprive me of your friendship? Was it because you thought me to blame for the death of Ida Holbert?"

"No."

"Why then? I'd like an honest answer."

"You shall have it: it was because of your affair with Fyodor."

"Is that it?"

"I know what was going on—you can't deny it."

Frederick Lord Leighton, *Study of a Nude*. Colnaghi's Gallery, London.

Otto Meyer-Amden, *Dialogue*. Kunstmuseum, Basel.

"I admit I can't."

"Now, perhaps, my attitude would be quite different, but at the time I didn't know very much and had given things very little thought. It was very painful for me, I must confess, because I thought I was losing you forever, and with you, the path to the beautiful in life."

Circling a glade, they continued to follow the same path, and the laughter of children playing ball came to them remotely.

"Tomorrow I'm supposed to be going to Bari, but I could stay; it depends on you: if your answer is no, send me a note saying 'go'; if it's yes, then write 'stay.'"

"What do you mean, 'no' or 'yes?'" asked Vanya.

"Would you like me to spell it out for you?"

"No, don't, I understand; but is this really necessary?"

"It has become unavoidable. I'll wait until one o'clock."

"I'll give you my answer, one way or the other."

"Just one more little effort and you'll grow wings. I can see them already."

"Perhaps—but the growing can be very painful," said Vanya with a wry grin....

After a sleepless night, he got up exhausted and with an aching head. He washed and dressed with studied deliberation. Without opening the blind, he went over to the desk, upon which stood a glass of flowers, and slowly traced the word "go"; after a moment's thought, still with the same sleepy expression, he added, "and take me with you." Then he threw open the window onto a street flooded with sunlight.

THOMAS MANN (1875-1955)

Thomas Mann, who was awarded the Nobel Prize for Literature in 1929, describes a disquieting, decaying world in his novels; a world which he knew, by which he was disturbed and to which he was drawn. The protagonist of *Death in Venice,* the ageing writer Gustave Von Aschenbach, finds himself in the beautiful Adriatic city during a heat wave. He had come there to find rest; instead he experiences a "death vertigo" and feels his moral uprightness slowly melting in the sun. Corruption, eroticism and morbidness fascinate him. He is haunted by the beauty of young Tadzio, a youth he sees at his hotel and wanders through the city in search of him. In this "story of sensuality and annihilation" written in 1912 (a year after the demise of Mann's great friend, the composer Gustav Mahler), death has the final word.

From DEATH IN VENICE

Aschenbach saw the boy Tadzio almost constantly. The narrow confines of their world of hotel and beach, the daily round followed by all alike, brought him in close, almost uninterrupted touch with the beautiful lad. He encountered him everywhere—in the salons of the hotel, on the cooling rides to the city and back, among the splendours of the Piazza, and besides all this in many another going and coming as chance vouchsafed. But it was the regular morning hours on the beach which gave him his happiest opportunity to study and admire the lovely apparition.... He had three or four hours before the sun reached its height and the fearful climax of its power; three or four hours while the sea went deeper and deeper blue; three or four hours in which to watch Tadzio....

Soon the observer knew every line and pose of this form that limned itself so freely against sea and sky; its every loveliness, though conned by heart, yet thrilled him each day afresh; his admiration knew no bounds, the delight of his eye was unending.... What discipline, what precision of thought were expressed by the tense youthful perfection of this form! And yet the pure, strong will which had laboured in darkness and succeeded in bringing this godlike work of art to the light of day—was it not known and familiar to him, the artist? Was not the same force at work in himself when he strove in cold fury to liberate from the marble mass of language the slender forms of his art which he saw with the eye of his mind and would body forth to men as the mirror and image of spiritual beauty?

Mirror and image! His eyes took in the proud bearing of that figure there at the blue water's edge; with an outburst of rapture he told himself that what he saw was beauty's very essence; form as divine thought, the single and pure perfection which resides in the mind, of which an image and likeness, rare and holy, was here raised up for adoration. This was very frenzy—and without a scruple, nay, eagerly, the ageing artist bade it come....

It came at last to this—that his frenzy left him capacity for nothing else but to pursue his flame; to dream of him absent, to lavish, loverlike, endearing terms on his mere shadow. He was alone, he was a foreigner, he was sunk deep in this belated bliss of his—all which enabled him to pass unblushing through experiences well-nigh unbelievable. One night, returning late from Venice, he paused by his beloved's chamber door in the second storey, leaned his head against the panel, and remained there long, in utter drunkenness, powerless to tear himself away, blind to the danger of being caught in so mad an attitude.

And yet there were not wholly lacking moments when he paused and reflected, when in consternation he asked himself what path was this on which he had set his foot. Like most other men of parts and attainments, he had an aristocratic interest in his forbears, and when he achieved a success he liked to think he had gratified them, compelled their admiration and regard. He thought of them now, involved as he was in this illicit adventure, seized of these exotic excesses of feeling; thought of their stern self-command and decent manliness, and gave a melancholy smile. What would they have said? What, indeed, would they have said to his entire life, that varied to the point of degeneracy from theirs? This life in the bonds of art, had not he himself, in the days of his youth and in the very spirit of those bourgeois forefathers, pronounced mocking judgement upon it? And yet, at bottom, it had been so like their own! It had been a service, and he a soldier, like some of them; and art was war—a grilling, exhausting struggle that nowadays wore one out before one could grow old. It had been a life of self-conquest, a life against odds, dour, steadfast, abstinent; he had made it symbolical of the kind of overstrained heroism the time admired, and he was entitled to call it manly, even courageous. He wondered if such a life might not be somehow specially pleasing in the eyes of the god who had him in his power. For Eros had received most countenance among the most valiant nations—yes, were we not told that in their cities prowess made him flourish exceedingly? And many heroes of olden time had willingly borne his yoke, not counting any humiliation such as if it happened by the god's decree; vows, prostrations, self-abasements, these were no source of shame to the lover; rather they reaped him praise and honour....

William Blake, *The Dance of Albion*. British Museum, London. Nonconformists like Beckford, Swinburne and more recently, André Gide, particularly appreciated Blake.

MARCEL PROUST (1871-1922)

By Way of Sainte-Beuve is a volume of unfinished essays written between 1908 and 1910 and published after Marcel Proust's death in 1922. Chapter 13, entitled "A Race Accursed," was begun after the arrest of Prince Philip of Eulenbourg, a German nobleman who was a great admirer of the French, and who was married and the father of eight children. The prince was accused of being a homosexual and convicted on the testimony of a boatman and a milk delivery boy. Proust, who was profoundly disturbed by the outcome of the trial, decided to write an essay on homosexuality. He himself was in love at the time with a young chauffeur, named Agostinelli, whom he had met at a seaside resort, and whom he made his secretary. Agostinelli died in a plane crash in 1914, and Proust later declared that this was the greatest blow to him since the death of his mother in 1905. "A Race Accursed" is in a sense a prologue to *Sodom and Gomorrah* in Proust's monumental psychological novel, *The Rememberance of Things Past*.

Time Regained, the concluding volume of *The Rememberance of Things Past*, was published in 1927. The male brothel described in this book really existed: it was partly financed by Proust himself. The proprietor, who is called Jupien in the novel, was in reality Albert Le Cuziat, a footman who had worked for Prince Radziwill (a turn-of-the-century aesthete who surrounded himself with a flock of beautiful lads to whom he gave pearl necklaces), the Prince d'Essling, Countess Greffulhe, and finally Count Orloff in whose drawing room Proust met Le Cuziat. The hyper-sensitive author of *Swann's Way* enjoyed Albert's company, and spent many an evening with him (rewarding him generously each time). Until 1905, the year his mother died, Proust associated with young men of his own social background—notably Reynaldo Hahn and Lucien Daudet, both of whom he was very fond of—but after that date, he gave in increasingly to his penchant for more manly, socially inferior lads, in some cases hiring them as his secretary, chauffeur or valet. In 1917, Proust lent Albert a considerable sum of money to open a homosexual brothel at no. 11, rue de l'Arcade in Paris. He also gave Albert his parents' furniture (which had been placed in storage since their death). Thus it was in a familiar (if not familial) setting that Proust would listen to Albert's latest stories about the peculiarities and whims of his clients. After Proust died, Albert told Maurice Sachs that Proust had been especially fond of apprentice butchers and had occasionally indulged in the bizarre pleasure of whipping and jabbing rats with a hat pin.

In a note appended to his description of Baron de Charlus (a character who may have been inspired partly by the aesthete Robert de Montesquiou and partly by Baron Doasan), Proust compares homosexual gatherings to a trading market for stamp dealers, with its "perfect understanding between experts and the fierce reality of collecting."

Proust saw homosexuality as a vice and a disorder, not as something idyllic. Nevertheless it seemed to him that the public opprobrium incurred by its devotees gave that "race accursed" a stature that was both heroic and tragic.

Marcel Proust, Doodlings from the author's notebooks. Bibliothèque Nationale, Paris. These drawings have no relationship to the text; they are expressions of the author's unconscious mind. "always searching, groping, feeling its way around its objects like a diver fathoming the floor of the sea." The figures represented often have the piercing eyes and the "curved, beak-shaped" nose of the Guermantes.

Anonymous, *Cicisbeo*. Italian, *c.* 1900. (Reproduced by permission of Mr. Cornette de St-Cyr.)

From BY WAY OF SAINTE-BEUVE

...as soon as I said those words to myself: "One would take him for a woman". I had understood, he *was* one. He was one of them. He belonged to that race of beings who are in effect, since it is precisely because their temperament is feminine that they worship manliness, at cross-purposes with themselves, who go through life apparently in step with other men, but bearing about with them on that little disk of the eye's pupil, through which we look at the world and on which our desire is engraved, the body, not of a nymph but of a youth, who casts his shadow, virile and erect, over all they see and all they do. A race accursed, since the thing which is for it the ideal of beauty and the food of love is also the embodiment of shame and the dread of punishment, a race compelled to live in falsehood and perjury, even when it comes to defend itself before the seat of justice and in the sight of Christ; since its desire, if it knew how to comprehend it, would be in some way unadmittable, because loving only those men who are completely manly, men who are single-sexed, it is only with such a man that it can appease a desire it ought not to feel for him, and which he ought not to feel in return—if the need for love were not an arch-cheat, and did not make it see in the most ignominious pansy the likeness of a man, of a real man like other men, who by a miracle would feel love for it, or stoop to it; since like criminals it must perforce hide its secret from those it holds dearest, dreading the grief of a family, the scorn of friends, the criminal code of a country; a race accursed, persecuted like Israel, and finally, like Israel, under a mass opprobrium of undeserved abhorrence, taking on mass characteristics, the physiognomy of a nation; all with certain characteristic features, physical features that are often repulsive, that sometimes are beautiful, all with a woman's loving, breakable heart, but with a woman's suspicions, her wilful, coquettish, tale-bearing nature, a woman's knack for being clever at everything, a woman's incapacity to do anything supremely well; cut off from family life, where they can never be quite open, from national life, where they would be regarded as undisclosed criminals, cut off even from their fellows, in whom they inspire the chagrin of discovering in their own bosoms the warning that the thing they believe to be a natural love is a sickly madness—as well as that womanliness which offends them; yet for all that, loving hearts, cut off from friendship because when a simple friendliness is all they feel, their friends may suspect an intention of something other than friendship and, if they should own to feeling something else, would not understand it....

("A Race Accursed")

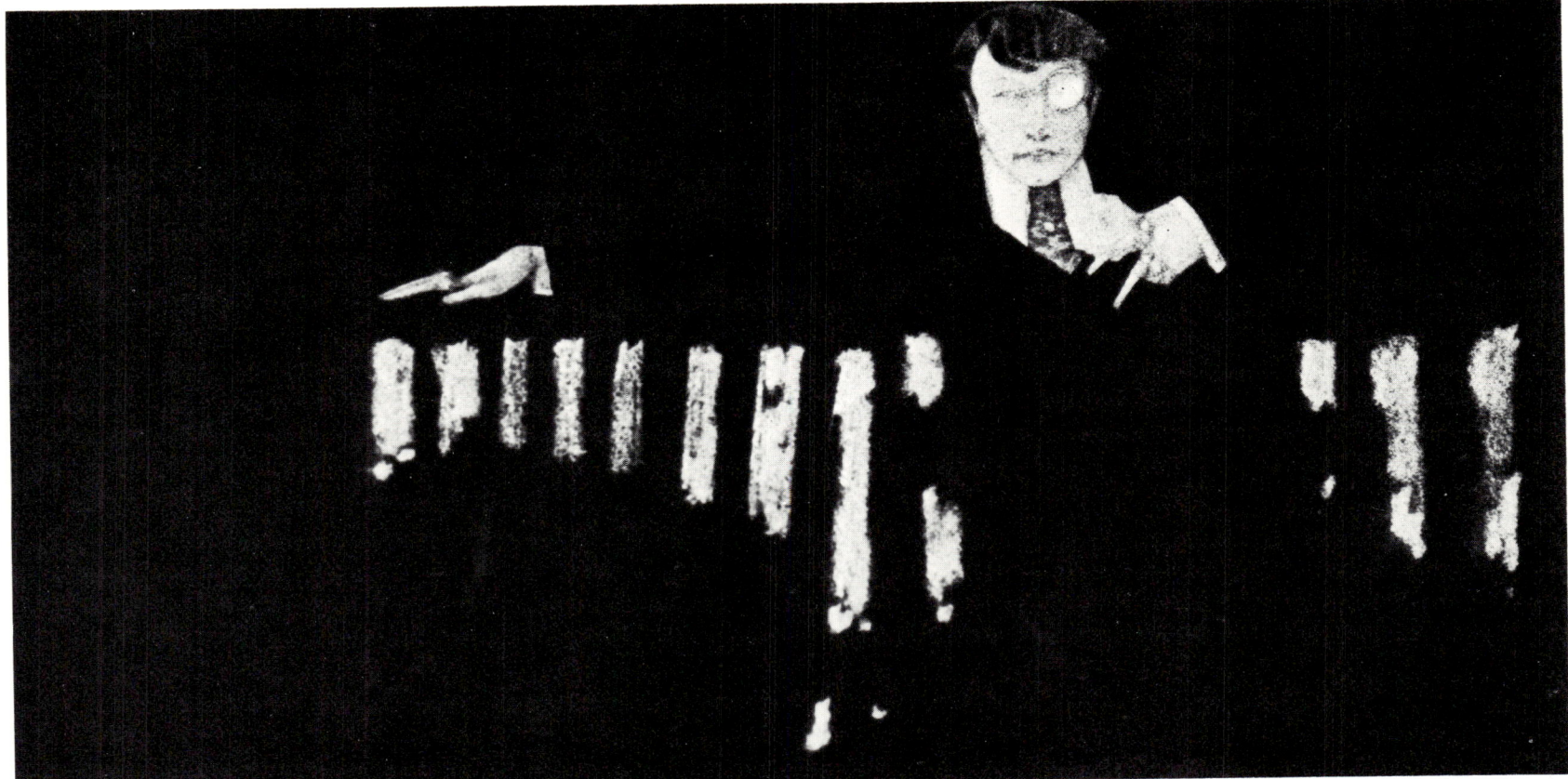

FROM TIME REGAINED
(The narrator is visiting Jupien's establishment.)

Presently I was taken up to Room 43, but it was so unpleasantly stuffy and my curiosity was so great that, having drunk my *cassis*, I started to go downstairs again, then, changing my mind, turned round and went up past the floor of Room 43 to the top of the building. Suddenly, from a room situated by itself at the end of a corridor, I thought I heard stifled groans. I walked rapidly towards the sounds and put my ear to the door. "I beseech you, mercy, have pity, untie me, don't beat me so hard," said a voice. "I kiss your feet, I abase myself, I promise not to offend again. Have pity on me." "No, you filthy brute," replied another voice, "and if you yell and drag yourself about on your knees like that, you'll be tied to the bed, no mercy for you," and I heard the noise of the crack of a whip, which I guessed to be reinforced with nails, for it was followed by cries of pain. At this moment I noticed that there was a small oval window opening from the room onto the corridor and that the curtain had not been drawn across it; stealthily in the darkness I crept as far as this window and there in the room, chained to a bed like Prometheus to his rock, receiving the blows that Maurice rained upon him with a whip which was in fact studded with nails, I saw, with blood already flowing from him and covered with blotches which proved that the chastisement was not taking place for the first time—I saw before me M. de Charlus....

Marcel Proust, Two sketches from his notebooks. Bibliothèque Nationale, Paris.

The Baron soon entered the ante-room, walking with difficulty on account of his injuries, though doubtless he must have been used to them. Although his pleasure was at an end and he had only come in to give Maurice the money which he owed him, he directed at the young men a tender and curious glance which travelled round the whole circle, promising himself with each of them the pleasure of a moment's chat, platonic but amorously prolonged. And in the sprightly frivolity which he exhibited before this harem which appeared almost to intimidate him, I recognised those jerky movements of the body and the head, those languishing glances which had struck me on the evening of his first visit to La Raspelière, graces inherited from some grandmother whom I had not known, which in ordinary life were disguised by more virile expressions on his face but which from time to time were made to blossom there coquettishly, when circumstances made him anxious to please an inferior audience, by the desire to appear a great lady.

Jupien had recommended the young men to the Baron's favour by swearing that they were all pimps from Belleville and would sell you their own sisters for a few francs. And in this he was at the same time lying and telling the truth. Better, more soft-hearted than he made them out to be, they did not belong to a race of savages. But the clients who believed them to be thugs spoke to them nevertheless with complete truthfulness, a truthfulness which they imagined these terrible beings to share. For a man given to sadistic pleasures may believe that he is talking to a murderer but this will not alter his own purity of heart, he will still be astounded by the mendacity of his companion, who is not a murderer at all but wants to earn a little easy money and whose father or mother or sister alternately die, come to life, and die again as he contradicts himself in his conversation with the client whom he is attempting to please. The client, in his naïvety, is astounded, for with his arbitrary conception of the gigolo, while he gets a thrill of delight from the numerous murders of which he believes him to be guilty, he is horrified by any simple contradiction or lie which he detects in his words.

Everybody in the room seemed to know him, and M. de Charlus stopped for a long time before each one, talking to them in what he thought was their language,

Jean Boldini, *Portrait of Count Robert de Montesquiou*. Musée National d'Art Moderne, Paris. Unlike Proust's character, Monsieur de Charlus, Count Robert de Montesquiou did not like to go slumming; his companions were the Dorian Gray type. Nevertheless, this aesthete refused to meet Oscar Wilde, whose scandalous behavior he disapproved of. It was Montesquiou who saw to it that Verlaine was awarded the title "Prince of Poets."

both from a pretentious affectation of local colour and because he got a sadistic pleasure from contact with a life of depravity. "You're disgusting, you are, I saw you outside the Olympia with two tickets in your hand. After a bit of brass, no doubt. Just shows how faithful you are to me." Luckily for the man to whom these remarks were addressed, he did not have time to declare that he would never have accepted "brass" from a woman, a claim which would have damped the Baron's ardour, but reserved his protest for the final phrase, which he answered by saying: "But of course I'm faithful to you." This remark gave M. de Charlus a lively pleasure, and as, in spite of himself, the kind of intelligence that was natural to him showed through the character which he affected, he turned to Jupien: "How nice of him to say that! And how well he says it! One would really think it was true. And after all, what does it matter whether it is true or not since he manages to make me believe it? What charming little eyes he has! There, I'm going to give you two big kisses for your trouble, my dear boy. You will think of me in the trenches. Things are not too bad there?" "Whew, there are some days, when a grenade just misses you...." And the young man proceeded to imitate the noise of the grenade, the aeroplanes, etc. "But one's got to do what the others do, and you can be absolutely sure that we will go on to the end...."

"But I don't think I have made the acquaintance of this charming, this delightful young man," he added, spying another whom he did not recognise or perhaps had not seen before. He greeted him as he would have greeted a prince at Versailles, and making the most of this opportunity to have a supplementary pleasure for nothing—just as, when I was little and my mother had finished giving an order at Boissier's or Gouache's, I would accept the offer of a sweet which one of the ladies behind the counter would invite me to select from those glass bowls over which she and her colleagues held sway—he took the hand of the charming young man and gave it a long squeeze, in the Prussian manner, smilingly fixing him with his eyes for the interminable time which photographers used to take to pose you when the light was bad. "Sir, I am charmed, I am enchanted to make your acquaintance." "What pretty hair he has!" he said, turning to Jupien. Next he went up to Maurice to give him his fifty francs, but first, putting his arm round his waist: "You never told me that you had knifed an old hag of a concierge in Belleville." And M. de Charlus went off into ecstatic laughter and brought his face close to that of Maurice. "Oh! Monsieur le Baron." said the gigolo, who had not been warned, "how can you believe such a thing?" Whether the report was in fact false, or whether it was true and the perpetrator of the deed nevertheless thought it abominable and one of those things that it is better to deny, he went on: "Me touch a fellow-creature? A Boche, yes, because that's war, but a woman, and an old woman at that!" This declaration of virtuous principles had the effect of a douche of cold water upon the Baron, who brusquely moved away from Maurice, having first handed him his money, but with the disgusted air of someone who has been cheated, who pays because he does not want to make a fuss but is far from pleased. The bad impression made upon the Baron was accentuated by the manner in which the recipient thanked him, with the words: "I shall send this to the old folks and keep a bit for my brother at the front as well." By these touching sentiments M. de Charlus was almost as gravely disappointed as he was irritated by the rather conventional peasant's language in which they were expressed. Occasionally Jupien warned the young men that they would have to be more perverse. Then one of them, as if he were confessing to something diabolical, would hazard: "Do you know, Baron, you won't believe

Philippe Jullian, Illustrations for an edition of Marcel Proust's masterpiece, *A la Recherche du Temps perdu* (1969): Editions Gallimard, Paris.

(a) *Monsieur de Charlus and Morel at la Raspelière.*
(b) "Every day Monsieur de Charlus went with Morel to tea at Jupien's...."

me, but when I was a kid I used to watch my parents making love through the key-hole. Pretty vicious, wasn't it? You look as if you think that's a cock and bull story, but I swear it's the truth." And M. de Charlus was driven at once to despair and to exasperation by this factitious attempt at perversity, the result of which was only to reveal such depths both of stupidity and of innocence. Yet even the most determined thief or murderer would not have satisfied him, for that sort of man does not talk about his crimes; and besides there exists in the sadist—however kind he may be, in fact all the more the kinder he is—a thirst for evil which wicked men, doing what they do, not because it is wicked but from other motives, are unable to assuage.

The young man realised his mistake and tried to repair it by saying that he loathed the sight of a copper and by insolently asking the Baron to "fork out a date" (meaning a rendezvous), but it was too late, the charm was dispelled. His remarks were obviously unauthentic, like the books of authors who force themselves to write slang. It was in vain that the young man described in detail all the "filthy things" that he did with his wife; M. de Charlus merely reflected that these "filthy things" amounted to very little. And in this he was not simply being insincere. Nothing is more limited than pleasure and vice. In that sense one may say truly, altering slightly the meaning of the phrase, that we revolve always in the same vicious circle.

ROBERT DESNOS (1900-1945)

Robert Desnos was one of the most lyrical poets of the Surrealist generation. He wrote *Love and Liberty* in 1927; this was followed by *Corps et Biens* (1930) and *Fortune* (1942). During World War II he wrote poems for the French resistance. He was captured by the Germans and interned in a concentration camp in Czechoslovakia, where he died of exhaustion and malnutrition in 1945. Like a number of his fellow Surrealists, Desnos prized manly friendship. Homosexuality seemed noble and romantic to him, expecially when, as in the following excerpt, it springs out of a physical struggle between two men.

From LOVE AND LIBERTY

I picture Roger as he appeared to my puffy eyes in the morning, when cruel daylight dragged its sleeve over our faces and turned its glare on the bed we had tumbled on together. His polished muscles, his smooth forehead, his even breathing, the powerful and supple rise and fall of his chest; everything gave him the physique of a perfect man, of the male. Myself, even though I've gotten old, I still have some of my strength, and I'm sure you'll have no trouble believing me when I tell you that I was lithe as a tiger and that my flat stomach, my high but solid waist, made me a fair specimen of the human race. So there we were, two males in the night, wrestling with each other for hours on end, yielding to each other by turns. There was nothing half-blooded about the way we made love. We were both full of scorn for fairies, or rather we scornfully ignored them. We pushed them out of our way, had no use for their women's hearts and their filter-paper brains. We stayed away from their gardens, and their irises, and their silly childish sentimentality which marks them as cheap perfume marks a housemaid. Their incalculable stupidity made us smile; and, though we usually sided with them against the famous common sense of the normal herd in the name of individual liberty and because we believed that everything is legitimate in love, we attacked them out of the same conviction when they started babbling about avoiding women at all costs—the truth is that they were impotent, or physical wrecks, or half-wits. We had discovered the madness of embracing, Roger and I, as a result of some argument which ended in a fight: we grappled with each other, and when we realized that neither of us had an edge on the other, our grapplings turned into embraces. So we made friends, knowing that our minds, despite the fact that they were opposed to each other, belonged to the same plane and could clash together without either being brought down.

We stayed together for several years. Our hearts and our souls rang against each other like fine blades growing sharper all the time.

There was nothing Platonic about our love. My arms still remember the exact curve of his hips; my lips still know how to match his. And if he were not dead, he would remember me just as clearly....

André Masson, *Le double ou l'assassinat de l'automate* [*The Double or the Assassination of the Automaton*], detail (1941). Galerie Georges Leiris, Paris.

RENÉ CREVEL (1900-1935)

René Crevel, the homosexual black sheep of the surrealist group. Viollet Collection, Paris.

Frank Kupka, *The Pal*. Musée National d'Art Moderne, Paris. "Little punk, with your shaved neck so white, half-hidden by a fine red foulard, behind your glass of liqueur you were waiting for a friend, someone to make you forget the rain and the loneliness of the night." (René Crevel)

René Crevel was born in Paris on August 10, 1900. His father, a printer who specialized in popular songs, committed suicide for no apparent reason when Crevel was fourteen. His mother had had him circumcised when he was three. These two events made a deep psychic wound which never healed. Death and castration loom large in Crevel's writing and apparently haunted him throughout his short life. "By the time I was a teenager, I sensed that the man who facilitates his own death is the docile and reasonable instrument of a superior force (call it God or Nature) which, having placed us all in the midst of earthly mediocrity, carries off the more courageous souls among us, far away from the waiting room of this world." Crevel's classmates remembered him as a sluggish youth who was "indifferent to whatever was said or done in class, nothing mattered to him, neither his teachers nor his fellow pupils... he was like a sleepwalker."

Then the war came, followed by the explosion of often desperate creativity in the post-war years: the Dada manifestoes, the jazz craze, the violent, nihilistic young artists who trampled everything that was held sacred by society, who posed as the dauntless enemies of capitalist bourgeoisie (which was more confident than ever during the "roaring twenties"). In 1921, during his military service, Crevel founded his first literary magazine *(L'Aventure)* with the help of fellow-draftees like Marcel Arland, Jacques Baron, Max Morise, Georges Limbour and Roger Vitrac (all of whom later became famous in French literary circles). This was followed by *Dés*. Both reviews were short-lived.

This literary activity brought Crevel into contact with André Breton and his Surrealist disciples. In 1922 the Dadaists and the Surrealists came to blows. Crevel, who had agreed to act in a play by the Dadaist Tristan Tzara, was slapped by the Surrealist poet Paul Eluard and called a "dirty little culture vulture" by Robert Desnos. This did not prevent Crevel from publishing a thoroughly Surrealist book in 1924 *(Détours)*.

Crevel was the only self-proclaimed homosexual in the Surrealist group. In theory the Surrealists were opposed to homosexuality, often attacking it with a violence which seems rather suspicious today: "I accuse pederasts," wrote André Breton, "of taxing human tolerance with a moral and mental deficiency which they tend to erect into a system that paralyses all the activities I admire." During a colloquium on sexuality the Russian author Ilya Ehrenbourg referred to Surrealism as a "pederastic activity"—which earned him a punch by André Breton, who was determined to avenge the honor of the Surrealists, those real men.

NIGHTTIME

Softly
so as to sleep in the black shadow of oblivion
tonight
I will kill the prowlers
the silent dancers
of the night
whose black velvet feet
torment my naked flesh
as gently as the wing of a bat
and so subtly they send
fright into the folds where skin quails, moved to
fiercer love and fear
at another body and the cold.
But what river for escape oh my mind this evening?
It is the hour of nightwalkers
and delinquents.
Two wide shadowy eyes in the dark
could be so sweet, so sweet to me.
I, the prisoner of mournful seasons,
am alone
a perfect crime for him.
Lurking over there on the horizon
a viper perhaps cold from not loving.
But where
where does the
river flow for my mind
to run away on?
Along the banks the girls go
with weary eyes and glistening hair.
I am wordless before these girls
whose apaches
whose proud pimps
are on the prowl.
I am alone a perfect crime for him.
Two great shadowy eyes in the dark
would be so sweet, so sweet to me.
It is the hour of nightwalkers.

ROGER PEYREFITTE (1907-)

Roger Peyrefitte is best known for his novel, *Special Friendships,* which describes in intimate detail the first erotic stirrings of two schoolboys. In *Singular Loves* he tells the story of Baron Gloeden who left Germany and settled in Taormina, Sicily, where he supported himself by selling nude photographs of well-endowed young rubes.

From SINGULAR LOVES

One day I photographed some village boys playing naked beside a beached boat. Not without some apprehension I mailed off the photographs to a German magazine. However, to provoke my fellow countrymen, I proudly signed the photographs, in the manner of a painting, *W. v. Gloeden fecit*. I waited for, if not a refusal, at least a reduced reproduction. Imagine my surprise—on the contrary—to see my young boys in the place of honor! They had made a good impression, for requests were arriving from everywhere asking for "photos of the same subject matter." My path was marked out; all I had to do was to follow it....

Perhaps the young visitor who entered my house that day naively thought himself protected by incognito. I had not, it is true, been received by his imperial family, but I had no difficulty recognizing in him the Prince August-Wilhelm of Prussia. He was seventeen and I admired him, not only for his good manners, but for the courage he showed by stepping through my door. I was tempted to send him away, realizing that his father might pick a quarrel with me. But I would have offended the gods who had offered me such sweet prey.

Ordinarily, I would begin by showing the country scenes and the "Sicilian models." This time, I hurried things along: I offered him, on the spot, the nude collections, as if I had nothing else. And I felt myself avenged with the Hohenzollern, when the prince broke into a blush. However he didn't falter and continued to turn the album pages with ease. I thought that the nudes were the object of his visit, and I wanted to defy him as much as to satisfy him. Besides that I was not unaware that one must be bold with the young for they will always be grateful for it. I had been more roundabout with Princess de Courlande, but then I had been helped by her husband, and the veil of the hymen had screened these nudities somewhat.

I was amused, when the young August-Wilhelm attempted to thicken the veil of incognito existing between us, saying to me that he was a painter and was searching for suitable subjects. Was he strengthened by this lie? He turned the pages less quickly; his attention was lingering: his mouth was certainly watering. In fact, he was worthy of his ancestry: any number of his ancestors could have proclaimed themselves honorary citizens of Taormina. He finally spoke, without raising his head:

"Are these models from around here"?

I bent my head forward:

"They are at the order of your Imperial Highness."

It was the first time I assumed a role other than that of a photographer, but it was a brilliant début. The Prince no longer blushed; turning his face towards me, he smiled; that was his reply. Until then, he was standing beside my table; now, he considered himself more at home and sat down in an armchair. Continuing to examine the albums he stopped and stared for a long time at one of the

Baron von Gloeden, Four photographs, Taormina, Sicily. *c.* 1900. Gérard Lévy Collection, Paris. (See also following page.)

photographs, then scanned others before returning to the one which first drew his attention. His eyes caught mine: we understood each other.

Esthetically, his choice was an honorable one; it was strange from a social point of view. My models ranged from goatherds to patricians—patricians of Taormina—the Kaiser's son could have fallen on one of the latter; unfortunately, he didn't even fall on a goatherd: his choice was a young cobbler. The Prince didn't show any displeasure over his choice, however, and the following day he was able to compare, at my home, the original with the photograph....

The opposite of this pleasant story was that of Krupp. Cruising near my home, the richest man in Germany [Krupp] had stopped to visit and complimented me on my work. He was searching for a site where he could install his summer residence. He had thought about Morocco, which was beginning to be very fashionable; later he told me it was I who made him prefer Italy. At one time, he had the intention of settling in Taormina: It was his misfortune not to have done so. There are secret virtues here which protect one against scandal, and Krupp would not have experienced the fate awaiting him at Capri.

For it was there that he settled, drawn by the memories of Tiberius. I made a stop-over at his home once during a voyage to Naples and was startled by his style of living. He had transformed the island into a factory of pleasure, just as he could have transformed it into a factory of cannons. He was too envied to permit himself to openly revive the "roman orgy" which, even among the Romans—without excepting Tiberius himself—always ended badly. He believed himself to have found a hiding-place, and instead it was a target. The solitude of Mount Ziretto would have been safer; there are also virtues of moderation in Taormina which would have been beneficial to Baron Krupp.

That which could not miss happening, happened: the new Caesar of Capri was violently attacked in Germany by the opposition's press. Photographs were published of nude groups, taken, it was said, in his own villa and which in reality, had been taken by me in Sicily. Krupp returned to Essen and committed suicide. I was astonished that he had not considered it more grandiose to kill himself on Capri.

T.E. LAWRENCE (1888-1935)

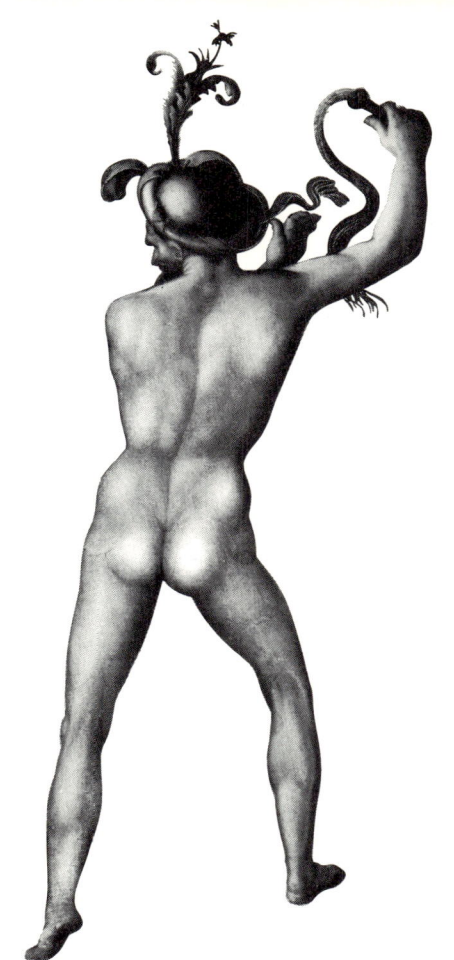

T.E. Lawrence (detail). Viollet Collection, Paris.

The Flagellation (details). Attributed to Perugino. Cook Gallery, Richmond.

T.E. Lawrence, the liaison officer between the Arab chiefs and the British army during World War I who engineered the decisive attacks against the Turks along the Damascus-Medina railway line, was the second son, born out of wedlock, of Sir Thomas Chapman. Despite a happy, protected childhood it seems that this illegitimate birth affected Lawrence profoundly in later life. To this was added a keen feeling of bitterness, after the war ended, with the failure of the British to fulfill what Lawrence considered their moral obligation to the Arabs. As he result he "resigned from the world," as the great French Arab scholar, Louis Massignon, has put it, "mortally wounded in his manly sense of allegiance, which is the virgin spot in any soldier's heart." He sat down to write *Seven Pillars of Wisdom*, resigned from government service, gave up his rank as lieutenant-colonel, took a new name and enlisted as a mechanic in the Royal Air Force. His routine life as an anonymous soldier gave him a certain peace of mind, especially in the last years of his life. His military studies of amphibious and air warfare gained him the respect of his superior officers. Two months after leaving the R.A.F. in 1935, Lawrence was killed in a motocycle accident.

When it appeared in 1927, *Seven Pillars of Wisdom* was an instantaneous and thoroughly deserved success. "It ranks with the greatest books ever written in the English language," pronounced Sir Winston Churchill. Almost immediately journalists and admirers of Lawrence began asking the inevitable questions: Who was the mysterious S.A. to whom the moving introductory poem is dedicated? What really happened at Deraa, where Lawrence was captured and tortured by the Turks? Lawrence kept stonily silent about this incident and usually answered the first question with quips like, "the book is dedicated to an imaginary person of "neutral sex." However a recent biography, *The Secret Lives of Lawrence of Arabia* (1969) by Phillip Knightley and Colin Simpson, establishes beyond a shadow of doubt that S.A. was a young donkey-driver named Salim Ahmed—or Dahoum—whom Lawrence met during an archeological expedition to excavate the site of Carchemish. Lawrence became attached to the boy (who was fourteen at the time) and helped him in various ways. In 1913 he even brought him to London for a visit. During the war he entrusted him with several intelligence missions. Salim died of typhus in 1918. In a note pencilled in the margin of one of his books, Lawrence wrote: "I tried desperately to get him his freedom, to bring light to his sad eyes, but he died while waiting for me; after that, I cast away my gift, and henceforth I will never find peace or rest anywhere."

Like many unconfessed homosexuals, Lawrence felt most at ease among simple, unpolished men. He enjoyed competing with them, excelling on their own ground, and hardening his body in their midst. Vyvyan Richards, his friend at Oxford, complained that "He paid no heed to the flesh or to any sort of sexual impulse. He accepted my affection, my sacrifice, in fact my total submission, as something that was owed him. He never gave the least sign of understanding my desire... I now realize that he was asexual, or at least that he was not conscious of being sexual." This raises a question in the light of what Lawrence has written in *Seven Pillars*: did his experience with sex begin and end with the humiliating incident at Deraa? Lawrence does not specifically say that he was raped, but a letter he wrote to Charlotte Shaw, the great playwright's wife, a woman in her sixties then and one of the very few people to whom Lawrence unburdened his soul, suggests that something of the sort may very well have taken place. (See below).

At any rate Lawrence's biographers, Knightley and Simpson, reveal that after his return to England Lawrence had himself periodically whipped by a young man called Bruce, whom he kept in his service for thirteen years. Lawrence had explained to this devoted, naive, nineteen year old lad that one of his uncles had threatened to make an embarrassing disclosure about his illegitimate birth unless Lawrence agreed to submit to a regular "punishment" of flagellation. Moreover, the "Old Man," as Lawrence called this uncle, insisted on seeing the marks left by these whippings as proof that they had been administered with adequate severity. Bruce apparently swallowed the story. As for Lawrence, one can only conjecture that this willful, masochistic self-humiliation must have been a source of sexual enjoyment; but also an expression of deep moral distress and self-contempt, to the point of being a form of partial suicide.

243

From THE SECRET LIVES OF LAWRENCE OF ARABIA

First, we must examine the dedicatory poem to "S.A." in *Seven Pillars.* The version as published is not as Lawrence wrote it, but as Robert Graves, his friend, arranged it. Graves toned down the more personal references and rewrote a complete stanza. To show what changes Graves made, here is the original with Graves's substitutions in italics:

I loved you, so I drew these tides of men into my hands
   and wrote my will across the sky in stars
     [*earn*]
To gain you Freedom, the seven-pillared worthy house,
   that your eyes might be shining for me
                       [*we*]
                      When I came
[*seemed*]
Death was my servant on the road, till we were near
                    and saw you waiting:
When you smiled, and in sorrowful envy he outran me
                    and took you apart:
                      Into his quietness
[*Love: the way-weary, groped to your body*]
                 [*our brief wage*]
So our love's earnings was your cast off body to be held
            [*ours for the moment*]
                    one moment
         [*hand explored your shape,*]
Before earth's soft hands would explore your face and the
                   [*grew fat upon*]
                blind worms transmute
                 [*your substance.*]
                 Your failing substance.
             [*that I set our*]
Men prayed me to set my work, the inviolate house,
               [*as a*]
              in memory of you.
But for fit monument I shattered it, unfinished: and now
The little things creep out to patch themselves hovels
                in the marred shadow
                Of your gift.

Lawrence described this poem as a cipher and did his best to keep it so. He told Graves that perhaps he had been in love with S.A. and that "S.A. was someone who had provided a disproportionate share of the Arabian adventure...."

Anonymous, *Prisoners.* c. 1930. François Duchêne Collection, Paris.

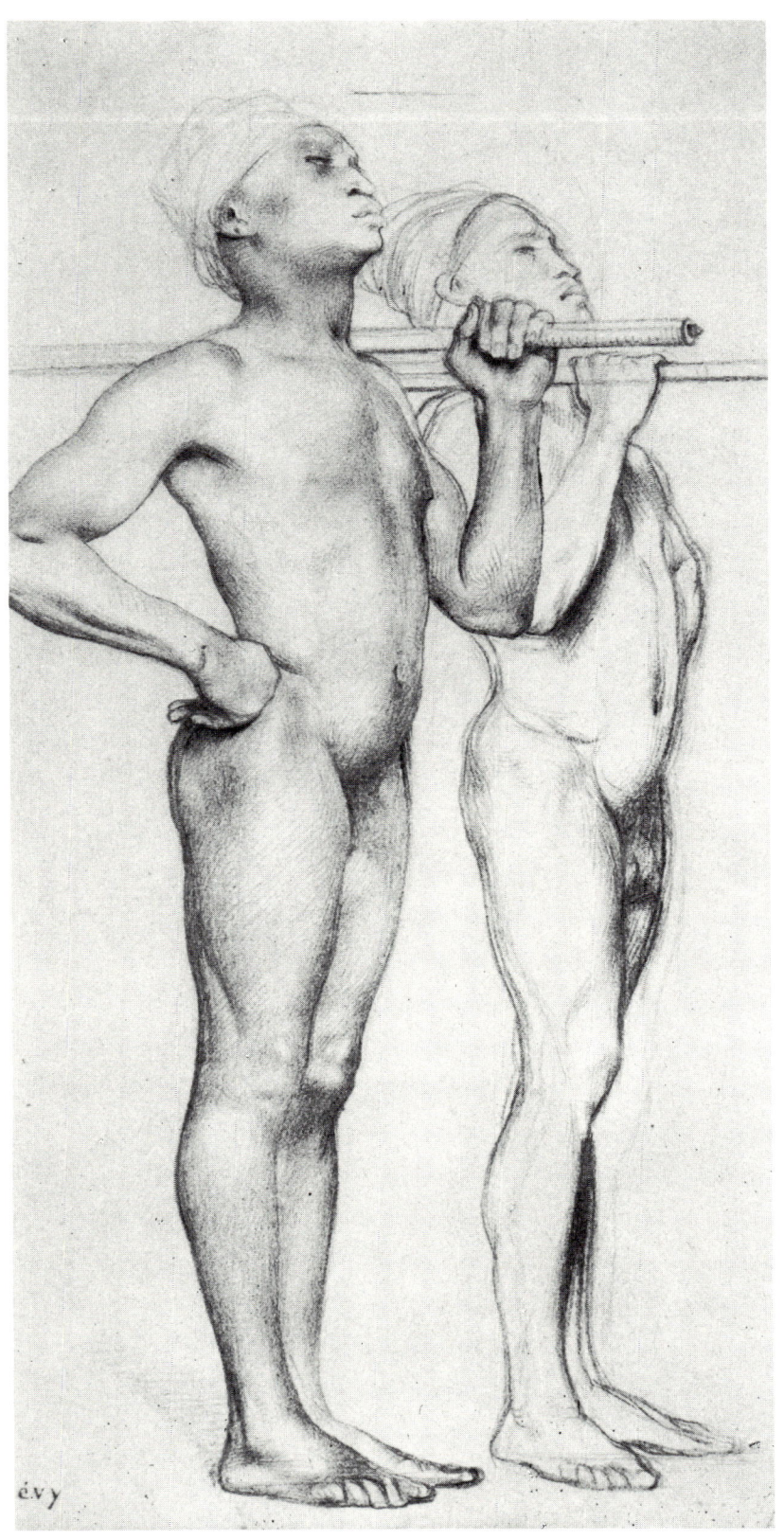

Emile Levy, *Madagascan Bearers*. Private collection.

...Anyone trying to probe the truth of the Deraa incident at this distance in time will find his investigations strewn with traps. In the researches necessary for the articles which appeared in *The Sunday Times* in June and July 1968, we came upon evidence which we believed offered an answer to the question beyond reasonable doubt and quoted two documents in support of this. The first, the secret report of June 1919 from Lawrence to the Chief Political Officer at GHQ Egyptian Expeditionary Force in Cairo ...recounts the story much as it appears in *Seven Pillars*, except that there is no mention of Lawrence's being flogged and he is unequivocal in stating that the Bey "never reported my capture and escape".

The second document is a letter to Charlotte Shaw in which Lawrence is much more specific as to what occurred. It is dated 26 March 1924:

"About that night. I shouldn't tell you, because decent men don't talk about such things. I wanted to put it plain in the book, & wrestled for days with my self-respect...which wouldn't, hasn't let me. For fear of being hurt, or rather, to earn five minutes' respite from a pain which drove me mad, I gave away the only possession we are born into the world with—our bodily integrity. It's an unforgivable matter, an irrecoverable position: and it's that which has made me forswear decent living, & the exercise of my not-contemptible wits & talents.

"You may call this morbid: but think of the offence, and the intensity of my brooding over it for these years. It will hang about me while I live, & afterwards if our personality survives. Consider wandering among the decent ghosts hereafter, crying 'Unclean, unclean!...' "

Jean Géricault, *Studies of Male Nudes* (deta[il]), Musée Bonnat, Bayonne. This French pai[nter] was fascinated by powerful, muscled, eve[n] brutal male bodies. There is something al[most] obsessional about his painting, which may spring from hidden passions.

Charlotte and Lawrence had none of these ups and downs. As their friendship deepened into complete trust, she revealed herself and her thoughts and doubts to him as she probably did to no one else. This was not easy for her and it did not happen before Lawrence had bared his own emotional scars—something that before he met Charlotte Shaw he found was a painful process. Gradually she drew him out, consciously helping to exorcise his shyness by talking to him about it. He became able to tell her about his moods, especially when he was depressed:

"I've changed, and the Lawrence who used to go about and be friendly and familiar with that sort of people is dead. He's worse than dead. He is a stranger I once knew. From henceforward my way will lie with these fellows in the RAF here degrading myself (for in their eyes and your eyes and Winterton's eyes I see it is a degradation) in the hope that some day I will really feel degraded, be degraded, to their level. I long for people to look down on me and despise me, and I'm too shy to take the filthy steps which would publicly shame me and put me into their contempt. I want to dirty myself outwardly, so that my person may properly reflect the distress which it conceals... and I shrink from dirtying the outside, while I have eaten, avidly eaten, every filthy morsel which chance threw my way.

I'm too shy to go looking for dirt. I'd be afraid of seeming a novice in it, when I found it. That's why I can't go off stewing into the Lincoln or Naveby brothels with the fellows. They think its because I'm superior, proud, or peculiar, or "posh," as they say: and its because I wouldn't know what to do, how to carry myself, where to stop. Fear again: fear everywhere...."

E.M. FORSTER (1879-1970)

E.M. Forster's *Maurice* is to homosexual literature what *Lady Chatterly's Lover* was to the modern heterosexual novel: a radical (but to us, a rather dated and over-solemn) plea for honesty. It is the story of a "mentally-torpid," respectable middle class young man (Maurice) who, through a Platonic affair with a classmate at Cambridge (Clive) discovers his own basic homosexuality, gradually comes to terms with it and finally fulfills it with a gamekeeper named Alec. Though written in 1914 (fourteen years earlier than Lawrence's novel), it was not published until 1971. Forster, who disliked scandal, had carefully prepared the manuscript for posthumous publication: but, with characteristic modesty, seems to have had doubts about its literary value: "Publishable—but worth it?" he had scribbled on the cover of the typescript. He had no doubts, however, about the worth of what he had attempted to do in the book. He explains in a terminal note that "I was determined that in fiction anyway two men should fall in love and remain in it for the ever and ever that fiction allows, and in this sense Maurice and Alec still roam the greenwood. I dedicated it 'To a Happier Year' and not altogether vainly."

Baron von Gloeden, Photograph, Taormina, Sicily. c. 1900. Gérard Lévy Collection, Paris.

From MAURICE

During the next two years Maurice and Clive had as much happiness as men under that star can expect. They were affectionate and consistent by nature, and, thanks to Clive, extremely sensible. Clive knew that ecstasy cannot last, but can carve a channel for something lasting, and he contrived a relation that proved permanent. If Maurice made love it was Clive who preserved it, and caused its rivers to water the garden. He could not bear that one drop should be wasted, either in bitterness or in sentimentality, and as time went on they abstained from avowals ("we have said everything") and almost from caresses. Their happiness was to be together; they radiated something of their calm among others, and could take their place in society.

Clive had expanded in this direction ever since he had understood Greek. The love that Socrates bore Phaedo now lay within his reach, love passionate but temperate, such as only finer natures can understand, and he found in Maurice a nature that was not indeed fine, but charmingly willing. He led the beloved up a narrow and beautiful path, high above either abyss. It went on until the final darkness—he could see no other terror—and when that descended they would at all events have lived more fully than either saint or sensualist, and would have extracted to their utmost the nobility and sweetness of the world. He educated Maurice, or rather his spirit educated Maurice's spirit, for they themselves became equal. Neither thought "Am I led; am I leading?" Love had caught him out of triviality and Maurice out of bewilderment in order that two imperfect souls might touch perfection.

So they proceeded outwardly like other men. Society received them, as she receives thousands like them. Behind Society slumbered the Law. They had their last year at Cambridge together, they travelled in Italy. Then the prison house closed, but on both of them. Clive was working for the bar, Maurice harnessed to an office. They were together still.

(18)

"Had I best be going now, sir?"

Abominably shy, Maurice pretended not to hear.

"We mustn't fall asleep though, awkward if anyone came in," he continued, with a pleasant blurred laugh that made Maurice feel friendly but at the same time diffident and sad. He managed to reply, "You mustn't call me Sir," and the laugh sounded again, as if brushing aside such problems. There seemed to be charm and insight, yet his discomfort increased.

"May I ask your name?" he said awkwardly.

"I'm Scudder."

"I know you're Scudder—I meant your other name."

"Only Alec just."

"Jolly name to have."

"It's only my name."

"I'm called Maurice."

I saw you when you first drove up, Mr Hall, wasn't it Tuesday, I did think you looked at me angry and gentle both together."

"Who were those people with you?" said Maurice, after a pause.

"Oh that wor only Mill, that wor Milly's cousin. Then do you remember the piano got wet the same evening, and you had great trouble to suit yourself over a book, didn't read it, did you either?"

"How ever did your know I didn't read my book?"

"Saw you leaning out of the window instead. I saw you the next night too. I was out on the lawn."

"Do you mean you were out in all that infernal rain?"

"Yes... watching... oh, that's nothing, you've got to watch, haven't you... see, I've not much longer in this country, that's how I kep putting it."

"How beastly I was to you this morning!"

"Oh that's nothing—Excuse the question but is that door locked?"

"I'll lock it." As he did so, the feeling of awkwardness returned. Whither was he tending, from Clive into what companionship?

Presently they fell asleep.

They slept separate at first, as if proximity harassed them but towards morning a movement began, and they woke deep in each other's arms. "Had I best be going now?" he repeated, but Maurice, through whose earlier night had threaded the dream "Something is a little wrong and had better be," was resting utterly at last, and murmured "No, no."

"Sir, the church has gone four, you'll have to release me."

"Maurice, I'm Maurice."

"But the church has-"

"Damn the church."

He said, "I've the cricket pitch to help roll for the match," but did not move, and seemed in the faint grey light to be smiling proudly. "I have the young birds too—the boat's done—Mr London and Mr Fetherstonhaugh dived splack into the water lilies— they told me all young gentlemen can dive—I never learned to. It seems more natural like not to let the head get under the water. I call that drowning before your day."

"I was taught I'd be ill if I didn't wet my hair."

"Well, you was taught what wasn't the case."

"I expect so—it's a piece with all else I was taught. A master I used to trust as a kid taught me it. I can still remember walking on the beach with him... oh dear! And the tide came up, all beastly grey..." He shook himself fully awake, as he felt his companion slip from him. "Don't, why did you?"

"There's the cricket-"

"No, there's not the cricket—You're going abroad."

"Well, we'll find another opportunity before I do."

"If you'll stop, I'll tell you my dream. I dreamt of an old grandfather of mine. He was a queer card. I wonder what you'd have made of him. He used to think dead people went to the sun, but he treated his own employees badly."

"I dreamt the Reverend Borenius was trying to drown me, and now really I must go, I can't talk about dreams, don't you see, or I'll catch it from Mr Ayres."

"Did you ever dream you'd a friend, Alec? Nothing else but just 'my friend', he trying to help you and you him. A friend," he repeated, sentimental suddenly. "Someone to last your whole life and you his. I suppose such a thing can't really happen outside sleep."

But the moment for speech had passed. Class was calling, the crack in the floor must reopen at sunrise. When he reached the window Maurice called "Scudder", and he turned like a well-trained dog.

"Alec, you're a dear fellow and we've been very happy."

"You get some sleep, there's no hurry in your case," he said kindly, and took up the gun that had guarded them through the night. The tips of the ladder quivered against the dawn as he descended, then were motionless. There was a tiny crackle from the gravel, a tiny clink from the fence that divided garden and park: then all was as if nothing had been, and silence absolute filled the Russet Room, broken after a time by the sounds of a new day.

FEDERICO GARCIA LORCA
(1899-1936)

Garcia Lorca, the Andalusian poet and friend of important modern cultural figures like Rafael Alberti, Luis Bunuel, Emilio Prado, Manuel de Falla and Salvador Dali, was a closet homosexual. There is a story that he rushed over to a friend's house one day, so upset that he had to lie down a while before he could speak. He finally blurted out on the verge of tears: "Paquito Soriano says I'm an invert!" True, Lorca was only twenty-one at the time. Later in life he confessed to his close friend Adriano del Valle: "I am an unfortunate boy, silently wracked with passion, who bears, like marvellous Verlaine, a white lily that can never be watered. To those who look on me with their untrained eyes I show a rose, a deep red one, of the sexual coloring of an April peony, but that is not the truth of my heart." In his last years Lorca was able to view the problem of homosexuality with more equanimity and detachment, although he violently attacked "mariquitas" [queens] in his "Ode to Walt Whitman" written after his visit to New York in 1929.

Lorca was murdered by Francoist thugs in 1936 at the outbreak of the Spanish Civil War.

From ODE TO WALT WHITMAN

...Not for a moment, manly and comely one,
on mountains of railroads and coal and advertisements,
but you dreamed yourself river, and slept like a river,
with that comrade who took to your heart
the little complaint of the ignorant leopard.

Not a moment, blood-brother, Adam, and masculine,
lone man in a sea, Walt Whitman, comely old man—
for look!—on the rooftops,
or huddled in bars,
or leaping in packs from the gutters,
or held between legs of the motorist, shuddering,
or whirling on platforms of absinthe,
the perverts, Walt Whitman, all pointing you!

This one—and this one! They fall
on your decent and luminous beard,
the blonde-headed northerners, the blacks from the sand-
    dunes,
a legion of gestures and outcries,
catlike and serpentine—
perverts—the pack of them perverts, Walt Whitman—
grimy with tears, so much meat for the whiplash,
for the boot or the bite of the animal-tamers.

Alastair, Illustration for *The Blind Bowboy* by Carl Van Vechten (1926). Private collection.

Ismaël de la Serna, *The Bullfighter's Moment of Triumph* (detail) 1920. François Duchêne Collection, Paris.

And this one! And this one! The taint of their fingernails
   point
to the brink of your dream
where the playfellow munches your apple
with a faint taste of gasoline,
and the sunlight sings out on the navels
of the boys at their games under bridges.

But you never went looking for the scar on the eye,
or the overcast swamp where the boys are submerged,
or the freezing saliva
or the contours, split open, like the sac of the toad,
that the perverts in taxis and terraces carry
as the moon whips them on into terrified corners.

You looked for a nude that could be like a river,
the bull and the dream that could merge, like seaweed and
   wheel,
sire of your agony, your mortality's camellia,
to cry in the flames of your secret equator.

It is fitting that no man should seek
in another day's thickets of blood for his pleasure
Heaven has shores for our flights out of life,
and the corpse need not make itself over at dawn....

Wherefore my voice is not raised
to admonish the boy who inscribes
a girl's name on his pillow, Walt Whitman, old friend;
not to shame the young man who dresses himself like a
   bride
in the dark of the clothes-closet,
or the stags of the dance-hall
who drink at the waters of whoredom and sicken,
or the green apparition of men
who cherish mankind and burn out their lips in the
   silence.
But you! against all of you, perverts of the cities,
immodest of thought and tumescent of flesh,
mothers of filthiness, harpies, sleeplessly thwarting
the Love that apportions us garlands of pleasure.

Always against you, whosoever bestow upon boys
the foul drop of death with wormwood of venom.
Against you to the end!
North American *fairies*,
Pajaros of Havana,
Jotos of Mexico,
Sarasas of Càdiz,
Apios of Seville,
Cancos of Madrid,
Floras of Alicante,
Adelaidas of Portugal.

Perverts of the world, dove-killers!
Toadies of women, dressing-room bitches,
brazen in squares in a fever of fans
or ambushed in motionless landscapes of hemlock.

No quarter! Death
oozes out of your eyes
and clusters gray flowers at the edge of a bog.
No quarter! Beware!
Let the pure, the bewildered,
the illustrious, classic, and suppliant
shut the festival doors in your face

And you, on the shores of the Hudson, handsome Walt
   Whitman, asleep
with your beard to the pole, open-handed.
In the delicate marl or the snow, your tongue always
   summoning
the comrades to watch your gazelle, disembodied in air.
Sleep on; for nothing abides.

A dancing of walls rocks the meadows
and America drowns under engines and tears.
I could wish for a stirring of wind from the deepest abyss
   of the night
to undo all the letters and flowers from the arch where
   you drowse,
while a black boy declares to the gold-getting white
kingdom come in a tassel of corn.

ANDRÉ GIDE (1869-1951)

Gide's *Corydon* is an outspoken apology for homosexuality. The book created a scandal when it appeared—anonymously—in 1911. A second edition, with Gide's name on it, was released in 1924 as a reply to Proust's *Sodom and Gomorrah*. Gide categorically rejected the suggestion that homosexuality was an illness or a sin. Basing himself on biology and on ancient Greek history he set out to show that, on the contrary, it is both admirable and natural. Today *Corydon* seems rather dated. For that reason we have taken passages from two other works, *If It Die...* and *Madeleine—Et Nunc Manet In Te,* where Gide appears more personal, more persuasive.

Gide saw himself as a combination of "a little boy who is having fun, and a Protestant minister who is boring him." But if one is to believe the autobiographical narrative, *If It Die....*, the minister's austere facade was easily circumvented by the slender bodies of Arab boys. *Et Nunc Manet In Te,* published after the death of Gide's wife, is a bold, heart-rending confession by a homosexual who looks back on his honeymoon trip with a young bride he sincerely loved and respected but never desired.

Herbert List *Rolf Düring in Rome, 1953.* (Photograph taken from *Herbert List: Photographien 1930-1970*, text by Günter Metken; Schirmer Mosel, Munich, 1976).

From IF IT DIE...

(Note: This passage was deleted—with André Gide's consent—from the standard English translation of *Si le Grain ne meurt* [*If It Die...*]).

Daniel B. went with me. Mohammed took us up to the fourth floor of a shady hotel over a bar where sailors were drinking noisily. The *patron* asked us for our names: I wrote *César Bloch* on the register. Daniel ordered a beer and a lemon soda, "for appearances' sake," as he said. Night had fallen. The room we entered was dark, lit only by the candle they'd given us downstairs. A waiter brought us the bottles and some glasses and set them on the table next to the candle. There were only two chairs. Daniel and I sat down on them; Mohammed chose the table. Placing himself between us, he lifted up the hem of the *haïk* he had slipped on instead of his usual Tunisian robe and stretched his naked legs towards us.

"One for each of you," he laughed.

Then, while I stayed sitting by the half-empty glasses, Daniel took Mohammed in his arms and carried him over to the bed which filled the back of the room. He set him down on his back across the edge of the bed. The next moment all I could see was two slender legs hanging down on either side of my panting friend. Daniel had not even bothered to remove his coat. Very tall in the poor light as he stood against the bed in his ankle-length over-coat, his face masked by locks of long black hair, Daniel looked gigantic. Seeing him bowed over that little body, which

251

Simeon Solomon, *Bridegroom and Sad Love*. Victoria and Albert Museum, London.

he almost entirely blotted out, you would have thought he was an enormous vampire feeding off a corpse. I nearly cried out in horror.

It always takes an effort of will to understand the loves of other people—their ways of making love. Even when you see animals at it (or perhaps I should keep that *even* for my fellow humans). It is one thing to envy birds their singing, their flight; to write:

> Ach! wüsstest du wie's Fischlein ist
> So wohlig auf dem Grund!

Even the dog devouring his bone strikes a chord of bestial sympathy in me. But nothing is more disconcerting than the movement, differing so greatly from species to species, with which each animal achieves his sexual goal. Whatever Monsieur de Gourmont, who makes a point of drawing unsettling analogies between man and the various animals, may say about it, I am of the opinion that this analogy exists only in the realm of desire—and that on the contrary it is in what Monsieur de Gourmont calls *la physique de l'amour* that the differences appear most marked, not only between man and animal, but often even between man and man—to the degree that, were we allowed to watch them, our neighbour's practices would seem as strange to us, as outlandish and—admit it—as monstrous as the couplings of batrachians, insects or (why search for such distant examples?) dogs or cats.

And it is doubtless for this reason that there is such a lack of understanding about these matters and why sexual prejudices are so fierce.

As for me, who can understand pleasure only when I am in direct contact with it, when it is reciprocal and not violent and when, as is often the case—as it was for Whitman—the most fleeting secretive touches are all I require; I was horrified, not only at Daniel's crude thrusting, but also at Mohammed's utter submission to it.

From MADELEINE—ET NUNC MANET IN TE

...it did not seem to me that I was unfaithful to her in seeking elsewhere a satisfaction of the flesh that I did not know how to ask of her. Besides, I didn't reason. I acted like an irresponsible person. A demon inhabited me. It never possessed me more imperiously than on our return to Algiers, during the same voyage:

The Easter holidays had ended. In the train taking us from Biskra, three schoolboys, returning to their *lycée,* occupied the compartment next to ours, which was almost full. They were but half clothed, for the heat was tantalizing, and, alone in their compartment, were raising the roof. I listened to them laugh and jostle one another. At each of the frequent but brief stops the train made, by leaning out of the little side window I had lowered, my hand just reached the arm of one of the boys who amused himself by leaning toward me from the next window, laughingly entering into the spirit of the game; and I tasted excruciating delights in touching the downy amber flesh he offered to my caress. My hand, slipping up along his arm, rounded the shoulder... At the next station, one of the two others had taken his place and the same game would begin again. Then the train would start again. I would sit down, breathless and panting, and pretend to be absorbed by my reading. Madeleine, seated opposite me, said nothing, pretended not to see me, not to know me....

On our arrival in Algiers, the two of us alone in the omnibus which was taking us to the hotel, she finally said to me in a tone in which I felt even more sorrow than censure: "You looked either like a criminal or a madman."

JEAN COCTEAU (1889-1963) AND HIS FRIENDS

Jean Cocteau, *Self-Portrait* (1923). Drawing published in *Souvenir des Ballets russes*.

It has been said that Jean Cocteau was the bandleader of the arts during the first half of the twentieth century in France. Poetry, the novel, painting, the theatre, ballet, films and jazz—everything interested him, including boxing. "I haven't stopped for a minute since I was fifteen," he once wrote, and indeed his perpetual youthfulness never ceased to amaze his contemporaries. He was a magician, who transformed everything he touched.

At the turn of the century elegant, flippant eighteen year old Cocteau was the darling of Paris society. With his cronies Maurice Rostand (who went about in high heels) and Lucien Daudet ("that curled, pomaded, powdered boy who spoke with a voice so frail that you could have slipped it into a fob pocket," as Jules Renard described him), Cocteau belonged to the group of young intellectuals like Marcel Proust, Reynaldo Hahn and the Noailles who brought wit and youth to the drawing rooms of the Emperess Eugenie. In 1908 one of Cocteau's more ardent (and wealthy) admirers rented a theatre for an evening and organized a reading of his protege's poetry introduced by Laurent Tailhade. Cocteau had just turned nineteen. Around the same time he managed to get himself accepted by the bohemian artists of Montmartre who disliked both the "rich" and the "fashionable." Despite the reticence of some of them—notably André Breton—Cocteau soon became fast friends with the likes of Picasso, Apollinaire and Max Jacob.

For these artists of the rising modernist generation who were shortly to be plunged into the inferno of World War I, the great event of the pre-War years was the season of ballet presented by Diaghilev's Russian troupe at the Théâtre du Châtelet in Paris in 1909. Cocteau later said that it gave him the feeling that "the slate had been wiped clean." The young poet-about-town was fascinated by Diaghilev, a bizarre person who invariably wore a thick opossum-lined cloak held shut with safety pins. In 1913 Diaghilev returned to Paris and staged Stravinsky's *Sacre du Printemps*—which caused a furore; Diaghilev was accused of being "Greek," of corrupting the youth of France, of accelerating the decadence of music and art; none of which bothered Diaghilev, who liked nothing more than to have himself talked about, whether for good

Jean Cocteau, *The Den of Iniquity* (1923). Taken from an album of drawings. Private collection.

Jean Cocteau, *Souvenir des Ballets russes* (1923). Showing Sergei Diaghilev and Nijinsky.

or ill. One day, as he was coming out of the theater, he turned to his irrepressible young companion, Cocteau, and, adjusting his monocle, demanded: "Astonish me!"

Cocteau did more than that a few years later (in 1917) when he staged his avant-garde ballet, *Parade.* The Cubistic set and costumes (designed by Picasso) and the irreverent music by Eric Satie roused the audience to such a pitch of fury that the theatre resounded with the angry shouts of "To Berlin!" "To Berlin!" Taken aback, and above all terrified, Diaghilev scurried into a hiding place; while Cocteau, Picasso and Satie took to their heels hotly pursued by a throng of outraged ladies armed with hatpins.

Jean Cocteau had no inclination for politics (or even reality); for him the real battle was the battle of modernism and not the war being fought in the fields of Flanders. Although deferred from active military duty, he nevertheless volunteered as an orderly in an ambulance corps organized by his friend Etienne de Beaumont. Knowing Cocteau well, Beaumont had warned him to

dress soberly—whereupon Cocteau went to the great couturier Paul Poiret and had him design a semi-military uniform. One evening the ambulance he had been assigned to pulled up in front of a small hotel in Flanders. While dinner was being prepared under the supervision of the writer Bernard Faÿ, Cocteau and Beaumont went upstairs to change into more comfortable clothes. Meanwhile General Haig arrived unannounced and installed himself at a table in the dining room. Enter the French section of the ambulance corps: Beaumont in black pyjamas followed by Cocteau in shocking pink pyjamas. Both men sported gold bracelets on their ankles. According to Bernard Faÿ, who relates the incident in his book, *Les Précieux,* Cocteau, on seeing the general, looked like "a bathing nymph surprised by intruders." We are not told what the general's reaction was; but, for safe measure, Faÿ tore out the page he and his friends had signed in the hotel register before leaving the next morning. Somewhat later Cocteau's ambulance unit was ordered to evacuate some wounded marines. "What charming heroes," gushed Cocteau, who was recalled to Paris by Beaumont who feared a new scandal. "I thought

255

Pablo Picasso, Costumes for *Parade* (1917).
Bibliothèque Nationale, Paris.

Léon Bakst, Watercolor of Nijinsky in *La Péri*
for the program of the Ballets russes (1911).
Bibliothèque Nationale, Paris.

that war could be a joyful thing," Cocteau wrote naively to his brother. But the heroic death of the pilot, Roland Garros, Cocteau's first great love, taught the poet that there was nothing enchanting about armies shooting at each other.

In 1918 Cocteau met fifteen year old Raymond Radiguet in Max Jacob's studio. He was enthralled by the precociousness, seriousness, breadth of knowledge and literary talent of this boy who still wore short pants and had been writing poems for a year; he was already trying to make a living by writing for newspapers. Radiguet had been sent to Max Jacob by André Salmon, at that time the literary director of a review called *Fantasio*. His "child's beauty, his large affectionate mouth and chapped lips" had immediately appealed to Max Jacob who took the boy under his wing, inviting him to lunch every day. Max was therefore rather unhappy when Cocteau got his hands on Radiguet and began taking him along to fashionable soirees, to concerts, to the circus and to the fun fair. Cocteau and his prodigy-protege became inseparable friends, even spending their vacations together. Despite their difference in age, Radiguet turned out to be the dominant partner in the relationship. His eighteenth birthday was memorably celebrated in a night-club called "Le Bœuf sur le Toit," the "in" spot frequented by the literary and artistic avant-garde of Paris including George Auric, Jean and Valentine Hugo, Darius Milhaud, Francis Poulenc, Tristan Tzara, Francis Picabia (who was painting his fresco, *"L'Oeil cacodylate"* there) and Marcel Jouhandeau's future wife, Caryathis.

Cocteau's affair with Radiguet was not always a bed of roses. Radiguet would have icy fits of anger, which Cocteau feared and hated; moreover the boy was extremely jealous of his independence and had rented a

room of his own at the Hotel Foyot where he had occasional trysts with women, like the beautiful Bronca Perlmutter. Modigliani's favorite model, the socializing poetess Beatrice Hastings, whose admirers included Ezra Pound and George Bernard Shaw, had fallen heavily for the boy-genius who had become an overnight celebrity when his first novel, *Le Diable au corps,* was published. Radiguet soon burnt himself out, though. Exhausted by his frantic pace of living, by drugs and alcohol, he caught typhus in Arcachon while correcting the proofs of his second book, *Le Bal du comte d'Orgel* (1923). He was brought back to Paris, where he died several weeks later.

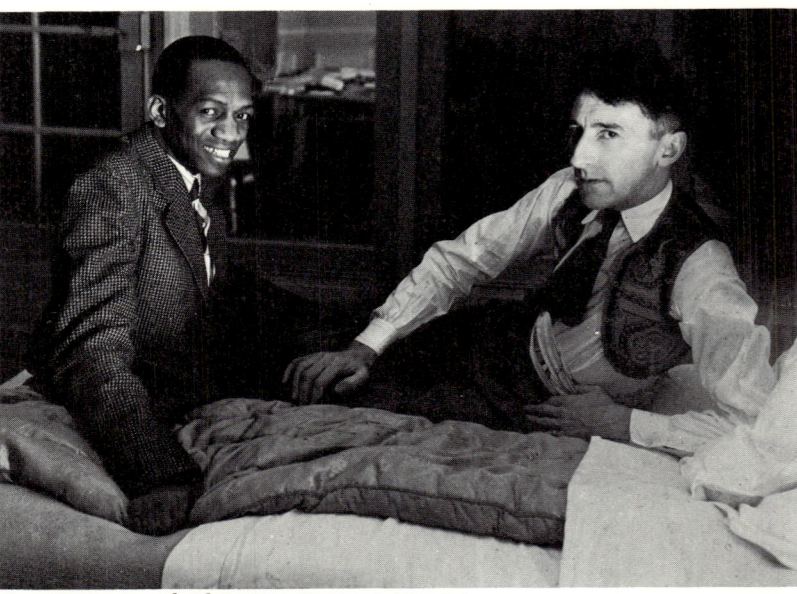

Jean Cocteau and Al Brown. François Duchêne Collection, Paris.

"I am going to be shot by God's firing squad," he whispered two days before his death at twenty-three. This blow plunged Cocteau into bottomless despair. "His death left me rudderless." Unable to stand his grief he took to opium. His best work—*Thomas l'Imposteur, Les mariés de la Tour Eiffel,* and his book of poems, *Plain Chant*—had been written during the years with Radiguet.

Drifting from one companion to another, caught in the hellish round of addictions and cures, surrounded by younger men who idolized but did not really understand him, Cocteau struggled with his anxieties and the "difficulty of living." The Catholic philosopher Jacques Maritain (a Protestant who had been converted by Léon Bloy) tried to help the poet and bring him back to God. He and his wife Raïssa took an interest in several of Cocteau's followers, notably Maurice Sachs. They became friends with Jean Hugo, Paul Claudel, Georges Rouault, Julian Green, Max Jacob, Chagall, Father Henryon and Henri Ghéon (who had shared André Gide's first homosexual experiences, but had later converted). Meanwhile Cocteau fell in love with Jean Desbordes, a twenty-one year old draftee in the navy, who wore his sailor's uniform "delightfully." Desbordes was the author of a book called *J'adore,* which had caused quite a scandal; but he could not replace Radiguet, whose talent and personality he did not possess. Cocteau gave him a part in his first film, *Blood of a Poet.* Another part (the "Hermaphrodite") was given to Barbette, the American trapeze artist who performed in drag at the "Bœuf sur le Toit." Cocteau was especially fond of this transvestite who always kept the same three books on his bedstand: James Joyce's *Ulysses,* Cocteau's novel *Le Grand Ecart* and a book by Havelock Ellis on masturbation.

In 1936 Cocteau adopted a new "son": the American boxer, Al Brown. Al Brown had lost an important fight and was on the decline. He had gotten a job in a music hall and was trying to forget his downfall with the help of drugs and alcohol. Cocteau urged him to start training again and generally took charge of his career, eventually organizing everything from newspaper coverage to the actual fights. On the day of Al Brown's comeback, Cocteau stood next to the ring encouraging him. Despite the fact that Al Brown was greeted with booes and angry shouts of "Poet!", "Dancer!" he won the fight—and went on to win ten more fights after that. Al Brown died several years later in a Harlem hospital while listening to a recording of Cocteau reminiscing about their days together. As for Jean Desbordes, he met with a tragic end: arrested by the Gestapo in 1944 he was tortured to death in a Paris cellar.

After the war ended in 1945, Cocteau noted sadly: "I am drawn to high-speed mechanisms which wear out tragically. Now my fatherly instinct warns me to stay away from them. I turn towards those who are not marked by the black star. The accursed star. I hate it. What is there left for me but to warm my old body in the sun?" But his days of love were hardly over: he met a young man named Jean Marais, an actor, who bore an extraordinary resemblance to the Grecian profiles of boys

Jean Cocteau, Comic drawing for François de Gouy and Russel Greely. P. Agoune Collection, Paris.

Jean Cocteau, *The Den of Iniquity* (1923). Taken from an album of drawings. Private collection.

Cocteau had been sketching for years. Moreover Marais was not marked by the "black star." Nor was another of Cocteau's "autumn loves," Jean Dermit, whom the poet introduced to painting and made the executor of his estate. Beginning in 1955 a series of honors fell on Cocteau's shoulders—much to his surprise: he was elected to the Académie française and to the Belgian Academy and was given an honorary degree by Oxford University. He was commissioned to decorate three chapels: Villefranche (1956), Saint-Blaise in Milly (1959) and Notre-Dame de France in London (1960).

Shortly before he died Cocteau surveyed his life and declared that it was like "running in zigzags for forty years in front of a hunting party, with horns sounding in my ears." But in the end Cocteau outfoxed his pursuers: the hue and cry had turned into acclaim.

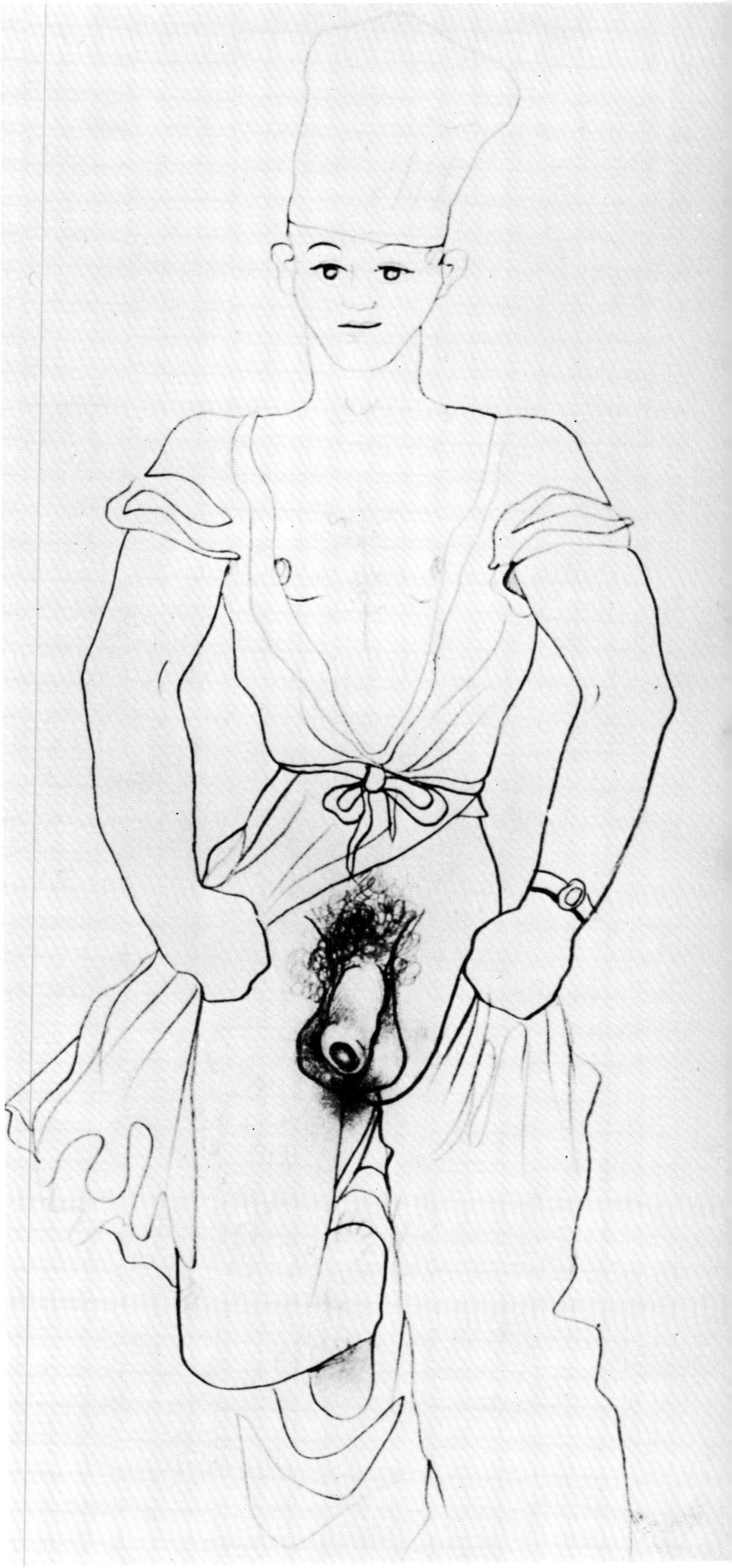

Jean Cocteau, *The Cook's Help*. Editions Jacques Damase, Brussels.

Marie Laurencin, *Portrait of Radiguet*. Editions Jacques Damase, Brussels.

Anonymous, *"Le Négligé"*. Illustration for *Thomas l'Imposteur* by Jean Cocteau. Editions Jacques Damase, Brussels.

From THE WHITE PAPER

...*Hell of a Fellow* was spelled out in letters of gold on the flat hat tilted down in front over his left eyebrow, his tie was knotted up over his Adam's apple and he was wearing those amply bell-bottomed pants which sailors used once upon a time to roll to the thigh and which nowadays the regulations find some moral excuse or other for outlawing.

In another place I'd never have dared put myself within range of that lofty stare. But Toulon is Toulon; dancing eliminates uncomfortable preambles, it throws strangers into each other's arms and sets the stage for love.

They were playing dipsy-doodly music full of sauciness and winning smiles; we danced a waltz; The arched bodies are riveted together at the sex; grave profiles cast thoughtful downward glances, turn less quickly than the tripping and now and then plodding feet. Free hands assume the gracious attitudes affected by common folk when they take a cup of tea or piss it out again. A springtime exhiliration transports the bodies. Those bodies bud, push forth shoots, branches, hard members bump, squeeze, sweats commingle, and there's another couple heading for one of the rooms with globe lights overhead and eiderdowns on the bed.

Despoiled of the accessories which cow civilians and of the manner sailors adopt to screw up their courage, *Hell of a Fellow* became a meek animal. He had got his nose broken by a syphon-bottle in the course of a brawl. Without that crooked nose his face might well have been uninteresting. A syphon-bottle had put the finishing touch to a masterpiece.

Upon his naked torso, this lad, who represented pure luck to me, had LOUSY LUCK tattooed in blue capital letters. He told me his story. It was brief. That afflicting tattoo condensed it in a nutshell. He'd just emerged from the brig. After the *Ernest-Renan* mutiny there'd been the inquest; they'd confused him with a colleague; that was why his hair was only half an inch long; he deplored a tonsure which wonderfully became him. "I've never had anything but lousy luck," he repeated, shaking that bald little head reminiscent of a classical bust, "and it ain't never going to change."

I slipped my fetish-chain around his neck. "I'm not giving it to you," I explained, "it's a charm, but not much of one, I guess, for it hasn't done much for me and won't for you either. Just wear it tonight." Then I uncapped my fountain pen, and crossed out the ominous motto. I drew a star and a heart above it. He smiled. He understood, more with his skin than with the rest, that he was in safe hands, that our encounter wasn't like the ones he'd grown accustomed to: hasty encounters in which selfishness satisfies itself.

Lousy Luck! Incredible—with that mouth, those teeth, those eyes, that belly, those shoulders and cast-iron muscles, those legs, how was it possible? Lousy luck, with that fabulous little undersea plant, forlorn, inert, shipwrecked on the frothy fleece, which then stirs, unwrinkles, develops, rouses itself and hurls its sap afar when once it is restored to its element of love. Lousy luck? I couldn't believe it; and to resolve the problem I drowned myself in a vigilant sleep.

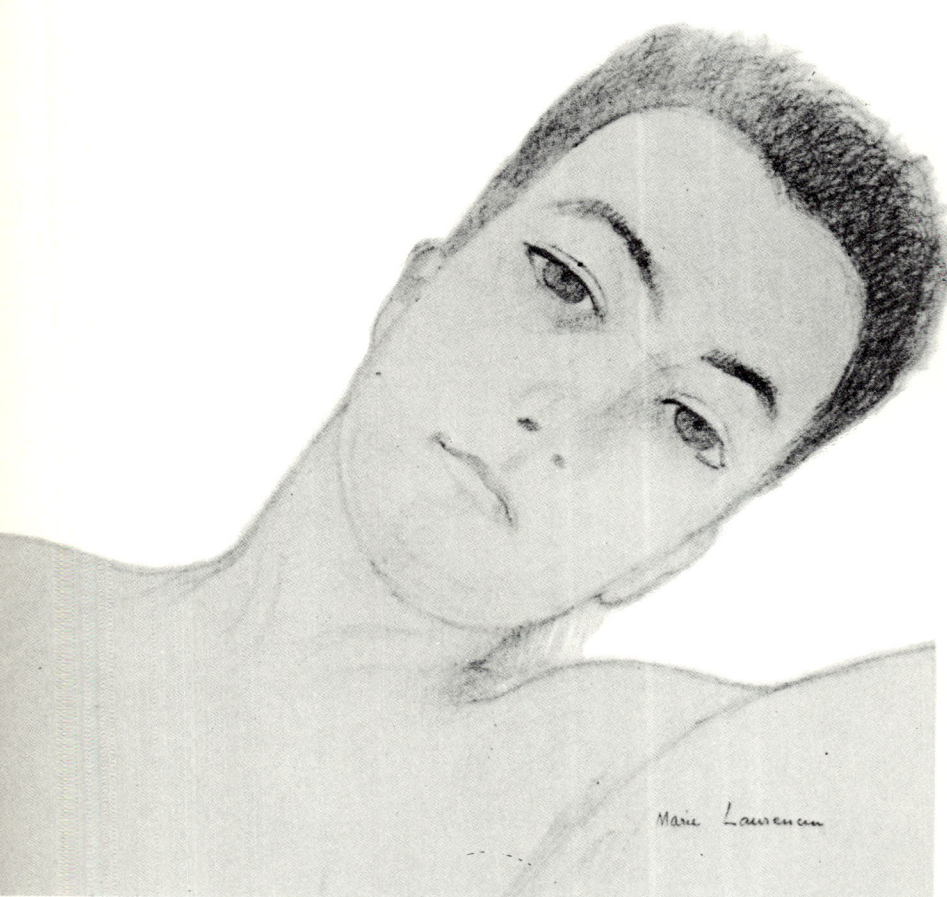

From PLAINSONG

Whoa, bed of love! Here, in this tall shadow,
We'll pull up, and talk while our feet are tranquil
Down at the other end like two horses side by side.
Now and then one lazily arches its neck across the other.

Nothing chills me more than the false lull of
    A sleeping face;
Your dreams are Egypt, and you the mummy
    With its mask of gold.

Where has your gaze flown beneath that painted cast
    Of a dying queen,
Now love's night has hollowed you, and recomposed
    You like a black embalmer?

Oh my queen, oh my migrator, leave
    The centuries and the seas;
Light on the breathing surface, joined to your reflection
    Risen back into your eyes.

Your lips folding back in laughter, rose petals,
Cancel my pique at your metamorphosis;
The dream is forgotten, since you are awake.
Once again I'm tied to your tree,
And you are tightening your knots around me,
And we are two plants sharing the same bark,
The same flame, the same throb of green,
Our mouths fusing the flower of unity.

Illustration for The White Paper *(1930) by Jean Cocteau, hand-coloured by M.B. and Armington. Editions du Signe, Paris.*

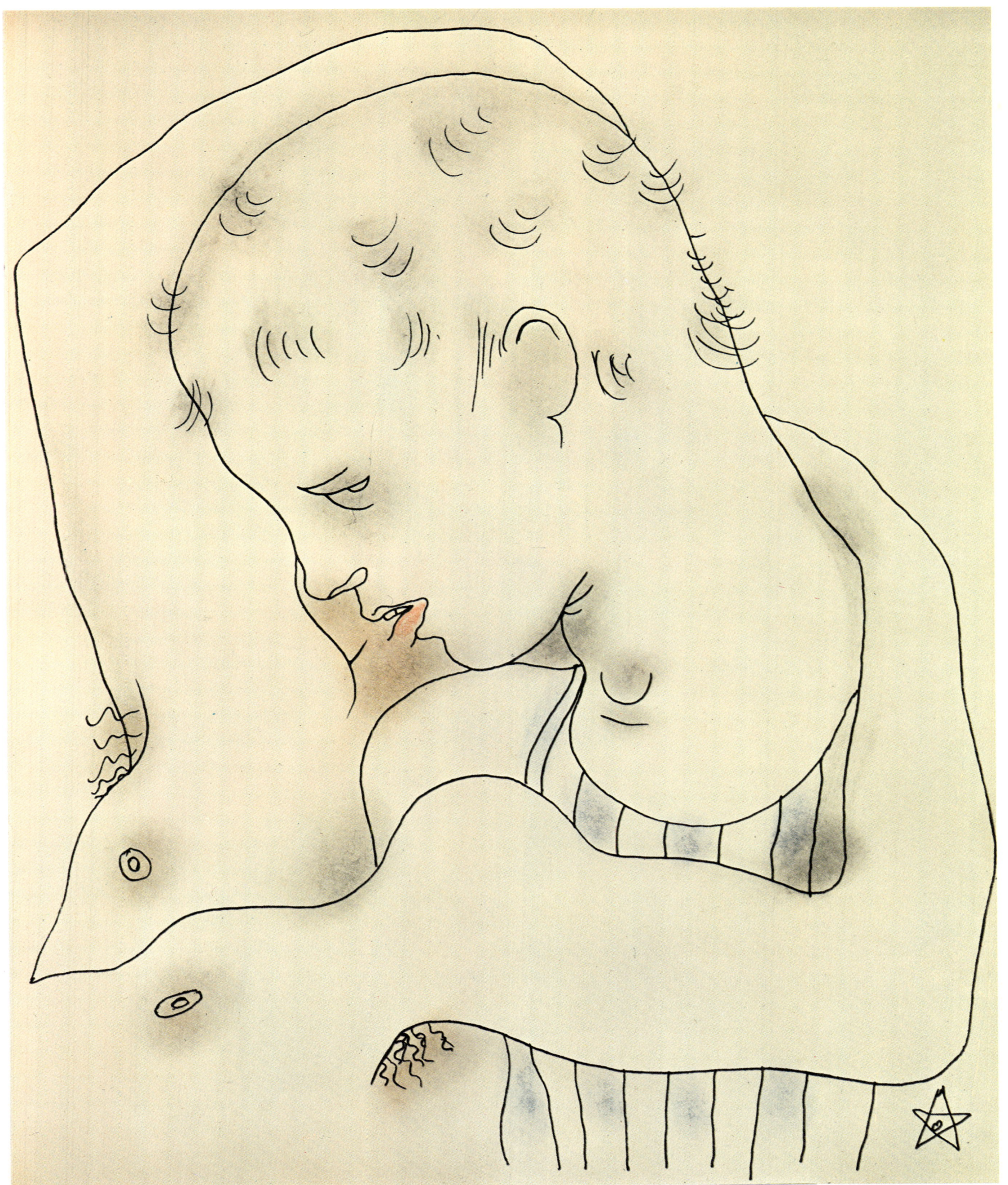

MAURICE SACHS (1906-1945)

Maurice Sachs's grandfather, a wealthy Jewish diamond-merchant, was one of the founders of the French communist daily, *l'Humanité*. His father, a lazy, dissolute man, left home when Maurice was still a child. His mother remarried, and ran up debts. By the age of sixteen, Maurice had to fend for himself. Through Jean Cocteau he met Jacques Maritain—and promptly fell in love with him. He decided to become a priest; and, on January 2, 1926 (he was seventeen) he entered a seminary. After six months in the novitiate he went to spend his holidays at his grandmother's house in the elegant, mundane resort of Juan-les-Pins. Two days later he succumbed to temptation in the form of a young man he ran into on the beach. The story made the rounds of Paris society vacationing on the Riviera. But for Maurice it was no laughing matter: the affair was a disastrous failure, and it brought him to the verge of committing suicide.

Thereafter his life became a succession of binges and drunken brawls, humiliations, betrayals and swindlings. Maurice Sachs went to the United States, got married there, promptly left his wife and returned to France with a lover. During World War II he was involved in all kinds of shady deals and finally signed up as a volunteer worker in Germany. To avoid hard physical labor, he offered his services to the Gestapo (where he was given the number G 117). Instructed to spy on his compatriots, he set about recruiting collaborators, preferably homosexuals. "I am like Lyautey," he explained, "I only work well with people I go to bed with." The Germans seem to have taken a dim view of Maurice Sachs's methods and jailed him on November 16, 1943. In prison he acted as a stool-pigeon. According to his fellow inmates he spent a great deal of time writing and became quite philosophical about his troubles. In April 1945 the prisoners of Fuhlbüttel, where Sachs was detained, were evacuated towards Kiel. Maurice Ettinghausen (the name on his Hamburg birth-registration) and a German who had been jailed for homosexual offenses, both exhausted by a forty-eight-hours' forced march, refused to continue any further and were shot on the spot by an SS officer.

Maurice Sachs was mainly a witty and lively chronicler of the "roaring twenties" in Paris, of that generation of intellectuals who had tried to forget that politics existed and who had revered Rimbaud and Lautréamont as the founding fathers of visionary modernism.

Even towards the end of his life, Maurice Sachs, who described himself as "thoroughly defiled and sated with excrement," nevertheless hoped to "restore his soul" one day. But he was never able to break out of the "infernal round of the witches' Sabbath."

Jean Cocteau, *The Den of Iniquity* (1923) Two drawings. Taken from an album of drawings. Private collection.

From WITCHES' SABBATH

(Note: The following excerpts from Maurice Sachs's autobiography, *Witches' Sabbath,* describe his first homosexual experiences in a fashionable boy's school, the Collège de Luza).

...a few months later, I experienced what must, despite my youth, be called true love. Though I was only twelve or thirteen, this profound and terrible love made me suffer no less than certain unhappy loves I experienced later.

The object of this passion was a delicate, pale boy my own age with long, straight, fine blond hair. He had a rather angelic expression. I was so troubled by his presence, I scarcely dared speak to him, and I forget how we managed to be walking together in the woods one day. A bower of fallen leaves suddenly appeared: we lay down in it at the same time and flung our arms around each other without a word. And soon, without knowing how, an extraordinary fever inflamed my whole body, and without even offering a helping hand, we were flooded by pleasure.

This unique incident made me understand the profound links that existed between love and pleasure; nothing seemed higher to me. But I learned on the same occasion what venality is, for this boy with his angelic face did not conceal from me that he longed for a fine tennis racket I had. I gave it to him, but the minute he received it, he withdrew from me quite openly.

This episode at least instructed me that there are better things in the world than a wallet, and I suddenly realized that what I had just done with Aser was a habitual practice throughout the school.

A great wave of sensuality swept through this institution. Lustful practices were rife, affected every grade, and it is no exaggeration to say that out of a hundred

Michel Henricot, Watercolor and ink drawing (1972). The artist's collection, Paris.

students, over fifty were making love together. Only the youngest and a few boys of a sturdy virtue who deliberately excluded themselves were exempt from our excesses. The older boys pursued the younger. In certain recreation periods, we would go in troups of eight or ten, sometimes, to roll together in the hay that filled a barn; we could come back exhausted, happy, covered with wisps of hay.

It was surprising that the authorities suspected nothing for so long; ultimately, of course, something gave us away and a major purge was instituted. As might be expected, I was high on the list of the students expelled so politely that our parents, luckily, had no idea of what had really happened.

I think the reason for this indulgence was the fact that more than one teacher, especially our British masters, was among the guilty.

Thus, ingloriously, ended my time at boarding-school....

It was at this period that I experienced the first strong passion of my life. It was for a boy whom I shall call Octave. We had met at the Collège de Luza. At home, my

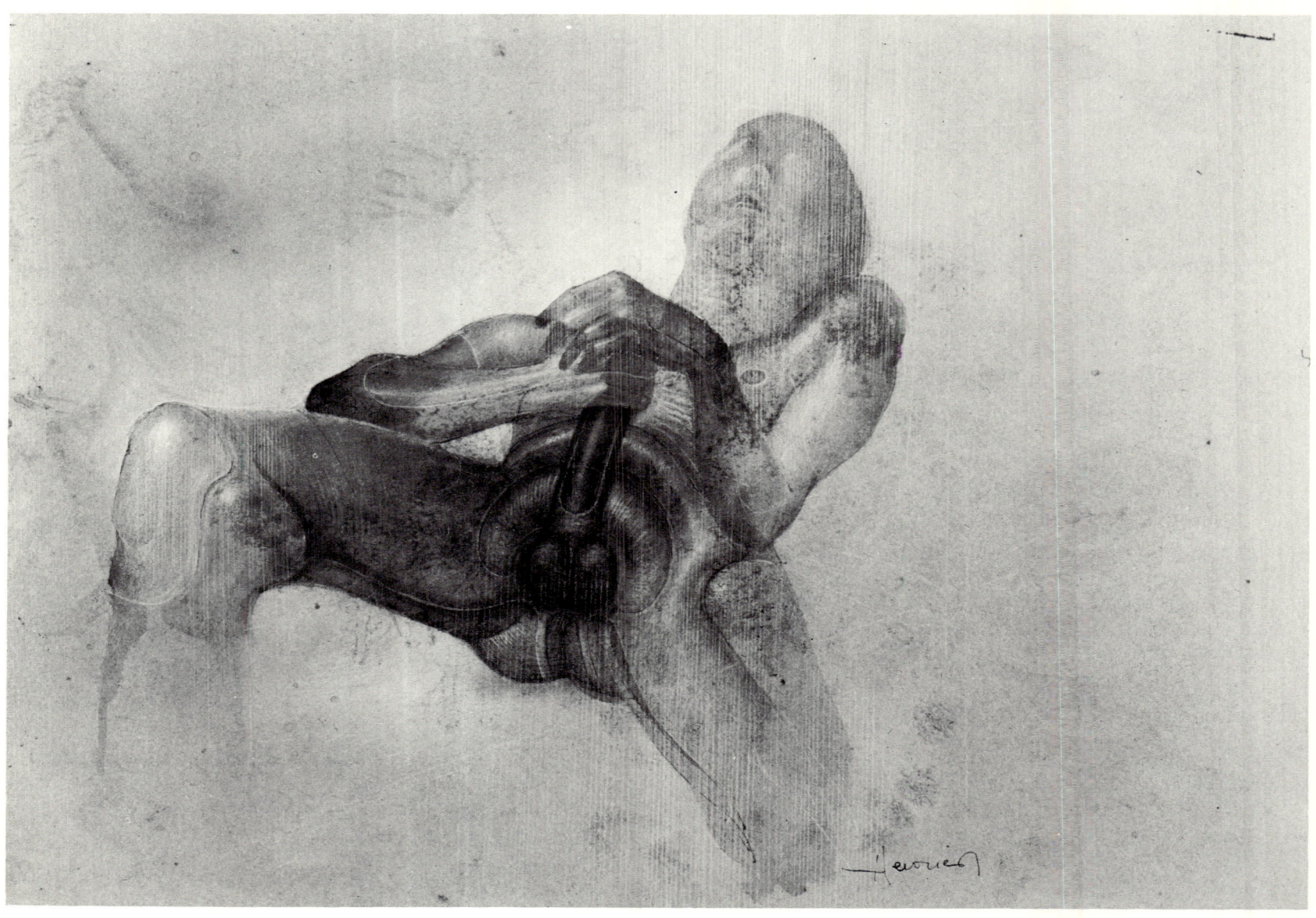

good behavior astonished everyone; there was no need to forbid me anything now. Indeed, as soon as dinner was over, I locked myself in my room and wrote enormous letters to Octave. I was happy: he loved me too.

It was an intense, sweet sentiment of which I have never been ashamed; our love, in its first bloom, was all the more like the kind teen-age boys and girls feel for each other, loving in a self-sustaining blaze from which they expect no other reward than its incandescence.

Blond, muscular, covered with freckles, Octave had something rather animal about him; he was if not younger, at least shorter than I, but I showed utter submission toward him, for unconsciously I had perhaps already developed a certain inferiority complex that has hampered my emotional involvements ever since, leading me to that victimization to which those who must buy love are subjected.

How had this affair begun? I no longer remember very clearly. It seems to me that I took the first step, I mean, that I wrote first. He answered, even before we had made any gesture toward each other more affectionate than those customary among schoolmates. And that was the paradoxical thing about our situation: we treated each other as "comrades" and wrote each other so passionately that anyone would have assumed, had they read what we wrote, that we were making love every day; for we used a conventional vocabulary, as children and uneducated people always do when they are surprised by their own feelings. But such pleasures preoccupied us singularly little. Doubtless they seemed the necessary fulfillment to such ardor, but we were not in any hurry to achieve it.

During recess periods, we kept apart from the others and talked endlessly (and it seems to me today, quite intelligently for our age). Sometimes we held hands, and given our extreme youth, this did not seem at all improper. Soon, the tone of our letters mounting, Octave got in the habit of spending an hour at my house in the afternoon.

We lay together on the couch in my bedroom, rather like puppies, while playing in the fashion of lovers. I remember those afternoons with deep emotion. Enthusiasm and innocence sorted well together, and so deep was the wellspring of tenderness we felt that I don't recall we felt any real guilt at all. And if I kept the door shut, it was rather out of modesty, out of respect for this emotion which I thought deserved secrecy, and out of fear that I would be accused of laziness, for my love in itself seemed innocent and beautiful. And if I felt some sense of inferiority, it was only toward this friend of whom I considered myself unworthy, for I thought him more handsome, more charming, more sensitive than myself.

I shall not claim that this relationship was entirely chaste. But I recall that we were not at all eager to seal it in the pleasure of the flesh, so greatly did we enjoy the exaltation of those embraces without any declared purpose, without ulterior motive. The day we touched each other more intimately we added nothing to our happiness, for at that age tenderness can still do without possession.

If the reader grants with me that the whole of our life is nothing more than an attempt to fulfill the dreams of our youth, he will understand that it is possible to search throughout the whole of one's life for a happiness one has enjoyed as a child.

For me, the memory of Octave and the endless, perhaps futile search for another Octave all too like the original confirmed me in my homosexual appetites and I no longer believe myself capable of other pleasures of the heart and of the body. Doubtless there is some infantilism in this, as the psychiatrists call it, and doubtless I would have rediscovered these innocent pleasures that Octave afforded me, so gentle yet so sensual, much more certainly in the arms of a woman my own age twenty years later.

But this is beyond my powers. I do not *believe,* in other words I do not believe that a woman can ever be Octave. She cannot even pretend to be. While a boy can give me that illusion.

C.P. CAVAFY (1863-1933)

Cavafy, the best-known of the modern Greek poets, was born in Alexandria, Egypt. He was a head clerk in the Office of Irrigation and wrote poetry in his spare time. Only a few of his poems were published during his life. As his French translator, Marguerite Yourcenar, observed, Cavafy's poems are like Near Eastern cafés: you never see a woman in them.

Gösta Adrian Nilsson, *Boxer* (1923), collage. Kulturhistoriska Föreningen För Södra Sverige Kulturen, Lund, Sweden.

Gösta Adrian Nilsson, *Dancing Sailors*, collage. Kulturhistoriska Föreningen För Södra Sverige Kulturen, Lund, Sweden.

BEAUTIFUL FLOWERS AND WHITE THAT BECAME HIM WELL

He walked into the café where they used to go together.—
It was here that his friend had told him three months before,
"We haven't a farthing. We are two boys who are completely penniless—reduced to the cheapest places.
I tell you this plainly, I can no longer go around with you. Someone else, you must know, is asking for me."
This "someone else" had promised him two suits of clothes and a few
handkerchiefs made of silk.— To win him back once more
he moved heaven and earth, and he found twenty pounds.
He went around with him again because of the twenty pounds;
but also, along with these, for their old friendship,
for the old love they felt, for their very deep feeling.—
The "someone else" was a liar, a regular guttersnipe;
he had only one suit of clothes made for him, and even that begrudgingly, after a thousand pleas.

But now he no longer wants either the suit of clothes,
or anything at all of the handkerchiefs of silk,
or the twenty pounds, or the twenty piasters.

On Sunday they buried him, at ten in the morning.
On Sunday they buried him, it is almost a week.

On his very cheap coffin, he placed flowers,
beautiful flowers and white that became him well,
that became his beauty and his twenty-two years.

In the evening when he went— on a job that came his way,
a need to earn his bread— to the café where they used to go together: a knife in his heart,
was the desolate café where they used to go together.

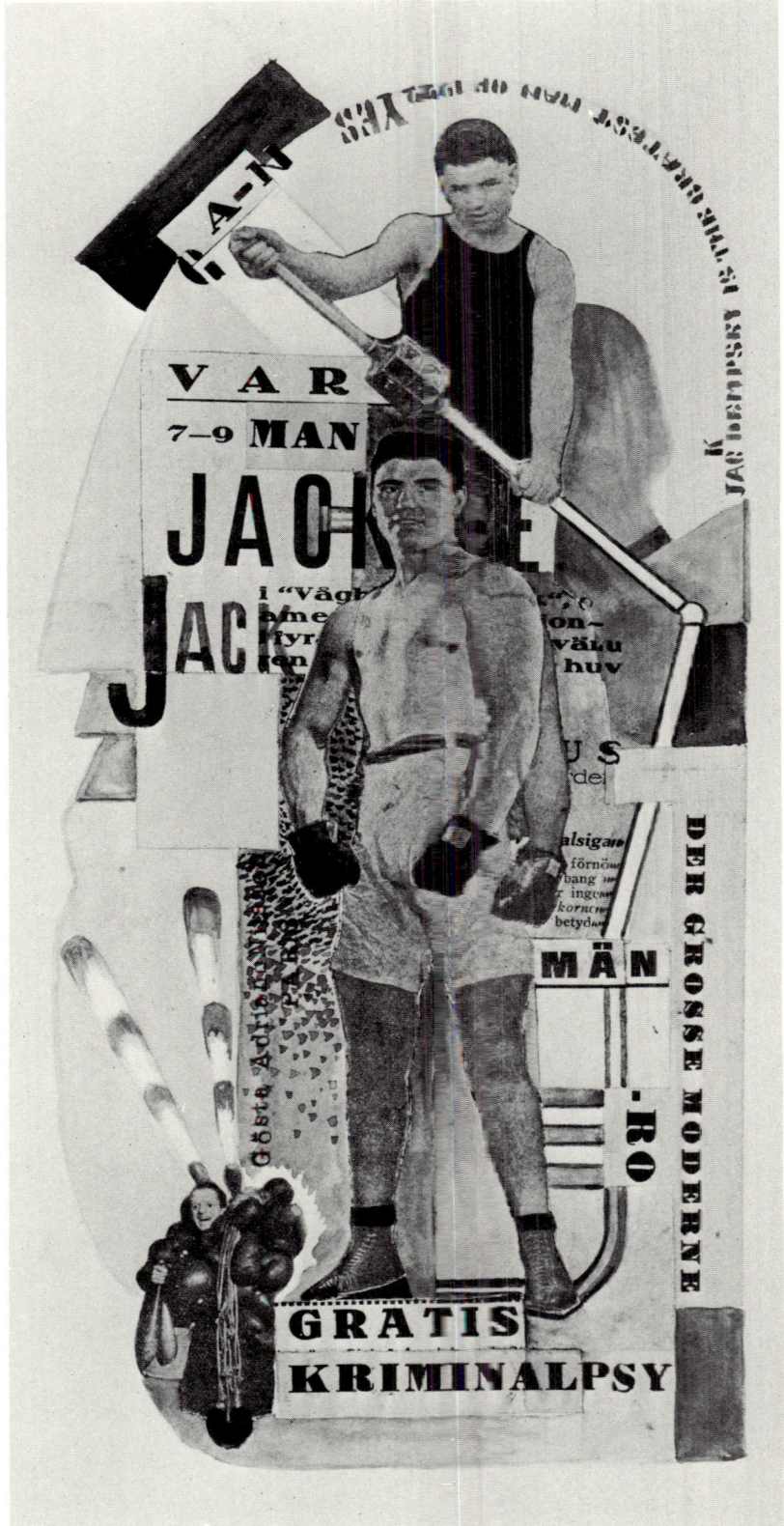

David Hockney, 1963 version of Hogarth's famous series, *The Rake's Progress*. Tate Gallery, London.

THE MIRROR IN THE HALL

The wealthy home had in its entrance
an enormous, extremely old mirror,
that must have been bought at least eighty years ago.

An unusually handsome lad, a tailor's employee
(on Sundays an amateur athlete),
stood holding a parcel. He delivered it
to someone in the house, who carried it inside
to fetch the receipt. The tailor's employee
was left by himself, and he waited.
He approached the mirror and took a look at himself,
and he straightened his tie. Five minutes later
they brought back the receipt. He took it and left.

But the old mirror that had seen and seen,
during the long, long years of its existence,
thousands of objects and faces;
but this time the old mirror was delighted,
and it felt proud that it had received unto itself
for a few moments an image of flawless beauty.

ONE NIGHT

The room was poor and squalid,
hidden above the dubious tavern.
From the window you could see the alley
filthy and narrow. From below
came the voices of some workmen
playing cards and carousing.

And there on the much-used, lowly bed
I had the body of love, I had the lips,
the voluptuous and rosy lips of ecstasy—
rosy lips of such ecstasy, that even now
as I write, after so many years!
in my solitary house, I am drunk again.

A YOUNG MAN SKILLED IN THE ART OF THE WORD

Henceforth brain, toil as well as you can.—
A half-enjoyment is wasting him
He is in a nervous state.
Every day he kisses the beloved face,
his hands are placed on the impeccable limbs.
He has never lived with such a great degree of
passion. But the beautiful consummation of love
is lacking; the consummation is lacking
that must be intensely desired by both of them.

(They are not both equally given to deviate sensual
 pleasure.
Him alone it has utterly mastered.)

So he is wasted, and he is completely unnerved.
Besides he is out of work; and that has much to do with it.
With difficulty he borrows some small
sums of money (sometimes he practically
begs for it) and pseudo-supports himself.
He kisses the adored lips; on the exquisite
body—that now however he senses
is only consenting—he takes his pleasure.
And then he drinks and he smokes; he drinks and he
 smokes;
and he drags himself through the cafés all day long,
he drags with boredom the languour of his beauty.—

Henceforth brain, toil as well as you can.

JEAN GENET (1910-)

The adoptive son of a blind singer, Jean Genet was sent to a reformatory for a minor offense at the age of fifteen. This was the beginning of a long career as an inmate of various correctional establishments. Self-educated (at one point between prison spells he tutored French in Prague), he came to know all aspects of the closed world of the penal system and became attached to many of his cell mates: homosexuals, thieves and murderers. He saw prison society as an astonishing world—with its heroes, its saints and its devils—in which homosexuality appeared a strange, baroque rite whose infinite variations he described in rich, lyrical prose. *Our Lady of the Flowers* was written in Fresnes prison in 1942 and published in 1948; *Funeral Rites* (1947) was Genet's first novel written outside of jail. It is dedicated to his lover, the resistance fighter Jean Decarnin, who was killed during the liberation of Paris. "I felt that I could only reply to the rigidness of his corpse with the rigidness of my penis." In writing this novel Genet released his fantasies of erotic encounters with Aryan victors in black uniforms bulging with virility, exterminating angels whose caresses are brutal. For Genet, to "screw" a man was to become a man doubly.

Jan Storm, *The Actor Jacques Catelain* (1926). Robert Walker Collection, Paris. This is the era described in the works of Jean Cocteau, Maurice Sachs and Jean Genet.

From OUR LADY OF THE FLOWERS

I shall speak again about Divine, but Divine in her garret, between Our Lady, the marble-hearted, and Gorgui. If Divine were a woman, she would not be jealous. She would be perfectly willing to go out alone in the evening to pick up customers between the trees on the boulevard. What would it matter to her that her two males spent their evenings together? On the contrary, a family atmosphere, the light of a lamp shade, would utterly delight her; but Divine is *also* a man. She is, to begin with, jealous of Our Lady, who is young and handsome and without guile. He is in danger of obeying the sympathies of his name. Our Lady, without guile and wily as an Englishwoman. He may arouse Gorgui. It would be easy. Let us imagine them at the movies one afternoon, side by side in the artificial darkness.

"Got your snotrag, Seck?"

No sooner said than done, his hand is on the Negro's pocket. Oh! fatal movement. Divine is jealous of Gorgui. The Negro is her man, and that little tramp of an Our Lady is young and pretty. Beneath the trees of the boulevard, Divine is looking for old geezers, and she is being torn apart by the anguish of a double jealousy. Then, as Divine is a man, she thinks: "I have to feed them both *together*. I'm the slave." She is becoming bitter. At the movies, well-behaved as schoolboys (but, as around schoolboys, who—and that's enough—lower their heads together behind the desk, there prowls, ready to leap, a mad little act), Our Lady and Gorgui smoke and see only the film. In a little while they will go for a glass of beer, unsuspecting, and they will return to the garret, but not without Our Lady's having strewn on the sidewalk little pistol caps with which Gorgui amuses himself by exploding them beneath his steel-tipped shoes; thus, like the whistle blasts between those of pimps, sparks blazed forth between his calves....

Divine has dug out for this evening her two 1890 silk dresses, which she keeps, souvenirs of former carnivals. One of them is black, embroidered with jet; she puts it on and offers the other to Our Lady.

"You're nuts. What'll the guys say?"

But Gorgui insists, and Our Lady knows that all his pals will have a laugh, that not a single one will snicker;

Jim Dine, Illustration for *The Picture of Dorian Gray* (1968) by Oscar Wilde. Ileana Sonnabend Gallery, Paris.

Alfred Courmes, *Saint Sebastian* (1935). The artist's collection, Paris.

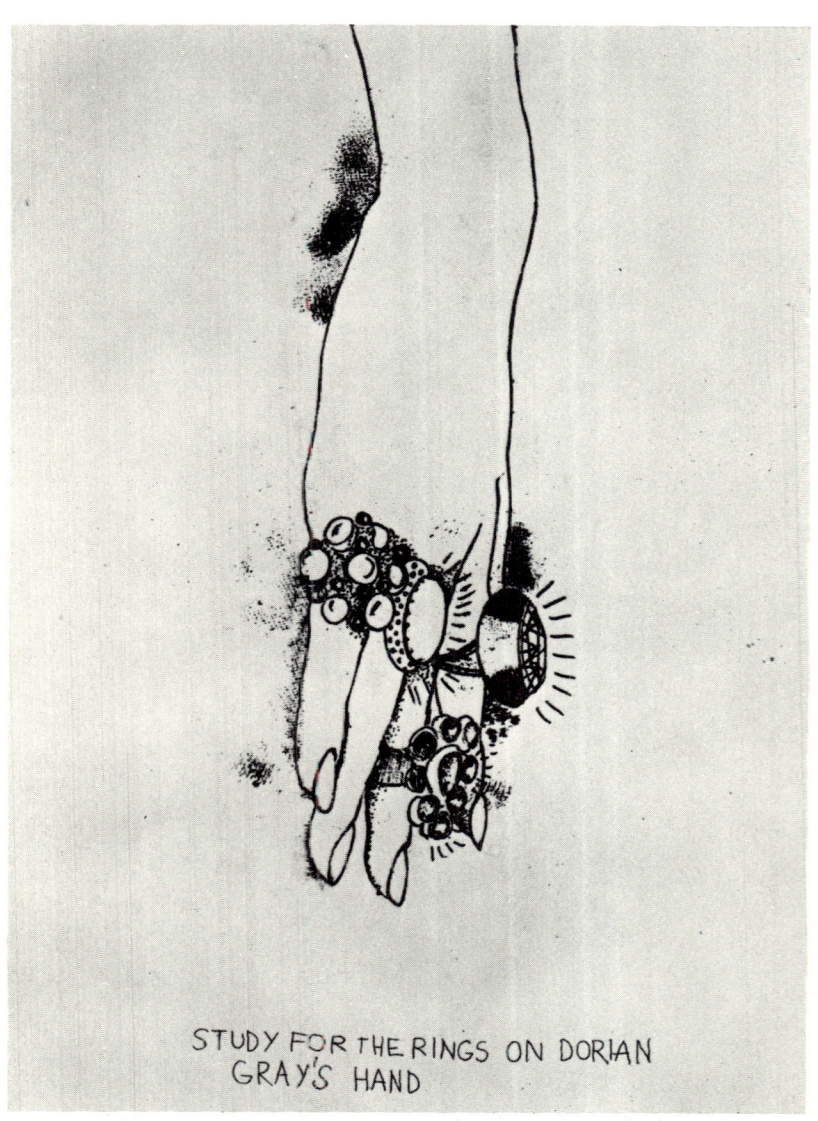

STUDY FOR THE RINGS ON DORIAN GRAY'S HAND

and high heels, but they are completely concealed by the flounces of the skirt. They dressed very quickly that evening because they were going out for real fun. Divine puts on her black silk dress and over it a pink jacket, and takes a spangled tulle fan. Gorgui is wearing tails and a white tie. Occurred the scene of the match being blown out. They went down the stairs. Taxi. *The Tabernacle*. The doorman, quite young and ever so good looking, leers three times. Our Lady dazzles him. They enter the brilliant fireworks of silk and muslin flounces which cannot fight clear of the smoke. They dance the smoke. They smoke the music. They drink from mouth to mouth. Our Lady is acclaimed by his pals. He had not realized that his firm buttocks would draw the cloth so tight. He doesn't give a damn that they see he has a hard-on, but not to such a point, in front of the fellows. He would like to hide. He turns to Gorgui and, slightly pink, shows him his bulging dress, muttering:

"Say, Seck, let me ditch that."

He barely snickers. His eyes seem moist, and Gorgui does not know whether he is kidding or annoyed; then the Negro takes the murderer by the shoulders, hugs him, clasps him, locks between his mighty thighs the jutting horn that is raising the silk, and carries him on his heart in waltzes and tangoes which will last till dawn....

they esteem him. The dress drapes Our Lady's body, which is naked under the silk. He rather likes the way he looks. His legs, with their downy, even slightly hairy skin, brush against each other. He bends down, turns around, looks at himself in the mirror. The dress, which has a bustle, makes his rump stick out, suggesting a pair of cellos. Let us put a velvet flower into his tousled hair. He is wearing Divine's tan shoes, the ones with ankle straps

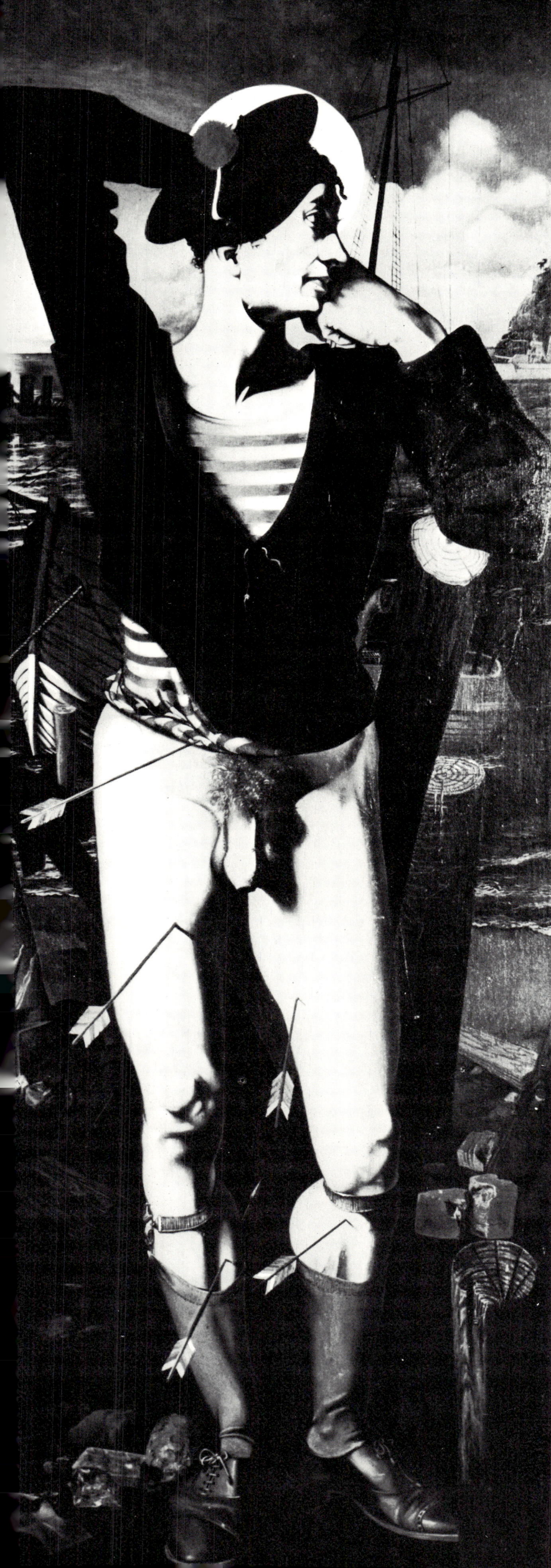

From **FUNERAL RITES**

...Erik and the executioner were locked in an embrace, face to face. Erik's underpants were torn. His khaki breeches were falling down and forming a thick heap of clothes between his legs, and his buttocks were crushed in the fog against the red bark, those soft-skinned, amber buttocks, as rich to the eye as the milky fog whose matter had the luster of pearl. Erik hung from the executioner's neck with both hands. His feet were no longer touching the wet grass, though his breeches were, having fallen down between his naked calves and his ankles. The executioner, whose prick was still stiff and was now between Erik's pressed thighs, held him up and dug into the rich earth. Their knees were piercing the mist. The executioner was hugging the boy to him and, at the same time, backing him up and crushing his ass against the tree. Erik was pulling the man's head. The executioner realized that the boy was solidly built and tremendously violent. They stayed in that position for a few seconds without moving, the two heads pressing hard against each other, cheek to cheek. The executioner was the first to break away, for he had discharged between Erik's golden thighs, which were velvety with morning mist. The position had lasted only a brief moment, but long enough to beget in the executioner and the morning's assistant a feeling of simultaneous tenderness: Erik for the executioner, whom he was holding by the neck in such a way that it could mean only tenderness, and the executioner for the youngster, for even though the gesture was necessitated by their difference in height, it was so winning that it would have made the toughest of men burst into tears. Erik loved the executioner. He wanted to love him, and little by little he felt himself being wrapped in the huge folds of the legendary red cloak inside which he cuddled at the same time as he took a piece of newspaper from his pocket and politely handed it to the executioner who took it to wipe his prick.

"I love the executioner and I make love with him, at dawn!"

273

MARCEL JOUHANDEAU (1888-)

The French writer, Marcel Jouhandeau, taught school in Paris from 1912 to 1949. In 1929 he married Cocteau's friend, the dancer Caryathis, who was the star performer at the "Boeuf sur le Toit" and for whom Erik Satie composed *La Belle excentrique*. Jouhandeau does not call on the forces of the imagination; rather, he writes about daily events (in a style "studded with gold," as Max Jacob has said) transforming them into a magical, occasionally disturbing, vision of reality. Under his pen, the most graceless men suddenly acquire movingly graceful gestures. Jouhandeau considers "abjection" detachedly as a peculiarity of the soul which must be studied with the patience of an entomologist—with the difference that in vice he sees the operation of the supernatural. He openly admits to his own homosexuality, pointing out that he never made any victims, having always chosen adult partners. *On Abjection* (1939) and *Tiresias* (1954), from which the following passages were taken, were both published anonymously.

From ON ABJECTION

I remember that a little later the landlord at 26, Rue Gay-Lussac consented, after a long delay, to rent me two attic rooms overlooking the Oceanographic Institute, but only if I agreed not to bring home any women: "I don't want to expose," he said, "my wife, Madame Bonnet, to some girl off Saint-Michel coming up the stairway." The landlord lived in the building. Both to ridicule him and avenge myself, starting the following month, I went for lunch in a seedy restaurant on Avenue d'Orleans, where I would invite home no matter whom—provided they weren't women—unemployed laborers, plumbers, mechanics and often no doubt petty criminals, thieves murderers; it could have cost me my life. When these individuals arrived in my room, I offered them a cigarette, a drink or a snack according to the time of day; and if I saw that their nails were too long or too dirty, I asked my guests to let me trim and clean them. It was my vice. So for a long time I held their hands captive in my hands, and I saw my guests departing a bit disturbed, asking themselves if I might not be a bit mad. One Sunday night a man with a limp arrived. I asked him to take off his shoes and have a foot bath. I cleaned his feet myself. He was, I believe, a plasterer, who was about twenty and rather good looking. Around his ankles and inside the spaces between his toes were traces of quick lime, leading me to believe a statue was coming to life under my fingers. Once my devotion to the feet of the poor was satisfied, after these little gestures of care, we often became more familiar, yet never to the point where my guests ceased having for one moment a sort of respect for me mixed with fear; so much so that the day I surprised one of them with his hand on my wallet, I had only to gaze sadly at him for him to give it back, although it's true after having first made a gesture of strangling me.

One afternoon, as I was returning home from lunch, waiting under my lily-lined porch, was the justice of the peace from C, the village where my family lives. He was surrounded by his seven children. He began bubbling out news from home, and I was in the midst of enjoying his account, when I saw approaching a pale boy, clad in large black velvet pants, held up by an even larger scarlet flannel belt: one of my guests leaving the hospital. I had only to make one gesture, and the Danger withdrew to where it came from. What exaltation of feelings the apparition, the very presence of these young strangers brought to my solitude! Some of them assumed the pose of slaves while I became their King. They adored me. Sometimes it occured to me that I was only a man whom the gods chose to visit, and for that reason I did everything possible to convince my young guests of my being an engraver by profession, which excused all my actions; then I would quite naturally request them to undress and stretch out across my bed. They would assume the pose most convenient for them, and I—armed with pen and paper—moved near and around them, without ever touching them; sometimes standing, kneeling, or sitting beside them. Once Endymion was sleeping, the pretending stopped....

This morning at seven-thirty under the archway, an Arab, about thirty, with lowered gaze, stands regarding his thumb. There is a gentleness in him which must resemble mine, the kindness of a shepherd or an Islamic wiseman. I can only imagine this man in a far off corner of Africa, crook in hand, watching over his flock, and perhaps at the same time seeing me in the guise of a shepherd, so that everyone seems finally to ask why this meeting of all the shepherds in the world inside this passageway of a city?

Anonymous, Illustration for *Querelle de Brest* (1948) by Jean Genet. Attributed to Jean Cocteau. Private collection.

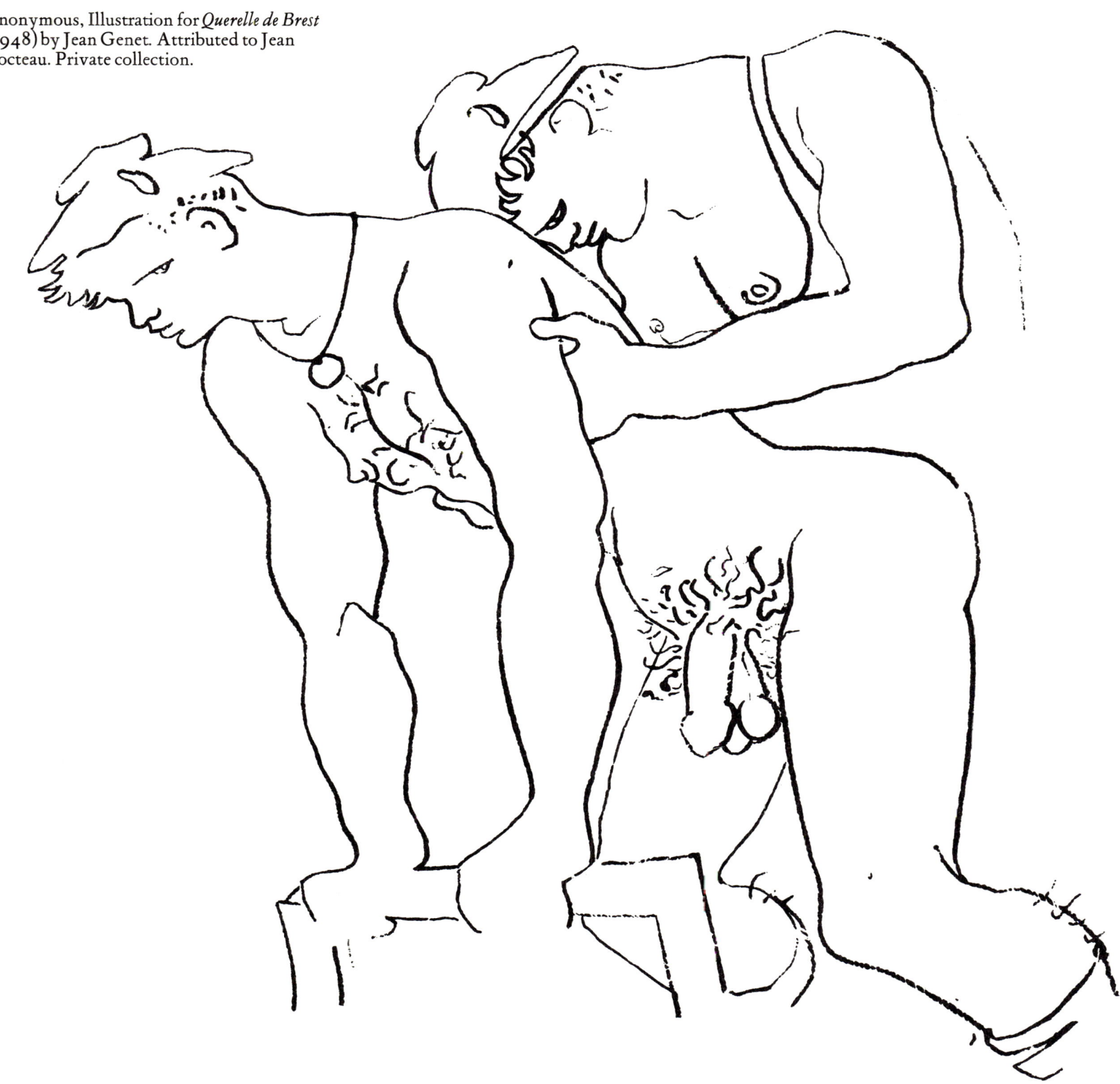

From TIRESIAS

We see each other, Richard and I, every Thursday. From then on, I only live from one Thursday to the next, or it is like wandering through a cave in search of daylight.

Barely do I move, breathe, for fear of upsetting something, of disturbing the delicate machinery that assures the workings of the world. Should an unpredictable accident take place in his life or mine, should his watch or mine be a little ahead or a bit behind, and we risk not being together! In the circumstances which govern his steps and mine, let one obstacle slide in and our affair is finished.

I know only his first name, and he knows only mine. I know where he stations himself for me between two-thirty and three, one given day out of seven and that is it. Five minutes before I arrive, somebody could take him from me. So handsome is he, that he would discover someone friendlier than me in the interval!

At the time I was telling him my name, why had I hesitated? Probably, at that moment I valued my liberty more than him. Now, no. What a difficult balance to maintain! One wishes to remain master of one's self and already one no longer is.

Today I had news of Jean-Jacques, of Little Louis and Richard I. The Circle of my boys going around inside of me!

275

Jean Cocteau. Illustration for *The White Paper* (1930). Editions du Signe, Paris.

Anonymous, Illustration for *Querelle de Brest* (1948) by Jean Genet. Attributed to Jean Cocteau. Private Collection.

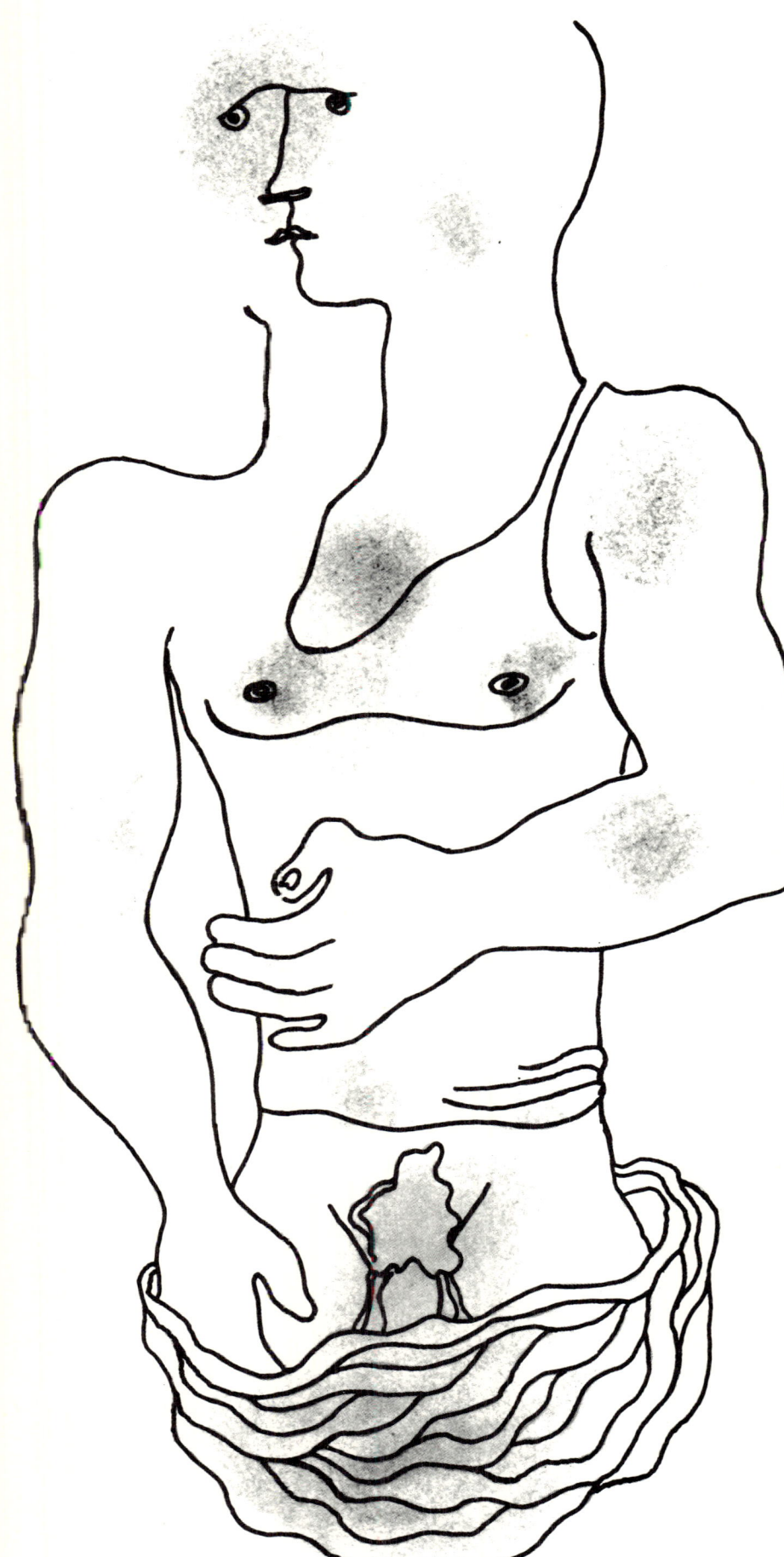

What affects me in Richard II, however, is the detail of his life. For example, he reports to me that he returns from celebrating so late at night that his lover's valet never gets any sleep, for the pleasure of tucking him in (his lover who keeps him in princely fashion is on vacation).

Around his neck he wears an old cross made from heavy gold; his linens come directly from the shirtmaker of the King of England, and every Thursday around three o'clock he waits for me among the vagrants who one of these days are going to kill him for his silk socks, not to mention all the rest.

He is kind enough not to hide the pleasure he takes in our games. Not for one instant is there any suspicion of blackmail, of conceit or of fatigue.

His beauty has reached the point of maturity that I've been seeking: half-way between adolescence and the completed man. He is more virile than graceful; hirsute, but his wild hair, supple, light and scattered, neither gets in the way nor weighs down in any way the graceful contour of his figure; in that way he is scarcely veiled, like a pulp. He always looks like he just stepped from the bath.

What amuses me in love between men is the mechanical side of the gestures as you look at them, the clinical and symbolic side of the actions, "when vases communicate," the penis readily taking on the shape of an alembic for experiments, to which no mysterious quest, no alchemical investigation, would be foreign. That is the alchemy of Pleasure.

Why not allow him to invade the Place, someone will say, why see this Sun but once a week? Discipline of the heavenly bodies who know what they are capable of together—at what distance they must hold off in order not to risk annihilation, burning each other up, in order to wander a long time in each other's company. There is no harmony more wonderful than the one which springs from obeying the Law inviting one to hesitate forever between supreme audacity and discretion, without entirely giving in either to the one or to the other.

When my hand grips the neck of his flask swollen with milk, he closes his eyes, like pigeons that one suffocates.

For a long time after having drawn near him, I avoided touching myself, for fear of erasing his trace.

UMBERTO SABA (1883-1957)

The author of several books of poetry, the major Italian poet Umberto Saba considered his first novel, *Ernesto,* written at the age of seventy, as "the finest thing I have ever written in prose." Nevertheless he was reluctant to publish it. In fact, the novel was never finished and was published as is after Saba's death in 1957. It is the story of a sixteen year old boy's first erotic experience. Ernesto, the protagonist, meets a docker and responds to his advances with naive curiosity, finding pleasure in the older man's embraces. In a letter to his friend Bruno Pincherle (June, 1953), Saba explained that his hero has no inhibitions, that he is not a "decadent" but on the contrary a "primitive." Later on Ernesto becomes involved with an affectionate, maternal prostitute who reminds him of the wet-nurse he had had as an infant. The novel ends at the moment when Ernesto meets a fifteen-year-old violinist with whom he falls truly in love. We shall never know the outcome of this idyllic relationship. In the episode given below Ernesto, who is employed in the office of a flour mill, meets the docker after work and begins conversing with him. As the French poet Claudel says, "Preserve us from the sin we commit when taken by surprise."

From ERNESTO

"We're alone today," said the man seeing Ernesto was not speaking. He had taken a needle and some heavy thread out of the pouch he always carried, but instead of setting to work he waited for the boy to say something that would recall their conversation on the previous day and encourage him. But Ernesto remained silent. He had moved close to the man (perhaps closer than usual) and stood there with lowered head toying with a label affixed to the opening of a sack; so that, after a while, the label came loose in his hand. He tore it into tiny pieces then, which he threw away.

"Alone," he at last said, "alone for an hour."

"It's many things can be done in an hour," replied the man quickly.

"Then you...what is it you would like to do?"

"Don't you remember what we spoke about yesterday? What you promised me, almost? Don't you know what I would be so pleased to do to you?"

"Fuck me in the ass," said Ernesto with tranquil innocence.

The man was somewhat taken aback by the crudeness of the expression and above all surprised to hear it on the lips of a boy like Ernesto. Taken aback, and afraid too. He thought that the little rogue, as he called him, had repented of his semi-acquiescence and was now taunting him. Worse yet: he may have spoken to others about it, perhaps even (this was what he feared the most) to his mother. But that was not it at all. For with that clear, precise utterance the boy had unknowingly revealed what was to become years later, after many experiences and much sorrow, his "style": his manner of going straight to the heart of things, to the incandescent core of life, stepping over resistances and inhibitions, neither resorting to paraphrases nor to futile circumlocutions. It would not matter to him whether the things were deemed base and vulgar (or even prohibited) or considered "sublime"—he would situate them all, as Nature does, on the same plane. But certainly at the moment none of this occurred to him. The phrase the journeyman had blushed at had sprung to his lips because the situation had suggested it. He had wanted to please and give pleasure to his friend, as well as to experience a new sensation, drawn to it precisely because of its novelty and strangeness. At the same time he had felt afraid of getting hurt. There had been no other considerations in his mind then.

"Is it that good?" he asked.

"The best thing in the world."

"For you maybe. But for me..."

"For you too. Have you never done it with a man?"

"Me? Never. And you, have you with other boys?"

"Lots. Nobody as good-looking as you though." The man raised his hand to stroke Ernesto, but the boy averted his face, avoiding the touch.

"And the others, what did they say?"

"Nothing. They said nothing. They were happy. Some of them even asked me."

Ernesto looked down and saw that the man was aroused.

"Let me see it."

"Sure," replied the man. He was about to give them both satisfaction when the lad stopped him.

"I'll take it out," he said, "all right?"

"Sure then, go ahead."

Intent on carrying out this caprice, Ernesto got so tangled up in the man's colored shirt that he had to be helped.

"It's big," he said, his voice wavering between fear and amusement; "it's twice as big as mine."

"That's because you're young. Wait 'till you're my age, why then..."

The boy reached out, but the man stopped him.

"Not with the hand, you'll make it come."

"Isn't that what you want?"

"Aye, but not in the hand."

"Oh." Ernesto withdrew his hand, as though from something forbidden. The man moved closer.

"I'm afraid," said Ernesto.

"Of what? Don't you know I'm your friend?"

"Yes, I believe you; otherwise...but I'm afraid you'll hurt me anyway."

"Me, hurt you? I know how to treat a lad who's never done it before—you especially."

"You won't put it all in, will you?" said Ernesto.

"Are you daft?" The man smiled. "Hardly anything, just the tip."

"Yes, that's what you say now, but afterwards, when you start to enjoy it..."

"He's an adorable lad," thought the man. And once

Elisar von Kupffer, *Innocent Games*. Sanctuarium Artis Elisarion, Minusio, near Locarno.

again he swore to himself that he would not hurt him at all, even if it meant feeling less pleasure.

"I'd rather pull out than hurt you," he said, trying to give him a kiss, which Ernesto ducked as he had turned from the man's touch a little earlier.

"Take down your britches," begged the man, "or time'll be up and we shan't have finished."

"You want to finish, is that it." laughed Ernesto.

"That's what you want too, isn't it what we're here for?" And hurriedly he added in a whisper: "Provided you won't be offended after."

"I already told you... But on one condition."

"What is that?" The man didn't grasp what Ernesto was alluding to. Had he not been poor and the boy (so he thought) rich, he would have thought it was a request for money, which would have spoiled everything.

"I want you to swear that when I say enough, you will stop—the moment I say it."

"Sure, you won't need to say it; but I'll promise anyway."

"Promising's not enough, you must swear it."

The man laughed.

"What do you want me to swear on."

"Don't laugh. You must give me your word of honor." The boy extended his hand, as though to seal a bargain. The man shook his hand.

"Whenever you say it, and the very moment," he confirmed. Ernesto looked reassured.

"All right then if you really want to..."

"God bless you! Now, take off your jacket (the man had already taken off his) and drop your britches."

"You too," said Ernesto.

"Aye, sure."

Then Ernesto had another idea.

"I'll take off yours, and you take off mine. All right?"

The man assented.

"And now," said Ernesto, "where do you want us to do it?"

"There." The man nodded towards a low pile of sacks on top of which was the one whose label Ernesto in his turmoil had detached and torn up. They were medium-sized sacks, filled with double-O flour, the whitest and finest quality there was (because of the price, few bakeries asked for it). Stacked beneath an archway in a remote corner of the warehouse, where no one—except for the

eye of God—could chance upon them, the pile of sacks seemed made for the purpose.

Ernesto did as his friend asked; he bent over, supporting himself against the sacks. The man came up behind him and slowly lifted the boy's shirt which, either through unconscious coquetery or more probably in the confusion of feelings sweeping through him, Ernesto had forgotten to pull up. (It was the last defense, the last bulwark between himself and the irreparable). Both the man and the boy were trembling.

The man stroked the buttocks he had just laid bare, but only for a moment, fearing that the boy would lose patience. For the same reason he refrained from speaking certain tender words that rose in his heart, words full of gratitude and admiration, which Ernesto would not have been able to appreciate and might not even have heard. Instead he muttered something brutal, as though in reply to what the boy had uttered a few minutes earlier that had made him almost blush.

Ernesto did not answer. Absorbed as he was by curiosity and fear he could not have spoken, even had he wanted to. Besides, what was there to say? He heard the man asking him to change his position a little, and he acquiesced as though it had been an order. The thought, "I am lost," flashed through his mind; yet he felt no regret, no urge to turn back. Then he experienced a strange, indefinable sensation of warmth (not without softness at first), as the man found him and established contact. Neither of them spoke, except for a soft cry of "angel" which the man uttered just before coming and a preventive "Ow" from the boy when it seemed to him that the man was pushing too hard. But the latter kept to his word; he did not hurt (and tried not to hurt) the boy. For that matter everything went faster and smoother than Ernesto had anticipated. He was about to stand up when the man asked him to stay still for another moment. "What does he want to do to me now?" thought the boy; but he relaxed when he saw the man pull a handkerchief out of his pocket. The man only wanted to wipe the boy (perhaps as a delicate attention, perhaps to rub out any trace of the act). Ernesto suddenly felt like a small child, lost and confused.

"You were good, good as fresh bread," said the man after they had both dressed and shaken the flour from their clothes.

Ernesto, albeit frowning, acknowledged the compliment.

"Did you enjoy it?" he asked.

"I was in sweet Heaven. But you enjoyed it too, confess."

"Not that much! A little at first, but then it hurt. I even yelled."

"Yelled?"

"Didn't you hear me when I yelled 'Ow?' But you, why did you call me angel?"

"Was I to call you something else?"

"Angels don't do those kinds of things," declared Ernesto almost severely. "They don't even have bodies."

"We came together," said the man.

"How do you know that?"

"I felt it when I came; you always feel those things. And look there."

"Where?" Ernesto was suddenly apprehensive.

The man pointed to a stain on one of the double-O sacks, precisely the one whose tag the boy had torn off and against which he had rested.

Ernesto stared, and felt ill.

"You can see it," he said. "The sack should be turned over. Don't you want us to turn it?"

"Who would ever guess what it is? But if you really want me to, I'll turn it over later."

Then silence fell between them, a feeling of embarrassment which lasted a rather long time. The man had become thoughtful, almost somber.

"What are you thinking about?" asked Ernesto, a little impressed.

"I'm thinking I must be telling you something, which I'd rather not be saying. Maybe I should have told you before. You won't speak of this to anyone?"

"Who should I be speaking to about it? I'm not stupid. I know very well what things one can say and what things one can't."

The man looked relieved. But the worst still remained to be said.

"You know that these things are dangerous. People don't understand them, and...you can even go to jail for them."

"I know that too," said Ernesto triumphantly. "I read about two fellows like us in the newspaper: a man and a boy. They were caught in a bathing cabin. The article was called, "The Ill-Effects of Bathing." The boy copped four months and the man six. "Ough!" concluded Ernesto, who knows why skipping over the r.

"When that happens," the man added mockingly, "there's nothing for it but to jump into the sea, for the shame of it." But immediately he repented tormenting the lad thus.

"Don't think about it anymore," said the latter to console him. "You just musn't get caught like those two idiots. It was the bathing attendant, who thought they had gone, he caught them when he opened the door; and instead of keeping mum, the fool shouted it out all over the place. Now me, without you even noticing, I made sure you had put the lock on the door."

Ernesto smiled. The man remained thoughtful, almost sad.

"It's something else I'm thinking about," said Ernesto.

"What is that?" asked the man anxiously.

"I'm thinking how can I look my mother in the face tonight?"

KURT MALAPARTE
(1898-1957)

Of Austrian descent but raised by an Italian peasant family, Malaparte signed up in the French army in 1914. In 1922 he joined the Fascist party, but resigned in 1931 and moved to Paris. In 1933 he was placed under house arrest in the Lipari Islands off Sicily. During World War II he was sent to the Russian front as a war correspondent—and was then expelled for having written anti-German articles. Malaparte's abhorrence of war is a central theme in his novels, *Blood* (1937), *Kaputt* (1944) and *The Skin* (1949), from which the following excerpt is taken. Malaparte gives a cynical description of the strange atmosphere under a fascist regime with its insidious homosexuality and ostentatious display of virility. For this author, who has admitted that he has an "instinctive aversion for homosexuality," perversion is the result of political thuggery and tyranny.

Numa Gillet, *Solitudo Refugium*. François Duchêne Collection, Paris.

From THE SKIN

...Gerda lived in the West End. The streets were dark and deserted. As they approached the West End suburbs the air became misty, the green foliage of the lime-trees floated in the starry sky, the thousand remote sounds of the city dissolved in the blue haze like a drop of coloured liquid in a glass of water, and all the while the transparent veil of mist had a light sonorous hue.

Gerda von H—— was wearing a long sky-blue gown, which fell about her bare feet in soft folds, like the grooves in a Doric pillar. With her fair hair swept up above her temples and gathered into a mass on top of her head she looked like Nausicaa emerging from the sea. There was something of the sea, indeed, in her slow, sweeping gestures, in the way she raised her knees as she walked along the sea-shore. Gerda von H—— had remained faithful to the ideal of classical beauty which was in vogue in Germany about 1930. She had been a pupil of Curtius at Bonn, had for some time frequented the little world of intellectuals and aesthetes who were initiated in the cult of Stephan George, and seemed to live and move and have her being in the conventional setting of Stephan George's poetry, in which the neo-classical architectural designs of Winckelmann and the scenes in the second part of *Faust* provide a background for the spectral Muses of Hölderling and Rainer Maria Rilke. Her house, to use her old-fashioned phrase, was a temple, in which she received her guests while reclining at her ease on a pile of cushions, in the centre of a group of young women stretched out on thick carpets—*comme un bétail pensif sur le sable couché.* A brilliant smile played about her sad lips. Her eyes were round, their gaze warm and steady.

Gerda von H—— took Lanza by the hand, and walking lightly on her bare feet led the way into the drawing-room, in which were assembled five girls. Tall and ephebic of frame, they had lean faces and calm, steady, lustrous blue eyes, which shone forth from under deep brows. Their lips were of a rich ruby colour, slightly modified by that faint green tinge which is sometimes discernible in the lips of blonde women. Their ears were small and pink, like stems of coral. But there was something indeterminate about their faces, that vague, nebulous quality which is apparent in a face reflected in a mirror, when the contrast with the icy brilliance of the crystal makes the image dull and remote. They wore low-necked evening gowns, which revealed their shoulders—sun-tanned, rounded, smooth, the colour of honey. They had somewhat thick ankles, as German girls do, but their legs were well-shaped, long and supple, with rather prominent, bony knees. She who appeared the boldest, and looked like Diana among the huntresses, said that they had spent the day boating on the Wannsee, and that they were still drunk from the sun. She laughed, throwing back her head, and the movement revealed her lean throat and her ample, muscular Amazonian bosom.

The champagne was tepid, and as the windows had been closed for the black-out the atmosphere of the room was humid and oppressive, and full of the acrid smell of tobacco. The young women and the two Italian diplomats talked of Rome, Venice and Paris. The girl who looked like Diana had returned from Paris a few days before, and the tone in which she spoke of the French gave Lanza and Ridomi a disagreeable shock: it was a tone in which affection was mingled with bitterness, and jealousy with spite. It seemed that she was in love with France and at the same time hated it. Here was the love of a woman who had been betrayed. "The French hate us," said Gerda von H——. "Why do they hate us?" As Lanza and Ridomi conversed their minds were far away, obsessed by the thought which was troubling them, and every so often they exchanged anxious glances. A dozen times already Lanza had been on the point of revealing to Gerda and her friends the reason for their perturbation, but each time an obscure sense of foreboding restrained him. Meanwhile time was passing, and the uncertainty in the minds of the two Italian diplomats was turning to anguish.

Lanza was already on the point of getting up, of drawing Gerda aside, of telling her the truth, of asking her for advice and help. He was already getting up, he was already going over to her, when she spread out her arms, rested a hand on his shoulder and said: "Would you like to dance?"

"Yes, yes!" cried the other girls, and one of them switched on the radio.

"It's late," said Ridomi. "All the stations have closed down."

But the girl was turning the knob, and in due course she picked up Rome. The sound of a dance orchestra filled the room. "*A whole night with you,*" sang a woman's voice.

"Wunderbar!" said Gerda. "Rome is still singing."

"It'll sing a lot more soon," said Ridomi.

"Why?" asked Gerda.

"Because..." answered Ridomi, but he said no more, because of that obscure sense of foreboding which, in his mind and in that of his companion, was gradually ripening into fear.

To the ears of the two Italian diplomats the voice sounded faint and very remote, like a thin mist of sound rolling through the night; and the two friends felt their hearts trembling within them, assailed as they were by the fear that at any moment that tender voice would become raucous and harsh, and proclaim the dread news.

"Dance with my friend," said Gerda, pushing Lanza into the arms of the girl who looked like Diana, and with innocent grace pulling the fat, slow-moving Ridomi towards her by the hand. The other four girls had split up into couples and were dancing languidly, each pressing her bosom and hips close against her partner's. Lanza's partner clung tightly to him and gazed into his eyes, smiling and constantly fluttering her eyelids. Lanza felt the vigorous beating of her heart close to his own, felt the motion of her flanks against his, felt her stomach pressing hard against his stomach. But his thoughts were else-

Otto Meyer-Amden, *Dancer*. 1915 (?).

where, and in his mind was a confused picture of Mussolini, the King and Badoglio indulging in a free fight, getting mixed up together, disengaging themselves, rolling on the floor, and trying to handcuff one another, like acrobats when they engage in a rough-and-tumble on a mat.

Suddenly the music stopped, the tender feminine voice was silent, and a hoarse, breathless voice announced: "Before we read the proclamation by Marshal Badoglio here is a summary of the latest news. At about six o'clock this evening the Head of the Government, Mussolini, was arrested by order of His Majesty the King. The new Head of the Government, Marshal Badoglio, has addressed the following proclamation to the Italian people..."

At the sound of that voice, of those words, Lanza's partner broke away from him, repelling him with a shove that seemed to Lanza like a blow of the fist. Each of the other couples disengaged themselves from their embrace, and before the eyes of the two bewildered Italian diplomats there occurred the most extraordinary thing imaginable. The movements, the postures, the smiles, the voices, the expressions of the girls gradually underwent an amazing metamorphosis. Their blue eyes darkened, the smiles died away on their lips, which had suddenly become pale and thin, their voices grew deep and harsh, their movements, which a moment before had been languid, became abrupt, their arms, just now plump and soft, grew hard and wooden, as when the branch of a tree is torn off by the wind, and, with the gradual drying up of its vital sap, loses its bright greenness, the sheen on its bark, that suppleness which is characteristic of trees, so that it becomes hard and rough. But the change which comes over a branch of a tree gradually was wrought in those girls instantaneously. As Lanza and Ridomi stood face to face with the young women they were conscious of the same bewilderment and terror as had seized Apollo when Daphne was transformed from a young girl into a laurel before his eyes. In the space of a few seconds those fair-haired, gentle girls turned into men. They *were* men.

"Ach, so!" said the one who a moment before had looked like Diana, in a harsh voice, staring at the two Italian diplomats with a menacing expression. "Ach, so! Do you think you can get away with it? Do you think the Führer will let you arrest Mussolini without bashing your heads in?" And turning to his companions, "Let's go to the camp at once," he went on. "I've no doubt our squadron has already received orders to start. In a few hours we shall be bombing Rome."

"Jawohl, mein Hauptmann," answered the four Air Force officers, clicking their heels loudly. The captain and his companions bowed silently to Gerda von H——, and without deigning to look at the two stupefied Italians departed in great haste with virile strides, making the floor ring with the sound of their heels.

CHARLES HENRI FORD
(1913-   )
AND PARKER TYLER
(1907-1974)

Gustave Moreau, *The Angels of Sodom* (detail). Musée Gustave Moreau, Paris.

The Young and the Evil, that classic of American avant-garde erotica, was published in Paris in 1933. A second edition appeared in the notorious green-jacketed Traveler's Companion series (Olympia Press, Paris) in 1960. Copies are almost unobtainable today. A lyrical novel throbbing with the rhythms of New York in the early 30s, it was written in collaboration by Charles Henri Ford, whose Surrealist inspired poems are a minor but durable feature of the prewar literary landscape in America, and Parker Tyler, who is best known as a film critic (he is the author of, among other books, *Homosexuality in the Movies*, New York, 1972). In *The Garden of Disorder and Other Poems* by Charles Henri Ford there is a sonnet entitled "Young Boy" which is dedicated to Parker Tyler. Its last four lines read:

> I do not call your innocence perverse
> Yet vastly fear to think of you in bloom,
> nor doubt the poison that is mine to pick
> is love enough in but one universe.

From THE YOUNG AND THE EVIL

It was a long ride on the subway to 155th Street but they hadn't the money for a taxi. Frederick was not in drag nor was Julian who wore striped pants with a coat that didn't match, his black shirt with an orange tie and a slouch cap. Frederick was not made up more than usual except his eyebrows were plucked thinner but Julian had on his face the darkest powder he could borrow, blue eyeshadow and several applications of black mascara; on his lips was orange-red rouge and a brown pencil had been on his eyebrows showing them longer. He wanted to be considered in costume and so get in for a dollar less. When they arrived at the Casino Palace policemen and others were about the entrance. They passed under the canopy and went in.

I hope we don't get arrested tonight Julian said. Your judgement of my trousers is true but your moral wrong he thought, getting his ticket cheaper than Frederick who said I wonder if money will ever be as unimportant as I think it is.

They had to wind up a long gold-banisterd staircase above which a terrible racket was taking serene form.

There is only one sex—the female said Frederick.

Now they are doing without beauty said Julian when he saw the first creation. It was all black lace but only stockings and step-ins and brassiere and gloves. Fanny Ward is supposed to come.

Yes my dear Frederick said. She's so young she has to learn to play the piano all over again!

The ball was too large to be rushed at without being swallowed. The negro orchestra on the stage at one end was heard at the other end with the aid of a reproducer. On both sides of the wall a balcony spread laden with people in boxes at tables. Underneath were more tables and more people. The dancefloor was a scene whose celestial flavor and cerulean coloring no angelic painter or nectarish poet has ever conceived.

This place is neither cozy nor safe Frederick said. It's lit up like high mass.

One was with blonde hair and a brown face and yellow feathers and another was with black hair and a tan face and white feathers. Some had on tango things and some blue feathers. One wore pink organdie and a black picture

hat. There were many colors including a beard in a red ballet skirt and number 9 shoes and some others who, conjuring with their golden-tipped wands against the voices of their mutually male consciences, yet remained more serious than powdered—they seemed to be always on their way to far off mistresses.

They found Tony and Vincent at a table with K-Y and Woodward. Vincent spoke with the most wonderful whisky voice Frederick! Julian! Tony was South American. He had on a black satin that Vincent had made him, fitted to the knee and then flaring, long pearls and pearl drops.

Tony dear aren't you overdressed! asked Frederick.

I suppose *you* would say overdressed Tony answered but I'm not Sheba surrounded by food and Mary what you look like in that outfit he said to Julian. Look at her!

Vincent had on a white satin blouse and black breeches. Dear I'm master of ceremonies tonight and you should have come in drag you'd have gotten a prize. He had large eyes with a sex-life all their own and claimed to be the hardest boiled queen on Broadway. Frederick he said you look like something Lindbergh dropped on the way across. Dry yourself Bella!

When are you going to remove your mask and reveal a row of chamber pots Frederick replied in his resonant voice which could also be nasal at the wrong time.

The music was playing wavy and sad and so true.

Let's dance Julian said to K-Y and they went on the floor.

You've mastered the art of makeup she said.

I must have he said when I did things that were pleasant surprises, not wicked because they were unusual and necessary.

Dancing drew the blood faster through their bodies. Drink drusic drowned them. A lush annamaywong lavender-skinned negro gazed at him.

They are looking this way so hard said Julian their eyes go through us and *button* in the back.

A boy with an innocent exterior said to him over his shoulder how is your dog bite?

My dog bite Julian said sweetly. Your mouth hasn't been that close to my leg all evening.

This is dreadully amusing said K-Y.

One may divide people into thrills and frills I think Julian said. What he was really thinking was that it must be the white-pink flesh like some Italians with the lippink scarlet as heliotrope and the black of hair and the eyebrows with the miraculous slant bespeaking benevolence. He knew the precise youth of it there and the vulgarity raw enough to be exhilarating. He saw another as they danced by a table and the sharkmouth of a hope tore his womb, carrying a piece of it away.

Someone shouted Bessie if you don't believe Heliogabalus died by having his head stuck in a toilet bowl you NEEDN'T COME AROUND any more.

They all ought to be in a scrap-book Julian said. Would blood, paste and print make them stick together?

No said K-Y. There is no holding people back. It will go on until it stops and then there will be something else.

JULIAN GREEN (1900-)

Luc Albert Moreau, Drawing. François Duchêne Collection, Paris.

Julian Green, an American writer who lives in France, says that he landed in the wrong century—like someone who gets out of an elevator on the wrong floor. For him, true love must transcend the senses—only then will it be immortal—for pleasure kills it. In his novels he describes the anguish of temptation as his heroes struggle feverishly to overcome their sexual nature. In *Youth*, an autobiographical narrative published in French in 1974, Green recalls how as a young man he had searched for a love relationship founded on something other than desire... and how he failed and what remorse he felt upon succumbing to "the hunger for beauty in the gluttonous enjoyment of the body." Yielding to temptation, becoming a sinner in his own eyes, Green nevertheless sees no moral difference between a man who "chases after boys" and a married man who chases after other women. Lust leads to atheism and to perdition, Green believes, but only those who want to lose themselves are actually lost.

From YOUTH

After several additional minutes of indecision, I started down the porch steps and began moving towards the river. Without knowing it, I took the *correct* direction, the one which leads straight to obscure regions from which a return is difficult. Someone was waiting for me, but placed there by whom? Starting from this moment, liberty, judgment, composure were confiscated from me until another time. I became a toy in the hands of power, habit was ready to function as always, like a mechanism of infallible precision. Each night would see me wandering, seemingly by chance, but already following the most favorable itineraries to places that a less observant person would have presumed deserted. That was my destiny. For how long?

Returning home that night I felt a strange and almost indescribable joy. Indeed, it seemed to me as if I had become my entire body, if these words mean anything. An extraordinary sense of well-being dissipated my customary worries: all the questions I ceaselessly asked myself about my future and my work. Sliding between my sheets I found myself laughing alone, as if the simple fact of being alive was sufficient to fill me with a sort of animal bliss. I kept reliving the scene which took place not too far from the Pont d'Iena, surprisingly without horror.

The horror came later. I will not abandon myself to a description of the stranger who approached me in the rain and the strange illumination of the street lamps. His face should have frightened me. With an almost hypnotic ugliness, he exuded the most monstrous lure of vice, and I could only acquiesce like the exhausted prey subdued by a hunter....

I made strong resolutions, but the same night—and it appeared comic to me, for the irony of the situation didn't escape me—a little before nine o'clock, I was outside. I can't remember if it was raining or clear, but I was attracted by a lighted window at the bottom of a building near Avenue Kleber where there was a bank. Bars protected the large square openings that overlooked a gymnasium, inside which could be glimpsed almost nude young boys learning how to box. I passed slowly by the window, then returned, hesitating to linger, for fear that someone would close the window which was filling my eyes, heart and imagination with a spectacle that burned up my blood. But why (this question often tormented me) this inexplicable desire to possess? Isn't it enough to experience beauty with the eyes alone? Where did this brutal pang of hunger come from? And what did possession mean? That which we possessed was immediately taken away from us. I suffered while coveting those inaccessible young boys. It wasn't sufficient to have subdued the yearning from the night before. The dreadful hunger clutched again like a disease gnawing at my insides, and so strongly was my attention directed at the window that I didn't immediately perceive the presence of another spectator who was brushing his shoulder against mine. A low voice murmured something into my ear with a foreign accent. I turned my head and walked on a few steps, but I was no longer alone.

He was Russian, having escaped from his country during the revolution. Reduced to earning a modest salary, he took me to his room on the fifth floor of a building near Les Galeries Lafayette. In the midst of a decor whose banality was almost sordid, I found the panicky joy of the night before—but it was destructive. Henceforth I was lost. I understood it this time walking down the narrow stairway which smelt of misery. Against my instinct, I could do nothing but obey. Henceforth, I would be the one who wanders and searches. I wasn't lost but I was losing myself, and I knew it but forgot because I wished to forget....

If my nights were licentious, my mornings remained studious and my life organized itself into a framework which didn't alter until the awesome events of 1939. Every night at eight-thirty I had a rendezvous with the devil. I knew it and yet didn't know it. I mean by that, if I had known it to the very marrow of my bones, I would have trembled to leave my house; consequently, I didn't know it, but I knew it all the same. He hid behind banality. A young man in the street asked me the time. What is more ordinary? The small talk that ensued didn't seem suspect. What remains of my metaphysical night-mares? Everything entered its way into the order of things by the force of events and their sterile magic. In general, the prince of this world had only a pitiful hotel-room to offer; and if he didn't change the decor, he would at least make it disappear in the delirium of passion. A bed in an isolated and concealed location—was that not enough? Finally, it is possible that disgust was taking hold of me, a subtle and pervasive nausea, but that was my own business. The fault was done and the tempter was far away, abandoning his victim to pangs of conscience. What troubled me the most, whatever my repulsions could have been, was the certitude that the following night I would start to run again.

GORE VIDAL (1925-   )

When it was published in 1948, *The City and the Pillar,* which had been written two years earlier by twenty-one year old Gore Vidal, became a best-seller and created a furore. *The New York Times* refused to carry advertising for it. Kinsey, the author of the notorious *Report,* and André Gide, the famed French novelist, publicly congratulated Vidal for his bold and courageous portrayal of a homosexual relationship (Gide even sent Vidal a copy of *Corydon*). Jim, the novel's protagonist, has never forgotten his first sexual encounter with his boyhood friend, Bob. But several years later Bob, who had gotten married and had become a father, reacts with outrage when Jim wants to repeat the experience. Jim's desire eventually turns into homocidal fury.

Pierre Yves Trémois, *Narcissus* (1955). The artist's collection, Paris.

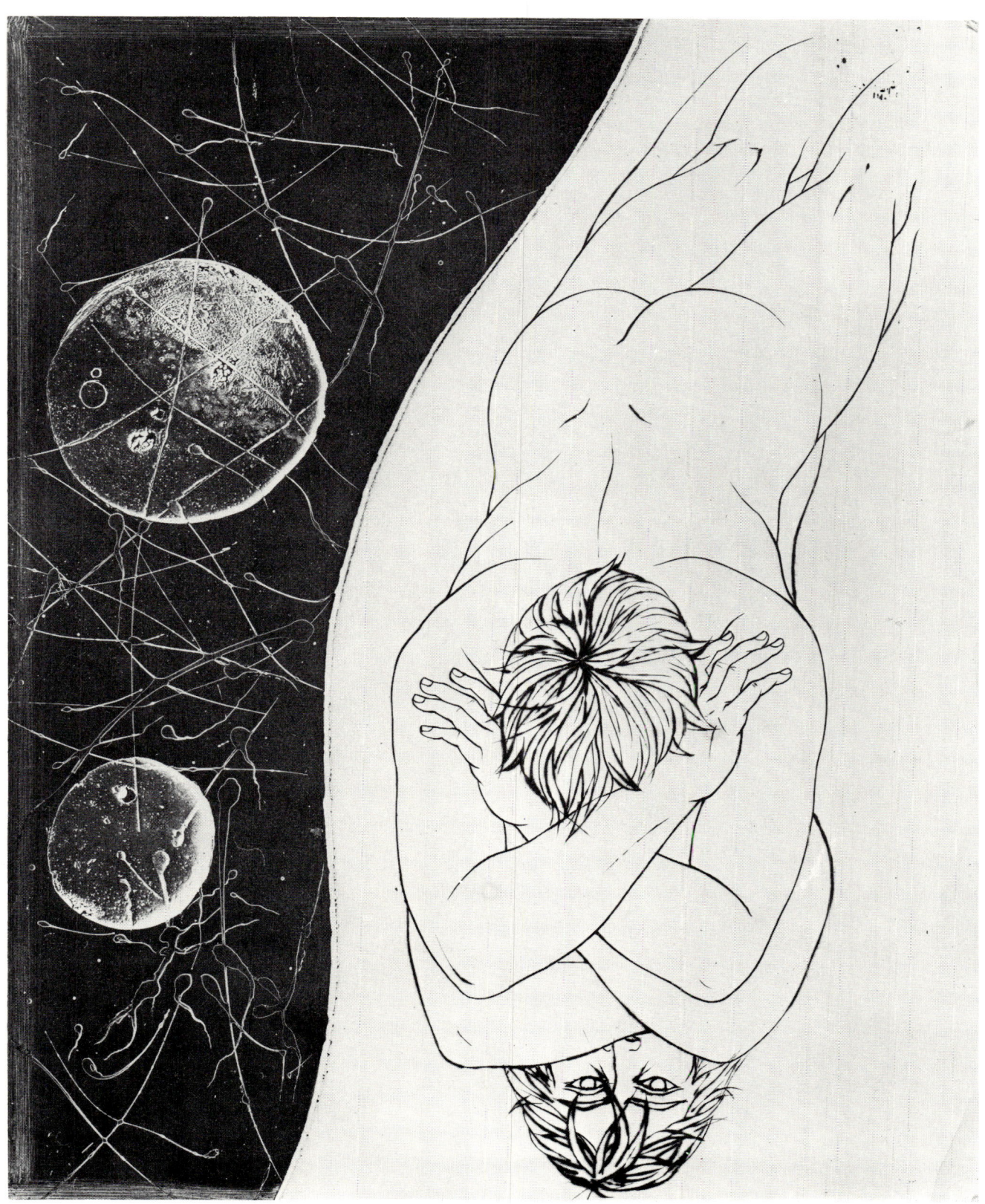

From THE CITY AND THE PILLAR

They drank together beneath the harsh white light of an electric bulb. The room was hot and they both took their shirts off. Jim was pleased that Bob's body had not changed. It was still muscular and strong and his skin was white and smooth, not freckled as is the skin of most people with dark red hair.

Finally, Jim began to talk of what was in his mind, had been in his mind for nine years. "You remember the cabin?" he said.

"The one down by the river? Sure."

"We had a lot of fun down there, didn't we?"

"I'll say. That pond was wonderful for swimming in."

"You remember the last time we went down there?"

"The last time? ... No, I don't think I do."

Could he have forgotten? Jim was panicky for a moment. No, he couldn't have forgotten. "You must remember. It was the weekend before you went North. After you'd graduated from school."

Bob nodded then. "Yes, I do remember now." He paused and frowned as he recalled. "We ... we fooled around quite a bit, didn't we?"

Yes, he remembered. Now it was coming. "I guess we did," said Jim. "It was a lot of fun."

Bob chuckled. "Kids always do that, I guess. They always do that together; though it's funny I never had done it with anybody until that time."

"Neither had I," said Jim.

"I guess we were just a couple of little queers at heart," said Bob, grinning.

"Did ... you ever do ... that again, with anybody else?"

"Any other fellow? Hell, no. Did you?"

"N ... no."

"Let's have another drink."

Soon they were both very drunk. Bob said that he was sleepy, that drinking made him sleepy. Jim said that he was too and that he had better go home but Bob insisted that he spend the night with him. They undressed, throwing their clothes on the floor. Bob stretched and Jim admired his long muscles. They got into bed and Bob turned out the light.

No longer thinking, but obeying his instincts, Jim reached out in the dark and took Bob in his arms.

"Hey! What's going on?" Bob sat up in bed. Jim said nothing, holding him still. Bob pushed him away. "What're you doing, anyway?" Then, when Jim didn't answer, he understood. "You're a queer," he said, "you're nothing but a damned queer! Go on and get your ass out of here!"

The fury came to Jim, took the place of love. He threw himself at Bob; he caught him by the shoulders. They rolled in the darkness, both drunk but both aware. It was like a nightmare. Jim was the stronger; his rage was the greater. They fell off the bed on to the floor. They fought silently.

Finally Jim had Bob by the throat; methodically he began to choke him. Bob twisted desperately on the floor but Jim was too strong. A long time passed before Jim released the now unconscious Bob and realized what had happened to all his dreaming. Exhausted, breathing painfully, Jim stood up and turned on the light. Bob lay quietly on the floor. There were red marks on his body and his face was discoloured. Tenderly Jim picked him up and put him on the bed. He was very heavy. Jim arranged his arms and legs and put a pillow under his head. He kissed him.

Then, calmly, Jim got dressed. He knew what he had done. Death was unimportant but the end of his love was important. He no longer cared what might happen to him. With Bob gone there was nothing left. The dream was shattered, lay white and bruised beneath the cold electric light. He left the room, leaving the light on. He went out of the hotel. He walked for a long time. Then he came to a bar and he went in. He would drink until the dream was completely over.

TENNESSEE WILLIAMS (1914-   )

Tennessee Williams's plays are set in the Deep South in an atmosphere of festering sexuality barely contained by fierce—and slightly rank—puritan prejudices. In a sense the characters—overripe women wracked by sexual longing and in love with brutal super-virile men, or misunderstood youths anguished by their deviant inclinations—are projections of their author's teeming psyche. "I believe that my work has always been a kind of psychotherapy for me," writes Williams. On the other hand, in his *Memoirs* published in 1975, the southern dramatist serenely relates the episodes of his tumultuous love life, the pleasure of "cruising" and picking up savagely good-looking young vagrants in tight jeans and leather jackets. Williams has described himself as "a puritan in appearance but a veritable little sexual demon underneath." He hopes to end his days in the company of a young boy with whom he would have both a spiritual and a physical rapport—for in Williams's eyes homosexuality is innocent.

Anonymous, Illustration for *Querelle de Brest* (1948) by Jean Genet. Attributed to Jean Cocteau. Private collection.

From MEMOIRS

I did know some very obvious types in New Orleans, however, when I first "came out." There was, for instance, one whom I'll call Antoine who walked about the streets of the French Quarter with a tiny cut-glass bottle of smelling salts in liquid form and at the approach of a woman or girl, would stop and lean against a wall with the stricken whisper of *"Poisson"*—and sniff his counteractive vial until the lady had passed; and even then he would affect a somewhat shattered condition...

I found him hilarious, but Antoine had a serious and gifted side to him, like most of our kind. He was not a brilliant painter but he had a distinctive and highly effective flair which later made him a successful designer in New York.

I remember an evening when Antoine, who had a charmingly decorated apartment on Toulouse, presented his production of *Four Saints in Three Acts*—the cast all homosexuals—and they did not camp it but presented it with true style and it was the best evening of Stein I've yet experienced.

I also remember, when I returned to New Orleans after my first exposure to the more discreetly organized gay world of New York, proselytizing my "gay" friends in the Quarter to conduct themselves in a fashion that was not just a travesty of the other sex. I told them, those who would listen, that that type of behavior simply made them distasteful, sexually, to anyone interested in sex ... and that it was "dated," as well.

Of course, "swish" and "camp" are products of self-mockery, imposed upon homosexuals by our society. The obnoxious forms of it will rapidly disappear as Gay Lib begins to succeed in its serious crusade to assert, for its genuinely misunderstood and persecuted minority, a free position in society which will permit them to respect themselves, at least to the extent that, individually, they deserve respect—and I think that degree is likely to be much higher than commonly supposed.

GEORGES EEKHOUD (1854-1927)

An orphan, born in Antwerp and raised by a strict, narrow-minded tutor in a stuffily bourgeois atmosphere, Georges Eekhoud was determined to be the bard of the poor, of rugged passions and of simple unadorned beauty. The hero of his novel *L'autre vue,* [*The Other View*] written in 1904, is particularly fond of dockers, marauders and guttersnipes. Though he is "tainted with perversion, there is no perversity in him"; nevertheless he is not understood by his community and is finally driven to commit suicide—for which he prepares by picking out an appealing little gravedigger, a cheery, saucy, down-to-earth (no pun intended) young lad. But after the burial the boy is suddenly tormented by what he thinks is a voice calling him. He returns to the cemetary and opens the grave—which gets him three months in jail. Pure and simple souls, so the moral of the story goes, are ever the victims of the tyranny of the bourgeoisie.

From THE OTHER VIEW

Many of them last but a short while, a single season of beauty. Then they pass like a flower or a rare insect. Precocious, they mature too soon. Nothing is more intensive than the atmosphere in which they grow up: inevitably they fade prematurely. Their life is but a dawn, an adolescence. Fortunately for my supreme pleasures, they are as prolific as they are ephemeral, and they are soon replaced by their offspring.

The age I prefer them at? Towards the age of conscription and even younger sometimes, when their apprenticing to a trade and their first escapades begin to give them a ruddy complexion; at the moment of their loss of innocence and of the appearance of fuzz on their lips and wild hairs on their chin; at the moment of puberty, so exasperating in lads raised according to the vagaries of chance and then taken in hand by unscrupulous initiators; at the climacteric moment their voice breaks and is at once arrogant, obstreporous, bragging of vice and cynicism, and full of wheedling awkwardnesses and naive hesitations; at the season they sow their wild oats, abandoning themselves with utter license to every postulate of their outright, pilfering, squabbling, pleasure-loving sparrow's nature.

Yes, I love you, all you urchins, wretches, dirty little devils, at whom the people of my class make a show of holding their noses, and at whom gentlemen cannot make disgusted enough looking faces—although their ladies ogle them on the sly perhaps. Yes, I find you closer to nature, more honest, freer, more generous, handsomer and pluckier. Ah, I am terribly weary of the falseness, the prudishness, the underhandedness of the grand folk. A fig for their art and their literature, which are as full of lies as their religion, their honor and their morals! They speak and write too easily, those people; they are like machines: wind them up, and off they go—only they haven't any more soul than their gramophones do. And their implacable, sinister good manners! Flowery talkers and sophists, the whole lot of them! They have never spoken so much about God as since they've stopped believing in Him. Whereas you at least, my poor street traipsers; you show yourselves for what you are worth neither more nor less, without imposing on us. You are straightforward and refreshing, like plants, fountains and birds; Oh, my beloved ones, you are as fraternal as wolves!

And here I am forgetting myself so far as to tell them about an old Spanish play, the *Damned for Lack of Faith* by the monk Tellez, applying to their situation the story of the unbeliever who was saved because he possessed the grace of the elect. I went on a long time in that apologetic vein.

They did not always understand me, but they listened to me with good will, looking me in the eye so as to read my thoughts there rather than on my lips; and from the caressing tone of my voice they guessed my sentiments.

Out of this humus there appeared a delightful flower: a little urchin with as fine a figure as one could wish. The prettiest lad in the group, he was subtle and greedy, a petty thief turned god, forever on the prowl nibbling fruit and sweets snitched from some store front. How many times have I not told myself at the sight of the boy: "Look at him well, engrave his form and his style into your memory; you will doubtless never again see him in such a becoming pose. What a scamp he is with his great dark eyes, his prominent cheek-bones—such an appetizing morsel you want to bite into him—and so precocious and wide-awake that he is

Anonymous, *Bull-Fighter*. c. 1940. François Duchêne Collection, Paris.

worth ten thousand rich kids, though he often goes about in a pair of trousers so badly worn that you see half of both his thighs beneath the loose tatters. Mark his pretty, irregular, almost scornful little face wrinkled by a deep-throated laugh, which rings with the puerile yet profound mockery of the guttersnipe who has already appraised social misery and knows that the best course is to make light of it so as to resign oneself to its inevitability. And do not forget the way he shrugs his shoulders while pouting, or the fold at the small of his back, or the way his jacket, which is too short, lifts up above his belt and his tucked-in shirt when he stuffs his fists into the pockets of his pants. Or his constant whistling, or his prowling pug nose, or the yellow strap holding up his breeches which serves on occasion as a sling shot or a whip, or even a leash when he has made away with someone's dog."

Like Tourlamain he excells at picking pockets. He practices this art with real virtuosity; more than anything it is the thrill of the risk he seeks out. He selects his victims carefully. He would feel bad about robbing a poor person. On the other hand he gives not a second's thought to pilfering from tarts, or from matrons displaying their geegaws of yellow metal, or from portly burghers exhibiting clinking trinkets on their protuberant bellies. He has never been pinched.

Now and then, to fool the vigilant eyes of the law, he judges it prudent to take on an honest job. Thus he has been seen as a pageboy at one of the large cafés on the boulevard. A nimbler, more resourceful bellhop had never been known in the annals of café employees. His performance was so impressive that the manager decided to give him a contract at an unheard of rate for a brat of his age. But the little swallow was too attached to his life of change and truantry. There was no way of keeping him working. Zwolu had his own code of honor: he never pilfered from his occasional employers. Towards Christmas and the gift season he expended treasure troves of ingenuity and clownish charm hawking the latest thing, the two-penny toy of the day. All of the ambulating merchants wanted to hire him....

WILLIAM BURROUGHS
(1914-   )

William Burroughs is the grandson of the inventor of the Burroughs Adding Machine. After getting his B.A. at Harvard in 1936, he traveled widely and lived briefly in Vienna, Paris and in Cairo. In 1944 he met Jack Kerouac and Allen Ginsberg in New York. Although Burroughs never associated himself with the Beat movement, the Beats acknowledged him as one of their masters. In 1945 Burroughs married Joan Vollmer who belonged to the small group of drug-users gathered around Jack Kerouac. He moved to Mexico in 1949 with Joan and their two children. One evening (the story goes) Joan rested her head on a glass and challenged Burroughs to shoot it out from under her. Burroughs, who was an experienced marksman, took aim and pulled the trigger. The bullet hit Joan in the head. Jailed and released on bail, Burroughs then traveled to South America before returning to New York where he moved in with Allen Ginsberg. From 1954 to 1956 he lived in Tangiers, constantly high on drugs. "I never cleaned or dusted the room. Empty ampule boxes and garbage piled up to the ceiling.... I was only roused to action when the hour-glass of junk ran out." Realizing that he had reached "the end of the junk line," he volunteered to take the apomorphine treatment in London and was cured. Kerouac and Ginsberg encouraged him to work on the notes he had written while on junk in Tangiers: the result was *The Naked Lunch*, finished in a small hotel in the Latin Quarter in Paris. *The Naked Lunch* is an apocalyptic vision (not without humor) of the white man's civilization, which Burroughs considers a calamity for the planet. It is written in the tradition of the *Satyricon* and the Spanish picaresque novels combined with American television shows. As in his other books—*The Soft Machine, The Ticket That Exploded, The Wild Boys* and *Exterminator*—Burroughs presents his readers with a hallucinatory spectacle of youths, monsters and dirty old men. There are no women. Burroughs's work, as Philippe Mikriammos has pointed out, is "a long commentary on the condition of homosexuals."

From THE NAKED LUNCH
hassan's rumpus room

Gilt and red plush. Rococo bar backed by pink shell. The air is cloyed with a sweet evil substance like decayed honey. Men and women in evening dress sip pousse-cafés through alabaster tubes. A Near East Mugwump sits naked on a bar stool covered in pink silk. He licks warm honey from a crystal goblet with a long black tongue. His genitals are perfectly formed—circumcised cock, black shiny pubic hairs. His lips are thin and purple-blue like the lips of a penis, his eyes blank with insect calm. The Mugwump has no liver, maintaining himself exclusively on sweets. Mugwump push a slender blond youth to a couch and strip him expertly.

"Stand up and turn around," he orders in telepathic pictographs. He ties the boy's hands behind him with a red silk cord. "Tonight we make it all the way."

"No, no!" screams the boy.

"Yes. Yes."

Cocks ejaculate in silent "yes." Mugwump part silk curtains, reveal a teak wood gallows against lighted screen of red flint. Gallows is on a dais of Aztec mosaics.

The boy crumples to his knees with a long "OOOOOOOOH," shitting and pissing in terror. He feels the shit warm between his thighs. A great wave of hot blood swells his lip and throat. His body contracts into a foetal position and sperm spurts hot into his face.

Donald Friend, *Sailors* (detail). Ink drawing, 1966. Reinhard Hassert Collection, Paris.

Francis Bacon, *Study of a Nude* (1970). Central panel of a triptych. (Reproduced courtesy of Marlborough Fine Art Ltd., London.)

The Mugwump dips hot perfumed water from alabaster bowl, pensively washes the boy's ass and cock, drying him with a soft blue towel. A warm wind plays over the boy's body and the hairs float free. The Mugwump puts a hand under the boy's chest and pulls him to his feet. Holding him by both pinioned elbows, propels him up the steps and under the noose. He stands in front of the boy holding the noose in both hands.

The boy looks into Mugwumps eyes blank as obsidian mirrors, pools of black blood, glory holes in a toilet wall closing on the Last Erection.

An old garbage collector, face fine and yellow as Chinese ivory, blows The Blast on his dented brass horn, wakes the Spanish pimp with a hard-on. Whore staggers out through dust and shit and litter of dead kittens, carrying bales of aborted foetuses, broken condoms, bloody Kotex, shit wrapped in bright color comics.

A vast still harbor of iridescent water. Deserted gas well flares on the smoky horizon. Stink of oil and sewage. Sick sharks swim through the black water, belch sulphur from rotting livers, ignore a bloody, broken Icarus. Naked Mr. America, burning frantic with self bone love, screams out: "My asshole confounds the Louvre! I fart ambrosia and shit pure gold turds! My cock spurts soft diamonds in the morning sunlight!" He plummets from the eyeless lighthouse, kissing and jacking off in face of the black mirror, glides oblique down with cryptic condoms and mosaic of a thousand newspapers through a drowned city of red brick to settle in black mud with tin cans and beer bottles, gangsters in concrete, pistols pounded flat and meaningless to avoid short-arm inspection of prurient ballistic experts. He waits the slow striptease of erosion with fossil loins....

"In Timbuctu I once saw an Arab boy who could play a flute with his ass, and the fairies told me he was really an individual in bed. He could play a tune up and down the organ hitting the most erogenously sensitive spots, which are different on everyone, of course. Every lover had his special theme song which was perfect for him and rose to his climax. The boy was a great artist when it came to improving new combines and special climaxes, some of them notes in the unknown, tie-ups of seeming discords that would suddenly break through each other and crash together with a stunning, hot sweet impact."

JAMES BALDWIN (1924-   )

Donald Friend, *The Boys in the Backroom*. Reinhard Hassert Collection, Paris.

Herbert List, *Lykabettos*, detail (1937). (Photograph taken from *Herbert List: Photographien 1930-1970*, text by Günter Metken; Schirmer Mosel, Munich, 1976).

James Baldwin was the son of a black minister. At the age of fifteen, he relates in his first novel, *Go Tell It to the Mountain*, he preached a sermon in a little church in Harlem. As a writer he is concerned mainly with homosexuality and the condition of the American black. His second novel, *Giovanni's Room*, describes the anguish of a boy torn between his love for the girl to whom he is engaged and his passion for an Italian barman. In *Another Country* the erotic permutations between whites and blacks, bisexuals and homosexuals, become exceedingly complicated. Eric Jones, a white actor, falls in love with Rufus Scott, a black jazz musician who enjoys humiliating Eric, as a representative of white America, by treating him like a woman. Rufus eventually commits suicide. Later Eric becomes the lover of a writer's wife, Cass; but it is not until he goes to France and meets Yves that he finds true love. Eric is obliged to leave Yves and go back to the States. Will his love for the boy survive? The latter, who is growing up, no longer requires protection. Nevertheless he is unwilling to forget Eric and goes to New York to see him. Smiling and "svelter than ever," Eric meets him at the airport. Yves's fears evaporate. "He was sure now that everything was going to be all right." As the French critic, Georges Michel Sarrote, has written in his study, *Comme un frère, comme un amant*, "However unconvincing it appears, let us nevertheless pay hommage to this attempt at ending a bisexual novel on a note of homosexual hope...." Why be pessimistic?

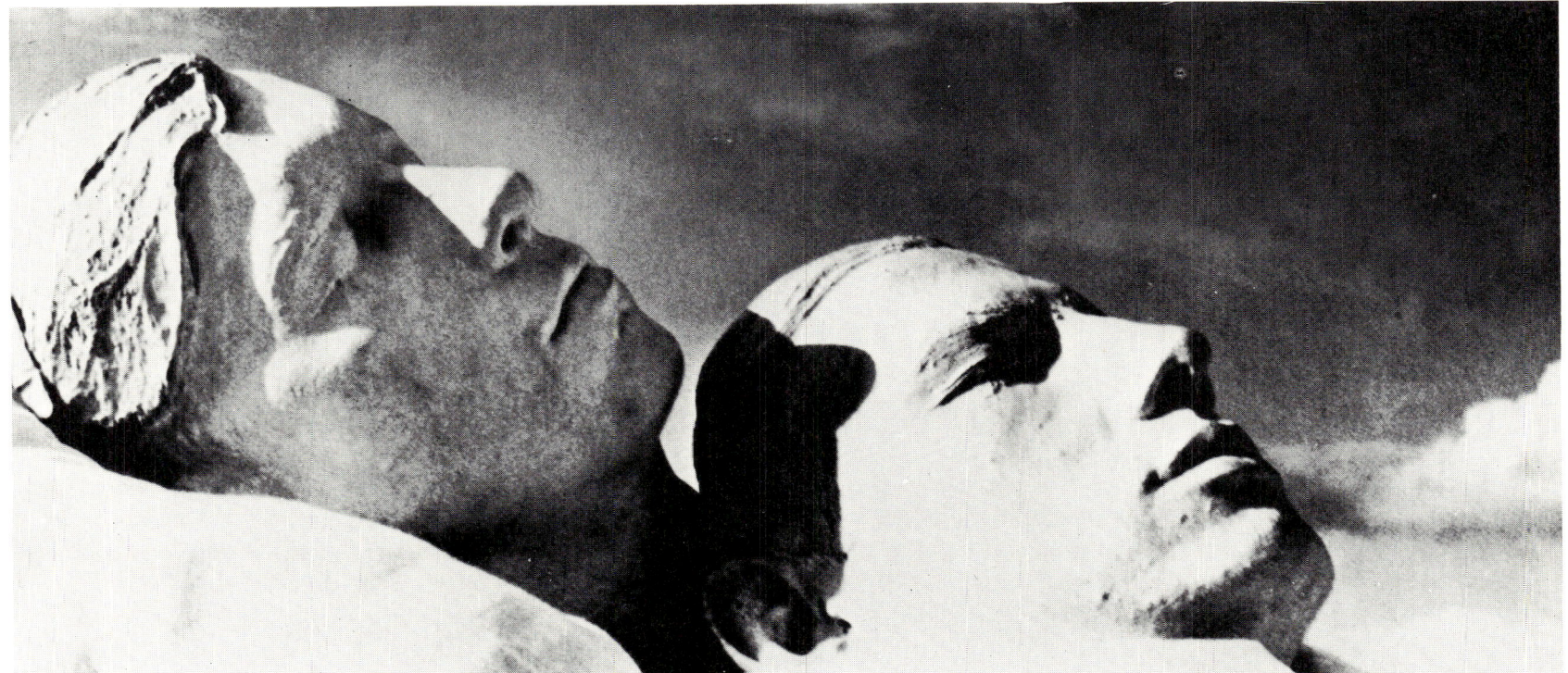

From ANOTHER COUNTRY

Eric rose and crossed to Yves, and they stood for a moment like two wrestlers, watching each other with a kind of physical calculation, smiling and pale. Yves always seemed, a moment before the act, tentative and tremulous; not like a girl—like a boy: and this strangely innocent waiting, this virile helplessness, always engendered in Eric a positive storm of tenderness. Everything in him, from his heights and depths, his mysterious, hidden source, came rushing together, like a great flood barely channelled in a narrow mountain stream. And it chilled him like that—like icy water; and roared in him like that, and with the menace of things scarcely understood, barely to be controlled; and he shook with violence with which he flowed toward Yves. It was this violence which made him gentle, for it frightened him. And now he touched Yves lightly and wonderingly on the cheek. Yves' smile faded, he watched Eric, they moved into each other's arms.

There were the wine bottle and the glasses on the table, their plates, the platter, the bread; Yves had left a cigarette burning in an ashtray on the table, it was nearly nothing but ash now, long and grey; and the kitchen light was on. "You say you don't care about the chicken?" Eric whispered, laughing. Yves laughed, giving off a whiff of garlic, of peppery sweat. Their arms locked around each other, then they drew apart, and, holding hands, stumbled into the bedroom, into the great haven of their bed. Perhaps it had never before seemed so much like a haven, so much their own, now that the terrible floodwaters of time were about to overtake it. And perhaps they had never before so belonged to each other, had never before given or taken so much from each other, as they did now, burning and sobbing on the crying bed.

They laboured together slowly, violently, a long time: both feared the end. Both feared the morning, when the moon and stars would be gone, when this room would be harsh and sorrowful with sunlight, and this bed would be dismantled, waiting for other flesh. *Love is expensive,* Yves had once said, with his curiously dry wonder. *One must put furniture around it, or it goes.* Now, for a while, there would be no furniture—how long would this night have to last them? What would the morning bring? the imminent morning, behind which were hidden so many mornings, so many nights.

And they moaned. *Soon,* Yves whispered, sounding insistent, like a child, and with a terrible regret. *Soon.* Eric's hands and mouth opened and closed on his lover's body, their bodies strained yet closer together, and Yves' body shook and he called Eric's name as no one had ever called this name before. *Eric. Eric. Eric.* The sound of his breath filled Eric, heavier than the far-off pounding of the sea.

Then they were silent, breathing hard. The sound of the sea returned. They were aware of the light in the living room, the light left burning in the kitchen. But they did not move. They remained still in one another's arms, in their slowly chilling bed. Soon, one of them, it would be Yves, would move, would light two cigarettes. They would lie in bed, smoking, talking and giggling. Then they would shower: *what a mess we are!* Yves could cry, laughing a laugh of triumph. Then they would dress, they would probably eat, they would probably go out. And soon the night would end. But, for the moment, they were simply exhausted and at peace with one another and loath to leave the only haven either of them had ever found.

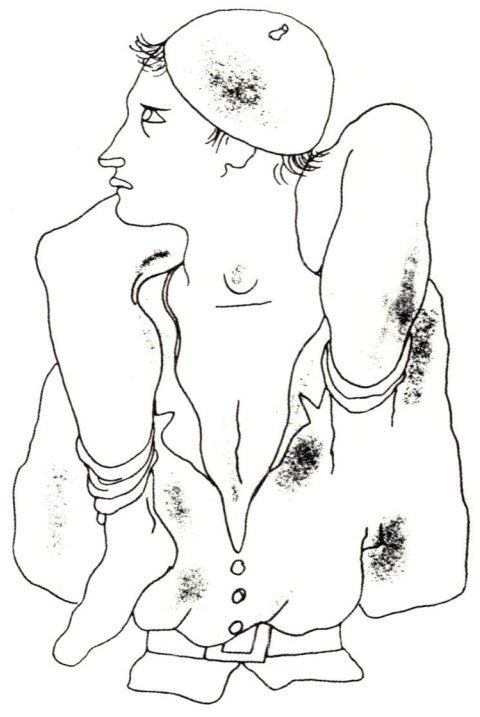

Jean Cocteau, Illustration for *The White Paper* (1930). Editions du Signe, Paris. Private collection.

SELECTED BIBLIOGRAPHY

Apollinaire, Fleuret Perceau. «L'Enfer de la Bibliothèque Nationale.» Reprint. Geneva: Stakins, 1970.

Chardans, Jean-Louis. *Histoire et Anthologie de l'Homosexualité: 1970.* Paris: Centre d'Etudes et de documentation pédagogique, 1970.

Cory, D.W. *The Homosexual in America: A Subjective Approach.* New York: Greenberg, 1951.

Daniel, Marc. and Baudry, A. *Les Homosexuels.* Paris: Editions Casterman, 1975.

Daniel, Marc, *Shakespeare et Gide en correctionnelle.* Paris: Editions du Scorpion, 1959.

—. *Hommes du Grand Siècle.* In *Arcadie.* Paris, 1956.

Forberg, F.C. *Manuel d'erotologie classique: De Figuris veneris.* Translated by Alcide Bonneau. Paris: J.Liseux, 1882.

Freud, Sigmund. *Un souvenir d'enfance de Leonard de Vinci.* Translated by Marie Bonaparte. Paris: Gallimard, 1927.

Havelock, Ellis. *Studies in the Psychology of Sex.* In The New American Library. New York, 1957.

Hirschfeld, Dr. Magnus. *Anomalies et Perversions sexuelles.* Paris, 1957.

—. *Le Sexe inconnu.* In Collection Etudes sexologiques. Paris, 1936.

Kinsey, Alfred, *Sexual Behavior in the Human Male.* Philadelphia: W.B. Saunders Co., 1948.

Lachèvre, Frédéric. *Le libertinage au XVIIe siècle.* Paris: H. Champion, 1909-1911.

Luppé, Marquis de. *Astolphe de Custine.* Paris: Editions du Rocher, 1957.

Perceau, Louis, and Fleuret, Fernand [Hernandez, Ludovic]. *Les procès en sodomie aux XVIe et XVIIe siècles.* Paris: Bibliothèque des Curieux, 1920.

Perceau, Louis. *Le cabinet secret du Parnasse.* Dijon: Cabinet du Livre, 1928.

Pia, Pascale. *Dictionnaire des oeuvres érotiques.* Paris: Mercure de France, 1971.

Reade, Brian. *Sexual Heretics: Male Homosexuality in English Literature from 1850-1900.* London: Routledge & Kegan Ltd., 1970.

Rowbotham, Sheila, and Weeks, Jeffrey. *Socialism and the New Life: The Personal and Sexual Policies of Edward Carpenter and Havelock Ellis.* London: Pluto Press, 1977.

Sarrote, G.M. *Comme un Frère, Comme un Amant.* Paris: Flammarion, 1976.

Spenser, Henri [Ashbee or Pisanus Fraxi]. *Index librorum prohibitorum.* n.p. 1877.

—. *Forbidden Books of the Victorians.* London, The Odyssey Press, 1970.

Young, Ian. *The Male Homosexual in Literature: A Bibliography.* Metuchen, N.J.: The Scarecrow Press, 1975.

ACKNOWLEDGMENTS

The author particularly wishes to thank Mr. François Duchêne, whose erudition was a precious aid in preparing this book, and Mr. Michael Taylor for his intelligent and witty translations. She is equally grateful to the museum curators, directors of art galleries and collectors, who so kindly authorized the reproduction of works belonging to them.

For the right to reprint the copyrighted material in this book, the author and publisher are indebted to the following persons and publishers:

AHM Publishing Corporation, Arlington Heights, Ill. for *Shakespeare: Sonnets*, edited by Hyder E. Rollins (New York, 1951) pp. 10, 21, 52, 72. By permission of the publisher.

Ardis/rlt for *Wings: Prose and Poetry* by M. Kuzmin (Ann Arbor, Mich., 1972) pp. 32-3, 107-08, 110. By permission of the publisher.

Edward Arnold (Publishers) Ltd. for *Maurice* by E.M. Forster (London, 1971) pp. 171-3. By permission of the publisher.

James Baldwin for *Another Country*, copyright © 1965 by James Baldwin (New York and London, 1965) pp. 174-7. By permission of the author.

Editions Bloud & Gay for *Oeuvres priapiques* by Aretino, English translation by Michael Taylor (Paris, 1970) pp. 41-2. By permission of the publisher.

The Bodley Head for *Vathek* by William Beckford, translated by Herbert B. Grimsditch, published by the Bodley Head (London, 1958) pp. 32-9. By permission of the publisher.

Calder and Boyars Ltd. for *Naked Lunch* by William Burroughs (London, 1964) pp. 94-6, 156-7. By permission of the publisher.

Chatto & Windus Ltd. for *By Way of Sainte-Beuve* by Marcel Proust, translated by Sylvia Townsend Warner (London, 1958) pp. 161-5. By permission of the publisher.

Rosica Colin Ltd. for *Funeral Rites*, copyright © 1969, Jean Genet; by Jean Genet, translated by Bernard Frechtman (Panther Books: London, 1971) pp. 63-4. By permission of the agent.

J.M. Dent & Sons, Ltd. for *Marlowe Plays + Poems*, ed. by M.R. Ridley, Everyman's Library Series (London, 1955) pp. 330-31, 390-92. By permission of the publisher.

Jean Dermit and Maurice Girodias for *The White Paper* by Jean Cocteau, (Olympia Press: Traveller's Companion no. 51, Paris, n.d.) pp. 46-51. By permission of the literary executor and the publisher.

Doubleday & Company, Inc. for *The Heresiarch and Co.*, by Guillaume Apollinaire, translated by Rémy Inglis Hall, Copyright © 1965 by Doubleday & Company, Inc. (New York, 1965), pp. 61-2. By permission of the publisher.

Leon Edel for Henry James's «Letters to Hendrik Andersen» in *The Treacherous Years: 1895-1901* by Leon Edel, (Lippincott: New York, 1969) pp. 295-7. Reprinted by permission of Leon Edel. Copyright © 1969 by Leon Edel.

The Estate of the late Vyvyan Holland [Mr. Merlin Holland] for *De Profundis: The Complete Text* by Oscar Wilde (Methuen & Co.: London, 1949) pp. 15, 20-1, 43-4, 53-4, 58-9. By permission of the estate.

Farrar, Straus & Giroux, Inc. for *Noa Noa* by Paul Gauguin, translated from the French by O.F. Theis (New York, 1961) pp. 42-52. Reprinted by permission of Farrar, Straus & Giroux, Inc., New York, NY.

Librairie Ernest Flammarion for *Les Amours Singulières* by Roger Peyrefitte, English translation by Michael Taylor and Steward Lindh (Paris, 1949) pp. 114, 144-9. By permission of the publisher.

Charles-Henri Ford and the estate of Parker Tyler for *The Young and the Evil* by Charles-Henri Ford and Parker Tyler (The Obelisk Press; Paris, 1933) pp. 151-5. By permission of the author and the estate.

Editions Gallimard for *La liberté et l'amour* by Robert Desnos, English translation by Michael Taylor (Paris, 1962) pp. 77-9; and *Si le grain ne meurt* by André Gide, English translation by Michael Taylor (Paris, 1955) pp. 344-6; and *De l'abjection* (Paris, 1939) pp. 76-7, 81 and *Tirésias* (Paris, 1954) pp. 59-62 by Marcel Jouhandeau, English translation by Michael Taylor and Steward Lindh; and "O Saisons, O Châteaux" in *Oeuvres complètes* by Arthur Rimbaud, English translation by Michael Taylor (Bibliothèque de la Pléiade: Paris, 1972) p. 88; and *Oeuvres poétiques complètes* (Bibliothèque de la Pléiade: Paris, 1962) pp. 136, 215, 521-2, 537 and "Hombres II" and "Mille e Tre" in *Oeuvres en prose complètes* (Bibliothèque de la Pléiade: Paris, 1972) by Paul Verlaine, English translation by Michael Taylor and Steward Lindh. By permission of the publisher.

Maurice Girodias for *The 120 Days of Sodom* by the Marquis de Sade, translated by Pieralessandro Casavini (Olympia Press: Paris, 1955) pp. 338-41. By permission of the publisher.

Robert Graves for *Suetonius: The Twelve Caesars*, translated by Robert Graves (A.P. Watt & Sons: London, 1962) pp. 21-2, 116, 200-01. By permission of the publisher.

Grove Press, Inc. for *Our Lady of the Flowers* by Jean Genet, translated by Bernard Frechtman; copyright © 1963 Grove Press

Inc. New York, N.Y. pp. 226-7, 229-30. Reprinted by permission of Grove Press, Inc.

Harcourt Brace Jovanovich, Inc. for *The Complete Poems of Cavafy,* copyright © 1961 by Rae Dalven. Reprinted from *The Complete Poems of Cavafy,* translated by Rae Dalven, by permission of Harcourt Brace Jovanovich, Inc. (Chatto & Windus: London and New York, 1968) pp. 60, 121, 145, 161, 165.

William Hodge & Company, Ltd. for *The Trials of Oscar Wilde* edited by H. Montgomery Hyde (William Hodge & Company, Ltd.: Glasgow, 1948) pp. 127, 133-4. By permission of the publisher.

Indiana University Press for *The Satires of Juvenal,* translated by Rolfe Humphries, copyright © 1958 by Indiana University Press (Bloomington, Ind., 1958) pp. 78-9, 114-15. Reprinted by permission of the publisher.

Alfred A. Knopf, Inc. for *Madelaine—Et Nunc Manet In Te* by André Gide, translated by Justin O'Brien, Copyright 1952 by Alfred A. Knopf, Inc. (London, 1952) pp. 36-8. Reprinted by permission of Alfred A. Knopf, Inc.; and *Death in Venice and Seven Other Stories,* by Thomas Mann, translated by H.T. Lowe-Porter. Copyright 1930 and renewed 1958 by Alfred A. Knopf, Inc. (London, 1955) pp. 48-51, 62-5, by permission of Alfred A. Knopf, Inc.

Guy Le Prat for "Hot Coals" by Artemon (p. 250) and "Musa Puerilis, No. 245" by Strato of Sardis in *Histoire de l'Amour grec* by M.H.E. Maier and L.R. Pogey-Castries, English translation by Michael Taylor (Paris, 1952). By permission of the publisher.

Winston Leyland for "Incantation" by Vsevolod Ivanov, translated by Simon Karlinsky in *Gay Sunshine* no. 29/30 (San Francisco, Cal., Summer-Fall, 1976). Reprinted by permission of the publisher.

Erich Linder and Editions du Seuil for *Ernesto* by Umberto Saba; French translation by Jean-Marie Roche, English translation by Michael Taylor. (Einaudi: Turin, 1975) pp. 14-21. By permission of the publishers.

The Loeb Classical Library for *The Speeches of Aeschinus,* translated by Charles Darwin Adams (1948) pp. 109-13; and "The Poems of Gaius Valerius Catullus" in *Catullus, Tibullus and Pervigilium Veneris* translated by F.W. Cornish (1950) p. 171; and *Lucian,* translated by M.D. Macleod (1961) vol. 7, pp. 283-91; (1967) vol. 8, pp. 169-77, 193-5, 231-3; and *Epigrams* by Martial, translated by Walter C.A. Ker (1947) vol. 1, pp. 235, 259; (1950) vol. 2, pp. 85-7; and *The Letters of Alciphron, Aelian and Philostratus* translated by Allen Rogers Beuner (1949) pp. 415-17, 505, 523-5; and *The Odes of Pindar,* translated by Sir John Sandys (1946) p. 585; and *Plato,* translated by W.R.M. Lamb (1953) vol. 5, pp. 225-33; and "Musa Puerilis, No. 93" by Rhianus in *The Greek Anthology,* translated by W.R. Paton (1948) vol. 4, pp. 327-29; and "Musa Puerilis, Nos. 4, 5, 200, 209" by Strato of Sardis in *The Greek Anthology,* translated by W.R. Paton (1948) vol. 4, pp. 285, 385, 389; and "XXIII—The Lover" "XXIX—The First Love-Poem", "XXX—The Second Love-Poem" by Theocritus in *The Greek Bucolic Poets,* translated by J.M. Edmonds (1950) pp. 279-85, 355-7, 359-61. All the above excerpts taken from the Loeb Classical Library (Harvard University Press: William Heinemann) by permission of the publisher.

Mercure de France for *L'autre vue* by Georges Eekhoud, English translation by Michael Taylor (Paris, 1914) pp. 44-7, 87-8; and *Journal littéraire (1873-1906)* by Paul Léautaud, English translation by Michael Taylor (Paris, 1954) pp. 45-6. By permission of the publisher.

William Morris Agency, Inc. for *The City and the Pillar* by Gore Vidal, copyright © 1949, Gore Vidal. (John Lehmann: London, 1949) pp. 262-4. Reprinted by permission of the agent.

Thomas Nelson & Sons, Ltd. for *The Secret Lives of Lawrence of Arabia,* by Phillip Knightley and Colin Simpson (London, 1969) pp. 184-5, 245-6, 292. By permission of the publisher.

New Directions Publishing Corporation for *Poet in New York* by Federico Garcia Lorca, translated by Ben Belitt. Copyright © 1955 by Ben Belitt. (New York, 1955) pp. 121-7. Reprinted by permission of New Directions Publishing Corportion, New York, Agents.

Pantheon Books and Martin Secker & Warburg, Ltd. for *Young Törless* by Robert Musil, translated by Eithne Wilkins and Ernst Kaiser, copyright © 1955 by Pantheon Books, Inc. (New York and London, 1961) pp. 131-3, 142-3. Reprinted by Pantheon Books, a Division of Random House, Inc.

Gérard Paresys for *Feuilles éparses* by René Crevel, translated by Michael Taylor. (Editions L. Broder: Paris, 1965) pp. 17-18. By permission of the literary executor.

Penguin Books Ltd. for *Lost Illusions,* by Balzac, translated by Herbert J. Hunt (Penguin Classics, 1971) pp. 634-5, 640-1, 649-50, 652, 654-5. Copyright © Herbert J. Hunt, 1971; and *Faust II* by Goethe, translated by Philip Wayne (Penguin Classics, 1959) pp. 276-9. Copyright © Philipp Wayne, 1959; and *The Confessions* by Jean-Jacques Rousseau, translated by J.M. Cohen

(Penguin Classics, 1973) pp. 72-3, 160-3. Copyright © J.M. Cohen, 1953. Reprinted by permission of the publisher.

Editions Plon for *Jeunesse* by Julian Green, English translation by Michael Taylor (Paris, 1974) pp. 131-4, 139-40. By permission of the publisher.

Peter Owen Ltd., Publishers for *The Letters of Michelangelo*, edited by E. Hartley Ramsden. Published by Peter Owen, London, (1963) vol. 1, pp. 180, 183-4. By permission of the publishers.

Oxford University Press for *The Orpheus of Angelo, Politian and the Aminta of Torquato Tasso*, translated by Louis Lord (London, 1931) pp. 99-100. By permission of the Oxford University Press.

Random House, Inc. and Chatto & Windus, Ltd. for *The Past Recaptured* [published as *Time Regained* in Britain] by Marcel Proust, translated by Andreas Mayor. Copyright © 1970 by Chatto & Windus, Ltd. (New York and London, 1970) pp. 154-7, 167-70. Reprinted by permission of Random House, Inc. and *If It Die* by André Gide, translated by Dorothy Bussy. Copyright 1935 and renewed 1963 by Random House, Inc. pp. 344-6.

Société d'Edition "Les Belles Lettres" for *Epigrammes* by Martial, compiled and translated into French by M.S. Isaac, English translation by Michael Taylor (Paris, 1933) vol. 2, pp. 28-9, 92. By permission of the publisher.

Stein and Day Publishers for *Witches' Sabbath* by Maurice Sachs, translated by Richard Howard (1965) pp. 31-2. Copyright © 1964 by Stein and Day, Inc. From the book *Witches' Sabbath*. Reprinted with permission of Stein and Day Publishers.

Editions Stock for *Plain Chant* by Jean Cocteau, English translation by Michael Taylor (Paris, 1959) pp. 130-1, 137. By permission of the publisher.

John Symonds for "A Ballad of Passive Pederasty" and "Go into the Highways..." in *White Stains: The Literary Remains of George Archibald Bishop, A Neuropath of the Second Empire* by Aleister Crowley (Smithers; n.p. 1898). By permission of John Symonds.

Mr. Julian Symons for *The Desire and Pursuit of the Whole* by Frederick Rolfe [alias Baron Corvo] (Cassel & Collier Macmillan: London, 1934) pp. 13-14, 45. By permission of the literary executor.

The University of Chicago Press for "Antique", "Vagabonds" and "Sonnet to the Ass-hole" in *Complete Works* by Arthur Rimbaud, translated by Wallace Fowlie. Copyright © 1966 by University of Chicago Press. (Chicago, 1966). Reprinted by permission of the University of Chicago Press, Publishers.

The University of North Carolina for *The Works of Stefan George*. Rendered into English by Olga Marx and Ernest Morwitz, 2nd, rev. and enl. ed. University of North Carolina Studies in the Germanic Languages and Literatures. No. 78. (Chapel Hill: The University of North Carolina Press, 1974) pp. 72, 257. Reprinted by permission of the publisher.

Tennessee Williams for *Memoirs*. Copyright © 1975 by Tennessee Williams (Doubleday: New York, 1975) p. 50. Reprinted by permission of the author.

The World Publishing Company for *Aristophanes: Five Comedies* (New York and Cleveland, 1948) pp. 152-9 Copyright © 1948 by the World Publishing Co. and *The Plays of Christopher Marlowe*, edited by Leo Kirschbaum (New York and Cleveland, 1962) pp. 276-7, Copyright © 1962 by the World Publishing Co. Reprinted by permission of the publisher.

Yale University Press for *The Odes of Anacreon*, translated by Erastus Richardson (New Haven, Conn., 1928) pp. 4, 20-1. Reprinted by permission of the publisher.

SOURCE NOTES:

The excerpts not mentioned in the previous acknowledgments are taken from the following sources:

[anon.] *Alcibiades in School*, English translation by Michael Taylor. (Published anonymously: Orange, France, 1652).

Bandello, Matteo. "The Tale of Porcellio" in *The Novels of Bandello*, prose translation by John Payne. (For private circulation only: London, 1890) vol. 1, pp. 94-98.

Barnfield, Richard. *The Affectionate Shepheard*, spelling and punctuation modernized by Michael Taylor. (Printed by John Danter for T.G. and E.N. and are to bee sold in Saint Dunstones Churchyard in Fleet Street, 1594).

Douglas, Lord Alfred. *Poèms*. (Mercure de France: Paris, 1896) pp. 22, 109-10.

Ducasse, Isidore [alias Comte de Lautréamont]. *The Lay of Maldoror*, translated by John Rodker. (Privately printed for subscribers only: The Casanova Society, n.p., 1924) pp. 245-7.

Goethe, Johann von. "Letters from Switzerland" in *The Autobiography of Goethe*, translated by Rev. A.J.W. Morrison. (Henry Bohn: London, 1849), pp. 262-3.

Gorani, Count Giuseppe. *The Secret Memoirs* in *Oeuvres complètes*, English translation by Michael Taylor. (Editions Buisson: Paris, 1793), pp. 299-302.

Lorrain, Jean. "An Asian Court" and "Trimalcion's Feast" in *Le Vice errant*. English translation by Michael Taylor. (P. Ollendorf: Paris, 1901), pp. 169-71, 256-9.

Malaparte, Kurt. *The Skin*, translated by David More. (Alvin Redman, Ltd.: London, 1952) pp. 130-7.

Michelangelo. "Sonnets XXVIII and LIV" in *The Sonnets of Michelangelo*, translated by J.A. Symonds. (Thomas Mosher: Portland, Maine, 1897).

Morlino, Gerolamo. "The Tale of the Youth Who Was Caught in the Act of Adultery and Sodomized and Flogged by the Husband" in *Contes et Nouvelles de J. Morlino* (Imp. Fiorentini, n.p., 1878); *Oeuvres galantes des conteurs italiens de la Renaissance: 1ère moitié du XVIe siècle*, translated into French by Van Bever, English translation by Michael Taylor. (Editions Gres: Paris, 1921), pp. 191-200.

Petronius. *The Satyricon*. [translation attributed to Oscar Wilde] (Privately printed for the Hogarth Press, Inc., New York, 1932), pp. 192-9 and excerpts from the introduction.

Philippe, Charles-Louis. "Les moutons à cinq pattes" in *Le Canard sauvage*, English translation by Michael Taylor. (Paris, July 26-August 1, 1903).

Saint-Pavin, Denys Sanguin de. "Epigram" in *Le libertinage au XVIIe siècle* by Frédéric Lachèvre, English translation by Michael Taylor. (H. Champion: Paris, 1909-11) vol. 2, pp. 85-6.

Tatius, Achilles. *The Loves of Cleitophon and Leucippe*. (Privately printed for the Athenian Society, n.p., 1897), pp. 95-6.

[anon.] *Teleny; or, the Reverse of the Medal: A Physiological Romance of Today*. (Cosmopoli: London, 1893).

de Viau, Théophile. "Theophile's Complaint to His Absent Friend, Tircis" and "Oh Phyllis, I'm Fucked" in *Le libertinage au XVIIe siècle* by Frédéric Lachèvre, English translation by Michael Taylor. (H. Champion: Paris, 1909-11), vol. 2, pp. 287-91, 393-94.

Voltaire. "Socratic Love" in *The Philosophical Dictionary* (London, 1765), English translation of footnote (1769) by Michael Taylor: and "A Letter to François de Moncrif" and "Poem to the King of Prussia" in *Correspondance* (Paris, n.d.), vol. 35, p. 391 and vol. 36, p. 210.

Whitman, Walt. *Leaves of Grass*. (Modern Library Series, Random House, Inc.: New York, n.d.), pp. 27-8, 99, 103-04.

Wilde, Oscar. *The Picture of Dorian Gray* in *The Works of Oscar Wilde*. (Collins Publishers: London, 1949), pp. 21, 23-4.

Wilmot, John, Earl of Rochester. "Sodom or the Quintessence of Debauchery" [by E. of R.] From the limited edition of the play reprinted in 1904 and in the archives of the City Library of Hamburg, Germany.

Winckelmann, Johann Joachim. "A Letter to Frederich von Berg" in *The Renaissance* by Walter Pater. (Mentor Books, The New American Library, Inc.: New York, 1959), pp. 130-1.

Xenophon. *Hiero*, translated by Rev. J.S. Watson. (George Bell & Sons, Ltd.: London, 1906), stanzas 31-7

PHOTO CREDITS

The publisher wishes to thank the following people and institutions for the use of their photographic material:

Belgium: Brussels—Musées Royaux des Beaux-Arts, 175, 176

England: Bambury—Blinkhorns, 148; Birmingham—Birmingham Museum & Art Gallery, 185; London—Apollo Magazine, Ltd., 109 (bottom), British Museum, 231, A.C. Cooper Ltd., 115, Deste, 272, Marlborough Fine Art (London) Ltd., 295, The National Gallery, 45, 95, Prudence Cuming Associates, 228, Roy Miles Fine Paintings Ltd., 147, John Symonds, 192, Tate Gallery, 178 (left), 183, 270, Victoria & Albert Museum 1(b + c), 51, 75, 109 (top), 131, 134, 253; Windsor—Windsor Castle, 97, 98

France: Albi—Musée Toulouse-Lautrec, 180; Bayonne—Musée Bonnat, 4; Paris—© 1977, Copyright by ADAGP, Paris and COSMOPRESS, Geneva, 207, 260, 283, 287, 289; Alinari-Giraudon, 78, Anderson-Giraudon, 14, 31 (left), 35 (both), 36, 37, 41, 81 (left), 84, 96, 243 (both), Anderson-Viollet, 83 (right), 100, 101, Archives Photographiques, 23, 82, 91, 111, 186, 235, Bibliothèque Nationale, 18, 19 (a + b), 21, 43, 58, 66, 87 (top), 92, 93, 94, 102, 103, 107, 121, 127, 128, 150, 164, 165, 190 (both), 211, 212 (bot.), 213 (both), 227, 232, 234 (both), 256, 257, Daniel Bourguignand, 273, Bulloz, 81 (right), 246, Collection François Duchêne, 201 (a + b), Collection M. Manoukian, 133, Collection Félix Marcilhac, 65, Collection Viollet, 46, 56, 71 (bottom), 167, 168 (both), 169, 171, 172, 177, 178 (right), 181, 182, 187, 238, 243 (center), Clichés des Musées Nationaux, 7, 12, 13, 17, 25, 26, 27 (top), 29, 31 (right), 39, 44, 48, 50 (bottom), 63, 74, 79, 85, 99, 104, 113, 118, 119, 137, 146, 163, 221, 239, Robert David, 86, Galerie Claude Bernard, 193, Garanger-Giraudon, 203, Giraudon, 76 (top), 77, 117, 143, Loïs Gosselin, 52, 69, 70, 71 (top), 76 (bottom), 87 (bottom), 144, 145, 158, 226, Harlingue-Viollet, 200, Jacqueline Hyde, 157 Philippe Jullian and Editions Gallimard, 236, Lauros-Giraudon, 120, 122, 160, 162 (both), André Morain, 59, von Plüschow, 240, 241, 242, 247, André Rogi, 258 (bottom), Georges Routhier, 22, 50 (top), 53, 61, 67, 68, 73, 105 (both), 129, 130 (both), 135, 136, 138, 140, 161, 173, 188, 189, 191, 205, 206, 210, 215, 216, 223, 237, 244, 249, 250, 254, 255 (both), 258 (top), 259 (both), 261, 263, 264, 265, 266, 271, 275, 276, 277, 281, 287, 291, 293, 294, 296, 298, Mr. Cornette de St-Cyr, 233, © 1977, Copyright, SPADEM, Paris and COSMOPRESS, Geneva, 200, 210, 255, 257, 259 (left), 263, 264, 265, 275, 276, 277, 291; Poitiers—Musée des Beaux-Arts, 47

Germany: Berlin—Jörg P. Anders, 106, Staatliche Museen Preussischer Kulturbesitz, 15, 42; Hamburg—Rolf Kleinhempel, 155, Kunsthalle, 149; Munich—Hirmer-Archiv, 9, 16, 20, 27 (bottom), 28, 33, 38, 57, 62, Herbert Litz and Schirmer Mosel/München, 251, 297

Italy: Florence—Gabinetto Fotografico—Sopr. Gallerie, Firenze, 112, Museo Nazionale del Bargello, 1 (d), 3; Rome—Alinari, 60, 141, Anderson, 54, 55, 64, 83 (center + left) 132, Museo Nazionale di Villa Giulia, 10, Vatican Museum, 1 (a)

Sweden: Lund—Kulturhistoriska Föreningen För Södra Sverige Kulturen, 208, 268, 269; Malmö—A.B. Allhem, 225; Stockholm—Nationalmuseum, 139

Switzerland: Basel—Hans Hinz, 49, 285, Kupferstichkabinett des Kunstmuseums, 229; Locarno—Alberto Celesia, 124, 125, 126, 151, 153, 159, 159, 179, 279; Zurich—Senta Meyer and Büchler Verlag, 219, 283

United States of America: Boston, Mass.—Museum of Fine Arts, 199; Fort Worth, Tex.—the Fort Worth Art Museum, 195; New York, N.Y.—Geoffrey Clements, 209, Metropolitan Museum of Art, 114; Philadelphia, Penn.—Philadelphia Museum of Art (Given by Mrs. John Wintersteen), 89; Saunderstown, R.I.—Winslow Ames Collection, 123; Washington, D.C.—Corcoran Gallery of Art, 197